BRITAIN & JAPAN:
BIOGRAPHICAL PORTRAITS

BRITAIN & JAPAN

BIOGRAPHICAL PORTRAITS

EDITED BY
IAN NISH

JAPAN
LIBRARY

JAPAN SOCIETY PAPERBACK EDITION Not for resale

BRITAIN & JAPAN: BIOGRAPHICAL PORTRAITS

First published 1994 by
JAPAN LIBRARY
Knoll House, 35 The Crescent, Sandgate
Folkestone, Kent, CT20 3EE

Japan Library is an imprint of Curzon Press Ltd
St John's Studios, Church Road, Richmond, Surrey TW9 2QA

© Japan Society Publications 1994

ISBN 1-873410-27-1 Cloth

British Library Cataloguing in Publication Data
A CIP entry for this book is available
from the British Library

Set in Bembo roman 12 on 12½ point
Typesetting by Bookman, Slough
Printed and bound in Great Britain by Bookcraft, Midsomer Norton, Avon

Table of Contents

List of Contributors

BALLHATCHET, Helen   Keio University, Tokyo

BARR, Pat   Freelance writer and lecturer, Norwich

BEST, Antony   Department of International History, London School of Economics

BLACKER, Carmen   formerly of Japan Research Centre, University of Cambridge

BUCKLEY, Roger   Department of International Relations, International Christian University, Mitaka, Tokyo

CHECKLAND, Olive   Honorary Research Fellow, University of Glasgow (to autumn 1993)

CONTE-HELM, Marie   Japanese Studies Division, University of Sunderland

CORTAZZI, Hugh   Chairman of the Japan Society; formerly British Ambassador to Japan

DORE, Ronald   Department of Political Science, Massachusetts Institute of Technology, Cambridge MA

HOARE, James   Senior Principal Research Officer, H.M. Diplomatic Service

HOTTA-LISTER, Ayako   Chinese University of Hong Kong

HUNTER, Janet   Saji Senior Lecturer in Japanese Economic and Social History, London School of Economics

IKEDA, Kiyoshi   Aoyama Gakuin University, Tokyo

LOWE, Peter   Department of History, University of Manchester

NISH, Ian   Professor Emeritus of International History, London School of Economics

PINNINGTON, Adrian   Department of Law, Waseda University, Tokyo

TAMAKI, Norio   Faculty of Commerce, Keio University, Tokyo

WILKINSON, Jane   Royal Museum of Scotland, Edinburgh

Introduction

IAN NISH

ONE THING that Britain and Japan have in common is mutual curiosity. This prompted the editor of the *Japan Weekly Mail* to write on 27 July 1872:

> 'Three years ago the name of the [Japanese] Empire was rarely seen in print in Europe or America. Now, it is hardly possible to open a newspaper without finding a reference to all this progress, and a kindly word in favour of those who are pursuing it. . . Meanwhile attention has been drawn to the spirited little Empire of the rising sun, which is sending its ambassadors abroad, appointing ministers to foreign courts, and sprinkling every university in Christendom with its eager scholars. . . Of its history, antiquities, geography, geology, its manners and customs, its art and its literature, we know little or nothing, and unless some definite effort is made to dispel this ignorance, we, or those who come here ten years after us, will know but little more. . . But how is all this information to be combined? By what means can it be thrown into focus, or how is it to be made accessible and available for the instructions of this community or the information of Europe?'[1]

The solution recommended was the formation of an Asiatic Society for Japan which came to fruition in 1874.[2] It performed the function of enlightening a wider public by publishing volumes of scholarly essays in its *Transactions* – a tradition which continues to this day.

Some seventeen years later, after a number of tentative steps and false starts, the Japan Society of London was formed in 1891 and began the publication of its *Transactions and Proceedings*, disseminating information on a wide range of scholarly disciplines to a wider readership. In 1991, its centenary year, the Society published under the editorship of Sir Hugh Cortazzi and Gordon Daniels, a volume entitled *Britain and Japan, 1859– 1991: Themes and Personalities.* The underlying intention was to pay tribute to those who had made a special contribution to Anglo-Japanese understanding, especially those connected with the Society. The volume took the form of pen-portraits of personalities, many of them strong personalities. But there were many personalities from the story of Anglo-Japanese relations who had to be omitted from the volume. Hence the decision to publish a follow-up set of pen-portraits.

The sub-committee charged with the task of choosing 'personalities' to be featured laid down the guidelines that there should be a balance between British and Japanese and, inevitably for the 1990s, that more 'women personalities' should be included. Such indomitable figures as Isabella Bird, Lady Ethel MacDonald and Otome Daniels more than meet that criterion (although they might have baulked at being so described), against a backcloth of journalists, diplomats, engineers, politicians, bankers, missionaries and literary figures, all of whom were male. We have been fortunate on this occasion to include the researches of Japanese contributors, who have provided insights into a few of the Japanese who were immersed in Things British. These studies are a useful reminder that, while some Japanese like Yoshio Makino and Admiral Tōgō liked Britain, others like Minakata and Natsume Sōseki did not. It was a mixed picture also for Britons in Japan.

★   ★   ★

The first group of essays deals with the Bakumatsu and Meiji periods. Here we find evidence of the fascination felt by the British towards the 'progress' and 'reform' which Japan had undertaken and the fascination of the Japanese at the 'progress' which Britain (like other countries in Europe) had made and the need to learn from her example. We draw on the experience of those nationals of one country who spent time, whether short or long, in the territory of the other and interpreted what they saw for the benefit of their countrymen.

It is fitting that the volume should begin with Sir Hugh Cortazzi's study of Sir Harry Parkes. Not that Parkes was wholly representative of Britain or of Britain's conception of Japan at the time. Arriving in Japan as envoy in 1865, he lived through the civil war leading to the Meiji Restoration and spent almost two decades in the country. Parkes, who was by reputation a workaholic and harsh task-master, laid the foundations of Britain's diplomatic and commercial position there. During his period at the Tokyo legation he gave abundant evidence of that energy, enterprise and initiative in dealing with what he saw as 'a developing country' that is usually associated with the Victorian age.

Then follow three chapters, covering professional groups. In describing British journalists in Japan (ch. 2), James Hoare includes such different personalities as John Reddie Black, Walter Dening, Robert Young, James Murdoch, F.V. Dickins, Francis Brinkley, and H. S. Palmer. Moving beyond the Treaty Ports, there was a large group of British missionaries in Japan (ch. 3) at the end of the nineteenth century. In her account of them Helen Ballhatchet includes such personalities as Dr Henry Faulds, Barclay Buxton, Arthur Lloyd, Bishop Evington and John Batchelor. Some of the journalists, notably Dening, Murdoch, Dickins and Brinkley acquired a good knowledge of Japanese, while the missionaries had, by the nature of their task, to learn at least the spoken language. Whereas the journalists were catering for the foreign community in the Treaty Ports, the life-style of the missionaries came closer to that of the Japanese.

The third group consists of Japanese in Britain, those Japanese engineers who came to Britain's universities for training and experience. Yamao Yōzō, Kikuchi Kyōzō, the scientists who came to study naval engineering and many others were to become famous when they completed their courses and returned home. Olive Checkland (ch. 4) builds on her earlier studies in the field by writing of their aspirations and those of their teachers in British universities. While Britain was largely the instructor and Japan the learner in this period, there was also a good deal of 'mutual learning'. But these early Japanese engineers were already looking to the day when they would catch on to their instructors' coat-tails.

If we have concentrated so far on group connections, there was still a place for individuals in Anglo-Japanese relations. For example, there was the individualism of Maejima Hisoka who visited Britain on an official delegation to clinch a loan for the Tokyo-Yokohama railway in 1870–71 and became determined to modernize Japan's communications (ch. 5). Dr Hunter tells how he developed in Britain a passion to convert from a courier system for mails to a national postal system. Because of this enthusiasm he was often to be described as 'the Roland Hill of Japan'. Of another kind was the individualism of Isabella Bird, Mrs Bishop, who made four journeys in Japan over the two decades from 1878 to 1897 (ch. 6). An indefatigable traveller and intrepid adventuress, she includes in her published letters some of the best descriptions of the Japanese countryside. Pat Barr relates how on her final departure from Japan, she said that she felt more at home in Tokyo than in the United Kingdom.

An individualist of a quite different kind was the eccentric scholar, Minakata Kumagusu, talented in many directions but not quite stable or in control of himself. He spent most of the nineties in Britain, mainly studying in the British Museum until his ticket was withdrawn in circumstances which are amusingly sketched by Carmen Blacker (ch. 7). With his fluency in English he produced copious writings on academic topics. The Japanese scholars who came to Britain at the tail-end of the nineteenth century like Natsume Sōseki, Noguchi Yone and Takakusu Junjirō, and the artist–writer Yoshio Makino (ch. 14) reacted variously to the country and the treatment they received, a mixture of kindness and inconsiderateness. In Minakata's case, the reaction could be explosive and violent.

The second group of essays deals with the period of the Anglo-Japanese alliance. The alliance lasted from 30 January 1902 until it was ended with the ratification of the Washington Four-Power treaty on 17 August 1923. By historical standards, it was a long-standing alliance of two decades though the post-war American-Japanese alliance (if, indeed, we may call the Security Treaty an alliance) has long outlasted it. But the Anglo-Japanese alliance affected all aspects of the relationship in this period of rapid development for Japan.

The Anglo-Japanese alliance was a naval alliance. Or at least it had a large naval element in it. Marie Conte-Helm deals with one important aspect of this, the supply of warships and naval technology from British yards to Japan in her essay 'Armstrongs, Vickers and Japan' (ch. 8). Many Japanese naval officers, both senior and junior, had experiences in Britain which greatly affected their subsequent careers and attitudes. Professor Kiyoshi Ikeda's essay on Admiral Tōgō Heihachirō, 'the silent admiral' (ch. 9), reminds us of the close and cordial relationship which he had with the Royal Navy so long as the alliance lasted.

Throughout his long public career, spanning the period from the 1870s to his death in 1934, Tōgō was one of the symbols of cordiality between Britain and Japan.

The influence of the alliance extended well beyond the naval sphere. Professor Norio Tamaki (ch. 10) places his focus on Finance Minister Matsukata's visit to the United Kingdom in 1902. He uses this to illustrate the relationship between the banking communities in the two countries following the Chinese Indemnity loan and Japan's adoption of the gold standard. He mentions in particular the two influential bankers, Nakai Yoshigusu and Takahashi Korekiyo.

No account of Anglo-Japanese history would be complete without a reference to Sir Claude and Lady Ethel MacDonald who presided over the British embassy in Tokyo from 1900 to 1913 (ch. 11). This was the time of national crisis for Japan, covering the Russo-Japanese war and the annexation of Korea, and the MacDonalds supplied friendly but not uncritical advice to Japanese statesmen who were still feeling their way in the world. Because of his long tenure of the post, Sir Claude was able to play some part in the first alliance treaty and was still in post when it was fundamentally revised in 1905 and 1911.

Ayako Hotta-Lister deals with the Japanese embassy in London for the same period, the senior Japanese embassy abroad at the time (ch. 12). Her paper describes the endeavours of the diplomats, a distinguished group including Komura Jutarō, Katō Takaaki, Mutsu Hirokichi and Yamaza Enjirō, as they laid the foundations of the Great Spectacular, the Anglo-Japanese Exhibition at the White City in the summer of 1910. Their intention would appear to have been to introduce Japan to the British people. It was not so much that British people were unaware of Japan's art and culture; it was her economic growth and political stability that they had not grasped. The object, it might be said, was 'Educating John Bull'. Matsudaira Tsuneo, the subject of a later essay (ch. 16) was already a junior member of the embassy staff at this time and was like his contemporaries Yoshida Shigeru, Shidehara Kijurō and Yoshizawa Kenkichi to rise to high office later in his career.

Frank Ashton-Gwatkin (ch. 13) makes a fitting conclusion to the alliance period. Having joined the British embassy as a language student in 1911, he represents that element of disillusion which crept into the alliance. He was deeply immersed in Thing Japanese but was not uncritical of Japan either in the novels (which he wrote under the pseudonym of 'John Paris') or as a shrewd bureaucrat, analyzing Japan from a political or economic point of view.

The next series of pen-portraits reflects the decline in Anglo-Japanese relations in the 1920s and 1930s.

The Ainu community had always held a fascination for British travellers. Isabella Bird had visited Hokkaido specially and described them in her writings (ch. 6). The Rev. John Batchelor had been posted as a missionary to Hokkaido in 1877 and became a great expert in the Ainu language and customs (ch. 3). Dr Gordon Munro went to Japan as director of the Yokohama General Hospital in 1897 but spent much of his leisure in the north among the Ainu. From 1930 he moved to Hokkaido to live in an Ainu village where he eventually died in 1942 (ch. 17). Jane Wilkinson who has special access to Munro material throws new light on his researches.

This is followed by essays on two distinguished craftsmen. Yoshio Markino (Makino), a water colour artist, lived in London from 1897 to 1942 – an interpreter of British landscapes and British city life. Carmen Blacker shows the impecunious conditions under which he lived in London and the generous assistance he received from admirers, both British and Japanese. Among the last was Shigemitsu Mamoru who gave Makino a flat in the embassy (ch. 14). A British craftsman who developed a special respect for Japan's traditional kiln pottery was Bernard Leach, whose connection with Japan spans the period from 1910 to his death. Sir Hugh Cortazzi's essay (ch. 15) entitled 'The Mingei Movement and Bernard Leach' deals with the mutual influences between Japanese and British potters.

On the political front, relations between Britain and Japan deteriorated as the thirties advanced. Among many who tried to arrest this deterioration were Matsudaira Tsuneo (ch. 16) and Sir Robert Craigie (ch. 18). Matsudaira was ambassador in London from 1929 to 1935, a popular and cultured figure in whom the British government had remarkable confidence. Craigie served in Tokyo after Matsudaira had returned there. Antony Best gives a reinterpretation of the man and his thinking, which have for long been clouded in controversy.

The last group of essays deals with Britain's approach to Japan after the war. First, we concentrate on the teachers. Adrian

Pinnington deals with R.H. Blyth who, after a long career as professor of English in the Imperial University in Seoul, Korea, came in 1945 to play an important political role in the run-up to the Emperor Hirohito's statement of New Years Day, 1946, renouncing his divinity (ch. 19). Meanwhile Frank and Otome Daniels were the most prominent teachers of the Japanese language in the United Kingdom (ch. 20). Lecturing at the School of Oriental and African Studies in London University, they were both pioneers in teaching methods and practitioners who educated a generation of students in Japanese language and culture during and after the war.

Politically, Britain had to accept a changed role for herself. After 1945 many of those like Craigie, Blyth and the Daniels lived on well into the post-war period and played an active role in Anglo-Japanese relations. Thus, Sir Robert Craigie took over as chairman of the Japan Society when it was reconstituted in 1949, continuing in office till 1958. But the atmosphere had changed. It involved an adjustment of attitudes. Britain's role in East Asia had changed as much as Japan's. One who had to make this adjustment was Sir Alvary Gascoigne, who had known Japan in the 1930s and became Britain's representative in Tokyo from 1946 to 1951. As depicted in Peter Lowe's portrait (ch. 21), his task was to re-build relationships with the Japanese but was more importantly, as one might expect in the occupation period, to cultivate, and to some extent appease, General Douglas MacArthur.

Another aspect of Britain's lesser role was her diminished responsibility for the allied occupation after the withdrawal of her military forces from Japan in the summer of 1947. This led in turn to some ambivalence towards the occupation and to measured criticisms of it. Britain's rather distinctive view of the occupation and the coming peace treaty with Japan is sketched by Roger Buckley through the eyes of British press correspondents there (ch. 22). The essay covers a cluster of journalists, Frank Hawley (who like Blyth had been imprisoned by the Japanese), Hessell Tiltman and Richard Hughes, while it also discusses authors like Richard Mason, Honor Tracy, John Morris and Christmas Humphreys and cultural attachés like Edmund Blunden and George Fraser. But, as Buckley stresses, 'British perceptions of occupied Japan depended largely on the efforts of relatively few reporters and writers' who held a wide variety of views.

★ ★ ★

Perhaps variety is the keynote struck in this volume. As one reflects on these essays, one has to conclude that there is no prototype for a British 'Japan specialist' or for a Japanese 'British specialist'. Some of the British portrayed here spent most of their lives in Japan, while others were merely birds of passage. Some Japanese like Yoshio Makino spent very long periods in Britain, others like Maejima merely a year. Some Britishers acquired a deep knowledge of Japan and Japanese by dint of hard work and private study, since professional training in advance was not readily available. Some turned into scholars like Frank Hawley who accumulated discriminating academic libraries and published small monographs[1]. On the Japanese side, Minakata, the pioneer ethnologist and botanist, attained through private study a remarkable proficiency in English which enable him to publish erudite articles in international journals.

Japan and Britain have become more accessible to each other recently than in the times to which these studies relate. It is easier now to gain a knowledge of their cultures through the greater availability of professional studies. With the change to air transport, there is the opportunity – at a price – to visit each other's country regularly. A far cry from the days of Meiji, Taishō and early Shōwa. In Victorian times, a visit to Japan was a once-in-a-lifetime experience for British nationals (*pace* the spirited Isabella Bird); hardly any of the British *o-yatoi* were able to re-visit the Horned Islands once they had left. Similarly, for the Japanese there was little expectation of return. And as for Minakata and Natsume Soseki who spent two years (1900–02) in London, they had to collect their materials frenetically in case they faced academic isolation on their return to Japan. Perhaps it gave them all a broader, international perspective. As the quotation in the title of the essay on Frank Ashton-Gwatkin says, 'In one day have I lived many lives'.

In conclusion, the editor would like to thank the members of the Japan Society sub-committee – Sir Hugh Cortazzi and Dr Carmen Blacker – for their good counsel. He would also like to express his thanks for the many kindnesses from those who have contributed essays.

Special thanks are extended to the Daiwa Anglo-Japanese

Foundation and its Director General, Mr C.H.D. Everett, CBE, for generous assistance in the publication of this volume. I also wish to acknowledge valuable help from the London School of Economics and its library. And finally, we are indebted to Mr Paul Norbury and the Japan Library/Curzon Press for wide-ranging assistance with this book which grew and grew.

IAN NISH

JAPANESE NAMES
In accordance with normal conventions, Japanese names are presented with the family name first.

.. F. Hawley, *Miscellanea japonica*, being occasional contributions to Japanese studies, vols. 1 and 2, Kyoto, 1954 and 1958.

1

Sir Harry Parkes, 1828-1885

SIR HUGH CORTAZZI

SIR HARRY PARKES was the British Minister to Japan over a period of eighteen years from 1865 to 1883. He was the longest serving British head of mission in Japan. His period of service coincided with the Meiji Restoration of 1868 and covered a period of unprecedented revolutionary change. What sort of a man was Sir Harry Parkes? How 'successful' was he as the chief British representative in Japan during his long term of office?

Sir Harry Smith Parkes GCMG, KCB was born in Staffordshire but was orphaned while still a boy. In 1841 he was sent to join relatives in Macao. He studied Chinese and in 1842 found employment in the office of the Chief Super-intendent of Trade in Hong Kong which had been occupied by the British in 1841 and became a British colony in the following year. When the British plenipotentiary to the Chinese Court, Sir Henry Pottinger, left Hong Kong in June 1842 for the Yangtse Kiang and Nanking, Parkes was a member of his party. He worked as interpreter under Sir Rutherford Alcock who became Consul in Amoy in 1844. Parkes was in due course promoted to be Consul serving in Amoy, Canton and Shanghai. He travelled extensively in China. He was a member of Lord Elgin's mission to Peking in 1860. In the course of this expedition he was arrested by Chinese authorities and imprisoned for three weeks during which he was laden with chains for eleven days and threatened with execution. Lord Elgin wrote of him:[1] 'Parkes is one of the most remarkable men I have ever met; for energy, courage and ability combined, I do not know where I could find his match; and this, joined to his facility of speaking Chinese, . . .

makes him at present the man of the situation.' Parkes was made a CB in 1860 and a KCB at the early age of 34 in 1862. In 1865, at the age of only 38, he was appointed Minister to Japan in succession to his old chief, Sir Rutherford Alcock.

Parkes was described[2] on his arrival in Japan by the legation doctor, William Willis, as 'slim and rather below-the-middle size with auburn hair and red whiskers, a pleasant countenance with refined features, hands and feet much too large for gentility. The front part of the head is bald, the top very high. The features all express thought rapidly passing into action, the various appetites are not strong, I conclude.' Grace Fox[3] said that 'A large head, impressive brow, and alert blue eyes dominated his slight, short stature.' In 1878 Isabella Bird[4] thought that he was then still '. . . young-looking . . . scarcely in middle life, slight, active, fair, blue-eyed, a thorough Saxon, with sunny hair and a sunny smile, a sunshiny geniality in his manner, and bearing no trace in his appearance of his thirty years of service in the East, his sufferings in the prison at Peking, and the various attempts on his life in Japan.' (Willis commented[5] that, if you saw him smiling, you would think him such an amiable mortal quite deserving his sobriquet of 'Sir Smiles' but Willis had heard that Parkes was then (1874) said to be '. . . gouty and livery and not up to his old standard of making everyone miserable over whom he holds power.')

'Sunshiny geniality' was not the quality which struck members of his staff, nor probably his family. Willis asserted that Lady Parkes had '. . . a goodly amount of scolding and snubbing to put up with.'[6] He had written earlier[7]: 'Lady Parkes appears of a melancholy disposition and I fancy there is not much domestic happiness in Sir Harry's nature. He is a bustling pushing man and I believe has objects of desire dearer to him than home or family. He never eats a meal in time . . . Fancy on Christmas day [1866] Sir Harry dined in Edo and Lady Parkes in Yokohama. There is as little domestic bliss in the house as any I ever heard of. I believe he is one of those pushing elbowing men who [will do nothing] or anything except in so far as it advances himself. He would be, I am quite sure, unmoved if an earthquake swallowed up his wife and family, so absorbed is he in the game of self. Of all hateful husbands I can imagine it is a man who never eats, drinks or anything else at the same time other people do so.'

Willis was being unfair. It is clear from other comments that

Parkes was a reasonably social person. He enjoyed an occasional dance and he entertained frequently. F.V. Dickins who, with S. Lane Poole, wrote the two-volume biography of Parkes which appeared in 1894[8] recorded that 'On Sunday evenings it was their custom to have some of the members of the Legation to dinner, and it was at these dinners I found it easiest to get him to talk on his life in China: he had the power of bringing the scenes he described before his listener with wonderful clearness, till one almost felt the excitement of the moment he was talking about.' Basil Hall Chamberlain[9] noted how, after his arrival in Yokohama, '. . . having been prostrated by a fever, I was hospitably taken in by Sir Harry and Lady Parkes as soon as it was possible to move me from the uncomfortable Yokohama hotel of those days to the British Legation on the Bluff.'

It is clear from Parkes' own letters that in fact he was very fond of his wife and children. When his wife died in England in November 1879, he was on his way home having obtained permission from the Foreign Office to come home on leave to see her. He wrote to F.V. Dickins[10] on 30 November: 'I left Japan by the first opportunity after receiving the earliest warning that her illness was attended with danger. I lost not an hour in crossing America – but I arrived too late to hear her last wishes and injunctions, to smooth her pillow, and to close her eyes . . . I have now six children to take charge of, and feebly indeed shall I replace her in that charge, while the Legation will have lost the bright and good spirit to which it owed entirely whatever attraction it possessed.'

Willis was also over-harsh in his judgement of Parkes' motives. Parkes was no doubt ambitious in the sense that he was gratified by the honours conferred on him and he doubtless welcomed the power which his position gave him. But, although by the standards of the time he was not badly paid (his salary on appointment to Japan was £3000 a year and he was granted a further £1000 for his outfit[11]), he was not motivated by pecuniary gain. In 1872 Parkes who was in London on leave and in attendance on the Iwakura Mission was questioned about diplomatic salaries by a House of Commons Committee. He considered[12] that all grades of the service in Japan were underpaid. In his case he had '. . . only just made both ends meet. I came away from Japan, after six years service there, poorer than I went.' When he was transferred to Peking[13] he accepted a reduction of £500 a year in the stipend attached to the Legation at Peking which had been demanded by a House of Commons Committee in a fit of economy. It has never been suggested that Parkes, unlike some of his diplomatic colleagues in Japan, ever profited from commercial transactions. Nor did even his detractors ever suggest that he was corrupt. His main motive was probably the old-fashioned one of carrying out his tasks as effectively and as conscientiously as possible.

Parkes was not demonstratively a religious man but in accordance with Victorian tradition he maintained a system of family prayers. Nor was he a profound man. But, as Dickins noted:[14] 'Men of action are not profound men, they are neither philosophers nor *erudits*. Their qualities are insight, decision, and courage moral and physical, and with these Sir Harry Parkes was abundantly endowed. If scantily "school'd he was yet learned" in the real knowledge of life, but he never lost a certain boyish ardour and simplicity. Although in his later time no student, he was always a great reader, a lover of poetry, and a devourer of as much modern literature as he could find time for. His wonderful industry extended to everything that bore upon his work.' He worked hard at his French. He was a '. . . most suggestive and stimulating President of the Asiatic Society.' A.B. Mitford, later Lord Redesdale who was a member of Parkes' staff in Japan, agreed[15]: 'Busy as his life was, he had read greedily, and he often took me by surprise in unexpected ways.' (Willis, however, disagreed[16]: 'Sir Harry never reads nor studies anything. He is shallow to a degree on every subject.') Parkes, despite the fact that he was an accomplished Chinese interpreter never seems to have worked at the Japanese language, but this is understandable. He was 38 when he came to Japan and was extremely busy. Moreover, he had able interpreters to work for him.

There can be no disputing his courage. Various attempts were made on his life while he was in Japan. The most dramatic of these was the attack by *ronin* on the British Legation party on its way to the Imperial Palace in Kyoto for an audience with the young Emperor on 22 March 1868.[17] One man rushed at Parkes, '. . . cutting and slashing as he went, but fortunately missing the Minister. Satow had a narrow escape, for his horse was wounded close to his rider's knee, and part of the poor beast's nose was sliced off.' When Mitford ran forward to see what had happened, he found Parkes '. . . sitting on his horse, quite unmoved . . . As

4

I came up with them I stumbled over something. It was a man's head.' As they wended their way back to the Chionin temple in Kyoto where the Legation was temporarily housed, Mitford was walking by Sir Harry's horse when Parkes turned to him and said: 'Sensation diplomacy this, Mitford.' Satow[18] said of him: 'I do not think that his coolness and fortitude in the moment of peril have ever been surpassed by any man not bred to war.'

Parkes was courageous in other ways too. He was fearless in defending what he considered to be right irrespective of the position of the person he was speaking to. In those days travelling to the East, although much faster and easier than in the days of sailing ships, was still long and uncomfortable. In the treaty ports of the East disease was rife with smallpox, cholera and typhoid endemic. Indeed it was typhoid fever combined with overwork which caused Parkes's death in Peking in 1885. Parkes never hesitated in the face of these discomforts and threats to his life.

Nor did anyone doubt Parkes's application and willingness to work indefatigably. He had an insatiable curiosity and expected his staff to work as long hours as he did. He was thus a hard task-master. Mitford and Willis both found Parkes a maker of work. Mitford described him[19] as '. . . a very bustling man' '. . . full of whims, and seeming to seek out discomfort as he does danger for its own sake.' Willis[20] found Parkes '. . . a little pestilently active. He gets up at 5 in the morning and works all day plotting and scheming to get up a sensation.' 'He is always muddling and meddling . . . He has the genius of misrule about him.'[21] 'Our chief is the most restless troublesome man you can imagine and seldom gives you leisure to do anything for one self.' Willis preferred a quieter life than he could obtain under Parkes! Satow[22] commented that Parkes was '. . . entirely absorbed in the duties of his post, untiring in his endeavours to obtain a correct view of his surroundings, never sparing himself, and requiring from his subordinates the same zealous assiduity.'

Parkes was, as Satow also wrote,[23] '. . . of an active inquisitive temperament.' In Niigata in 1867 Parkes '. . . signalized himself in the eyes of the natives by scrambling up to the top of a large shed under which a junk was in the course of construction, to get a view of the surrounding country, much to the horror of Mitford and myself, who were so orientalized by this time in our notions that we longed to see our chief conduct himself with the impassive dignity of a Japanese gentleman.'

5

If Parkes cared little about dignity he was determined not to be set down by any of his diplomatic colleagues. Parkes's *bête noire* in the diplomatic corps in the days before the Meiji Restoration was Leon Roches, the French Minister. Mitford described Roches[24] as: '. . . a handsome swashbuckler, who had been an interpreter in the French army in Algeria. He was far more a picturesque Spahi than a diplomatist . . . It is not too much to say that Parkes and Roches hated one another and were as jealous as a couple of women . . . One day Parkes came into my room like a whirlwind, his fair, reddish hair almost standing on end, as was its way when he was excited. "What is the matter, Sir Harry?" I asked. "Matter!" was the answer. "What do you think that fellow Roches has just told me? He is going to have a *mission militaire* out from France to drill the Shogun's army! Never mind! I'll be even with him. I'll have a *mission navale!*" – and he did.'

Parkes's relations with some of his other colleagues were friendly enough. In particular he seems to have got on well with Von Brandt, the Prussian Minister. He did not, however, care for some of his American colleagues whom he suspected of double dealing.

Parkes was undoubtedly domineering in his manner. He was also very quick-tempered and his language was frequently most undiplomatic. In 1866 Willis[25] thought Parkes' manner with Japanese officials '. . . rather rough . . . he scolds them. Our last interview was the most rugged one I have yet seen.' Of a later interview with the *Gorōjū* Willis commented that this was 'A most stormy badgering style of interview. I can tell you Parkes is not overburdened with politeness to the Japanese. I almost fear he will goad them too far.' Satow who had to act as his interpreter in many of these interviews recorded how in Tokushima in 1867 '. . . Sir Harry [who had been kept waiting while Satow tried to procure three palanquins] lost his temper and swore he would not be kept waiting for all the d–d *daimios* in Japan.'[26] In February 1868 Satow was pleased to be able to record[27] that Sir Harry was then '. . . in high spirits and in very good temper. We had no more of the interviews with Japanese officials at which he used strong language, and interpreting for him which used to be a painful duty, was changed into a labour of love.' Unfortunately, this situation did not last and Satow recorded[28] how in December 1868 Parkes '. . . lost his temper over the arguments used by Kido [over the treatment of

Christians by the Meiji government] and made use of very violent language such as I do not care to repeat.'

Even Dickins noted[29] that Parkes's relations with Japanese representatives were often difficult and stormy: 'With the Japanese Ministers in the sixties, his manner was not always admirable, but the conviction of those who knew him best is that he often lost sight of the Minister altogether, and thought only of some act or proposition that in his opinion – and his opinion was never hastily formed or unsupported by an ample basis of facts – militated against British interests or the welfare of Japan herself. As he grew older the irritability or whatever it was lessened and finally disappeared altogether.' Satow did not agree with this view.[30] Grace Fox[31] concluded: 'Granted that his outbursts of temper and arrogance often offended the sensitive, increasingly self-confident Japanese, the Meiji ministers sought and respected his advice from the beginning of their government.' Basil Hall Chamberlain[32] wrote of him: 'His outspoken threats and occasional fits of passion earned for him the dread and dislike of the Japanese during his sojourn in Japan. But no sooner had he quitted Tokyo than they began to acknowledge that his high-handed policy had been founded on reason . . . a high Japanese official . . . said to a friend of the present writer: "Sir Harry Parkes was the only foreigner in Japan whom we could not twist round our little finger."'

Parkes's actions were often not as rough as his language. After the Bizen incident in Kobe on 4 February 1868 when there had been trouble between men of the Bizen clan and the foreigners who had moved from Osaka to Hyogo (Kobe) because of the disturbances in Osaka, the Japanese officer considered to be responsible for the incident, Taki Zenzaburō, was ordered to commit *seppuku*. Parkes had taken a very strong line after the incident but, when the heads of diplomatic missions considered the Japanese plea for clemency, it was Parkes[33] with the support of his Netherlands colleague who argued forcefully for clemency but they were overruled by the others who demanded that the punishment be carried out. After the attack on him in Kyoto in March that year Parkes very readily accepted the apologies of the Mikado's ministers. He could be and frequently was magnanimous despite extreme provocation.

His relations with members of his staff were also much better than his irascibility might suggest. He took care to commend good work in writing to the Foreign Office and did not claim for himself all the merit due to the Legation. Satow[34] who never cared for Parkes recorded that '. . . he was strict and severe in service matters, but in his private relations gracious to all those who had occasion to seek his help, and a faithful friend to all who won his goodwill. Unfortunately, I was not one of these, and the result was that from the beginning we were never friends, down to the very last, though he never had reasons to complain of sloth or unreadiness to take my share of the work.' It is possible to surmise that Parkes disapproved of Satow's private life (he had a Japanese mistress and two children by her). Parkes may also have resented Satow's independent ideas.

Satow got across Parkes at a very early stage. In August 1866[35] Parkes, having given Satow and Siebold a quantity of official documents to translate, they addressed letters to him asking him to recommend that they should receive an extra £100 a year. 'This brought down his wrath upon our heads.' Satow wrote to his father that the service was not worth remaining in. He soon received a telegram telling him to come home. Satow then approached Parkes and asked for his resignation to be accepted. 'After a little humming and hawing, he finally produced from a drawer a despatch from Lord Clarendon [then Foreign Secretary], which had been lying there for several days, granting the applications of both Siebold and myself, and I consequently abandoned my intention of quitting the service.' In March 1868 Parkes, on the curious grounds that Satow had not been presented at the British court, decided that Satow could not accompany him on his call on the Emperor. He took only Mitford into this interview while Satow and others remained outside. This rule did not prevent Satow from being presented to the Emperor in May that year when Parkes handed over his credentials in Osaka. Was this snobbery or spite?

Willis[36] thought that 'Parkes killed a poor fellow called MacDonald by worrying his life out of him . . . McDonald died of softening of the brain brought on, I believe, by the acute general unhappiness of having to deal with Parkes every day.' John MacDonald, first assistant in the Legation office, died in May 1866 of apoplexy and softening of the brain.

Dickins[37] wrote: 'Out of his officers he got as much work as he could, but he never spared himself. With them his relations were most cordial (though he could both speak and act sharply at times) . . . His purse was always open to those in need of assistance, after a frank and generous fashion that veiled the service . . . Though in official matters he went at once and straight to the point, and was apt to be somewhat brusque and exigent, especially with men of slow or confused minds, in all private relations he was one of the most long-suffering, friendly, and courteous of men. There was not an atom of factitious dignity about him, but one saw at a glance that the earnest and busy Minister was not a man to be trifled with – and no one ever attempted to trifle with him.'

All the above comments show that Parkes had outstanding qualities of courage, energy, drive and dedication. He was a difficult man to work for and his irascibility must have made him often insufferable but he was obviously an outstanding head of mission. What did he achieve?

★   ★   ★

Any fair assessment of Parkes must take into account his upbringing, the attitudes of Victorian England, the nature of British power in the second half of the nineteenth century as well as attitudes in Japan towards foreigners and their behaviour towards the first foreigners who came to work in Japan.

Parkes was largely self-educated. He had worked very hard to achieve his appointment to Japan at only 38 and was understandably contemptuous of those who were not ready to work as hard as he did or were not as quick in their perceptions. He certainly did not suffer fools gladly. He had had some bitter experiences in China and encountered many examples of official deceit. These all tended to make him highly suspicious of oriental officials.

Britain in the second half of the nineteenth century was at the height of its power. The Victorians believed that their achievements were the result of their own efforts and that Britain had much to teach developing countries of which Japan was one. British business needed markets and sources of supply and the Victorians were not in the mood to tolerate their business being frustrated by xenophobia or the seclusion policies of other countries.

Rutherford Alcock, Parkes' predecessor as Minister to Japan, had found the officials of the *bakufu* with whom he had to deal deceitful, incompetent and frequently powerless. There were no proper criminal or civil codes in Japan. Torture was an accepted practice in dealing with criminals and executions were common. The xenophobia which the authorities did nothing to curb led to frequent attacks on foreigners and life in the treaty ports in the 1860s was distinctly insecure. The hierarchy of Japan which put the merchants at the bottom of the pile seemed topsy-turvy to the foreigners who found the merchants with whom they came in contact generally dishonest. It was thus hardly surprising that the merchants who came out from Britain included a number who were themselves dishonest. Life was nasty, brutish and short in the treaty ports in those early days and the chance to win a quick fortune tended to attract the rough and tough as well as the charlatans.

Parkes' instructions from Lord Russell, then Foreign Secretary, were modelled on those given to Alcock, his predecessor[38] and he was given freedom to act as the state of affairs in Japan seemed to warrant. He was to seek '. . . the abandonment of any pretence on the part of the Mikado or the Tycoon to violate treaties, and banish foreigners from Japan.' He was also to seek to ensure '. . . the faithful execution of these treaties [and] confirmation of the Treaties by the Mikado, or the formal admission that the Tycoon . . . required no sanction from the Mikado.' He was also to obtain '. . . the trial of all persons accused of murdering British subjects and their execution, if convicted.'

Parkes carried out these instructions faithfully. The American missionary and writer about Japan, W.E. Griffis,[39] declared: 'English scholarship first discovered the true source of power, exposed the counterfeit government in Yedo, read the riddle of ages and rent the veil that so long hid the truth. The English minister, Sir Harry Parkes, who risked his life to find the truth, stripped the Shogun of his fictitious title of "Majesty", . . . recognized the new National Government, and thus laid the foundation of the true diplomacy in Japan.' Ignoring the hyperbole, it is fair to say that it was largely due to Parkes that the Mikado's acceptance of the treaties was confirmed. This in its turn further undermined the Shogun's position and contributed to the fall of the shogunate.

In 1866, Clarendon, then Foreign Secretary,[40] instructed Parkes '. . . not to take sides or express an opinion for or against either party in the approaching contest. Britain's aim in Japan was not to seek political influence but to develop commerce.' In 1867 Clarendon's successor, Lord Stanley, reaffirmed the policy of neutrality, but[41] Parkes might '. . . promote as far as you can any system which, by securing to the Daimios a fair share in the commerce of Japan, will enlist their sympathies in behalf of foreign nations and so promote the development of trade.' Parkes[42] proclaimed British neutrality in the civil war of 1867/9 and called for 'a strict and impartial neutrality' by all British subjects. This proclamation did not endear him to some British merchants but Parkes did his best to ensure that the proclamation was observed. Grace Fox, however, noted that[43] 'His consent to the withdrawal of the allied neutrality proclamation in February 1869 hastened the government's defeat of the rebels in the north that June.'

Professor W.G. Beasley has concluded[44] that in his reports: 'Parkes shows himself as politically "neutral" in the sense that he was not greatly concerned about who won the struggle in Japan, provided foreign interests were defended . . . In fact, the one respect in which he can be said to have "interfered" was that he invariably gave his approval – often openly – to any plan that might result in greater stability.' Beasley stresses[45] that 'Parkes was more concerned to see law and order established in the country, that is, an environment in which foreign trade could flourish, than he was in the question of which of the rival groups should establish it.' 'In so far as Parkes went beyond his purely diplomatic brief, defined in terms of defending British interests, it was more in the service of "enlightenment" (*bummei kaika*) than of Satsuma-Chōshū power.'[46] Parkes defined his own objective in 1867 as being: '. . . to divert their [i.e Japanese] attention from military glitter to industrial enterprise.'[47]. He also constantly reminded the leaders of Japan of the need to make Japan '. . . into one firm and compact State, governed by uniform and just laws.'[48]

If Parkes himself was 'neutral', Satow and Mitford who were members of his staff were certainly not neutral. They cultivated the representatives of the *tozama daimyō*[49] with Parkes' approval. Parkes no doubt justified this in his own mind as an essential means of gathering information and intelligence. But he could not have condoned Satow's famous *Japan Times* articles of 1866[50] without compromising his neutrality. Satow asserted:[51] 'As far as I know it never came to the ears of my chief, but it may fairly be supposed to have been not without its influence upon the relations between the English Legation and the new government afterwards established in the beginning of 1868.' It is difficult to believe that Parkes who was very well informed did not get to know that Satow had written these articles. Perhaps he decided to turn a Nelsonian blind eye to them in the hope that they could be turned to British advantage. But Satow's disobedience of the clear instructions from London may have been a factor in the coolness between the two men.[52]

Did Anglo-French rivalry and the jealousy between Parkes and his French colleague Roches who firmly supported the Shogunate make Parkes more inclined towards the supporters of the Restoration? This may have been a sub-conscious factor but there is no evidence to suggest that it was a material one.

The conclusion must be that in the first years of his mission Parkes's achievements were outstanding. He had certainly protected and furthered British interests and had for his part maintained a neutral position.

★   ★   ★

During the second part of his long stay between 1869 and 1883 one important issue which took up much of Parkes's time was the problem of the formerly 'hidden' Christians who continued to be persecuted by the new Meiji government. This was wholly unacceptable to Western governments and public opinion. Parkes[53] '. . . counselled that Western remonstrances should continue to be urged "with consideration and discretion". He understood the Japanese government's position. Roman Catholic proselytism at Urakami [in Kyushu] had assailed its dignity and authority. It was compelled to act if only to satisfy popular opinion which seemed to be vehemently directed against native converts . . . Events in time confirmed Parkes' faith in his personal influence with important Japanese ministers.' The persecutions were maintained but Parkes[54] '. . . continued to view the Japanese explanations tolerantly. He understood their intense national pride, their well-founded fear of Catholic proselytism, and the precarious position of the Emperor's government.' Britain and the United States opposed the view of the French Minister, M. D'Outrey,[55] that '. . . a strong and united demonstration of force by European powers would be the only effectual mode of preventing the recurrence of such acts and checking the intolerance of the Japanese government.'

Dr Gordon Daniels has asserted[56] that '. . . Parkes' approach to this problem was largely shaped by his hostility to Roman Catholicism, and particularly its Jesuit missionaries.' This is not supported by Grace Fox's account and it could be that Parkes was being politically sensitive and practical. Daniels goes on to note that, when on 9 February 1872 Parkes met representatives of the Evangelical Alliance, he rebutted their criticisms point by point: 'On this potentially emotive occasion Parkes exhibited qualities which are rarely associated with his East Asian diplomacy: finesse, sensitivity and extreme courteousness. He countered many criticisms with simple factual statements, and explained the complexities of Japan's religious difficulties. He concluded by urging patience in dealing with an enlightened, well-meaning government.'

Parkes devoted much effort to helping and advising the Meiji government in its efforts to modernize the country. In doing so, he was doubtless motivated to a considerable extent by the desire to gain commercial benefits in the long run for Britain, but he also wanted to help the development of Japan. As Hazel Jones has pointed out,[57] Britain provided the largest number of foreign employees. Between 1868 and 1900 employees of British origin provided 4353 man-years of service. The next largest figure of 1578 man-years was France followed by Germany (1223) and the USA (1213). Parkes played an important part in this process. To give one example Parkes was primarily responsible for the appointment in 1868 of Richard Henry Brunton, the first of the *o-yatoi gaijin* of the Meiji government to construct lighthouses throughout Japan in accordance with the supplementary agreement of 1866. Brunton's appointment was as Chief Engineer to the Lighthouse Department of the Japanese government.

Throughout his service in Japan Brunton had the backing of Parkes.[58] He summarised his difficulties with other foreign employees and with his Japanese colleagues and assistants in these words: 'The conscientious and efficient conduct of work in Japan was a task which presented the most perplexing difficulties . . . Resignation, insubordination, absence from duty, drunkenness, and other aberrations of conduct among Europeans employed in the Japanese government service, became frequent and distressing. On the other hand, the semi-ignorance of the native servants of the Emperor, and the self-esteem, craftiness and corruption of the Japanese underlings rendered cooperation by an honourable foreigner with them extremely irritating.' These latter problems frequently had to be taken up by Parkes and inevitably brought him into conflict with Japanese ministers. It is difficult not to sympathize with Parkes and the more honourable British employees in their difficulties. No doubt they would have done better to exercise greater restraint and tact but such reservations are readily made with the hindsight of history.

Among the many areas in which Parkes actively campaigned on behalf of British interests were telegraphs in which, after the Restoration, according to Grace Fox[59], Parkes 'forestalled' a Shogunate concession to the Swiss and Austrian governments. Parkes was also an advocate of improved communications especially roads; but he also backed the Japanese desire to build railways. This involved his old crony and old China hand, H.N. Lay, but, as Grace Fox has pointed out[60], 'There seems to be no evidence that Parkes or Her Majesty's Government tried to defend Lay when the Japanese government cancelled his commission . . .'

But, according to Hazel Jones[61], Parkes sometimes overdid his interventions on behalf of British employees, for example, in the case of Alexander Pope Porter, harbour master at Hakodate, who was given a contract in 1874 as sailing master: 'The truculent Parkes took umbrage at the clause rejecting his mediation and charged Japanese officials with nefarious plotting. When he received no satisfaction, he carried his argument with Foreign Minister Terajima Munenori [with whom his relations were frequently strained] to irrational lengths.'

But the most serious and contentious problem which Parkes had to face in these years was the question of treaty revision and the related issue of free trade versus protection. Dr Daniels has declared[62] that 'To Parkes treaty revision was a process that should proceed at a gradual, organic speed. This approach not only emanated from his basic philosophy, it coincided with the opinions of the British merchant community, which he sought to represent.' In fact, although Parkes' views were important, he remained the servant of the British government and the latter, no doubt primed by the arguments produced by Parkes, saw no need to hurry over treaty revision. Indeed, in London it was regarded as essential that, before extraterritoriality could be abolished, the Japanese should not only enact a 'civilized' criminal code and code of criminal procedure but should prove that they could operate if effectively and fairly. It was also felt to be essential for the sake of commerce that Japan should have adequate civil and commercial codes. At the Preliminary Conference on Treaty Revision held in Tokyo in 1882 Inoue Kaoru, its Japanese president, produced on 1 June[63] '. . . an altogether novel scheme of jurisdiction under which extra-territoriality wholly disappeared.' The American Minister nodded his approval, but Parkes submitted a memorandum in which he argued that, while the British government would sympathize with '. . . any efforts that might be made to bring the laws of Japan into such a condition as to allow of the entire abolition of the consular jurisdictions, . . . the new Penal Code had only been one year in operation, and '. . . neither civil nor commercial codes were yet in existence. As late as the close of 1879 an able Japanese publicist declared that the laws did not duly protect the lives, liberties, and property of the Japanese themselves, and required very considerable reform before they could be generally approved by the Japanese people.'

At the conference which ended in July 1882 there were no fundamental differences of opinion[64] over the tariff question, although the President of the conference proposed a rise in the general *ad valorem* tariff from 7 to 10% in order to increase 'the stock of specie in the country'. But many leading Japanese preferred the protectionist system of the USA to the free-trade principles advocated by the British. They also resented the fact that Japanese tariffs remained fixed by the tariff convention of 1866 which Parkes had worked so hard to achieve at that time.

Revision of the so-called 'unequal' treaties had become a major Japanese national objective and aroused Japanese xenophobia and nationalism to such an emotional pitch that any Japanese who attempted to propose any compromise, such as Count Ōkuma Shigenobu, was subject to violent attacks. Parkes' objections to treaty revision, however well founded at the time, inevitably provided fuel for his enemies.

Parkes would not, however, allow British subjects to abuse the privileges of extraterritoriality. In 1876 J.R. Black published without Japanese permission (Japanese press censorship was severe) a vernacular newspaper called the *Bankoku Shimbun*. This was stopped by the Japanese authorities who fined Black and appealed to Parkes to prohibit the publication of Japanese newspapers by British subjects. 'Sir Harry[65] saw the absurdity of so interpreting the extraterritorial privilege as to enable the native press to evade the laws of the land by the simple expedient of placing itself under the protection of a foreign power.' He accordingly used the powers granted to him by Order in Council to prohibit such evasions. His action aroused the praise of Japanese leaders but the condemnation of some foreigners.

Parkes' efforts to influence Meiji government policies were often unsuccessful as Dr Daniels has pointed out.[66] In particular he failed in his efforts at deterring the Japanese expedition to Formosa in 1874, although Sir Thomas Wade, the British Minister in Peking, was able to help with the final settlement and was duly thanked by the Japanese for his efforts.

By the early 1880s Parkes who had lost his wife and was increasingly unwell appears to have become still more arrogant and irritable in his official dealings with the Japanese. In a letter to Dickins[67] in 1881 Satow wrote: '. . . you would not credit to what extent he is the bugbear of the Japanese public; in the popular estimation he occupies much the same position as "Boney" with us fifty years ago. It has been going on for the past ten years . . . no one can deny his great qualities and his fitness to meet any dangerous crisis. His talents are however thrown away here. There is no analogy at all between the circumstances here and in China, where he learnt his diplomacy . . . here it is the square peg in the round hole.' Satow concluded that Parkes was not a 'diplomatist of the Talleyrand type' able to respond to the nuances and subtleties of Japanese behaviour. Satow was no friend of Parkes but his comments cannot be dismissed as simple prejudice if only because they match what we learn from other sources.

There can be no doubt that, if the Japanese had requested his recall, the British government would have had to comply. But perhaps some Japanese officials feared that such a step might jeopardize other Japanese interests or there were influential people in the Japanese government who appreciated Parkes' talents and help. His enemies instead used elaborate and indirect means to secure his removal.[68] The American journalist, E.H. House[69], '. . . was employed to write anti-British propaganda, and in a single year, 1875, wrote two pamphlets which were designed to create consternation in the British Legation.

Between 1877 and 1880 House received further subsidies to support the publication of the *Tokio Times*, a largely anti-British newspaper. In this paper House[70] '. . . attacked British economic policy, criticised Parkes bitterly, and argued violently for the abolition of extraterritoriality.'

Sir John Pope Hennessy, the Governor of Hong Kong,[71] caused a great deal of trouble on a visit to Japan. Parkes in a letter of 1879[72] said that he had invited him and his wife to dinner. He '. . . had had to have an explanation with him in consequence of the way in which he has been talking among the Japanese and foreigners. I told him that, if I had visited Hongkong, I should not have presumed to interfere with his business in the same way as he has done with mine, and much other plain language, for I wished him to know my mind. He defended himself but faintly, saying that he had been misrepresented, which, however, I know is not the case. I don't think he is accustomed to get a good setting down from any one, and I think I gave him one. We managed, notwithstanding, to part apparent friends, though he is a man with whom I shall never be on good terms, as I utterly mistrust him.'

Another tiresome character for Parkes was Sir Edward J. Reed KCB, MP. In January 1879 Parkes noted[73] that 'Reed, the late constructor of our navy – who built the three new ships for the Japanese – is now here, the guest of the Japanese Government who are making a great fuss about him. It remains to be seen what each wants from the other, but I doubt whether Japanese finances will permit of their giving Mr Reed [as he then was] orders for more ships.' At the end of Reed's stay of three months Parkes recorded that he had not seen much of Reed: 'He told me that the only expenditure needed by the Japanese was *brains*.' Parkes[74] believed that Reed had influenced the Japanese government to terminate the contracts of the remaining twenty-three members of the British naval mission in 1879 and had offered the Japanese men of his own selection.

Reed and Hennessy appear to have had contacts with House who[75] travelled to Britain at Japanese expense in 1881 to contact editors, politicians and men of influence and to undermine Parkes' position.

Parkes, despite his declining health, was still only 55 when he was transferred to Peking in July 1883. He clearly deserved another post and he was well qualified to return to China where he had spent his formative years. Peking was then regarded as a more important mission than Tokyo.

Whatever the frictions which had existed for many years between Parkes and Japanese leaders, he left with many expressions of thanks and goodwill. Were these just *tatemae* or did they represent Japanese *honne*? It is not possible to reach a final judgement so many years after the event but it is hard to believe that they were not at least to a considerable extent sincere. At a farewell luncheon given to him by the Emperor on 22 August 1883, to which all the members of the Japanese cabinet had been invited, the Emperor in a gracious speech[76] declared that, if British regulations had permitted, he would have conferred on Parkes the Grand Cordon of the Rising Sun but, because of the rules of the British court, he presented Parkes instead with a censer and flower vase '. . . which have been in my possession . . . as a token of my high regard for you.' On the evening of 27 August a farewell address was presented to Sir Harry on behalf of the British and foreign residents of Yokohama expressing their gratitude for all he had done to promote the well-being of the settlement. On Parkes' death Inoue Kaoru, then Japanese Foreign Minister,[77] sent a telegram saying 'His Imperial Majesty's Government cannot but feel great grief at the death of one who contributed so much to the improvement and progress of this country, and whose long residence has won so many friends among Japanese officials.'

Dr Daniels[78] has said that: 'Fundamental to Parkes' outlook was a critical view of Japan which failed to take account of its considerable achievements.' He went on to assert that such views were echoed by many people in Britain until the 1960s. It is hardly fair to make such a comment on Parkes who was in Japan at a time of revolutionary change and when Japanese xenophobia had been at its height. Japanese achievements were in those days largely confined to the cultural sphere and Parkes had little time to study Japanese culture. It is moreover the duty of a diplomat to take a critical view of the countries in which he serves. We may be sure that Japanese diplomats take a critical view of Britain. It is, however, essential that the critical view should be well based on observation and should be as fair as possible. Parkes was assiduous in collecting information and his judgements were, as Professor Beasley has pointed out, generally balanced although they were inevitably to some extent coloured by the age in which he lived and had been brought up.

Parkes' achievements cannot be dismissed lightly. They probably could have been greater if he had managed to exercise more restraint and tact. He was left in Tokyo for too long and British interests would have been better served if he had been transferred in the first half of the 1870s. But Parkes had received his appointment at the early age of 38 and the only obvious alternative post for him was that of Minister in Peking and this was not available at that time or Parkes was not then considered the top candidate. To have forced Parkes to retire early would have been unjust to a distinguished public servant and it is at least debatable whether in the long run his extended term of service in Japan was as harmful to British interests as Satow clearly thought it was.

Parkes cannot be faulted for lack of industry and application. Nor did he ever neglect British commercial interests. He rates a high place in the list of great British diplomats of the nineteenth century – a period when heads of mission, if only because of the slowness of communications, had much more discretion to act independently than they have today.

I would not have wanted to serve under Sir Harry Parkes (I have sadly been unable to find any evidence that he had much sense of humour and an ability to laugh at his own foibles). But I have to admire his fortitude and dedication.

2

British Journalists in Meiji Japan

JAMES HOARE

JAPAN'S TREATY-PORT PRESS

BY THE TIME OF THE MEIJI RESTORATION, the foreign-language press, the majority of whose journalists were British, was an established feature of Japanese treaty-port life. This was not surprising. From humble beginnings at Canton in 1827, newspapers had spread to most foreign settlements in East Asia. They were sometimes little more than advertising sheets but they met a local need and 'mail editions' gave the foreign communities an international voice.[1] Their history is often obscure, though much can be gleaned form the publications themselves, especially from the editorial quarrels which enlivened their pages and from the court cases which sometimes resulted. John Reddie Black was the only journalist to write a book on local history.[2]

The first foreign-language newspaper in Japan, the *Nagasaki Shipping List and Advertiser*, started at Nagasaki in 1861. Its founder was A.W. Hansard, an auctioneer and jobbing printer. The annual subscription was $20 Mexican, the accepted currency in the Japan ports, for four sides of news and advertisements four times a week. In subsequent years, over forty newspapers and some thirty magazines and periodicals were published in settlements whose foreign population, excluding the Chinese, was at its maximum about 5000. Most were produced in Yokohama where, by the mid-1890s, some 2500 Western residents lived. One contemporary noted, perhaps tongue in cheek, that this showed 'a remarkable degree of journalistic activity', indicating 'a positive craving for news on the part of the public'.[3] Other factors included international rivalries, personal ambitions and subsidies. A craving for news was probably low on the list.

Even successful papers seldom sold more than five hundred copies. The result was high subscription rates averaging $24 per year, with overseas or special editions extra. Advertisements were lucrative; Yokohama rates in 1882 were up to four times those of major London newspapers. Also important was job printing. One British official in 1885 claimed this was the chief source of profit for many papers, and another wrote in 1897 that it was 'highly lucrative . . . far more so than the newspaper', for one Nagasaki publisher.[4] Capital equipment was cheap. The *Japan Gazette* was still printed on hand presses in 1891. In 1893 the presses of the *Rising Sun and Nagasaki Express* were valued at only $1000, although paper and binding materials were worth $7000. Salaries were a major cost. They varied from $20 to $25 a month paid to Japanese compositors (who replaced the earlier Portugese in the mid-70s) and translators, to $500 paid briefly to the editor of the *Japan Gazette* in 1891, five times more than the *Kobe Chronicle* paid Lafcadio Hearn three years later. The usual rate was $150— 200 in the 1890s. Another cost was telegram subscriptions, though few paid the high rates charged by the Japanese government – four times the Shanghai rate – after the telegraph reached Japan in 1871. Some papers managed without; others poached.

THE BRITISH JOURNALISTS

Although newspapers and periodicals were published in a wide variety of languages, most were in English, and the majority of journalists were British. There were many Scots and Irish, while the 'first professionally trained newspaperman in Japan', was the Cornishman, J.E. Beale, for many years the managing editor of the *Japan Mail*.[5] Some of the British might now be Australians or New Zealanders. The founder of the *Nagasaki Shipping List and Advertiser*, A.W. Watkins, had lived in New Zealand before coming to Japan. John Reddie Black, born in Scotland, had later lived in South Australia.[6] John Henry Brooke, owner of the *Japan Herald* from 1870 to his death in 1902, was born in Lincolnshire. He, too, emigrated to Australia, was active in politics and arrived in Japan in 1867. To contemporaries and themselves, all were British.[7]

Most journalists were men, but Alice Mildred Vaughan Smith (or Vaughan-Smith), also worked as a professional journalist in Japan. She began as a leader writer on the *Japan Gazette* and correspondent for the *North China Daily News* in 1889. In 1891, she fell foul of the *Gazette's* editor, Walter Dening, and was dismissed. The owners of the *Gazette*, unable to afford Dening, then appointed her editor, a post she held until 1893. She later edited various China coast papers and was a correspondent for others and for the London *Standard*. She wrote two books about Japan and died in London in 1908.[8]

THE MAIN NEWSPAPERS: YOKOHAMA

Nagasaki was a backwater even in 1861. In November 1861, therefore, Hansard moved to Yokohama and established the weekly *Japan Herald*. Yokohama thus became the centre of foreign journalism in Japan, a position it held without dispute until the 1890s. The *Japan Herald* remained British until 1902, when it was bought by the *Deutsche Japan Post*, which ran it as its English-language edition until both were suppressed in 1914.[9]

To many, the *Herald* became synonymous with treaty-port journalism, especially after it was bought by J.H. Brooke in 1870. Opposed to Japanese policies, firm in defence of foreign rights, against treaty revision, it was the mouthpiece of 'John Bull' in Yokohama and Japan. Brooke's role in local affairs reflected this stand, and he was very opposed to treaty revision. To one British minister, he was 'a professional agitator of a rather vulgar class', willing to accept Japanese money when it suited him.[10] But his views struck a chord, and the *Herald* was one of the Yokohama papers most frequently quoted in British periodicals in the 1870s.[11]

This conservative role did not go unchallenged. Chronologically, the *Japan Times* came first, but is was the *Japan Gazette* which most contemporaries linked with the *Herald*. Like other papers, the *Gazette's* allegiance could waver if money was available, but it generally took a conservative stance. It was founded in 1867 by John Reddie Black, a man of many talents who had a great influence on both foreign and Japanese journalism.[12] He had been part proprietor of the *Japan Herald*, but he was a bad businessman, and by 1867 was forced to leave the *Herald*. He started the *Gazette* on a shoe-string, using wooden type and an old press. It was an evening daily, which also led the *Herald* to switch to evening publication. Under Black, the *Gazette* was moderately critical of the Japanese government.[13]

By the early 1870s, Black had new interests and he sold the *Gazette* in 1874. It passed to a consortium including J.R. Anglin, who had come to Japan in the mid-1860s with the British army. He purchased his discharge, and stayed on as a compositor and part owner of the *Japan Times*, then joined the *Japan Gazette* as a foreman printer. He became sole owner from 1884 or 1885 until his death in 1891. His interest was the technical side of the paper, and he left editorial matters to others.[14]

The first of Anglin's known editors was A.H. Cole. He ceased to be editor in 1877 or 1878 but he continued to write for the *Gazette*. In an obituary in 1884, the *Gazette* noted that he was well-educated and a good writer, but lacked steadiness and force of character, and did not get on with his colleagues.[15]

Cole was succeeded by W.H. Talbot. Despite claims that Talbot was 'a renegade American', he seems to have been British, with family connections elsewhere in East Asia. He was an accountant and loss adjuster, active in many aspects of treaty-port life, and had been manager of the *Japan Times*. By the early 1870s, he was Reuters' Yokohama agent. He later joined the Nippon Yusen Kaisha (NYK) as company secretary, and for a time was its Shanghai representative.[16] Under Talbot, the *Gazette* became more critical of the Japanese. It was not invariably hostile; it supported the government's policy over Korea in the early 1880s, for example. But its usual tone was disapproving, and like the *Herald*, it was a firm defender of foreign rights. It particularly opposed attempts to control trade or tamper with the currency. Talbot also conducted a bitter campaign against Martin Dohmen, one of Sir Harry Parkes's protégés in the British consular service.[17]

The shift which Talbot introduced in 1877 remained evident until the end of the century, under different editors. These included Alice Vaughan Smith and Walter Dening. Dening worked on other papers and was a scholar of distinction. Two others, Henry Tennant and Robert Hay, were both experienced journalists.[18]

The third of the major Yokohama papers was the *Japan Mail*. This began in 1865 as the *Japan Times*, the brainchild of Charles

Rickerby. Rickerby arrived in Japan about 1863 as the Yokohama manager of the Central Bank of Western India. He left banking under a cloud – one US consul described him as 'a disgraced, discharged, English bank official'. He was briefly an auctioneer and a founding member of the Yokohama Chamber of Commerce. He may have been connected with the Portugese-owned *Japan Commercial News* published from 1863 to 1865, and he was certainly a member of the consortium including Benjamin Seare and J.R. Anglin, which bought the plant in 1885. Anglin worked solely on the production side, and Seare left in 1866 to join the Japanese customs.[19] Rickerby thus became the editor. He began with sonorous statements of principle and fine editorials, and for a time enjoyed success. It was believed that the *Times* was close to the British legation, and it was in its pages that Ernest Satow published parts of his 'Eikoku sakuron' was well as anonymous editorials.[20]

The success was short-lived. Rickerby's editorials became hostile to British policies and he was a poor businessman. By 1869, he was in trouble and had to sell. He then held a variety of jobs while occasionally writing for various newspapers. He restarted the *Japan Times* in 1878, eventually merging it with the *Mail* while also writing for the *Gazette*. He was regularly in the courts either pursued by creditors or himself pursuing former employers. It was a heavy load and in spring 1879 he left for Britain, where he died that September.[21]

The *Japan Times* was bought by W.G. Howell, a British merchant, and H.N. Lay, formerly of the British consular service and the Chinese Maritime Customs, then in Japan to negotiate a railway loan. They changed the name to the *Japan Mail*, and it appeared under this title on 31 January 1870, though its masthead claimed it had been founded in 1865. It continued until 1917, when it merged with a third, Japanese-owned, *Japan Times*. Lay fell out with the Japanese over the railway loan and with Howell over the paper. Howell was left on his own; forty years' later, he was still bitter.[22]

The *Mail* projected itself as more respectable than other Yokohama papers. Its staff were active in public affairs and in the Asiatic Society of Japan. Howell was a council member of the Society until his departure from Japan in 1877, and the *Mail* often published the texts of the Society's papers and other learned treaties. It was magisterial in style, affecting to despise the petty quarrels of the other papers. A number of its editors acted as Japan correspondents for the London *Times*, which perhaps increased a sense of importance. The high moral tone, however, rarely prevented a *Mail* editorial from being as cutting as one from the *Herald* or *Gazette*.

The *Mail* had another characteristic, its alleged connection with the Japanese government. Allegations of subsidies were not infrequent, and probably every newspaper wrote to order at one time or another. In 1890, the British minister, Hugh Fraser, noted: '. . . English newspapers [in Japan] are of two kinds, those which are actually retained by the Japanese government, and those which do not happen to be under any official engagement . . .' and implied that the latter could be swayed by a switch in government advertising.[23] The relationship between the *Japan Mail* and the Japanese government was seen as different. As early as 1871, Rickerby claimed in court that the real purchasers of the newspaper were not Howell and Lay but the Japanese government. This was not denied, and it was repeated in the *Tōkei Journal* in 1874. In a later court case, however, and in a letter to the *Japan Gazette* in 1881, Howell stated that it was only in October 1873 that he had signed an agreement with the Japanese government to report 'the facts' about Japan's development to the outside world. Under this agreement, the government would pay for five hundred copies of each issue to be sent abroad. Howell retained the right to criticize the Japanese government, and had done so – the *Mail* was notably critical of the 1874 Formosan expedition. Whatever the nature of the agreement, it did not survive open hostility to Japanese policies, and it was apparently terminated in March 1875.[24]

Howell owned the *Mail* until January 1877, when he left Japan. He was briefly the proprietor of a horticultural journal, and subsequently the London-based secretary of the Shanghai Waterworks Company. He never returned to the East, though he regularly wrote querulous letters on Asian affairs.[25] The *Mail* was bought by G.C. Pearson, who continued Howell's more critical tone, but sold the paper at the end of 1877. The new owner was F.V. Dickins (1838–1915), a prominent Yokohama lawyer who had worked for the Japanese government and was a friend of Parkes, whose biographer he later became, and of Satow. There was a marked change of tone under his editorship but, in the summer of 1878, he had a breakdown and Charles

Rickerby became editor. Dickins retired to London. He later recovered, taught Japanese for a time and became registrar of London University.[26]

Rickerby's involvement was also short-lived, and the *Mail* passed through a succession of hands until it was acquired by Captain Francis Brinkley in January 1881. Brinkley owned it until his death in 1912. Brinkley was a Royal Artillery officer when he arrived in Japan in 1867. He was employed as a naval gunnery instructor and English and mathematics teacher, first by the Fukui *han* and then by the Japanese navy, though he remained on the British *Army List* until 1882. He acquired a considerable knowledge of Japanese and became an authority on Japanese art in general and porcelain in particular. He published several books. To visitors and some residents he was a courteous host, willing to share his delight in Japanese art. To others he was devious and too close to the Japanese.[27]

Under Brinkley, the paper continued its magisterial tone. The link with the London *Times* was re-established. Brinkley being its main correspondent from the early 1880s until after 1900. The *Mail* continued to be more literary than the other papers and it reflected Brinkley's artistic and scholarly interests. It also resumed a pro-Japanese stand. The treaty-port view was not ignored but the Japanese case was sympathetically presented. Some attributed this to Brinkley's absence from Yokohama, for, although the *Mail* was produced there, Brinkley lived in Tokyo, leaving the day-to-day work to J.E. Beale. Others testified to his wide range of contacts and his ability to talk to leading Japanese as factors leading him to a sympathetic and positive view of Japan, as was his marriage to a Japanese.

The less charitable attributed the *Mail*'s position to Japanese money. Brinkley may have acquired the *Mail* with Japanese assistance.[28] He was certainly an adviser to the government and to NYK at various times. During the 1884–5 Korean crisis, his role was important enough for the Japanese to contemplate decorating him, but British objections prevailed. The *Japan Punch* suggested that he should wear an appropriate costume, like the Koreans' German adviser.[29] (Later, he was to receive the Order of the Sacred Treasure, Third Class, a standard award for senior advisers.)

In a sense, therefore, he did receive Japanese money. He also admitted some Japanese involvement with the *Mail*. In February

1881, he published correspondence with Inoue Kaoru in which he noted that the Japanese government had a number of subscriptions to the newspaper but asserted his right to editorial independence. Such an arrangement was similar to that which Howell claimed to have in the early 1870s, and to that later offered to the *Kobe Chronicle* in 1892. In addition, Brinkley made no secret of his views. He wrote in one editorial that he had lived long in Japan, knew and liked the Japanese, though realising their faults, and thought Western policies 'illiberal and injudicious'.[30]

His fellow journalists saw it differently. 'Left his Queen and Country to become a Japanese flunkey', wrote the *Japan Punch* in October 1882. In 1906, the *Eastern World* carried an editorial which said in black capitals that 'Ex-Captain Francis Brinkley, R.A., editor of the *Japan Mail*, the organ of the Japanese Government, is an infamous and cowardly liar and slanderer.'[31] There were a host of similar, if less strident, claims that Brinkley was suborned.

Brinkley undoubtedly helped spread a positive image of Japan. The extra copies paid for by the Japanese explain the relatively full runs of the *Japan Mail* or *Japan Weekly Mail* found in some Western countries, and provided a counterweight to the 'righteous indignation and gratuitous advice' of more hostile papers.[32] By the time of Brinkley's death, the Japanese government had its own foreign-language newspaper, the third *Japan Times*, founded in 1897. Its editor paid tribute to Brinkley's services and avoided the old charges of how those services had come about, while the *Jiji Shimpō* attributed to him '. . . no other motive save a desire to explain the conditions of Japan to the outside world'.[33]

THE OTHER SETTLEMENTS: NAGASAKI, KOBE, TOKYO

After Hansard's departure, it was not until 1869–70 that newspapers were again published at Nagasaki. One was the *Nagasaki Express*, established in 1870 by an American, which was taken over in 1874 by two Britons, John Clark and Charles Sutton, and renamed the *Rising Sun and Nagasaki Express*. Clark soon left for Shanghai where he had a distinguished newspaper career, while Sutton, by trade a stevedore, left the running of the newspaper to the printer, C.A. Norman, also British. When Sutton died in 1892, Norman bought the paper. He was certified insane in 1896, and died the following year. The paper was briefly under the control of the British consul in Nagasaki, who persuaded E.A. Morphy, later editor of *The Straits Times,* to run it for a time. It was then sold. Renamed the *Nagasaki Express,* it lasted until the 1920s. Under Norman it was another staunch and uncritical defender of foreign rights.[34]

Kobe was the second most important foreign settlement. Here the *Hiogo News* and the *Hiogo and Osaka Herald* both established in 1868, vied for influence until the mid-1880s. Britons were involved with both. A.W. Hansard's son-in-law, A.T. Watkins, and briefly owner of the *Japan Herald,* was a founder of the *Hiogo and Osaka Herald* in 1868, though he did not long maintain his connection with the paper. Francis Walsh, a master printer from Shanghai who had worked in Nagasaki, bought out the owners of the *News* in 1869, and owned it until he retired to Britain in 1888.[35] A third paper, the *Kobe Herald,* began in 1886. It was owned and edited by A.W. Curtis, who had worked for Mitsubishi and NYK. The *Kobe Herald* may have been started with Japanese assistance, as a counterweight to the anti-Japanese *Hiogo News.*[36]

Kobe's best known paper, and the only rival to the Yokohama papers, was the *Kobe Chronicle,* established by Robert Young in 1892. Young was another Scot, born in 1858. After newspaper work in Britain, he arrived in Japan in 1885. He worked on the *Hiogo News,* which he left because of its anti-Japanese stand. The *Chronicle,* too, began with Japanese assistance, but Young claimed that, once it was clear that this involved uncritical support for the government, the link was broken.[37] Renamed the *Japan Chronicle* in 1902, it survived until 1942.

A few newspapers appeared in Tokyo, of which the best known was the *Tokio Times* (1877–80), owned and edited by the American, E.H. House. House's pro-Japanese stand and bitter editorials about Sir Harry Parkes and British policies in Japan led to attacks in the British-owned press and the usual claims of bribery. The *Tokei Journal* (1874–5), is sometimes credited to J.R. Black, but this is not certain. James Murdoch, another Scot with Australian links, a classical scholar and historian of Japan, was editor of the short-lived *Japan Echo* (1890–91).[38]

As noted earlier, some treaty-port journalists were foreign correspondents for other newspapers. The first was probably Charles Wirgman (see below), often described as the Japan correspondent of the *Illustrated London News*, though it is not clear if he contributed text as well as illustrations. Others included Alice Vaughan Smith and several of the *Mail*'s editors. But the most influential correspondent was probably none of these but Major General H.S. Palmer of the Royal Engineers who wrote for *The Times* and the *Manchester Guardian*. In 1883, Parkes suggested to the Japanese that they employ Palmer, then visiting Japan, as an adviser on the construction of Yokohama's waterworks. Soon afterwards, Palmer started to write for *The Times*, favouring the Japanese position on treaty revision. In 1887, having retired from the army, he was awarded a contract for harbour works at Yokohama. Hugh Fraser, the British minister, later claimed that there was a direct link between Palmer's reporting and the contract. Palmer continued to write and work for the Japanese until his death in 1893.[39]

THE PERIODICAL PRESS

The first rival to the *Japan Herald* was Charles Wirgman's *Japan Punch*, which began in 1862 at Yokohama. Wirgman's career was similar to more conventional journalists. He arrived in Japan via the Indian Mutiny and the Anglo-Chinese wars, where he had worked as an artist for the *Illustrated London News*. He contributed to the *ILN* from Japan for some years. He was a close friend of Satow, sometimes interpreter for the British legation, and an influence on Japan's artistic development. But his main preoccupation was the *Japan Punch*, which he produced until 1887. The *Japan Punch* has not worn well. The topical allusions are sometimes obscure; and standards of humour have changed. Yet it provides a good idea of life in Yokohama and Tokyo and the issues which concerned the treaty ports. Wirgman had rivals but, with the exception of the Frenchman, Georges Bigot, none approached him in ability or output. To Japanese, he is the father of the modern Japanese cartoon.[40]

Wirgman may have published another periodical, *The Far East,* in 1866–7, but no trace remains. Another *Far East* appeared in 1870, one more of J.R. Black's projects. It was published at Yokohama until 1876, then in Shanghai. Originally planned as a newspaper, it became a magazine 'illustrative of native life in the far East'.[41] It was fortnightly at first, then monthly, and in its heyday carried papers by Satow, F.V. Dickins and W.E. Griffis.

Its main feature was the use of real photographs, individually pasted into each copy. After Black moved to Shanghai in 1876, there was reduced coverage in Japan. It was Black's last journalistic effort. In Shanghai, he began writing *Young Japan*, and died while it was in progress.

From 1881 to 1883, Britons helped produce *The Chrysanthemum*, later *The Chrysanthemum and Phoenix*. 'A monthly magazine for Japan and the Far East', published by Presbyterian missionaries. Although it initially attracted a wide audience, it gradually became too missionary-dominated for most readers. Other missionary-inspired publications had little success outside the ranks of the committed.[42]

THE JAPANESE LANGUAGE PRESS

Britons were also pioneers in this field, though foreign involvement did not last long. Japanese interest in Western newspapers predated the opening of the ports in 1859, and publications received via the Dutch at Nagasaki were translated for the Bakufu. After 1861, the treaty-port papers were similarly translated. The first attempt at a Japanese-language newspaper was made by Joseph Heco (Hamada Hikozō), whose *Kaigai Shimbun* (Overseas News) appeared in 1864. Others followed, including the *Bankoku Shimbunshi* produced by the chaplain to the British legation, Buckworth Bailey, between 1867 and 1869. These publications avoided comment and enjoyed considerable popularity. They were left alone by the Japanese government.[43]

In 1872, J.R. Black established the *Nisshin Shinjishi* (Reliable Daily News). This broke new ground, for it carried political comment, and Black claimed it was well on the way to success by 1874. But by then there were several Japanese-owned papers as well, and the government determined to introduce effective press controls. There was no frontal attack on Black, to avoid a clash with the Western powers, but he was first offered government employment, then persuaded to remove his name from the *Nisshin Shinjishi*. He thus lost editorial control and his nominal editors rejected his writings. He also found his work for the Japanese was non-existent.

In June 1875, a new press law appeared which stated that newspaper proprietors, editors, temporary editors, and managers must be Japanese subjects. Foreigners believed that they were exempt from Japanese laws, whether they published in English or Japanese. Black, therefore, decided to establish a new vernacular newspaper. On 6 January 1876, the *Bankoku Shimbun* (News of the World) went on sale. The government again made no frontal attack, but issued regulations banning Japanese subjects from selling or distributing it. They also approached Parkes, pointing out the dangers to Japan if foreigners could freely publish in Japanese. On 7 February 1876, Parkes issued a regulation banning English subjects from publishing in Japanese. This would have repercussions far beyond journalism, but its immediate effect was to end foreign involvement in the Japanese-language press. The Japanese would later ignore some missionary publications in the vernacular, but no other political or commercial paper in Japanese appeared under foreign auspices.[44]

CONCLUSION

The importance of the foreign press can be disputed. These were tiny enterprises even by contemporary standards and many survived but a short period. Their direct influence on Japanese affairs was also limited. Few Japanese understood Western languages and fewer read the treaty-port press. Western diplomats generally had a low opinion of the treaty-port press, and such views may have influenced the Japanese. Whatever their concerns about the vernacular press, the Japanese government did not seek to control the foreign-language press before 1899, preferring to pay to make sure that Japanese views were made known. To the Japanese authorities, the foreign press was not nearly as important as it considered itself, but merely reflected the views of small and often faction-ridden communities, rather than the views of foreign governments.

Yet to Japanese historians, the foreign newspapers are an important part of their country's history. From them, the Japanese newspapermen acquired much technical knowledge, even if the Japanese papers, with their much greater readership, quickly moved beyond the small presses and short runs of the treaty-port press. The Western newspapers also contributed by comment and criticism to the development of Meiji Japan. Perhaps if there had been a little less criticism and more constructive advice, they would have had greater influence, but they did have an effect. Some argue that Japanese journalists obtained their first lessons in editorial freedom and responsibility from the treaty-port press. Others note the role of the foreign press in introducing Japan to a wider international audience. Whatever the final verdict, the British, always the majority among owners and editorial staff and always prominent in both positive and negative portrayal of Japan, played a major role.[45]

3

British Missionaries in Meiji Japan*

HELEN BALLHATCHET

MISSIONARIES formed a numerous and distinct group among the British in Meiji Japan, with a very special relationship with both Japan and the Japanese.[1] Whether they devoted themselves to direct evangelistic activities or worked indirectly, through caring for the sick and disadvantaged, as administrators of church affairs or as teachers of English, their object was to spread knowledge of Christianity and ultimately to convert. In other words, they aimed to bring about a fundamental change in both individuals and in the society as a whole, and believed that they had divine sanction for their activities. This meant that their involvement with the country was not only deeper but also more intrusive than that of other foreigners.

Unlike most of their fellow countrymen in Japan, all British missionaries learnt to speak Japanese, at least to an elementary level; some became very proficient and many could also read and write to a certain extent. They had daily contacts with ordinary Japanese people, and tried to develop close relationships with them. In remoter areas, especially in the early Meiji period, missionaries were the only foreigners most Japanese were ever likely to see. Conversely, extracts from the reports and letters which they wrote to their missionary societies were featured in missionary publications, and became an important source of information about Japan for the many supporters of missionary activity in the British Isles.

Meiji Japan (1868–1912) was not a typical mission field. The relatively mild climate, and high standards of public order and hygiene, meant that it did not offer the chances of heroic suffering and martyrdom found in archetypal missionary destinations such as 'teeming' China and 'darkest' Africa. The missionary to Japan must have been guiltily aware that he did not fit in with the romantic Livingstonian stereotype which so caught the Victorian imagination and encouraged the British to finance missionary activity.

In other words, everyday life was 'not one of . . . unmixed hardship and self sacrifice'.[2] British missionaries usually lived in Western-style houses with servants, and where possible ate Western food. In Tokyo, Kobe and Nagasaki in particular, they tended to live in close proximity to other foreigners. They would provide English-language religious services in such places if there was not enough money to employ a chaplain, and a friendly relationship could develop. This appears to have been the case at Kobe.[3] However, strains existed under the surface there, since many foreigners were 'living in the grossest sin.'[4] As for the foreign employees of the Japanese government living in neighbouring Osaka,

> '. . . they do not help but hinder the missionary in his work; for their impure lives, their indifferance [sic] to all religion and in some cases their avowed infidel principles too often prejudice the natives against . . . Xty.'[5]

On the other hand, with the exception of the group organized by Barclay Buxton, which will be discussed later, missionaries clearly wished to preserve a distance between themselves and the Japanese. They did not want their children to 'mix freely with the natives' because of the danger of 'moral evil', although an exception could be made in the case of 'natives of higher rank', who were 'of greater delicacy of character than is possible as yet in India & China'.[6] Their whole way of life served to cut them off from the majority of the Japanese, as one senior missionary was to recognize:

> '. . . we are looked upon as very well off by the major part of the population amongst whom we work. Our houses and furniture, our manner of living . . . are all such as are out of reach of our converts and so we are believed by them to be wholly free of such anxieties which are . . . most real to them.'[7]

When itinerating, 'European missionaries' were permitted to travel 2nd class by rail and 1st class by steamer; 'Japanese agents' on the other hand were to go 3rd class by rail and 2nd class by steamer.[8] There was a similar difference in salaries.

Missionaries did have legitimate reasons for wishing to keep themselves aloof apart from worries about the bad influences on their children. If it was difficult for them to feel completely at ease with the foreign community, their relationships with Japanese were likely to be even more delicate. The missionary 'must be at his best in mind temper patience [sic] for enquirers at all times',[9] constantly under the strain of wishing 'to present (oh! humbug yet striving words!) "the perfect man"'.[10] Although in some cases missionaries seem to have been on close, almost paternal, terms with converts, paternalistic attitudes were not always welcome. As one bishop warned those with catechists under their charge:

> 'Do not when you have received from them the names of the candidates for baptism . . . make them feel they are not trusted by your taking each candidate and examining him or her . . . Why we have lost some of the tools we had is because we would not trust them but hindered them by our criticism . . .'[11]

Even in their letters to the home missionary society, missionaries were ill advised to relax their guard:

> 'May I . . . beg of you not to let *any part* of the letter appear in print, as it is far too personal, & might do untold harm in the work here, where so many can read English . . . I know our Pastor here receives the magazines and I should be *so* sorry if any unpleasant feelings were to arise.'[12]

Another difficulty, which must have affected missionary relationships with Japanese people, lay in the language itself. In the early period, in particular, there were few textbooks, no Japanese–English or English–Japanese dictionaries, and no experienced teachers. One can only sympathize with remarks such as the following:

> '. . . while I am not disappointed on the whole, it would be untrue to say that I do not at times suffer from despair & despondency at the apparent hopelessness of, in any estimable period, *mastering* this dreadfully hard language. . .'[13]

It was even pointed out that '. . . the study of Japanese has often a serious effect in disarranging the functions of the brain'.[14]

It was presumably as a result of these various stressful problems that the main threat to missionary health appears to have been psychological in nature:

> '. . . I can now count up over a dozen men and women of the English Church Mission in Japan, who had suffered more or less from nervous breakdown since I came to Japan less than 8 years ago. More than half of these have had to lay down their work here altogether.'[15]

The mental strain must also have been a factor contributing to the most un-Christian relationships which so many missionaries seem to have had with each other. As a bishop wearily remarked: 'Very few people know the amount of energy, which is wasted, through disagreements of missionaries.'[16]

THE MISSIONARY TASK

This was the general background against which missionaries pursued their task of converting Japan and the Japanese. Their work was neither easy nor straightforward, and again it differed significantly from the stereotype of missionary activity. This missionary was supposed to be a heroic warrior of Christianity and civilization, battling against the forces of heathenism and culturally backward countries where the ignorant natives knew nothing better. Missionaries in Japan grew on this stereotype, particularly in the early decades of the Meiji period, with reference to '. . . the awfully lowering influence of heathenism – a darkness that can be felt'[17] and the use of military metaphors: '. . . the hosts of hell encamped around this place . . . the little army of God's saints like a thin white line . . .'[18] This almost ritualized language must have helped them to express their cultural alienation, and reinforced the bonds linking them to their missionary colleagues elsewhere.

However, the stereotype did not fit. Even on an everyday level, there was a great gap between the heroic ideal of missionary endeavour and the mundane reality:

> 'I find, contrary entirely to what I hoped & expected would be the case, that being engaged in missionary work is not necessarily conducive to one's own spiritual growth. The daily intercourse & acquaintance with heathenism is too apt to render the soul callous and indifferent to sin . . .'[19]

On a deeper level, too, tensions existed. Meiji Japan was changing rapidly. The tendency to associate heathenism with backwardness and Christianity with civilization naturally meant that the positive attitude of the Meiji government to reform on Western lines encouraged initial optimism about the prospects for evangelization. In 1875, the same year in which he complained about his low morale, the missionary quoted above was predicting that '. . . the rapidly rising tide of civilization can hardly fail to sweep in Religious Toleration along with itself';[20] a few years later, another was observing 'the gradual spread of Christian truth' alongside the more general '. . . continuance of this Empire in the path of progress and Enlightenment.[21]

However, it gradually became clear that secular 'progress' did not necessarily mean religious change in the direction of Christianity. Despite its influence among Westernizing intellectuals and the early appearance of outstanding Japanese Christian leaders, and despite periods of optimism such as the mid-1880s and the early 1900s, Christianity in general, and British missionaries in particular, had relatively little success in Japan — at least in terms of numbers of converts. To the detached observer this might not be surprising, given the overall religio-political situation, but it was hard for the faithful to accept that Christianity might hold less appeal to the average Japanese than more indigenous beliefs, or no beliefs at all.

From very early on, in fact, it had been pointed out that the general eagerness to adopt Western learning was also encouraging a high degree of interest in the rationalist and scientific arguments being used against Christianity in contemporary Britain:

> '. . . the battle lies no more . . . between Christianity and heathenism but between Christianity and infidelity . . . here as at home this same fight goes on.'[22]

It seems likely that the majority of missionaries were not equipped to deal with such sophisticated objections. In the mid-1870s, for example, one missionary reported how a catechumen had asked him about the reason for the creation. He replied that it was 'the general outflow of Divine goodness' and suspected the questioner of 'captiously questioning' when he appeared unsatisfied by this answer.[23]

When Edward Sylvester Morse, an American biologist, began

to spread an anti-Christian version of the theory of evolution in lectures in Tokyo in 1877, missionaries were clearly upset by the enthusiastic reception which his ideas were given in educated circles:

> '. . . the Japanese want all the benefits and blessings possessed by Christian nations, but they do not want the Gospel. They want the effect without the cause.'[24]

Dr Henry Faulds of the mission of the (Scottish) United Presbyterian Church was one of the few foreign committed Christians in Japan who was able to provide a convincing refutation of what he described as 'modern scientific dogmas, which are believed by many christians to be simple blunders of the "scientific imagination"'.[25] In lectures, which were also published in Japanese,[26] he presented a theistic view of evolution and showed how it was possible to interpret the Bible in a way that accorded with a modified version of Darwin's theory. His efforts were clearly appreciated within Japanese Christian circles;[27] however, it is not clear how broad his overall influence was. Certainly, Western science was still being used as a weapon against Christianity when he left Japan in 1885.

As the Meiji period continued, with military victories and the signing of the first Anglo-Japanese Alliance in 1902, missionaries became witnesses of '. . . the extraordinary phenomenon of a fully civilized nation that does not know, nor believe in, Christ'.[28] The association between heathenism and backwardness was absolutely shattered, leaving bewilderment in its place:

> 'One could scarcely believe that Japan, with all her culture and enlightenment, with all her learning and progress, could still produce in this one town hundreds, nay, thousands of people to pay homage at such a shrine! Yet such is the case.'[29]

Missionaries worried that Japan's material progress might lead to the idea that their efforts were no longer needed, on the grounds '. . . that a nation like this might be left to herself'.[30] Even their own evangelistic zeal was in danger, since it was easy to forget that 'underneath all this there is the same terrible want here as in other less civilized lands'.[31]

One response to all such doubts was to emphasize that Japan's modernization tended to be superficial, 'mere materialistic prosperity', beneath which '. . . hoary-headed idolatry and superstition still hold sway'.[32] And some at least were aware of the socio-economic problems which existed underneath the apparent prosperity. From around the 1890s a few British missionaries started to work among the newly-emerging industrial poor, notably coal miners in Kyushu and factory workers in Osaka. They were distressed by the conditions which they found:

> 'The factory hands form an almost distinct, uneducated, and more or less neglected class of society . . . I could never have believed or realized what I now know. Crowds are living in dirt and weariness and sins.'[33]

However, their solution was to spread knowledge of Christianity, both among the workers, when one of their objects seems to have been to exert pressure on management by making them '. . . alive to the fact that someone does care for the factory hands and therefore they must . . .',[34] and among the managers themselves, in the belief that Christian managers would be more humane.[35] In other words, the emphasis was on ameliorating conditions through spreading knowledge of Christianity on an individual basis rather than through trying to promote changes in social conditions directly.

Despite this knowledge of the sacrifices which were being made by some, missionaries on the whole reacted positively to Japan's material progress, and particularly to the military successes which this made possible. They believed that Japan's victories were a result of divine help, admired the bravery and patriotism of the people, and even hoped that national crisis would make both Christians and non-Christians more aware of their need for Christianity.[36]

EVANGELISTIC CAMPAIGNS

However, the rapidly changing situation affected the scope and nature of missionary work. Some, as we have seen, were moving in a direction which might lead them to call for social as well as religious changes; as the number of Japanese priests and catechists grew, an increasing number of missionaries became involved in educational and supervisory activities rather than direct evangelization. But new, contrasting, tendencies can also be discerned in evangelistic methods. The first of these was characterized by an emphasis on immediate conversion through revivalistic preaching by charismatic individuals, the second resulted from the idea that points of contact existed between Christianity and Japanese religion.

Of course, charisma had always been an important element in direct evangelistic work; as at least one missionary pointed out, rational presentation of Christianity was not necessarily enough:

> '. . . experience shows what a mistake it is to suppose that if only the truths of Christianity be known its reasonableness & superiority in point of morality as compared with other religions be admitted a man *must* become a Christian. Many here do know and admit all this and yet go no further.'[37]

From around the 1890s, however, some missionaries began to experiment with organized evangelistic campaigns of the type associated in Britain and America with popular revivalists such as Dwight L. Moody. In the West such campaigns are often seen as a reaction against the influence of liberal theology; this may also have been responsible for their appeal in Japan, at least among missionaries. A nationwide inter-denominational drive for conversions in 1901 was based on these techniques. The assumption was that preaching in Japan could be carried out in the same way as in Britain or the United States, despite the differences in basic knowledge of Christianity and general ideas about the nature of religion on the part of the audiences. Meetings were publicized in advance, through newspapers and leaflets, in order to attract large audiences, sometimes in the region of 800, and members of the audience were encouraged to make an individual commitment on the spot, possibly by signing 'a paper expressing their belief in God in Christ as Saviour – and their own desire to be a Christian'. After-meetings were provided for those who had come forward so that they could be given more individual attention, and more information about Christianity than would have been the case in a nominally Christian country such as Britain.[38]

A central figure in introducing such methods was the Rev. Barclay Buxton. Buxton came from a wealthy evangelical family; his grandfather, Thomas Fowell Buxton, had been famous for his involvement in the movement for the emancipation of slaves. Always a serious Christian, his intellectual faith received spiritual confirmation when he attended a meeting presided over by Moody, and was 'born again'. Troubled by the feeling that he was not yet spiritually clean, however, he prayed for the baptism of the Holy Spirit and achieved '. . . a personal knowledge of Him who alone can make us strong and successful soldiers of the Cross' which allowed him to '. . . get back to Apostolical Christianity in its supernatural power'.[39]

When Buxton went out to Japan as a missionary in 1890, working for the CMS but with his own private group of co-workers, it was to bring this message of sanctification and direct baptism by the Holy Ghost. He believed that Japanese religions were the work of the devil and that there was no salvation without knowledge of Christ, but on the other hand he also believed that it was possible to work in Japan '. . . just as I should in England, for I feel that men's hearts are the same everywhere.'[40] Unlike many missionaries, he was able to accept that it was possible for someone to be truly converted on their first hearing of the Gospels, and that sincere Japanese converts were his spiritual equals, capable of holding positions of responsibility, despite their having been brought up in a 'heathen' land.[41] He also soon began to wear Japanese dress, since he felt that it brought him closer to ordinary Japanese people.[42] Buxton's group became the Japan Evangelistic Band; he influenced both Yamamuro Gunpei of the Salvation Army and the indigenous Holiness Church.[43]

Although he was criticized by some mainstream missionaries for doctrinal reasons,[44] Buxton was really practising an extension of the traditional evangelical approach to missionary work. It was the cultural approach which involved a radical rethinking of the Protestant missionary position. As was pointed out above, the image of heathenism was important in motivating the majority of missionaries and in providing a framework of reference for their experience in the mission field. Missionaries, therefore, tended to reject Japanese religions as resulting from human ignorance, or even as the work of Satan. However, there were signs of more positive attitudes, particularly from the late nineteenth century. These changes occurred for various reasons, and probably from a combination of several: as a result of individual encounters with aspects of Japanese beliefs, in the process of trying to understand why Japanese religions were not disappearing as quickly as expected, and under the influence of the development of the comparative study of religions as an academic discipline and the related general movement for greater appreciation of non-

Christian religions and cultures.

Glimpses of changed attitudes can be obtained from chance remarks in missionary writings, but evidence of organized rethinking is rare. One example is available in the ideas expressed in 1898 by Evington, an Oxford graduate who joined the evangelical Church Missionary Society, arrived in Japan in 1874 and was appointed Bishop of Kyushu twenty years later. In two sermons and a paper on evangelistic methods presented to the CMS United Conference in Japan, he called on missionaries to become more sensitive to the strong points of Japanese culture, and the weak points of their own. They must study the Japanese, their culture and society, since, '. . . we ought to know more their code of morality that we may appreciate in it of the Land of God'. Only through such study could they:

> '. . . speak straight to the heart in language and illustrations which will be at once understood and received . . . Our continual use of illustrations drawn from homehabits (sic) of life will tend to separate rather than unite . . .'[45]

The missionary should think of what he could gain through missionary work, not of what he had given up in order to become a missionary. He should seek fellowship with Japanese Christians and draw inspiration from their spiritual experiences, for:

> '. . . the absolutely different point of view from which a Japanese sees almost everything to what we do, a fact too, which it takes years for many to fully appreciate, makes it probable . . . that they will afford opportunities for the manifestation of Divine grace . . . different from those of our own experience, but none the less instructive if our minds are free to receive teaching. Their ignorance of some of our customs, their freedom from some of our prejudices, too, will enable them to see some things more clearly . . . than we can, and so again we may learn.'[46]

JAPANESE RELIGIONS

Some missionaries even suggested that Japanese religions in some way showed traces of divine revelation. John Batchelor, the famous evangelist to the Ainu, denied that they were without true religious feelings since God '. . . had, in all likelihood, manifested Himself to them as He has to the world at large'; they believed in a chief god called 'the maker of worlds and places' and 'the possessor of heaven', 'truly grand conceptions' which reminded him of Genesis.[47] Other missionaries made similar comments about Japanese religion.[48]

The logical implication of such thinking was the systematic study of Japanese religion in order to find points of contact with Christianity. While Japan did not produce scholar missionaries of the calibre of James Legge, the missionary to China who produced highly-valued translations of the Confucian classics, Arthur Lloyd, an Oxford graduate who went out to Japan as a missionary of the High-Church Society for the Propagation of the Gospel to Foreign Parts in 1885, devoted himself to the study of Pure Land Buddhism. Like Timothy Richard in China and other missionaries, he was struck by the similarity between the Pure Land teaching of rebirth in the Western Paradise as a result of even one sincere invocation of the name of Amida, and the Protestant doctrine of salvation through faith alone.

Embarking on what he called a 'new and dangerous missionary experiment',[49] Lloyd examined this and other resemblances between Christianity and Buddhism and searched for evidence of the Christian influences on Buddhism which he believed were the origin of these resemblances. Unlike Batchelor in the article referred to above and Meiji Japanese Christians such as Uemura Masahisa,[50] he was not prepared to accept that non-Christian religions might be in receipt of a direct revelation from God. However, his efforts to promote dialogue between Christianity and Buddhism seem to have been valued by the Meiji philosopher, Inoue Tetsujirō.[51]

All foreigners in Meiji Japan were witnesses to an unprecedented transformation as it became the first non-Western country to industrialize and develop into a world power. For many this must have meant some sort of readjustment of their world-view. Missionaries had to accept that the changes had been possible without the adoption of Christianity. Although none of them would have accepted that this meant that Christianity had 'failed' in Japan, they had to change their preconceptions of what a non-Christian country was and develop patterns of work to fit the new conditions.

Two new approaches to evangelistic activity emerged in place of the traditional idea of the missionary battling against the forces of uncivilized heathenism. On the one side were those who chose to deny the importance of cultural differences, on the grounds that the direct spiritual message of Christianity transcended all barriers. They adopted revivalist methods similar to those used in contemporary Britain in what was really an extension of the traditional Protestant missionary drive for individual conversions. On the other side were those who emphasized a sensitive awareness of cultural differences but were prepared to accept the existence of points of contact between Japanese religions and Christianity, and even the possibility of a universal divine revelation. The logical implication of this approach can be found in the present-day interest in inter-faith dialogue. However, both sides – and of course the majority of missionaries were probably influenced to varying degrees by both extremes – acknowledged the existence of basic similarities between the Christian and the non-Christian: on an individual level in the case of the charismatic approach, and on a cultural level in the case of the other. British missionaries came to Meiji Japan intending to transform it, but found that Japan was changing so rapidly that they had to transform themselves as well if they were not to be left behind.

4

'Working at their Profession': Japanese Engineers in Britain before 1914

OLIVE CHECKLAND

A NEW PROFESSION

WHEN ITŌ HIROBUMI visited Scotland,[1] during the travels of the Iwakura Mission, he met John McQuorn Rankine,[2] professor of Engineering at the University of Glasgow. The question which Itō then posed was: 'How can an efficient factory to make cannon be established in Japan?' After some consideration, Rankine answered 'First of all you must educate and train engineers in a proper engineering college'.[3]

Rankine was a notable engineer who had had much success in cooperating with John Elder, a gifted ship designer and ship builder on the Clyde. Rankine had always 'cultivated the harmony between theory and practice in Mechanics' writing: 'In theoretical science the question is – what are we to think? But in practical science the question is – what are we to do?'[4]

Shortly after the discussion between Itō and Rankine, the Imperial College of Engineering[5] was set up at Toranomon, Tokyo, where it remained a separate, expensive and privileged institution, under the Ministry of Public Works (*Kōbushō*), until 1886 when it became part of the Faculty of Engineering in the reorganized Imperial University of Tokyo, under the Ministry of Education (Mombushō). Although staff for the College came from a variety of backgrounds, a good proportion, including the principal, Henry Dyer,[6] were Scots from the University of Glasgow. There is no doubt that under Dyer's guidance the

45

College effectively married theoretical teaching to practical engineering work.

Graduates from the Imperial College of Engineering and from other colleges of the University of Tokyo, men taught entirely in English, became the first generation of Japanese engineers to seek advanced education and work experience in the United Kingdom (and elsewhere in Europe and America) during the Meiji era.

The future of Japan's new industrial economy rested on the slim shoulders of a handful of young Japanese engineers who, because of their aptitude for the 'new' Western science and technology, were sent abroad by their government. They were only too conscious of their responsibilities. It was Fred T. Jane, whose study of the *Imperial Japanese Navy* was published in 1904, who designated young Japanese naval engineers as '. . . working at their profession'.[7] The singlemindedness, and the determination to do their best, which these Japanese engineers displayed impressed everyone who knew them.

It was the keenness, and the deference, of the Japanese which endeared them to those British engineers with whom they came into contact. As A.E. Sutton remarked about his six Japanese student engineers: '. . . in helping to educate those Japanese, I can honestly say that they educated me, for the result of my teaching was the production of my first book largely as a result of the crucial questions which my (Japanese) pupils put to me'.[8]

Japanese engineers were in Britain working in every form of engineering endeavour, including armament-making, ship engineering and shipbuilding, railway and other civil engineering, textile engineering and the manufacture of textile machinery. As individuals they are difficult to trace although in Japan there are some biographical studies. In Britain, occasionally, Japanese names do appear in the apprentice books[9] of large engineering firms, but this is exceptional. Japanese 'apprentices' were, of course, different; normally graduate engineers, their presence in the company was negotiated at the highest level. Often contracts signed by the Japanese stipulated the employment of their own 'apprentices' in factory, workshop or shipyard.[10] Care was taken to ensure that the British company agreed to allow the Japanese to work in several departments so that they could learn something of the business overall. With fierce competition from other countries, including Germany and the United States, British businesses were not in a position to refuse Japanese requests. In any case, very few British engineers, at this time, could believe that the Japanese would ever constitute any sort of threat. Traditional Western attitudes ensured that the Japanese were seen, in perpetuity, as pupils.

Although a few worked in London, the principal centres for the Japanese engineers were in the industrial centres, of Scotland, especially Glasgow, the north-east coast, Newcastle-upon-Tyne, Middlesborough, and Sunderland, Sheffield and Barrow-in-Furness, as well as in royal naval dockyards. There were also Japanese, with a particular interest in the cotton industry, to be found in and around Manchester.

Many Japanese working as engineers in Britain were, in addition, following university academic courses. It is sometimes easier to trace these men through University and College records.

IN LONDON

There were Japanese engineering students in London, from the 1860s, before the Meiji Restoration at University College. There may have been Japanese at King's College as well as the School of Chemistry, the Royal School of Mines and the Royal School of Science which, later, made up the Imperial College (founded 1907). Of these University College was the most famous, receiving in 1863, before the Meiji Restoration, the 'Chōshū five'.

The five in question were Itō Hirobumi, Inoue Kaoru, Nomura Yakichi (known in Japan as Inoue Masaru), Yamao Yōzō and Endō Kinsuke, had arrived in London, through the good offices of Hugh Matheson, and they presented themselves to Alexander Williamson (1824–1904) at University College. These Chōshū men, all destined later to play important parts in Meiji Japan, studied a variety of scientific and engineering subjects but, despite their 'student' status, they were primarily in Britain to examine Western industrial progress.

IN GLASGOW

The university system in Scotland was markedly different from that in England, and was much appreciated by the Japanese because of the ready availability of advanced courses in science and engineering. The Scottish universities were enjoying a particularly fruitful period. It should be explained that:

> 'Lord Kelvin (Sir William Thomson) succeeded to the chair of Natural Philosophy in Glasgow in 1846 and began his great electrical researches leading to his successful scientific and business exploits in cable laying in the 1860s and after. Around Thomson clustered a galaxy of professors, as pupils, teachers and business partners – Lewis Gordon, Fleeming Jenkin, P.G. Tait, Alfred Ewing – active in university science in Scotland and entrepreneurship in the electrical industry. Products of the Scottish universities, and usually of the Cambridge Mathematic Tripos also, were amongst the finest flower of Scottish Victorian culture, and in their presence the Scottish universities were confident enough to hold to their traditions.'[11]

The Japanese came particularly to Glasgow because the Chair of Engineering, like that at University College, London, had been founded (by the Crown, against the wishes of the University) in 1840. In 1833 the establishment by the University of Glasgow (founded 1451) of the Elder Chair of Naval Architecture, the first in the world, confirmed for the Japanese the importance of this ancient University, adjacent to the Clyde shipyards, for Japanese engineers.

The first Japanese in Glasgow was Yamao Yōzō, one of the original Chōshū five who studied in the city between 1866 and 1868. Yamao worked at Napier's shipyard during the day and attended classes at the Andersonian University[12] in Glasgow at night. Yamao was proud of his Scottish experience, which he never forgot, and it may be that his understanding of the advantages of Glasgow were later influential with successive generations of Japanese. To this day his grandson in Tokyo proudly displays the saw and plane used by his grandfather at Napier's shipyard.

The Japanese in Glasgow were primarily scientists and engineers who were registered for classes in Natural Philosophy (physics), mathematics, engineering, chemistry and naval architecture. Some Japanese did register for full degree courses, graduating BSc[13] and CE, others came to work as apprentices in the shipbuilding yards and so attended academic classes, on a part-time basis, either in the evenings or during the summer.

From time to time Japanese students dominated prize lists at the University of Glasgow. In 1881–2 Japanese received first, second and seventh prize in the Natural Philosophy class.[14] These men Shida Rinzaburō, Takayama Naomoto and Minami Kyoshi, recent graduates from the Imperial College of Engineering in Tokyo, were regular prize-winners. Earlier in Tokyo, Shida had worked with William Ayrton, then professor of Physics at the Imperial College of Engineering, on telegraphy. After graduating he came to Glasgow to work under Kelvin, as indeed Ayrton himself had done earlier. Shida, who won the Cleland Gold medal in Natural Philosophy '. . . for the best experimental investigation of Magnetic susceptibility', was an outstanding student who, until his early death, at the age of 37, in 1892, worked in Japan in charge of the new and expanding telegraph service.[15]

The University of Glasgow certainly encouraged those Japanese who aspired to become students. In 1901 Fukuzawa Sampachi,[16] the third son of Fukuzawa Yukichi, applied to the University to use Japanese as his necessary foreign language for entry. Thanks to the intervention of Dr Henry Dyer, former principal of the Imperial College of Engineering in Tokyo, the University granted his request.[17] The external examiner in Japanese on this first occasion, for which he was paid a fee of four guineas, was Natsume Soseki, then resident in London. Later several other aspiring Japanese engineering students took the opportunity of taking the entrance examination in Japanese.

AT ENGLISH CIVIC UNIVERSITIES

The provincial university movement of the later years of Queen Victoria's reign brought advanced education to Manchester, Newcastle (with Durham), Leeds, Bristol, Sheffield, Birmingham, Liverpool and Nottingham. These small new universities were interested from the beginning in teaching science and engineering, as well as the arts subjects, and they soon became important in their own right. In the case of Manchester, for example, Professor Sir Henry Roscoe taught chemistry, a subject clearly important in the textile industry. He remarked of his Japanese students, that he found them all extraordinarily persevering and painstaking men. He was also astonished at the response of one Japanese student, who, finding himself placed only second in his second year, when he had achieved first place, out of a class of 150, in his first year, regarded himself as disgraced.[18]

The case of Kikuchi Kyōzō (1859–1942) is also helpful in illuminating the Manchester connection. Kikuchi, born of a wealthy family in remote Ehime prefecture, Shikoku, travelled at the age of 17 years with his brother to Osaka, to attend school and to learn English. Kikuchi determined to study engineering and moved to Tokyo where he applied to the Imperial College of Engineering which he entered in 1879. He graduated with the highest honours as *Kōgakushi* (engineer) in 1885, having specialized in mechanical engineering. After two other jobs, Kikuchi was recruited by the Hirano Spinning Company as company engineer, but first he insisted that he travel to England to learn about the textile trade. He spent one year in Lancashire, studying spinning at the Manchester Technical School, while visiting and working at a spinning mill. He bought ring-spindle machines from Platts of Oldham before returning to Japan. His subsequent career as a highly competent engineer-manager demonstrates well the crucial role of these new men in Meiji Japan.[19]

Newcastle was another centre which attracted Japanese students, the dominance of the coal-mining and shipbuilding industries was reflected in the high level of advanced technical education which was available in the city. Haramiishi Motereru[20] [?Mototeru] was sent in 1890 as a shipbuilding apprentice to Messrs Armstrong Whitworth on the Tyne. He had studied earlier at Tokyo Technical School although it is not known if he enrolled in a college in Newcastle. He remained in the north-east for no less than nine years, before returning to Japan where he was employed in the ship and design office of Mitsubishi Shipbuilding and Engineering Company.

NAVAL ENGINEERS

During the later years of the nineteenth century many ships for the Imperial Japanese Navy were built in British yards. Contracts were awarded on condition that engineering naval officers should have access to, and supervision of, the day-to-day work, in the yard. There were, therefore, Japanese engineers living and working over years in Sheffield, which made high-grade steel for the plates for the outer skin of the ships, as well as in ports including Barrow-in-Furness, Newcastle-upon-Tyne and Glasgow.

Japanese naval engineer officers had, according to the contracts signed when Japanese orders were given to British yards, full authority to supervize the building of ships day by day in the shipyard. The contract invariably included phrases such as '. . . the inspector can see any drawings and details' and '. . . examine all construction materials'. It may, therefore, have come as something of a shock to British shipbuilders to find that the Japanese, unlike other foreign owners, who left such supervision to their agents, posted their own nationals to the shipyard to do their day-to-day inspections themselves. The presence of the Japanese 'inspectors' was resented; certainly the Japanese felt unwelcome. One example may be helpful.

In 1895, writing from Japan, Professor (later Sir) John Harvard Biles of the chair of Naval Architecture at the University of Glasgow, reported on the difficulties with the *Chiyoda*, a protected cruiser built on the Clyde by J. & G. Thomson (later John Brown & Co). He believed that '. . . the boilers would not steam with the Japanese coal on account of the small diameter of the tubes, these tubes being readily choked by the sooty deposit from the Japanese coal.' Biles' report continued:

'a considerable amount of prejudice had been created in the minds of several of the officials by statements which had been made by some of the Japanese people who were at Clydebank during the building of the *Chiyoda*. These statements were generally of the nature of complaints that the wishes of the Japanese officials had not been attended to in many matters, and that they had been treated as if they knew very little of the subject of construction.'[21]

It should be noted that Biles himself was chief designer at J. & G. Thomson when the *Chiyoda* was under construction.

In later years matters were easier. Dr S. Yokota wrote to William Denny's, shipbuilders, Dumbarton, on the lower Clyde, (9 September 1907):

'I have duly received your letter of yesterday informing me the price for the extra winch with copper piping. I ask you to give me a little more detailed estimate, about this, as my own estimate comes out to be different from yours, and I like to be a correct reporter as advised by your good Mr John Denny. Perhaps my own estimate may be wrong, but I would like to see the cause of the difference.'[22]

One reason for the easier time which the Japanese naval engineers had in Britain, undertaking difficult supervisory jobs in shipyards, was the presence, in the later Meiji years, of Honorary Japanese Consuls. These British businessmen, with the support of a strong local network, also acted as agents for the Japanese government. The Honorary Consulates were in Glasgow (1890–1941), Middlesborough (1898–1922), Manchester (1907–1941) and Liverpool (1889–1986).[23]

THE HONORARY JAPANESE CONSUL

The best known Consul was Albert Richard Brown (1839–1913) who, as Captain Brown had been in government service in Japan, in charge of the Japanese lighthouse tender and other shipping concerns, for twenty years when he resigned in 1889. He left Japan and established himself as Honorary Consul[24] in Glasgow, where he set himself up as an agent for the Japanese, or any other foreign government, in ordering and supervising the making of ships from Scottish or other British shipyards.

There can be no doubt of Brown's importance in providing a ready welcome for those Japanese, then living and working in Britain. With Brown's help Japanese were drafted into offices in Glasgow and onto ships operating from the Clyde. When Albert Brown died in 1913, a letter of condolence was sent by the Japanese Glasgow Society in Tokyo. It was signed by eleven Japanese representatives, headed by A. Tanakadate.[25] The Japanese consulate in Glasgow was finally closed, by the neutral Swiss, with the outbreak of war at the end of 1941.

CAN WE COMPETE?

Young Japanese engineers who were working in Britain were an unusual élite, in that they were being trained in disciplines hitherto of low esteem in Japan. Could there be any justification for the Japanese to take up these subjects? One man who agonized over these matters was Tanakadate Aikitsu (1856–1952) who, originally determined, as a traditional *samurai*, to study government, persuaded himself to become a student of physics which is '. . . the basis of all science to make up in full measure for our country's deficiencies'.[26] Tanakadate had been trained in Tokyo by Cargill G. Knott (D.Sc. Edinburgh), but subsequently he was in Glasgow, working under Kelvin (1888–91) on ammeters. Tanakadate became the foremost Japanese physicist of his generation, and served as Professor of Physics, and Director of the Physical Institute at the Imperial University of Tokyo.

On the occasion of Lord Kelvin's eightieth birthday in 1904 six of his former Japanese research students sent 'hearty birthday greetings'. The telegram, carefully preserved by the recipient, in the notebook he was then using, was signed by Masuda, Taniguchi, Watanabe, Mano, Gotō and Tanakadate.[27]

Notwithstanding the friendliness between the young engineers and their British teachers, the Japanese were on the defensive. Were they good enough to compete against a world consortium of research scholars from whom they were learning? And there was some resentment. In 1888, when Tanakadate Aikitsu was working in Glasgow, his young colleague in Tokyo, Nagaoka Hantarō, expressed his annoyance at Western attitudes, writing:

'We must work actively with an open eye, keen sense and ready understanding, indefatigably and not a moment stopping . . . There is no reason why the whites should be so supreme at everything and as you say, I hope we shall be able to beat those *yatta hottya* (pompous) people in the course of ten or twenty years . . . another great prerequisite in beating those whites is to make our own work known. This is a great difficulty. As a first step we cannot write in Japanese and make the Westerners understand our writings. We must borrow their language and make the Westerners understand our writings.'[28]

This sense of competitiveness, although not understood by those other than Japanese, was always present as the Japanese struggled to close the gap between them and their competitors. There can be no doubt of the determination and dedication of those Japanese who experienced the challenge of working at their engineering profession in Britain before 1914.

Maejima Hisoka (1835–1919) – Founder of Japan's Postal System

JANET HUNTER

THE NOW LITTLE USED Y1 stamp in Japan has long borne the head of Maejima Hisoka, known to several generations of Japanese as the founder of the country's modern postal service. Maejima's achievements made a major contribution to the process of change and industrialization in the later decades of the nineteenth century. The frequent references made to him as 'Japan's Roland Hill' inevitably suggest a debt to the British inventor of the Penny Post and, while Maejima himself devised the broad outlines of Japan's new communications services of the 1870s–1880s, a trip to Europe at the beginning of the 1870s, and his exposure to the British experience, had a major influence on his subsequent activities. This brief paper will consider the extent of the British influence on Maejima in the context of his overall career.[1]

MAEJIMA'S EARLY CAREER

Maejima Hisoka personified what might be called 'Meiji Man'. His life embraced a huge variety of activities: bureaucrat, politician, businessman, educationalist and campaigner for language reform. His interests were diverse, from poetry and music on one hand to charitable activity on the other. He had a large and close family, and enjoyed close friendships with many of the great names of his day, including Ōkuma Shigenobu, Ōkubo Toshimichi and Shibusawa Eiichi. His active life spanned a period of unprecedentedly rapid change in Japan, and by the time of his death in 1919 at the age of 84 he had participated fully in many aspects of it. It is for his work on the postal service, however, that he remains best known.

Born in 1835 in the *fudai* domain of Takada, in rural Niigata prefecture, Maejima was the second son of a low-ranking member of the warrior class, whose income came mainly from farming.[2] Maejima's father died when he was still a baby, and he was brought up in straitened circumstances, although his uncle ensured that he received much of the classical education deemed fitting for a member of the warrior class. Following the advent of Perry's mission in 1853 he determined to become something of a *rōnin*, and spent many months travelling the length and breadth of Japan, engaged in a relentless pursuit of knowledge about his country and the problems which it faced. This unusual upbringing provided him with an interest in communications which was to dominate the course of his career. His relative freedom within the constraints imposed by the old regime made him realise the importance and possibility of overcoming existing barriers to human and physical communication. His youth also stimulated in Maejima a national consciousness which was to become progressively more marked during the course of his life. He decided that his interest in communications would be used to build Japan into a strong, united nation.

During his youth, apart from his traditional education, Maejima gleaned some knowledge of Western affairs, of medicine and of shipping activities, and a limited amount of English. In 1866, believing that only the Bakufu was likely to be able to act as a nationally recognized government – something which was essential given the current foreign relations crisis – Maejima applied for adoption into a Tokugawa retainer family, thus allying himself formally with the shogunate. Two years later, of course, the Tokugawa fell from power. Maejima spent around two years in the limbo which many Bakufu retainers encountered in the difficult aftermath of the Restoration of 1868, although he made some valuable contacts at this time, including Shibusawa Eiichi.

In January 1870, Maejima took up an appointment as a lowly official in the new government's Ministry of Civil Affairs (*Minbushō*), a body which contained many former Bakufu officials and which, until its functions were subsumed by other ministries during 1871, spearheaded many of the new regime's plans for economic and social transformation. Among Maejima's tasks here was the development of plans for taxation. He was also requested by Ōkuma Shigenobu to draw up estimates for the construction of a railway line from Tokyo to Osaka. Maejima had, of course, never seen a railway line, but still managed to produce an estimate acceptable even to Western experts.[3] He became an ardent advocate of the need for railways in Japan, and the importance of government activity in promoting them for the benefit of the nation. Then, in June 1870, he was appointed to the post of Acting Head of Communications. Now given the chance to act in a field which had long obsessed him, he was delighted: 'I was in the happy position where the accumulated hopes of years had been brought to fruition,' he wrote, 'and truly I cannot speak about the joy which I felt.'[4]

Transport and communications in Tokugawa Japan were mainly a function of the courier system.[5] The system remained unchanged in the first two years after the Restoration, but its efficiency was rapidly deteriorating under increasing pressure of business. Its operation was largely dependent on corvée labour, which caused much resentment. The sending of personal communications was difficult and prohibitively expensive. Restoration officials realized the deficiencies of the old system, but had little idea of what should replace it. The Bureau of Communications prior to Maejima's appointment had gone through no fewer than five heads, none of whom had the remotest idea of what should be done to improve the system.

In Western Europe during the nineteenth century communications developments had been exceptionally rapid. In Britain, the establishment of the Penny Post in 1840 clearly established access to the passage of letters, regardless of political power and income. The new system reduced prices, increased correspondence, and transformed communication from the upper class prerogative it had been to a right possessed by the whole population.[6] Similar systems were adopted by a succession of European countries. However, the first Japanese who went abroad found these systems incomprehensible. Fukuzawa Yukichi, for example, confessed that he would never forget '. . . the terrible trouble I had in understanding how the postal system worked'.[7] Wondering reports by other Japanese, and by Maejima's friends who had travelled abroad, proved to be of little practical use when it came to devising a new system.

Maejima's own knowledge of the Western postal system was almost as scanty as that of his colleagues. However, he had a sense of mission, convinced that the provision of an efficient and comprehensive communications system was a prerequisite for the establishment of a great nation. He was also sure, having received the accounts for the Tōkaidō courier system, that the expenses already being disbursed were more than enough to provide for a new, more efficient system. The principal barrier was ignorance.

In a submission to government leaders in June 1870,[8] Maejima proposed that a new government courier service be established, to run initially along the Tōkaidō daily in both directions. The service would take thirty-six hours to carry letters between Tokyo and Kyoto, and thirty-nine hours from Tokyo to Osaka. Both official and private communications would be carried at a low standard rate, with customers undertaking prepayment through the use of stamps. The new system, it was suggested, would gradually be extended to cover the whole country. Maejima proposed the use of the word *yūbin* to distinguish the new service from the old courier (*hikyaku*) system, and the adoption for stamps of the word *kitte*, already extensively used in commercial circles to denote certain kinds of receipt. The proposal received the approval of the government, and Maejima began to look to its practical implementation. Within a fortnight, however, Maejima was ordered in mid-July to leave his post at the Communications Bureau. He was to join an official delegation to Europe, where the mission's main task would be to sort out problems relating to a loan for the building of the Tokyo-Yokohama railway. The delegation was to be headed by Ueno Kagenori, a senior official in the Ministry of Finance, and Maejima was to be his deputy. The visit overseas was an opportunity for which he had long hoped, and he prepared to depart, confident that on his return he would be better able to complete his unfinished work on the post.

TRIP TO THE WEST, 1870–71

On 22 July 1870, Ueno's delegation sailed from Yokohama on a ship belonging to the Pacific Mail Steamship Company, arriving in San Francisco on 12 August.[9] Activities over the following few days included sightseeing, purchasing Western clothes and reading about the course of the Franco-Prussian War. Much amazement was expressed at the unfamiliar surroundings and customs, not least at the presence of women at a social gathering. On 18 August, the group departed by train for New York. Ueno's diary records their sighting of American Indians, and their astonishment on hearing that the Mormon leader, Brigham Young, had no fewer than eighteen wives. From New York the party boarded a Cunard liner for Europe, arriving in London on 19 September 1870.[10]

During the months after their arrival in London the members of the mission were engaged in a variety of tasks. While Ueno tried to sort out the confusion over the railway loan, which involved an Englishman named Horatio Nelson Lay,[11] Maejima visited Frankfurt, where he commissioned a firm to print banknotes for the Meiji government, thereby hoping to minimize counterfeiting, which was prevalent. The Oriental Bank was entrusted as the Japanese government's agent with contracts for paper-making machines. More important, perhaps, were the investigations which Maejima was able to make into the workings of postal services. He was away from Japan for more than a year, and was determined to make the most of his trip in making himself better informed about his chosen area of activity.

Only six days out from Yokohama, Maejima had discovered that the Pacific Mail ships were in receipt of a subsidy from the United States government to carry US mail. Moreover, he could actually write letters back home while on the ship, and have them taken to Japan by other Pacific Mail ships they met en route, instead of waiting to post them in San Francisco. The ship's captain also explained to Maejima the use of the postmark to prevent the re-use of stamps, and Maejima wrote of these new discoveries to his friend, Sugiura Yuzuru, who had taken charge of the Communications Bureau in his absence.[12] On reaching the United States, he was amazed to find not only that there was a government monopoly on all mail, but that his opposite number held ministerial status.

It was in England, though, that he had the opportunity to make more extensive observations, and it was with an air of revelation that day after day he made a succession of discoveries which caused him amazement. One thing which particularly struck him about the system introduced by Hill, was the levying within the country of equal rates regardless of distance. A letter from London to Birmingham cost the same as a letter from

London to Aberdeen, as did one from London to Guildford. This seemed to him an important step towards national integration, to facilitate the movement of goods, labour and information in a way which reduced discrimination against those further from the centres of economic and political activity. Moreover, whereas the introduction of a new postal system in Japan had been viewed by many as an operation far too costly for an impecunious government, in Britain the postal system was actually a major source of government revenue. The country had also implemented a postal savings system, which provided small savers with an accessible means of depositing, and earning interest on, their limited funds.

It was not sufficient, though, just to discover these things. Maejima needed to have more information on their practical operation if he was to have any chance of adopting the same policies in Japan. After all, his colleagues back in Japan could not help, and there is no evidence that the other members of the Ueno group could summon up an equivalent enthusiasm on this particular topic. Here he was on his own. Using his official status as a Japanese government official, he spent much of his free time in visiting the relevant government departments, attempting to find out details on the actual operation of the system, and the legislation relating to all aspects of the service, including postal orders and postal savings. He made multiple visits to post offices, sometimes pretending to be a client, so as to experience from the customer's point of view the services which were available. Perhaps because of his relatively low official status, he found the Post Office officials at the GPO initially uncooperative. On his first visit, he was received by a haughty individual who, he commented, treated him like a barbarian, and informed him with disdain that any kind of private postal service (such as the old courier system in Japan) was unheard of in 'civilized' countries. Later on, they proved to be more helpful. Maejima was provided with a considerable number of government publications, which he subsequently found to be of great use.[13] By the time of the delegation's departure for Japan in July 1871, Maejima had made sure that he was not only the member of the Japanese bureaucracy most committed to the development of a more efficient communications network, but also the only individual among his fellow countrymen with the knowledge and expertise to implement it.

DEVELOPMENT OF THE POSTAL SERVICE

By the time Maejima arrived back in Tokyo on 29 September 1871, his original plans for a new postal service had already been implemented. On 20 April of that year the Tōkaidō service had commenced operation. It carried all official mail, but there was little private mail, as the service was undercut by the private couriers, and the new service was disadvantaged by not serving Yokohama, which lay off the main route. At the same time there were vociferous complaints from the couriers at the loss of the lucrative Tōkaidō public mail. Shortly before Maejima's return, however, responsibility for communications had been passed to a highly conservative individual called Hamaguchi Gihei, who believed that, once the new service was successfully established, it would be passed over to the private couriers,[14] perhaps one of the first examples of Meiji privatization. Maejima was horrified. Convinced that his 'destiny' allowed of no demonstration of modesty, he submitted to government leaders a petition, requesting that he be allowed to replace Hamaguchi as head of communications. The granting of his request in early October meant that he was able to return to the work he had left unfinished a year previously, but with one difference: the system could now be worked out with reference to foreign models.[15]

From this time until his resignation almost ten years later, the postal service was the overriding concern of Maejima's life, and he presided over its development into an internationally recognized system, offering a range of services on a par with any of the systems of Western Europe or America. By July 1872, the newspapers could proudly announce that the network of regular services had been extended to all the major towns of Japan, excluding the northern part of Hokkaido. There were many problems to be overcome. Finance was in short supply and, although the whole business was meant to be self-financing, income for many years lagged behind expenditure. The printing and perforation of stamps was only carried out successfully after 1872. The first stamps had been made of very thin paper to prevent their re-use, and it was due to Maejima's Western trip that postmarks came into use.[16] It took a long while to persuade many of his colleagues of the importance of the post, and Maejima operated from a shabby building in Edobashi, near the old fish market. He had no separate room, and complained that he had constantly to contend with the smell of fish and the noise from a nearby army canteen.[17]

As the business developed, however, it became apparent that Maejima's direction of its expansion was indeed informed by what he had learnt while he was in Europe, and particularly in England. With regard to the financing of the enterprise, he adhered to what he regarded as the British principle, namely the lower the standard rate charged for sending a letter, the greater would be the volume transported, and hence the amount of profit accruing to the operation. While his purpose was essentially good government, efficient communications and a satisfied people rather than financial gain, he had little choice but to choose a policy of profit maximization. This he did by attempting to make the service cheap and accessible to all. Another major feature of the service in which Maejima followed the British model was the eventual establishment of a government monopoly on the carriage of mail. As we have seen, Maejima had little concept of the possibility of such a thing before his visit to the West. Yet an official submission by Ōkubo Toshimichi and Inoue Kaoru in October 1871, shortly after Maejima's return, stressed the need for government enterprise in the post and drew attention to the existence of government monopolies in other countries. Maejima's preamble to the new Postal Regulations of spring 1872, called attention to the deficiencies of a private system:

'For long the business of letters in our country has been entrusted to private merchants, and exchange has stagnated more than if the government had participated; that is to say, a man from Ōu wanting to send a letter to Hizen can do nothing but wait for a chance traveller, which may take years or months, and he may not know the way. Somewhere as far away as Hokkaido is as though unattainable. . . [In future] there will be no place which does not receive letters, however rural and remote. . . The basis of an increase in trade and production, this business of the post, which is of such great benefit to the people, will be administered by the Bureau of Communications.'[18]

This, then, was a clear suggestion that the government's role in the field of communications was regarded as crucial. In January of the following year, 1873, an article in the *Yūbin Hōchi*, still the official organ of the Post Office, laid the ground for a full monopoly. The article stated that, while Western countries operated uniform rates regardless of distance, if this were done in Japan while private competition still existed, the government service would incur heavy losses, since it would end up carrying long distance mail only. The official announcement in March of a full government monopoly, therefore, came as little surprise. Objections from the erstwhile private couriers were calmed by Maejima's strategy to incorporate them into a new domestic transport company, which would be entrusted with the carriage of all parcel post at the behest of the new service, and would discharge a range of other official commissions. This company, which became in 1875 one of Japan's earliest joint stock companies, eventually developed into the famous Nihon Tsūun Kaisha. Along with the monopoly came the introduction of a uniform rate for carriage. As a transitional measure a three-tier rate was adopted, with the final shift to a uniform rate being made only in 1880, but the principle was clearly established at this time.

In two fundamental features of the new system – the operation of a government monopoly and the charging of a uniform rate regardless of distance – the British model as observed by Maejima was, therefore, of fundamental importance. As the service expanded, it became apparent that there were other ways in which policy-makers were following the European model. Contracts were made with some of the new railway and shipping companies to carry mail in return for specified subsidies, as Maejima had first discovered with the Pacific Mail Company in 1870. A system of postal orders to send remittances by mail was also introduced. Maejima had made extensive investigations into the British system, and had drawn up a plan for implementation in Japan, but this had not initially been carried out due to a shortage of set-up funds. Eventually starting in 1875, the service expanded rapidly. The same month Maejima was able to state proudly to a friend that the business was already flourishing, and thousands of transactions had been undertaken.[19] British influence was just as evident in the postal savings system, which gradually spread through the country from 1875. The system had been introduced in England as recently as 1861, and by 1871, when Maejima was in Europe, the only other country to have introduced such a system was Belgium. Japan was thus relatively early in moving into this field.[20] Maejima saw the postal savings system as helping his fellow countrymen to provide for their own futures, as well as supporting the efforts of the nation by helping investment in areas such as infrastructure. While the system got off to a slow start, it was well established by the time Maejima left office in 1881, and its historical and contemporary importance as an institution for mobilizing scarce capital, and as a major locus for small personal savings, is universally recognized. [21]

ANGLO-JAPANESE POSTAL NEGOTIATIONS

Nationalist that he was, it was not enough for Maejima for his postal service to be acknowledged as a success by his fellow Japanese. In a Japan still bound by the unequal treaties and the operation of extraterritoriality for foreign nationals, foreigners operated their own postal services on Japanese soil, unwilling to entrust their communications to what was considered to be a second-rate Japanese service. It became for Maejima an overriding goal and an article of faith to achieve international recognition of the service he offered, and to abolish extraterritoriality in the sphere of postal communications.[22] While the first step towards postal autonomy was taken with the conclusion of a treaty with the United States implemented in 1875, agreement with Britain took five more years to complete. The exchanges were acerbic and resentful, the negotiations prolonged and difficult. Success critically depended on two factors: one was the opinion of the service entertained by the British community, the other the views of the British Minister, Sir Harry Parkes.

The British community's view of the new service was initially unfavourable, and it was, perhaps, not surprising that Parkes should react with some hostility when Maejima first raised the issue, following conclusion of the treaty with the United States:

> 'The Minister put on an extremely discontented expression, and said that he himself had as yet no idea as to what the Japanese post was like, what sort of laws there were, or what sort of learning and experience the officials possessed. Moreover, he declined to do anything, being so rude as to say that he had no way of knowing that Japanese officials had the skill needed for handling the communications of foreign countries.'[23]

The result of the meeting was several communications by Parkes to the Foreign Office in London, reporting unfavourably on the situation, and warning that any change which allowed Japanese to handle British communications would be extremely detrimental to the welfare of British citizens.[24] Maejima, therefore, had to fight a long battle to reverse these hostile opinions. In mid-1876, following a chance meeting, Maejima persuaded Parkes to visit the Post Office for an inspection. While Parkes' comments were positive, he was more guarded in his report to the authorities in London:

'I may mention to your Lordship that I had not met Mr Mayeshima since the interview which I reported in my Despatch No.98 of 1873, when his manner had not favourably impressed me. He then appeared to think that Japan had only to ask for a Postal Convention in order to obtain it, and gave me no information as to the plans of the Japanese Government respecting the proposed development of their Postal System, or the means at his disposal for carrying their plans into execution.

On the present occasion he exhibited a very different feeling. . . I accordingly visited the General Post Office, on the 22nd Ultimo, and found Mr Mayeshima quite ready to give me information on the working of that establishment. . . I observed to. . . Mr Mayeshima that no one watched with greater interest than I did the advance of the Japanese Postal System, but that before giving them any promise, or making a further report to my Government on this subject, I must wait for the information to be given in the next annual report, which Mr Mayeshima informed me will probably be published in November or December next.'[25]

December came and went, with little advance. While Parkes continued to keep the British government informed of his, usually negative, thoughts on the subject, Maejima perceived only inaction, and accused Parkes of prevarication. The balance began to change with Japan's being admitted to the Universal Postal Union[26] in June 1877. The U.P.U. treaty, signed by the British postal authorities and not the Foreign Office, gave all signatories equal and reciprocal rights, which rendered the existing Anglo-Japanese situation untenable. The British Foreign Office officials, however, failed to issue the requisite instructions, which would have permitted Japanese mail to be carried on board British steamers. Clearly the G.P.O., unlike the Foreign

Office, had ample confidence in the efficiency of the Japanese service. The potentially embarrassing difficulty was eventually resolved by a certain amount of restraint on both sides, and the G.P.O. saw no reason for an extra convention with Japan, in addition to the U.P.U. treaty, but the Foreign Office disagreed. Parkes was accused of obstructing the conclusion of a treaty not only by the Japanese government, but even by the foreign community in Yokohama. He became increasingly irate over the matter.

Formal negotiations eventually took place in 1879, against a background of controversy in the local English language press. While some of the papers read by foreigners approved of the proposed change, one, the normally pro-Japanese *Tokio Times*, was little short of vituperative. Ironically, this appears to be the only cutting which Parkes forwarded to London:

> 'In plain words, the local administration is utterly and inexcusably defective. It is so bad at times that it could not well be worse, and retains the slightest hold upon the general confidence. The transmission of mails between this capital (Yedo) and Yokohama in particular, is marked by irregularities which may properly be characterized in the strongest language of rebuke. The carelessness shown in many instances is little short of criminal, and the sense of official responsibility which should here be strained to the utmost degree of delicacy, seems blunted to the extent of complete indifference. For several months past evidence of inefficiency has been accumulating without, so far as can be learned, producing a sign of effect in the way of reformation.'[27]

Whether or not this was an attempt at a last ditch stand in unclear. If so, it was not successful. Negotiations reached a satisfactory conclusion after only two meetings, and a formal agreement was signed in October, to come into force at the end of that year. Reactions were, on the whole, favourable, though leading British business interests, including Butterfield and Swire, Finlay Richardson, Mather and the Hong Kong and Shanghai Bank, regarded the discontinuation of the British service to Hong Kong as a serious blow to British trade and commercial interests.[28] Maejima, predictably, was delighted:

> 'With this we could recover to the full our national rights in the field of communications, which had been so violated.

That it was my own humble efforts. . . which had brought this thing about, was a source of unceasing joy. . . To recover even one part of our national rights was surely a matter of very great joy for the country. However, even concerning this matter, there was no awareness of it among either people or government. Indeed, the Japanese were a nonchalant people.'[29]

The negotiations over international recognition of Japan's postal service thus offered Maejima a contrasting angle on the British experience and their place in the world. While his first encounter with Britain, on British soil, had been not only a learning process but a revelation, his second, this time on Japanese soil, was a source of considerable conflict, and proof, if any were needed, of the irrational unwillingness of the leading treaty power to acknowledge that in some spheres at least the Japanese had achieved the high standards set by the West. In both cases the exposure made a marked impact on him.

CONCLUSION

Although Maejima left his post in charge of the development of communications in the political upheaval of 1881, he continued for the remainder of his life to regard the postal service as his greatest achievement. During a subsequent career in politics, education, business and charitable work he contributed to many spheres of activity, but his elevation to the peerage in 1902, the twenty-fifth anniversary of Japan's joining the U.P.U., was open recognition that this was Maejima's greatest legacy to posterity. In this critical phase of his career, during the 1870s, Maejima was, as we have seen, exposed to Britain and some of her representatives in Japan. His experiences were both highly positive and extremely negative, and to that extent they perhaps reflect as well as anything else the ambiguity felt in Meiji Japan towards the treaty powers of the West.

6

Isabella Bird, 1831–1904

PAT BARR

MISS ISABELLA BIRD'S arrival in Japan in May 1878 marked her first real encounter with the continent of Asia which was to remain the chief focus of her interest and enthusiasm for the rest of her life. She had already achieved something of a reputation as a traveller and writer following the published accounts of her earlier adventures in Hawaii and Colorado, *Six Months in the Sandwich Isles* and *A Lady's Life in the Rocky Mountains*.[1] And British residents in Japan who had read those accounts of her pioneering, hard-riding, mountain-climbing exploits were probably surprised to find she was a small, dumpy, middle-aged lady with a low voice, clear gaze and a gracious, mild demeanour quite in keeping with her upbringing as the elder daughter of an English clergyman. For Isabella was, for most of her life, two people: the respectable, middle-class Christian lady and the reckless, energetic adventurer who yearned to go alone to the uttermost wilds of the world.

It was the former face forward when she first landed in Yokohama, one of those 'hybrid cities'[2] of the East she never liked. She stayed at the Oriental Hotel and, thanks to the many introductory letters that had preceded her, received thirteen callers on the first day. Among them were Sir Harry Parkes, the British Minister, and his wife who 'brought sunshine and kindliness into the room and left it behind them'.[3] That meeting was the beginning of a firm friendship and within days Isabella was installed in H.B.M.'s Legation in Tokyo which became her base for the remainder of her stay.

It was a truly English home, she noted, though the butler and footman were 'tall Chinese with long pigtails' and the other servants Japanese. The Parkes' two daughters, their nurse and Rags, the Skye dog, completed the family circle which she found most congenial. The Parkes fell in enthusiastically with all her travel plans and offered practical advice – for example, not to buy a pony that would undoubtedly fall sick and keep losing its shoes. Sir Harry helped to map out her proposed route northwards to Yezo (now Hokkaido) and Lady Parkes took her to the Naval College for tea. She drove her own 'flying phaeton' with a pair of beautiful chestnut ponies between the shafts and a *bettō* running ahead to clear the way.

Isabella then spent a week in Yokohama with the venerable missionaries, Dr and Mrs Hepburn. Hepburn's 'extensive information, scientific attainments, calm judgements and freedom from bias'[4] greatly impressed her but, despite his long experience of the country, he was not, she reported, sanguine about the future of the Japanese in any respect. Nor was he sanguine about her proposed journey and advised her against it. He argued, for one thing, that she would lack the proper nourishment, and all foreigners warned her that such 'necessities' as milk, meat, coffee, wine, bread and butter would be unobtainable. But, as the man she later married[5] was to say, Isabella had 'the appetite of a tiger and the digestion of an ostrich' and these considerations did not deter her. Travelling with a lot of impediments was not Isabella's style and she commented: 'Were I to accept much of the advice given to me as to taking tinned meats and soups, claret and a Japanese maid, I should need a train of at least six pack-horses.'[6]

She did, however, concede the necessity for a Japanese guide/interpreter and, while she was in Yokohama, interviewed several applicants for the post, including a sprightly youth sporting a starched shirt, watch-chain, a cane and a felt hat whose sartorial splendour would obviously 'enhance prices everywhere' and besides, 'I should feel perpetual difficulty in asking menial services from such an exquisite'.[7] She eventually engaged one Itō, a 'bandy-legged', strong-looking eighteen-year-old with no recommendations and a furtive glance. But she followed her instinct, hired him for twelve dollars a month – and did not regret it.

Returning to Tokyo, she found that Sir Harry Parkes had secured for her a passport written in Japanese that permitted her to travel anywhere north of the capital and in Yezo – an unusual degree of freedom for a foreigner at that time. She tried to find out more about that northern region, but neither Japanese nor foreigners were of much help. The government department she approached returned her proposed itinerary '. . . leaving out 140 miles of the route . . . on the ground of insufficient information'. At which Sir Harry cheerfully remarked that she would just have to get her information as she went along and it would be 'all the more interesting'.[8] Lady Parkes had also been busy on her behalf, providing her with two baskets with oiled-paper covers for the sides of a pack-horse, an india-rubber bath and a folding chair. Her final travel 'outfit' also included an air-pillow, a canvas stretcher-bed with long legs designed to secure her from fleas (which it failed to do), bundles of yen and sen, volumes of Asiatic Society *Transactions* and Ernest Satow's Anglo-Japanese dictionary.

She had made the acquaintance of Ernest Satow, then the legation secretary, when she first reached Tokyo and records that his reputation for scholarship was 'unequalled' even among Japanese. Whenever she asked them '. . . questions concerning the history, religions and ancient customs' of Japan, she was deflected with: 'You should ask Mr Satow, he could tell you'.[9] Indeed she *did* ask for Satow's help and advice then and on many subsequent occasions and a lasting friendship developed between them.

But now she was ready for off into the 'real Japan', clad in her travelling-dress of dust-coloured, striped tweed, strong laced boots and a bowl-shaped bamboo hat – '. . .very light and infinitely to be preferred to a heavy pith helmet'.[10] It was in character that she never made any effort to look like a typical English colonial lady and, as time went on, wore individual ensembles of Eastern and Western dress which looked a little strange but were comfortable and practical.

NORTHERN JAPAN

The account of the three months she spent in the 'northern wilds' forms the bulk of her book *Unbeaten Tracks in Japan*, published in two volumes by John Murray in 1880, and arranged in the form of letters written, more or less on-the-spot, to her younger sister, Henrietta. 'Hennie' was of a patient, timid, unselfish disposition, a perfect complement to Isabella's inquiring, restless, fearless, determined character. One who had known them from childhood wrote: 'What one lacked, the other possessed and thus together they formed a perfect combination.' Isabella herself recognized this and some of her unpublished letters contain phrases such as 'its being', 'its own pet' – a term of mutual endearment suggesting that the two felt themselves to be, in some ways, a single entity.[11] The letters Isabella wrote to Henrietta (edited before publication) are an honest, unsparing, vivid, occasionally humorous description of her travels, and also include a wealth of accurate, detailed information about the region – its landscape, local products, natural resources, institutions (such as hospitals and schools), and the everyday lives of its people.

Her trials were several, and the miserable, harsh conditions in which the rural poor lived were even worse than she had anticipated. The further north she went, the more she – a lone foreign lady – became an object of insatiable curiosity. Crowds of peasants surrounded her constantly, 'both sexes half-nude', 'apathetic', their skins covered with 'dirt and sores', their stares 'vacant', and they poked holes in the *shoji* of inn-rooms to watch her every movement – which must have been rather unnerving. Most of the inns were choked with charcoal and tobacco fumes, draughty, reeking of sewage, humming with fleas and mosquitoes; at night they were noisy with people eating, drinking, and playing the samisen, that 'instrument of dismay'; the food they served was just as execrable as she had been told. It consisted mostly of rice-mush and sour rice-dough, pickled vegetables, half-raw salt fish, ancient eggs and watery cucumbers.

Water was everywhere because it unfortunately turned out to be the wettest summer for thirty years. Streams and rivers overflowed, roads, already deeply rutted and precipitous, became treacherous swamps and mildew flourished everywhere – on her always-damp bedlinen, towels, boots and between the pages of the Asiatic Society *Transactions*. She had also to contend with the local breed of pack-horse, 'horridly fierce-looking creatures' who kicked, reared and bit. The very first one she mounted '. . . broke his head-rope . . . and proceeded down the main street mainly on his hind feet, squealing and striking out savagely with his forefeet'. She contrived to stay on its high-peaked saddle (for she was a very skilful horsewoman) until, '. . . as it surged past the police-station, four policemen came out and arrested it'.[12] There were many similar equine tribulations which aggravated the spinal pain that had dogged her for years. Despite all this, Isabella found much to give her pleasure: the splendour of the mountain scenery, the beauty of the peaceful thatched villages and the simple kindness, honesty and generosity of the ordinary people to which she often pays tribute.

Unlike most of her contemporary foreign travellers, Isabella even found much to like in the Ainu people whom she encountered in Yezo. She spent about three weeks there, galloping freely over the plains and staying with the Ainu who welcomed her into their isolated settlements. And that, she wrote, was the most interesting of all her travel experiences. It was not long since European anthropologists had begun to wonder if these docile, sturdy, hirsute people might provide a clue to the elusive 'missing link' of human evolution. And, as little was known about them, Isabella asked innumerable questions about their everyday habits, their religion, customs, legends, their methods of bear-hunting, tattooing, fishing, house-building, weaving and so on. This was an occupation she enjoyed, both for its own sake and because she hoped she was contributing her mite to the sum of human knowledge.

When she returned to Hakodate, where she stayed at the Church Mission House with Mr and Mrs Dening,[13] it was time to part company with Itō. In the course of their journeying together, she presents a shrewd but not unsympathetic portrait of this vain, moody, brash youth with his thoroughgoing patriotism, his admiration for all 'things Western', his genuine shame at the 'backwardness', deprivation and squalor they encountered in the remote interiors of his beloved country. He had proved to be clever, energetic, resourceful and she had learned to trust and depend on him. To some extent, he represented the failings and virtues of Meiji Japan itself and, understanding this, she learned to like him. And he certainly liked and admired her – for her tenacity, her physical courage, her sense of fair-dealing, her lack of pomposity. In later years, Itō guided foreign tourists round Nikko and apparently 'dined out' for the rest of his life on stories of his adventures with Miss Bird in the wilds of the north.[14]

BACK TO TOKYO

Miss Bird travelled south again in late September and spent another three months in Japan. But the high points of her stay were over once she returned to the comparatively developed and 'civilized' areas of the country. She invariably detested cities and Japan's capital proved no exception. She had little sense of the grandeur of its past and new Tokyo was merely a city 'of "magnificent distances" without magnificence'.[15] It was low-lying, straggling, grey with numbers of 'repulsively ugly Europeanized buildings'. She catalogues its main features with care but little enthusiasm and was attracted only to its older central area where canals were jammed with boats and roadways with carts, rickshaws and the infamous pack-horses. 'No streets of Liverpool or New York present more commercial activity,'[16] she noted.

She spent more time at the legation, but Sir Harry and Lady Parkes were absent, worn out by the enervating climate and too much work and society. So she shared the pleasant house with the dog Rags and Basil Hall Chamberlain,[17] who proved a very pleasant companion, being such 'a thorough lover of Japan'. He was never bored by her many questions on the subject, 'even though many of them are trivial and unintelligent'.[18] (It is hard to imagine Miss Bird asking a stupid question!) Another Victorian lady traveller, Miss Gordon Cumming, turned up while she was there. They tended to follow each other round the East, though not intentionally, and Miss Cumming was certainly not Miss Bird's equal either as an adventurer or writer. The relationship between them was cool, and Isabella's only comment, recorded in a letter home, was that 'Miss Gordon Cumming is beautifully dressed and is strong and well.'![19]

One afternoon the two ladies and Mr Chamberlain attended an 'afternoon entertainment' in one of the Emperor's palaces where they met Mori Arinori, Vice-Minister for Foreign Affairs and a true 'progressive'. He, she claimed, 'would tolerate anything', regarded Shinto only as a 'useful political engine' and was in favour of 'Women's Rights'.[20] She put that last in quotation marks for she, like most female travellers of her age, did not take them very seriously. On the whole, they were far too single-minded, apolitical and individualistic to be concerned with such issues and seldom held the majority of their sex in very high regard.

A few days after the Japanese reception, that was merely an imitation of an English one, she was invited by Ernest Satow to a reception à la Japonaise which she enjoyed much more. His house was furnished in the 'perfection of Japanese and European good taste and simplicity'; the drawing-room was pure Japanese with fine *tatami*, the occasional Persian rug and bronze ornament. After dinner, there was a concert by an amateur orchestra led by a 'Japanese composer who aspires to be the Wagner of Japan'. The setting was delightful, but the music was, to her, excruciating. In fact, she confessed, 'Oriental music is an agonizing mystery to me' – though 'Mr Satow's calm, thoughtful face showed no trace of anguish.'[21]

Miss Bird's last excursion from the capital was over the well-beaten tracks. First to Kobe, where she enjoyed the hospitality of the Gulicks,[22] American missionaries with whose family she had stayed several years before in Hawaii. And you can imagine, she wrote to Hennie, '. . . how we revel in Hawaiian talk . . .' and how, in their company, '. . . I dream my tropical dream once more'. She was not, however, uncritical of missionary conduct and deplored their habit of actively discouraging their Japanese pupils from the observance of 'all the graceful native courtesies', with the result that 'missionary manners' (a term used by Itō) meant bad manners in Japanese eyes. 'I abhor the denationalization of nations' she stated, 'and should like to see Japanese courtesies studied and met at least half-way'.[23]

She made these views clear to the Gulicks, arguing that '. . . the Christian religion is unpopular enough in Japan, without weighting it with the mill-stone of an implied and practised antagonism to the ancient laws of good breeding which . . . fit the people and from which we might advantageously learn not a little.'[24] She and Mrs Gulick went on a tour of the 'sights' in Kyoto, Nara and Ise which she enjoyed, though it was all rather tame small beer compared to where she had already been. In true globetrotter style, she bought vases, bronzes, paintings on silk and a 'daimyo's bath' which later held pot plants in her Edinburgh home. And, like many other foreigners, she found things to admire everywhere, while deploring the crude over-adornment of modern objects made to please Western taste.

By the time Miss Bird returned to Tokyo for the last time, the Parkes' home had been 'broken up' by the departure of Lady

Parkes and the children for England. She paid great tribute to all their kind hospitality and said that Lady Parkes '. . . used all the opportunities within her power to win the confidence and friendship . . .' of the Japanese women in her circle.[25] Her absence was 'mourned by everyone' and the recent parting of husband and wife was a sadder occasion than anyone realized, for they did not meet again. Isabella maintained her friendship with Lady Parkes when she returned home, but the latter continued to suffer much ill-health and died the following year. Isabella attended her funeral, but Sir Harry, urgently sent for, unfortunately arrived in England the day after it.

Isabella herself steamed out of Yokohama on 19 December and visited Malaya, which she describes colourfully and joyously in her rather neglected book, *The Golden Chersonese*. She eventually reached Tobermory on the Isle of Mull, where Henrietta had a cottage, in May 1879 and, despite a bout of ill-health (which seemed always to beset her once she returned home!), set about organizing her notes and research for a book about Japan. All seemed set fair. Her reputation as an original traveller and a writer of substance and popularity was confirmed by the success of her earlier works, and she was reasonably content to stay on Mull, visit friends and 'toil to finish' her new book. But in June 1880 disaster struck: Henrietta died of typhoid.

Isabella was utterly shattered by the death of the one who had been her main anchor, her best friend and soulmate, the '. . . inspiration of all my literary work', she told John Murray, and the other half of her. For months she was wrapped in a '. . . rigidity of grief that chilled and devitalized her', as a friend put it. That autumn, copies of *Unbeaten Tracks in Japan* reached the Tobermory cottage where she mourned alone and were put aside unopened. But her interest was eventually kindled by its many favourable reviews. The book was praised for its vivid personal account of her northern journey, for its comprehensiveness, for its candid and keen assessment of Japanese society and politics at the time. It was rightly pointed out that Miss Bird's descriptions of Japan were nearer to the truth than the cherry-blossom pretty scenarios conjured by the majority of globetrotters who seldom ventured beyond the popular resorts.

Her professional success did little to comfort Isabella's personal desolation, however, and it must have been mainly to relieve this that, in December, she agreed, as she put it to Murray, to accept 'a very faithful love that had long been mine'. She was to marry Dr John Bishop, a devoted admirer who had frequently ministered to the Bird sisters during their many illnesses. The marriage took place the following spring; Isabella Bird was fifty years old; the bridegroom was forty; she wore deep mourning in honour of Henrietta; there were no wedding guests.[26]

Mrs Bishop made conscientious efforts to play the domestic role of a doctor's wife in Edinburgh, but it was a sorry time. She suffered from various physical ailments, boredom, irritability, a 'morbid obsession' over Henrietta's death; then her husband contracted erysipelas in the course of his work. Pernicious anaemia followed and she nursed him devotedly during his gradual decline until his death in 1886, two days before their fifth wedding anniversary.

Again Isabella mourned, for now she was bereft of all close emotional ties – but slowly she allowed the hope of further travel to shape her future. In January 1889, after much prevarication and armed with the justifications of researching medical missions and '. . . bringing back a cargo of knowledge', she returned to her beloved East. During the next eight years she accomplished some extraordinary feats of exploration and endurance. She journeyed to the borders of Tibet, to Persia and Kurdistan where she camped among the 'ruffian tribes' of the Bakhitiari, she floated along the Korean River Han in a sampan and made an astonishing three-thousand mile journey through China from Shanghai to the Tibetan foothills by Yangtze river junk and sedan chair.

LAST THREE VISITS TO JAPAN

During this period Japan became her refuge for rest and recuperation after the rigours of less comfortable countries. But the three visits she made there are barely mentioned in her later books, *Korea and her Neighbours* and *The Yangtze Valley and Beyond*, and, in the absence of unpublished material, we cannot glean much about them. In the summer of 1895 she apparently stayed with Bishop and Mrs Bickersteth in Tokyo and the latter wrote to Anna Stoddart: 'It is impossible to say what her friendship was to us, or how we rejoiced in intercourse with that cultured mind and loving heart, always full of sympathy for our concerns, whether of the Mission or of private life and yet also delightfully ready to pour out her stores of knowledge and experience, with a complete absence of self-consciousness and a perfect command of language which made listening to her a treat indeed.'[27] Even though Isabella was so welcome at the Bickersteths, she soon longed to escape the city and spend two summer months in the mountain village of Ikao in a little rented house, working on her book about Korea and developing photographs – which was a new hobby.

On her last visit to Japan in 1896 she stayed for several weeks with Ernest Satow, now British Minister, at his summer residence at Lake Chuzenji. She described to a friend her '. . . quiet, serene life, in scenery absolutely lovely, in a little Japanese house, where everything goes like clockwork – but without the tick . . .' She goes on: 'Sir Ernest and I are great friends now and have been for some time; but we did not always get on together – far from it!' Their routine was leisurely: lunch about 1 p.m., 'open-air tea at 5', a row on the lake (she often took an oar) till 6.30, then dinner and 'talk on the verandah till about ten'.[28] The only other guests were Harold Parlett, a consular secretary, and Reverend Lionel Cholmondeley who mentions their interesting conversations in his reminiscences. The affairs of Japan and other Eastern nations were naturally main topics, and they also discussed literature – Isabella strongly urging Satow to read Lord Beaconsfield's *Tancred*.

During that summer, Isabella also visited the nearby spa of Yumoto and called in for tiffin at the summer house of Baroness d'Anethan, who gives this amusing picture of her in her memoirs.[29] It was raining as usual and Isabella '. . . looked a curious sight as she crawled forth from her covered jinrickshaw. She was dressed in a jinrickshaw man's mushroom-shaped hat, and wore a Chinese upper garment of some pale blue cotton stuff over her European clothing. The costume was a peculiar mixture of Japanese, Chinese and European. She was very interesting and related to me many of her experiences in the interior of China . . .'. The d'Anethans were close friends of Sir Ernest's and there were several other social contacts that included Isabella and the renowned German Dr Baelz, who was also staying in Chuzenji. At the end of the season the d'Anethans returned to the capital and, writes the Baroness, '. . . travelled with Mrs Bishop, whom we looked after'. Considering Isabella's long record of perilous and rigorous travel in Asia, it is hard to imagine she required any 'looking after' between Nikko and Tokyo!

After leaving Japan for the last time, Isabella spent several months in Korea and, early in 1879, told Murray that she was contemplating a return to England, but '. . . with a very bad grace. I am far more at home in Tokyo and Seoul than any place in Britain except Tobermory, and I very much prefer life in the East to life at home'.[30] Perhaps she should have stayed there, for her last homebound years did not give her much pleasure – their high point was probably a madcap fling to Morocco in her seventieth year when she rode a 'huge black stallion' to visit the Berber Arabs in the Atlas Mountains. That really was her final adventure and she died peacefully in Edinburgh in 1904. Even on her deathbed, Anna Stoddart records that she was fascinated by the progress of Japan's war against Russia. For her heart was still in the East and her trunks were still packed ready for another Asian journey.

Minakata Kumagusu, 1867–1941:
a Genius now Recognized

CARMEN BLACKER

UNTIL the late 1980s the name of Minakata Kumagusu was scarcely known in Japan. His collected works in twelve volumes had always attracted admirers, enthusiasts for the extraordinary erudition displayed there for natural history, folklore, classical learning in a dozen languages, and for the odd, unorthodox passion for human knowledge which had lain behind the erudition. But these enthusiasts were few and specialized. Professor Tsurumi Kazuko's book of 1978, *Minakata Kumagusu*, with its scholarly assessment of Minakata's peculiar genius, reached only a limited readership. The general public knew nothing of him, and in academic circles he was dismissed as a mere antiquarian, whose random writings were unified by no consistent 'theory', and whose lack of a single disciple to perpetuate his memory proved him to be academically negligible. His odd habits, moreover, forgetting while the *furor scribendi* was upon him to eat and sleep, or to wear any clothes in summer, or to dry himself after a hot bath, proved him to be a notable outsider, a *kijin* rather than a serious scholar.[1]

Five or six years ago, however, a remarkable change occurred. A 'Kumagusu-boom' had arrived. Books, magazine articles, videos and films about his life began to appear. His collected works were reprinted; his diary was published in four volumes. The citizens of his home town, Tanabe, on the Kii peninsula, suddenly aware that at the beginning of the century they had harboured a genius in their midst, were quick to publish posters proclaiming him to be one of the Three Great Men of Tanabe.

The boom reached a climax in 1991, the 50th anniversary of his death. In that year an exhibition in his honour was held at the Odakyū department store in Shinjuku, featuring memorabilia of every kind. There were photographs, notebooks and diaries filled with his distinctive tiny writing, boxes of dried fungi and insects, and even a 'nenkin-corner', where the primitive variety of mycetozoa, nenkin, in which Minakata had taken a special interest, was fully explained. Here for 200 yen a 'nenkin-kit' could be purchased, enabling anyone to propagate nenkin for themselves just as Minakata had done.

He was even hailed as a pioneer of a new mode of thinking. No longer a mere antiquarian, he was now a 'shackled giant'. His very loneness, his refusal to join any group or community, or to encourage any disciple to carry on his work, was now seen not as a mark of failure but as proof that his thought had transcended the conventional limits of scientific and rational knowledge. He was a pioneer for a new holistic view of the world. The strange diagram found among his writings, which to uninitiated eyes looks like an arbitrary scrawl, was now seen to be a 'minakata-mandala', a model for a new non-sequential mode of thought which could only be ascribed to a genius.[2]

His extraordinary library, moreover, has been opened, dusted and catalogued. For forty-five years it was left in much the same state as it was at his death in 1941, with rough wooden shelves piled with thousands of books in a dozen languages, with match-boxes and cigarette boxes dating from the 1920s filled with dried insects and fungi, fossils, minerals, shells and caramels, and bottles of insecticide dating from the 1930s. White powder for killing bookworms still lay scattered on the floor, and a voluminous and miscellaneous collection of papers still lay unsorted in boxes and shelves.

The books and papers have now been sorted and catalogued by Dr Matsui Ryūgo. The same scholar has also made an exhaustive list of the 600 odd books that Minakata used in the British Museum Library, and from which he copied passages into fifty-three large notebooks.

For the connection between this eccentric genius and Britain was an important one. From 1892 to 1900, Minakata spent eight years in London, for four of which he had a reader's ticket to the library of the British Museum. Here he was able, with ferocious energy and concentration, to read hundreds of books in a dozen languages, and to copy passages from the rarer volumes into his fifty-three notebooks. He was able to write the learned and unusual articles for *Nature* and for *Notes and Queries* which brought him to international notice. He was able to acquire a firm basis of scholarship which lasted him for the rest of his life.

Long before his arrival in London, however, he had shown signs of precocious brilliance. As a child in Wakayama he had displayed a photographic memory of such vividness that he could memorize an entire book after reading it through only once; each page was visualized in his mind's eye with such clarity that he could 'read off' the contents as though it were on a screen. At the age of thirteen he apparently memorized in this fashion not only the *Taiheiki*, but also three large encyclopaedias containing the names of thousands of plants and animals.

These were Kaibara Ekken's *Yamato Honzō*, compiled in the early eighteenth century and describing more than 1,300 plants; the sixteenth-century Chinese herbal *Pen-tsao kang-mu*, which again describes hundreds of plants and the diseases they were believed to cure. And, most impressive of all, the *Wakan Sansai Zue*, published in 1713 and containing descriptions of what the author, Terashima Ryōan, hoped was everything known to man. Animals, birds, fish, precious stones, ordinary stones, maps of China, musical instruments, foreign savages and dragons are all found arranged in sections on the traditional model of the Chinese encyclopaedia. The number of Chinese characters used in this work is immense; not less than 10,000 is a conservative estimate. Yet Minakata at the age of thirteen is said to have held this complex book in his memory so vividly that he was able to copy it out, from each visualized page, over the space of three years.[3]

It was said also that as a child he conceived a renaissance ambition for omniscience, for a general 'knowledge', *hakubutsu-gaku*, which would explain the universe. His hero, on whom he decided to model his life, was the sixteenth-century Swiss polymath Conrad von Gesner, author of the bestiary *Historia Animalium*, from whom our well-loved Topsell derived much of his material.

Despite these amazing mental gifts, however, Minakata was uninterested in conventional education. His father, one of the richest merchants in Wakayama, sent him to Tokyo University. But the lectures bored him so much that he failed the final examinations. His father then sent him to America, where he was expelled from two colleges for drunken and disorderly behaviour. The five years he spent in America were largely passed in hippy-like wanderings over the mid-West, Florida and Cuba, collecting specimens of insects and fungi.[4]

MINAKATA IN LONDON

He arrived in London from America in 1892 and took lodgings at ten shillings a week over a stable in a dingy mews in Kensington, 15 Blithfield Street. But, despite this unpromising address, it was not long before he made his first leap into scholarly recognition. He happened to see in the journal *Nature*, the most prestigious scientific journal of the period, a query about the grouping of stars into constellations. He composed a reply in English entitled 'The Constellations of the Far East', in which he described the traditional Chinese method of grouping stars into 'inns', 'palaces' and 'seats'. He tells us that he only had half a dictionary at his disposal, the A to Q half, lent by his landlady, the R to Z half being missing. It was accepted and published in October 1893.

The erudition of the work and the recondite nature of its content, for little was known of Chinese astronomy at the time, attracted immediate and excited attention. Who was this unknown Japanese?

Notices appeared in the newspapers, and he was invited to a dinner of roast goose by Sir Augustus Wollaston Franks, Keeper of the Department of British and Medieval Antiquities in the British Museum, President of the Society of Antiquaries, and author of a number of learned books.[5] This kind and eminent man became the first of Minakata's scholarly English friends, and it was through his introduction that Minakata gained entry to the place in London which was to figure most prominently in his life for the next five years, the Reading Room of the British Museum.

Here at last he found a wealth of the kind of learning for which he had been craving for so long: natural history and the folklore of natural history. He read, he copied long passages from rare works unobtainable in Japan, and he continued to compose more learned articles for *Nature* on an extraordinary variety of subjects.[6]

'Some Oriental Beliefs about Bees and Wasps', for example, published in May 1894, discusses the odd belief that bees can be born from the carcase of an ox. 'The Antiquity of the Finger-print Method', December 1894, cites many learned authorities to show that the Chinese were the first to use finger-printing as a method of personal identification. 'The Mandrake', April 1895 and August 1896, demonstrates that there exists in China a plant Shang-lu, *phytolacca acinosa*, round which congregate a cluster of beliefs uncannily similar to those attributed in Europe to the mysterious plant mandrake. 'The Story of the Wandering Jew', November 1895, draws attention to a figure from the Buddhist scriptures, Pindola Bharadvaja or Binzuru, whose legend bears a remarkable resemblance to that of the Wandering Jew in Europe.

In all he contributed no less than fifty articles for *Nature* between 1893 and 1914, of which thirty-five were written in London and the rest sent from Japan after 1900.

The other learned journal to which he contributed extensively was *Notes and Queries*, then in its heyday and containing a fascinating medley of learned queries on matters of history, classical literature, heraldry and folklore, together with the replies proffered by readers. Minakata did not begin to write for *Notes and Queries* until 1899, the year before he left England, but in that year he published no less than sixteen contributions, mostly Replies to other people's queries, and drawing on an extraordinary range of erudition. He continued to send contributions of varying length to *Notes and Queries*, adding up to a grand total of 307, until 1933. All are written in his own special style of English, which abounds in learned Latinisms like that of Sir Thomas Browne. He speaks of a percutient implement, an anthropophagous crab, an ogreish monopode and quotidien ague.

The learning revealed in these essays is astonishing. He is on terms of easy familiarity with the great Mahayana Buddhist canon in Chinese, with Chinese dynastic histories, herbals and materia medica; with Japanese history and literature, including little known collections of folklore and local history; with a whole range of ancient works on natural history such as Pliny, Olaus Magnus and von Gesner; with the narratives of old travellers to strange lands, such as Purchas's *Pilgrimes*, Tavernier's *Six Voyages*, Yule's *Ser Marco Polo*, Humboldt's *Narratives*, Ramusio's *Navigationi e Viaggi*; with all the current periodicals on folklore, sinology and natural history, and with a mass of miscellaneous reading – Herodotus, Giraldus Cambrensis, Voltaire's *Dictionnaire Philosophique*, St Francis Xavier's *Lettres*, Boccaccio's *Decameron*, Haiton's *Histoire Orientale des Tartares*, Bennet and Murray's *Handbook of Cryptogamic Botany*, to quote a random few.[7]

He further quotes from works in Italian, French and Spanish, and cites others in Arabic, Persian and Armenian. For it appears that during this fertile period he taught himself, by a strange intuitive method which Yanagita Kunio found astonishing, to read nearly a dozen languages.

A random sample of the titles he contributed to *Notes and Queries* gives us: 'Footprints of Gods'; 'Flying Cups'; 'Born with Teeth'; 'The Purchasing of Dreams'; 'Easter Hare'; 'The Asiatic Orpheus'; 'Extraordinary Fountains in Ireland and Brittany'; 'Legless Spirits in Lithuanian Folklore'.

Miscellaneous though these titles may seem, their content shows a unity of intention: an earnest, even aggressive, desire to show Western readers that China and Japan contained treasures of folklore, literature and antiquarian study which they had never before suspected. He is concerned to supply learning from the Far East which might compare and contrast with the known body of learning from Western sources. Little was known in the 1890s of the folklore, history and literature of China and Japan. Mahayana Buddhism was as yet little explored, the Confucian and Taoist classics had not long been translated, and the translations had reached only a very limited public. Minakata, in quoting from the Mahayana sutras, the Chinese Official Histories, from Bakin and Arai Hakuseki, from the Kojiki and the voluminous smaller works in the *Gunsho Ruijū*, was offering knowledge from an area relatively unknown in the West.

So, when he writes that there is a figure in the Buddhist canon remarkably similar to the Wandering Jew, that there is a Chinese plant uncannily similar to the mandrake, that there are folktale types in China and Japan very similar to those found all over Europe and which had been assigned to the heritage of the Aryan people alone, that there are magic fountains in Japan which have the same miraculous properties as those in Ireland, that there are Buddhist priests in Japan whose holy powers can cause their begging bowls to fly through the air in exactly the same manner as Marco Polo relates of Kubla Khan's magicians – all this was new to the readers of *Notes and Queries*.

When a query was published asking for stories of children born with teeth, Minakata was able to cite Benkei: '. . . born after a uterogestation of three years and three months, with hair growing down to his shoulders, and with teeth, both front and molar, fully developed'.[8]

To an enquiry about magic stones found in eagles' nests which were believed to aid the process of parturition, Minakata replied with a *tour de force* of erudition, quoting sources from Pliny's *Natural History*, de Plancy's *Dictionaire Infernel*, 1845, the Chinese herbal *Pen-tsao kang-mu*, and the story of Solomon's temple in the first book of Kings.[9]

Minakata's English writings are in fact a little encyclopaedia of curious and little-known lore about China and Japan. Its arrangement is far from systematic, but it is a unique compendium.

During this same period he made several influential friends. Sir Robert Douglas, Keeper of Oriental Books and Manuscripts, and Professor of Chinese at King's College, London, was constantly kind and helpful, giving him a part-time job of cataloguing in the Library, with a small salary attached. So also was F.V. Dickins, who had been a medical officer of the Royal Navy stationed in Yokohama, a barrister, and became Assistant Registrar (1882–96) and Registrar (1896-1901) of London University. In collaboration with this kindly scholar, Minakata published a translation of the *Hōjōki*, with learned footnotes, which appeared in 1905 under the title of *A Japanese Thoreau of the 12th Century*. Both translation and notes were originally Minakata's, but were revised by Dickins who wrote on the first page: 'My friend Mr Minakata is the most erudite Japanese I have ever met, equally learned in the science and literature of the East and the West.'[10]

Another friend was Sun Yat-sen, the prime mover of the Chinese Revolution of 1911, to whom he was introduced by Sir Robert Douglas in 1897. Sun had arrived in London the previous year and had been kidnapped by the Chinese authorities and imprisoned in the basement of the Chinese legation in Portland Place, from which he was rescued two or three days later, thanks to the initiative of Dr James Cantlie. Sun was then thirty-two, Minakata thirty-one. Minakata's *London Diary* indicates that between March and July 1897 he and Sun met twenty-seven times, either in the British Museum, or in Sun's lodgings, or in the Maria Restaurant at Hyde Park, or in Kew

Gardens. But alas, there is not a word recorded of what they talked about during their brief friendship.[11]

His *London Diary*, indeed, kept regularly, if briefly, during his years in England, gives us some idea of the tenor of his daily life. On 30 January 1893 he had for dinner, 'Soup and Turnip, Goose Liver and coffee, 6 Cigars'. The next day he had for breakfast ham and eggs and coffee, and took nine cigars with his dinner. On 20 March he had 'Ham and Eggs, 4 cigars not paid, 2 Bottles Beer unpaid'.[12] In fact he spent nearly all his money on books, a fair amount on drink – he would sometimes leave the Museum at 8 pm and walk back to Kensington, stopping to have a drink at every pub he passed on the way – very little on food and least of all on his lodging. His room at 15 Blithfield Street was said to be so crammed with books and boxes of specimens as to be impossible to keep clean. There was also a strong smell of horse, said to come from the stables below. But his daughter Fumie tells us in her memoir of her father that in later years he used to keep a tray of horse manure in his room for the propagation of the *nenkin* or slime mould. If the habit was acquired in London, where horse manure was readily available, we can understand why the celebrated entomologist, Baron Osten-Sacken, who visited him there in the hope of discussing his article in *Nature* about bees and wasps, was so overcome by the smell of horse as to be unable to accept the cup of tea that Minakata hospitably offered him.[13]

It would be wrong, however, to assume that these years were passed by Minakata in an uncloudedly serene pursuit of omniscience. It is now believed that much of the demoniacal drive behind his concentrated quest for knowledge was fired by resentment against the assumptions, which he must have encountered outside his circle of sympathetic friends, that Western culture was unarguably superior to any other. Many of his learned articles, which we have seen to be concerned to supply knowledge of the traditions of China and Japan as yet unknown in the West, may have been stimulated also by resentment against such assumptions based on ignorance. Could his conversations with Sun Yat-sen in the Maria Restaurant in Hyde Park have included expressions on both sides of exasperation at the arrogance, and the ignorance, of many London citizens?

Such irritations, together with worries over money, for his

allowance from his family in Wakayama was drying up, and with the impoverished diet that his *London Diary* indicates, are now believed to be behind the signs of increasingly uncontrollable temper, rage and paranoid fancies that he was being insulted, that he showed from 1897 onwards.[14]

In 1897 he records two occasions when he actually attacked women in the London streets because he fancied they were laughing at him. On 28 April he writes that four policemen were needed to drag him to the nearest police station, so violent was his behaviour. But he was released after 2 am as they were apparently at a loss as to what to do with him.[15] He mentions that it was after 6 o'clock, when the pubs were open, so possibly he may have been drunk. He records in his diary other occasions when 'much drinking and wild words' heightened his aggressiveness.

MINAKATA AND THE BRITISH MUSEUM

It was one such outburst of violent temper which was responsible for the sudden end of this happy and productive period of his life. On 8 November 1897, in the middle of the Reading Room, crowded to capacity with quiet and sober readers, Minakata suddenly and violently assaulted another reader by punching him on the nose. *Hageshiku sono hana wo uchishi koto ari*, 'I gave him a hard blow on the nose', he recorded. He was ejected from the Room and the matter reported to the Standing Committee of the Museum. This body met on 13 November and considered a report dated 8 November which stated that: 'Mr Kumagusu Minakata (a Japanese) had that day violently assaulted another Reader, Mr G. St Leger Daniels, in the Reading Room, and was with difficulty induced to leave the Room.'

The Committee also considered two letters from Mr Minakata, dated 11 and 12 November, 'offering full apology, but alluding to provocation received'. The Principal Librarian reported that he had suspended Minakata's admission as a Reader, and was directed by the Trustees to enquire further into the matter. On 11 December the Trustees, having scrutinized another letter from Minakata 'undertaking to keep the peace under any circumstances within the walls of the British Museum', sanctioned his readmission to the Reading Room. None of Minakata's letters on this occasion have come to light, so we have no inkling of his own explanation of the affair.

He was, in fact, let off lightly, his reader's ticket having been suspended for only six weeks. All would have been forgotten and forgiven. But alas, a year later, on 6 December 1898, he again 'caused a disturbance in the Reading Room'. What exactly he did this time is not clear. His Diary for 7 December (not 6th) merely records that he had complained about some women chattering in loud voices, but had not been listened to. It is possible that he may himself have 'caused the disturbance' by shouting.

The Standing Committee once more considered an 'explanatory letter from Mr Minakata dated 7th December', but this time they were adamant. No pleas could shake them. The novelist, Arthur Morrison, whom Minakata had befriended, appealed on his behalf to the Prince of Wales, the Archbishop of Canterbury and the Lord Mayor of London. But not even these illustrious persons could make the Museum authorities budge. He was expelled from the Reading Room. All that the Committee would concede, after receiving two letters from Sir Robert Douglas, was that he could read, not in the Reading Room, but in the Oriental Students' Room 'under conditions that would prevent any disturbance in the future', and under the personal supervision of Sir Robert.

These restrictions were rejected by Minakata as humiliating. At the end of 1898, therefore, to his own great misfortune, Minakata left the British Museum for good.[16]

The 'explanatory letter dated December 7th' was discovered in 1990 by Dr Matsui Ryūgo in the course of his tireless inventory of Minakata's library at Tanabe. It proves to be a document of exceptional interest. It is a long petition to the Trustees, covering nine typewritten pages, and purporting to explain why, for a second time and after due warning, he was driven to such an outbreak of violence in the Reading Room.[17]

The reader whom he had assaulted the previous year, he declared, had subjected him over many months to repeated insults. Merely because Minakata had sneezed near his desk, this man had threatened to have him taken to a police court. Time and again he had offended Minakata 'by repetitions of dirty curses, funny grimaces and menacing talks, pointing to my face'. Even more insultingly, '. . . he always spat on my side with a countenance quite grotesque to our senses grinning his teeth like a baboon at the Zoo'.

Nor was this one reader the only offender. Others would come and seat themselves near his desk, putting to him noisily audible questions. 'e.g. how we call in Japanese *girls*, p. . ., v. . ., d. . ., (these being the names for very obscene things)? whether I am circumcized? whether I eat pork; and cat? and rat? how many sweethearts I have? whether can I render "God save the Queen" into Pigeon Chinese? . . . Some would squat down near me for a quarter of an hour, and regardless of my great disinclination, would narrate me the biography of certain Arthur Dissy, a grand Hungarian Philogist and wine dealer. . .'

Others would stare him in the face 'and squeak with weasel-like voice, Johny, Johny, Johny'. Worst of all, on 4 November 1897, two days before his first outburst, someone put 'a quill pen dripping with jetty ink' into his expensive silk-hat. This insult was the last straw, and '. . . at last resolved me to chastise him with my determined action'. He begs the authorities to understand that he was provoked beyond endurance, and that his only wish was to pursue his research in the Reading Room.

It is difficult to believe that readers in the British Museum Reading Room would stoop to uttering audible obscenities to another Reader, merely because he was an obvious foreigner. But such insults have an ugly ring of street taunts to Jews and Muslims, and by extension to other foreigners, and it is possible that, in his visits to pubs or in his frequent walks through the rougher purlieus of London, he was subjected to such offensive language. In his excitement as he defended himself, he conflated the insults he had received in such places with the conduct of G. St Leger Daniels.

The people, on the other hand, who at such tedious length recounted to him the life story of Arthur Diosy may have been well meaning members of the Japan Society urging him to join the club.[18] To one immersed in Dioscurides' Herbal they could have been equally irritating.

We should take account likewise, when attempting to assess the situation, of the record in Minakata's London diary of a third 'incident', which did not come to the notice of the Trustees. He states that on 7 February 1898, between the two other incidents recorded, he spat at the *yatsu* whom he hit last year. As Matsui Ryūgo remarks, this was clearly an unprovoked insult on Minakata's part and renders him by no means blameless in the affair.[19]

His last two years in England, after his expulsion from the Reading Room, were less happy. He lived in great poverty, his allowance from his family having ceased, and none of his efforts to earn money proving of any avail. He wrote sixteen articles for *Notes and Queries*, including another on the Wandering Jew. F.V. Dickins tried unsuccessfully to secure him a lectureship in Japanese at London University. At last he had no alternative but to return to Japan. He left England on 1 September 1900 in the steerage class of the *Tamba-maru*, with luggage of mountainous proportions. He took with him the vast numbers of books he had bought in London as well as the boxes containing 6,000 specimens of insects, lichen and fungi he had collected in America. But so penniless was he that he had to borrow five yen from one of the ship's officers for the incidental expenses of the voyage.[20]

RESEARCHES IN JAPAN

The rest of his life, until his death in December 1941, Minakata spent in Tanabe in a further unflagging pursuit of knowledge. In this quiet town, with the mountains of the Kii peninsula near to hand, he continued with unquenchably ferocious energy to collect specimens of spiders, to propagate slime moulds, to write nearly 300 articles for *Notes and Queries*, and to write in Japanese the fascinating works which have come down to us in the twelve volumes of his *zenshū*. His family saw to it that he was respectably married, to the daughter of a Shinto priest, and that he was kept free of money anxieties; that he was free, in short, to pursue his passionate quest for omniscient knowledge, for ancient traditions which showed how our ancestors had viewed the things of the natural world, and in what patterns they had interpreted the dispositions of the stars, or the spots on a ladybird's back. His eccentric habits, going about stark naked in summer, forgetting when he had had his last meal, working in his library regardless of the difference between night and day, won him the reputation of a *kijin*, or odd genius, a human type not unappreciated in Japanese literary history.

His external quiet life was diversified by few adventures. In 1906 he fought manfully against the tyrannous policy of the Meiji government of 'merging', or destroying, most of the small shrines in the land and indeed went to prison for eighteen days for his defence of the ancient small shrines of the Kii district. In 1929, when the young Showa Emperor visited the Kii peninsula in a battleship, Minakata was invited to lecture to him on the local varieties of slime mould. He was photographed wearing, for the only time in his life, a frock coat and a tie, and presented to the Emperor a parcel of slime moulds propagated by himself. So touched was the Emperor that he composed the following poem:

Ame ni keburu Kashima wo mite Kii no kuni no
Umishi Minakata Kumagusu wo omou[21]

CONCLUSION

A short essay can do no proper justice to the range of Minakata's work and its special quality. His complete works comprise ten volumes, and their range matches that of his English contributions to *Notes and Queries*. Notable amongst them is *Jūnishi-kō*, a study of the folklore and legends, worldwide, of eleven of the twelve animals of the Chinese zodiac. There is no *magnum opus*, nor is there any work dealing with the theory of knowledge. He wrote great numbers of short studies on a great many subjects, and contributed liberally to *Kyōdo Kenkyū*, *Minzoku*, *Tabi to Densetsu*, *Minzoku to Rekishi* and other learned journals on anthropology, zoology, folklore and astronomy. His letters to Yanagita Kunio and to the Tendai Buddhist priest, Togi Hōryū, are often as long and as erudite as his essays and articles.

Natural history, and the folklore of natural history, were the areas which chiefly absorbed him. He was preoccupied, in other words, with the 'patterns' which different peoples have discerned in the things of the natural world.

His very thinking was accomplished in patterns. In his library there have come to light huge sheets of paper, as big as a double spread of *The Times*, entirely covered with little squares and oblongs of tiny writing, like a patchwork of barely legible characters. These were notes for articles, and notes from reading. Where others preferred the sequential order of a notebook, Minakata chose to think in patterns arranged on enormous spreads of paper. It was through such patterns, Matsui asserts, that he hoped to arrive at his *issaichi* or knowledge of the whole world, a central truth which can be discerned radiating into all nature and consequently a key to the fundamental workings of the universe.[22]

We may wonder why, after fifty years of virtual neglect, his genius is only now coming to be properly valued and assessed. In Japan the same question has understandably been asked. Could it be because his very loneness, his fierce individualism, his contempt for the ordinary conventions of social life, which formerly branded him as an outsider, now raise him to the status of a hero who transcends the crippling and belittling strictures of the *kanri-shakai*, the over-controlled, over-managed society which find no place for such characters? Does he invite nostalgia for the paradisal freedom of one's Original Nature, where conventions are left behind on the other shore?

And at the same time his passionate quest for 'knowledge of the whole', *hakubutsugaku*, for a kind of key to the universe which cannot be found by rational arguments or empirical investigation, is seen more clearly now that science in Japan ceases to be a matter of competitive 'face', and Newtonian science is recognized to be the dark agent which has distorted primal ecological harmony. To see Minakata as a hero, and a pioneer of a new kind of knowledge, may prove to be an interesting chapter in Japan's cultural history.

There is evidence to show that Minakata first hoped to find his 'key' by investigating, as Chu Hsi had recommended, as many things and places as possible, and by travel to Tibet, India, Mecca and Persia. But the fact that during his eight years in England he scarcely moved out of London, seems to indicate that he had realized that the whole can after all be known from its parts. From a single spot you can know the whole leopard. The rare spider, the lowly slime mould, can, when so viewed, become my original face before I was born. With a single microscope, focused even on a *nenkin*, you can perceive the macrocosm, and even the one beyond.

But without his eight years in London, without Pliny or von Gesner as examples of the view that the universe is comprehensible in its entirety, would his genius perhaps have remained at the stage of collecting strange facts, of loving 'spots' of antiquarianism for their own sake, and missing the vision of the whole leopard?

8

Armstrong's, Vickers and Japan

MARIE CONTE-HELM

JAPAN'S SHIPBUILDING links with Britain are but part of a
shared history of technology-transfer dating back to the pre-
Meiji era and continued in much-altered form today. In the
north of England, the shipbuilding firms of Sir W.G. Armstrong,
Whitworth & Co. Ltd at Elswick on the Tyne and Vickers, Sons
& Maxim Ltd at Barrow-in-Furness were to furnish Japan with
warships that would contribute to her naval victories in the
Russo-Japanese War of 1904–5 and see her through to the
successful production of vessels of war from her own shipyards in
the post-1914 period.

Such firms were peopled with individuals who met and
entertained their Japanese customers on British soil or visited
Japan in pursuit of business and to monitor the performance of
British-built ships. For their part, Japanese Admiralty officials
came to both the north-east and the north-west seeking to order
the most sophisticated of vessels; Japanese shipbuilding engineers
to absorb the latest technology and to ensure that their
specifications were met; and Japanese sailors to learn to operate
the guns and ships that they would take back to Japan as yet
another link in the chain of modernization.

Many British and Japanese personalities were involved in this
process. This essay will attempt to focus upon the British builders
of ships for Japan and their Japanese customers. It is a subject rich
in social history which tells us equally of the ambitions and
aspirations of the Japanese during the Meiji period and of the
skills, ingenuity and self-confidence of British business in the
Victorian age.

The more general cultural awakening of one to the other is yet another dimension of such early Anglo-Japanese business relations. In focusing on this time span, we look back to the years leading up to the Anglo-Japanese Alliance of 1902 and beyond and to the men and the women who contributed to the process of its development and to the spirit of its enactment.

ARMSTRONG'S CONNECTIONS WITH JAPAN

Of all the individuals who were to forge lasting links with Japan during this period, Sir William G. Armstrong (1810–1900), the celebrated inventor and industrialist, was a key figure. One of the north-east's most famous sons, Armstrong established his business reputation first in the field of hydraulic engineering. W.G Armstrong & Co. was opened in 1847, one-and-a-half miles to the west of Newcastle, concentrating on the manufacture of hydraulic cranes, accumulators and mining machinery.

Armstrong's career was to take a different turn, however, with his development and improvement of the breech-loading gun during the Crimean War (1853–6). What became known as the Armstrong gun was, in 1859, to earn Armstrong a knighthood as well as an appointment as Engineer of Rifled Ordnance to the War Department. Nine months later, he was elevated to the post of Superintendent of the Royal Gun Factory at Woolwich.

It was in this capacity that Armstrong would have experienced his first direct contact with the Japanese when the Bakufu party which had come to England in 1862 to negotiate the postponement in the opening of further treaty ports in Japan came to Woolwich. The group made several excursions to the Royal Arsenal to observe the casting and fitting of Armstrong guns and displayed intense interest in the sophisticated weaponry. John MacDonald, the legation officer who accompanied them, was to remark upon the intensity of their reaction:

> 'No visitors among our own countrymen, or foreigners, had displayed such earnest and untiring interest, even in the most minute detail connected with the manufacture of the Armstrong gun, as the Japanese.'[1]

In February 1863 Armstrong resigned his government appointments and turned his energies to the development of the Elswick Ordnance Works. Given Armstrong's previous role, the company had been pledged not to supply guns to foreign governments. After 1863, however, this was to change and the Japanese would become one of many important foreign customers.

The performance of Armstrong guns was observed at first-hand in Japan during the conflict in September 1864 which resulted from Chōshū clan interference with foreign vessels.[2] When Chōshū leaders were subsequently given the opportunity to inspect the British ships that had fired upon them – all of which were fitted with Armstrong guns – another lesson of modernization was driven home to them and Japan's need for modern naval gunnery underlined. These future leaders of Meiji Japan were to see in Armstrong's firm a source for the technology that would transform their country in the years to follow.

Armstrong's factory on the Tyne received an initial Japanese order for guns and ammunition in 1865 from Thomas Glover, the British agent for Jardine Matheson & Co. in Nagasaki. While this order was placed on behalf of the Bakufu government, Glover similarly supplied Armstrong guns and other armament to pro-Imperial domains during this period.[3]

The growing diversity of Armstrong's business interests was to ensure Japan's future custom for, in 1867, a collaborative agreement between Armstrong and Charles Mitchell, owner of the Low Walker shipyard, was signed. From that date, warship production was initiated at the Walker yard with the armament supplied by Elswick. Armstrong's had taken the step which would lead to a generation of first-class warships emerging from Tyneside, built for a host of foreign governments, including Japan.

The culmination of this collaboration took place in 1883 with the amalgamation of the two firms to form Sir W.G. Armstrong, Mitchell & Co. Ltd. When the new Elswick shipyard was opened in 1884, warship production was concentrated at Elswick with merchant ships built at the Walker yard. In the intervening years, Japan had experienced major political change and the formation of a new government with the Meiji Restoration of 1868. The business relationship that had begun with orders for guns in the 1860s was to flourish in the 1880s and '90s as Armstrong-Mitchell became a major supplier of warships to Japan. Its acceleration and elaboration must, at least in part, have been due to the personal relationship that Armstrong and his colleagues forged with the Japanese.

IWAKURA MISSION

The ambitions of the Meiji government for the new Japan were well-illustrated by the sending of the Iwakura mission to Europe and America in 1871. While the revision of the 'unequal treaties' was on their political agenda, the mission members mounted a comprehensive fact-finding tour of western industrialized centres that was to greatly influence the course of Japan's future modernization programme.

The Iwakura mission arrived in London in August 1872 and gradually made their way around Britain's leading industrial cities. A party of mission members, accompanied by Sir Harry Parkes, Britain's Minister to Japan, arrived in Newcastle-upon-Tyne on the evening of 21 October 1872. The following morning they were met by Sir William Armstrong who would act as their guide and instructor on the wonders of north-east industry during the course of their stay.

Kume Kunitake's journal of the Iwakura mission dwells particularly on the delegation's visit to the Elswick Engine and Ordnance Works. Kume recorded the tour in detail from the inspection of hydraulic engines, the erecting and fitting departments, bridge shop, turning and boring shops, to the various stages of manufacture of the Armstrong, Gatling and other types of guns. At Elswick, the Japanese visitors were joined by Captain Andrew Noble and George Rendel, joint managers of the company. Rendel was responsible for the shipbuilding and armaments side of the business while Noble was essentially a gunnery expert. It was Noble who would eventually take over as managing director of the firm and, with his sons, Saxton and John, develop ever-closer links with Japan.

In Armstrong's company, the members of the Iwakura mission went on to visit Gosforth Colliery, mining technology being of increasing importance to Japan. They toured the River Tyne, viewing leading factories along the river, and were methodically introduced to the strengths of the north-east region. The persona of Armstrong must be numbered among these for his intellectual curiosity and inventiveness marked him as a man of his age and, for these particular visitors, the best possible guide to this heartland of heavy industry.

During their stay in Newcastle, the Iwakura party dined with Armstrong at his house in Jesmond just as, in future years, so many important Japanese naval officers and prospective business partners would be his guests at Cragside, the country house at Rothbury in Northumberland to which Armstrong gradually retired from the 1880s. That he cut an awesome, if somewhat contradictory, figure is alluded to by Kume's subsequent description of the then 62-year-old industrialist as '. . . taller than seven "shaku" (approximately one foot per shaku) and of mild demeanor'.[4] A letter from Armstrong to Stuart Rendel in November of the same year makes reference to a very fine gift of two large porcelain vases sent by the Japanese in appreciation for his efforts on their behalf.

With the establishment of this personal association in 1872 and the later opening of the Elswick shipyard in 1884, Armstrong's company began to make significant inroads in Japan. By November 1884, the Japanese had placed orders with Armstrong-Mitchell for the protected cruisers, *Naniwa-kan* and *Takachiho-kan* at a cost of £546,980.[5] At a dinner following the launch of the *Naniwa-kan* on 18 March 1885, Armstrong spoke of the personal impact made upon him by this contact with Japan as a result of his business dealings. Admiral Seki, who was present at the dinner, later quoted him as follows:

> 'He well recollected, when he was a boy, looking upon Japan as a strange and mysterious state, inhabited by an unknown people who might as well be the inhabitants of another planet. In those days he little thought how much he should ultimately have to do with the Japanese. The result of his intercourse with them, and it had now been considerable, was that he had learned to regard them as one of the most interesting nations on the face of the world.'[6]

Armstrong never actually visited Japan. He disliked travel and only once ventured beyond Europe to tour Egypt in 1872.[7] Despite this, his firm's increasing Japanese business dealings from the 1880s to his death in 1900 and his own personal commitment to undertakings in Japan paved the way for a flourishing trade in ships and guns. The Cragside Visitors' Book is filled with the signatures of Japanese guests from this period and subsequent generations of the Armstrong family were to maintain this tradition of Anglo-Japanese hospitality. In 1895, Armstrong's continuing involvements with Japan earned him the 'Order of the Sacred Treasure of the Rising Sun'. He was also, in this last decade of his life, to be elected one of the first Vice-Presidents of Britain's recently-formed Japan Society.

NOBLES AND JAPAN

As noted previously, Andrew Noble went on to become sole managing director of the Elswick Works following Armstrong's 'retirement'. He adopted the role of foreign ambassador more literally and travelled to Japan on the company's behalf. His first son, Saxton, was also to visit Japan in the course of his career with the firm but it was John Noble who formed a deeper and more lasting relationship with Armstrong's premier customer in the East at a later stage in the company's business dealings there.

The autobiography of Yamanouchi Masuji (1914) conveys something of the personal efforts which Andrew Noble put into the cultivation of friendly relations with visiting Japanese naval delegations.[8] To demonstrate to Yamanouchi the underlying principles of the quick-firing breech-loading gun, Noble specially arranged a deer-shooting expedition in Redesdale, Northumberland for him. This resulted in subsequent orders for the firm. Yamanouchi later wrote that while the French and the Germans has initially been approached for guns, the Japanese came to prefer their dealings with the English.

Sir Andrew Noble (as he later became) and his sons thus made a considerable direct contribution to securing Japanese business for Armstrong-Mitchell. Like Armstrong, Noble was awarded the Order of the Sacred Treasure of the Rising Sun in 1895 for assistance rendered to Japan during the Sino-Japanese War of 1894–5. Japan's victory led to the passing of the Ten-Year Naval Expansion Programme in 1896. This resulted in extensive orders directed to British yards, with Armstrong's playing a major role in the building and arming of new vessels for Japan.

Sir Andrew did not leave the acquisition of such orders to chance. Shortly after his return to Newcastle in July 1896, following a strategically-timed visit to Japan, a number of contracts were signed with the Japanese. In July 1900, quickly responding to rumours of a new naval programme under consideration by the Japanese government, he proposed to send his son Saxton to Japan.

The years leading up to the Russo-Japanese War of 1904–5

were important years for British shipbuilding interests in Japan. This was also a time of corporate change for Armstrong's. In 1897, a merger with Joseph Whitworth's Openshaw Works in Manchester resulted in the formation of Sir W.G. Armstrong, Whitworth & Co. Ltd. Orders from Japan continued to be filled and the firm's reputation enhanced with the technological advances each new ship came to represent.

The Imperial Japanese Navy, by the onset of the Russo-Japanese War, could claim considerable success in its modernization programme. The six principal battleships of the Japanese fleet — *Fuji, Yashima, Hatsuse, Shikishima, Asahi* and *Mikasa* — were all British-built. The *Yashima* and *Hatsuse* had been built at Armstrong's yard on the Tyne. Sir Andrew Noble was to later boast that '. . . all the ships engaged in the Battle of the Japan Sea (Tsushima) were armed with guns from Elswick'.[9]

VICKERS AND ARMSTRONG'S

There was intense competition between British yards to secure Japanese orders. While Armstrong's had built up a steady trade with Japan from the 1880s, another northern firm, Vickers, Sons & Maxim Ltd of Barrow-in-Furness in Cumbria (created through the amalgamation of various businesses in 1897), was to make more belated inroads into the Japanese market.

The *Mikasa*, Admiral Tōgō's celebrated flagship in the Russo-Japanese War, was the first major Japanese battleship order secured by Vickers-Maxim. Its guns were supplied by Armstrong's. The launch of the *Mikasa* at Barrow in November 1900 would be followed by further launches of major new battleships for Japan; the *Katori* in 1905 and the *Kongo* in 1912. In the years from 1897 to 1914, Vickers-Maxim was to present a serious challenge to Armstrong's in both the shipbuilding and the armaments industry.

By 1903, Vickers, Sons & Maxim Ltd were operating through the Japanese agents, Messrs Mitsui & Co., who had had an office in London since 1877. When tenders for new ships were invited from various yards in 1903, the choice of armaments supply was clearly a matter of price competitiveness between Armstrong's and Vickers alone.[10] As a newcomer to the Japanese trade, Vickers was well aware of Armstrong's established reputation with the Japanese Admiralty and of the need to make particular efforts in this quarter. One member of the firm wrote in June 1903 of the forthcoming visit of a Japanese naval delegation as follows:

> 'I am especially pleased because such a visit will give the Japanese officers a real insight into what Vickers really are and what they can do . . . I feel certain that if you treat them well all the reports which these fellows make to their masters here and to their people in Japan will have great weight on the Japanese authorities and that your kindness and attention will not be thrown away.'[11]

Despite the rivalry that existed between them, Armstrong's and Vickers went on to collaborate in a major business venture in Japan with the establishment of the Japan Steel Works (Nihon Sei-Kō-Sho) at Muroran on Hokkaido in 1907. Concerned that the nation should have an indigenous ordnance facility following the Russo-Japanese War, the Japanese government invited Armstrong's and Vickers, as well as other foreign companies, to enter into arrangements with Japanese financiers for the founding of a large ordnance factory.[12] The outcome was a joint-venture agreement between Hokkaido Tanko Kisen (the Hokkaido Coal and Steamship Company), Armstrong Whitworth, and Vickers-Maxim, providing for the manufacture of war material and other steel and iron products in Japan. An agency agreement allowed for the sale of the British-made products of the two northern firms in Japan. Armstrong's and Vickers entered into the agreement as equal shareholders, with a 50 per cent interest in the company which was founded with a capital of £1,000,000.[13] The Japan Steel Works was fully operational by 1911 and, for several decades, benefited from a steady flow of British technological expertise into Japan in return for the initial investment and the government orders it ensured.

The company's first prospectus highlighted the value of Britain's export of manpower to Japan during the Meiji period and the contribution made to her industrial fortunes. This 'British teacher–Japanese pupil' relationship was echoed in the running of the Japan Steel Works. While some Japanese employees of the Steel Works came to the UK for training, references in the Armstrong Directors' Meetings' Minutes suggest a regular flow of specialist labour from the north of England to Japan in the company's early years. In 1911,

Armstrong Whitworth reported sending a designer and gunnery expert from Elswick and an accountant, a foreman and four steel smelters from Sheffield to Japan.[14] In 1912, George Adams Atkinson, an engineer from the Elswick Works, was issued with 'a passport to travel to Japan' where he was to provide instruction in the manufacture of large naval guns at Muroran.[15] A Mr Trevelyan was also sent to Japan by the company in 1912 to assist in the management of the Japan Steel Works; by 1913 he was put forward for appointment as resident director.[16]

It is not always evident how much time such troubleshooters spent in Japan. The success of this joint-venture agreement must be credited, however, to Armstrong's and Vickers' willingness to despatch employees with a particular knowledge-base to Japan to engage in the training of local staff and the running of operations at Muroran.

From the outbreak of the Russo-Japanese War through to the establishment of the Japan Steel Works, Sir Andrew Noble's second son, John, was to spend increasing periods of time in Japan. Armstrong's maintained close contact with the Japanese Navy throughout the war and sent experts to advise on the operation and maintenance of the ships and gunnery produced on the Tyne. John Noble and his wife, Amie, were virtually resident in Tokyo from 1904 to 1905. She was to later recall the spring of 1905 when '. . . war conditions needed Johnny's advice at the Japanese Admiralty where most of his days were spent'.[17]

This was the first of several visits to Japan for Amie Noble. She returned with John in 1906 and 1908 and, finally, in 1939. As with so many diarists before her, Amie's initial reaction to Japan makes familiar reading:

'How wonderful to have been wafted here to Japan. My only picture of it so far had been that play, "Madame Butterfly", showing a western idea of a geisha girl's emotions and kimonas (sic.).'[18]

Married into this family of arms dealers, Amie disapproved of the nature of their business interests while revelling in the opportunities for exotic travel which they generated. A committed pacifist, she had even attempted to persuade John Noble to change careers and become a barrister.

The lifestyle of the young Nobles in Japan seems to have been exciting as well as select. They moved in fashionable circles, attending many grand social events. In 1905, there was lunch at the palace with Prince Fushimi, brother of the Emperor of Japan, and a steady round of engagements with the foreign expatriate community. Sir Claude MacDonald, head of the British Legation, and his wife Ethel, were to become close friends, as was Captain Pakenham, the British naval attaché. Pakenham periodically made her privy to confidential naval manoeuvres at the time of the Russo-Japanese War which she guarded even from her husband. She was later to recollect:

> 'Captain Pakenham used to tell me if and when he was going into action at Port Arthur where he stood on the bridge of an Elswick battleship directing the Japanese captain. I had to swear great secrecy until news came through as to the results of the fight . . .'

When not attending 'At Homes' or 'bandage-rolling afternoons' at the various foreign legations, Amie Noble frequently passed her days shopping in Yokohama. Her memoirs describe in vivid detail the embroidered silks, china, tortoiseshell, lacquerware and other craft items which she collected and which were still so enthusiastically being received into Europe. While her views of Japan were coloured by what was clearly a protected expatriate experience, Amie Noble's recollections provide yet another dimension in the story of Armstrong's business relationship with Japan.

For his part, John Noble was to play an important role in the setting up of the Japan Steel Works at Muroran. He entered into negotiations over the Armstrong-Vickers joint-venture from March 1905 and spent extended periods in Japan each year from 1905 to 1909. While the Minutes of Armstrong Board meetings and assorted business documents chart his movements during this period, it is only his wife's subsequent memoirs which give a fuller flavour of the Nobles' experience of Japan.

TŌGŌ VISITS NORTHERN ENGLAND

1911, the year in which the Japan Steel Works became fully operational, was to mark another important landmark in the association between Armstrong's, Vickers and Japan. Admiral Count Tōgō, the 'Nelson of Japan' and naval hero of the Russo-Japanese War, had come to Britain to attend the coronation of George V as part of Prince Fushimi's party. In July, he ventured beyond the capital to visit Vickers-Maxim's yard at Barrow-in-Furness and Armstrong's shipyard on the Tyne. For Tōgō, these were visits of pilgrimage to the yards that had supplied some of the key ships that had led the Japanese fleet to victory in the Russo-Japanese War.

Tōgō closely inspected the Vickers-Maxim yard during his stay in Barrow-in-Furness from 10 to 12 July 1911. He was officially received by the Mayor of Barrow and presented the town with a Japanese imari-ware bowl in commemoration of the special relationship which they shared. During his visit, Tōgō was treated as an honoured guest by both the company and the town where even a street bears the name, Mikasa. A specially-arranged excursion to Grasmere on the Furness Railway was to introduce him to the beauties of the Lake District and another aspect of the heritage of north west England.

A full account[19] exists of Tōgō's visit to Elswick. On 18 July 1911, he arrived in Newcastle, accompanied by his aide-de-camp, Commander Taniguchi and Commander Saito. For the next two days they were to be the guests of Sir Andrew and Lady Noble at Jesmond Dene House. The following day was fully occupied with Tōgō's inspection of the Elswick Works. Guided by Saxton Noble and various other company directors, the Japanese visitors toured the steel works and ordnance department and observed models of Elswick warships built for Japan before going on to view the latest Elswick-built ships.

Armstrong's gave Tōgō the welcome he deserved as his visit represented the fulfilment of a collaboration which had benefited both partners greatly. As he toured Elswick, notices of welcome were prominently displayed and even tools and castings had been arranged on the floor of the forge to read, 'Welcome to Admiral Togo, O.M.'. On his final day in Newcastle, Tōgō embarked from the Elswick shipyard for a cruise down the River Tyne. The Armstrong Whitworth vessel that conveyed him to the landing at North Shields was aptly named *Armstrong*.

At a Mansion House luncheon hosted by the Lord Mayor of Newcastle and the Tyne Commissioners, Admiral Count Tōgō paid homage to the city and the firm that had contributed so much to the modernization of the Japanese navy:

'It is a well-known fact that the name Newcastle is inseparable from the pages of the history of the Japanese navy, so many men-of-war have been either built or armed by the famous works of Elswick, which the city of Newcastle is very proud to possess. A great number of our officers and men have studied in this city how to build ships and how to make guns. I believe I am not flattering you too much if I say that, but for the kind help of your people, the history of the growth of the Japanese navy might have been written in a different way.'[20]

Armstrong's and Vickers' Japanese involvements generated a steady flow of British business travellers to Japan as well as visits by such distinguished Japanese figures as Admiral Tōgō to Britain. Some mention must be made, however, of the more mundane contact that resulted from Japanese orders for ships being lodged with these two northern firms. There were, after all, many Japanese students, shipyard engineers and sailors resident for periods of months in such shipyard towns. Both Newcastle-upon-Tyne and Barrow-in-Furness were to play host to large numbers of Japanese in the course of this trade and to witness a wider social interaction of British and Japanese as a result.

The presence of Japanese seamen in northern ports also led to orchestrated episodes of cultural exchange. On 23 May 1898, for example, the crew of the protected cruiser, *Takasago*, in Newcastle to collect and train on their Elswick-built ship, staged a 'Programme of Variety Entertainment' for the citizens of the town. The programme consisted of eight traditional items of entertainment including costumed dances, a fencing display and a performance of Scene Seven of *Chushingura* (*The Tale of the Forty-Seven Ronin*).[21] The First Newcastle Artillery Band juxtaposed Wagner with Sullivan and ended their performance with 'Kimigayo', the Japanese national anthem, followed by 'God Save the Queen'.

Interaction with the Japanese navy led to similar cultural exchanges at Barrow-in-Furness. On 8 November 1900, Baroness Hayashi presided over the launch of the *Mikasa* which was conducted with much pomp and celebration. The Japanese crew subsequently spent a five-month period in Barrow training on the ship.

Prior to their departure for Japan, the Mayor of Barrow arranged an evening reception at the Town Hall for the officers and crew of the *Mikasa* on 23 December 1901. *The (Barrow)*

News[22] recorded a scene of diverse entertainments in the banqueting room including a cinematograph exhibition, comic juggling and dance performance as the *Mikasa* crew mingled with the other guests. Gifts were exchanged in turn and likewise special tributes paid to the Japanese crew for their exemplary conduct during their stay and to the people of Barrow for their reciprocating friendliness and goodwill.

A farewell service for the officers and crew of the *Mikasa* took place at St James's Church in Barrow. Large crowds assembled along the route from the Devonshire Dock to the church to witness the 350 officers and men on parade, marching four-abreast in two squads, with Captain Arima in command. The service was simple and interpreted in Japanese and included a portion of scripture from St Luke's Gospel read in Japanese by Lieutenant Shirai. It was concluded with the singing of the 'Hallelujah Chorus'.

There were many such episodes surrounding the selling of ships to Japan. The *Kashima* was the last of the great battleships to be built for Japan at Elswick. On completion, in 1906, her crew came to Newcastle to collect the ship and were duly feted as war heroes. The spirit of the Anglo-Japanese Alliance and Japan's recent success in the Russo-Japanese War combined to generate a welcome which would be remembered long beyond their stay. On 24 April 1906, a Town Hall luncheon for the officers of the *Kashima* was followed by a celebratory football match at St James's Park. When the 150-strong crew of the *Kashima* arrived at the football ground to watch the match, they were welcomed with signs written in Japanese. It was later to be reported[23] that:

'. . . they received a hearty cheer on ascending to seats on the stand, and the crowd again cheered when the officers stood at attention during the playing of the Japanese national anthem.'

The *Kashima's* sister-ship, the *Katori*, was launched at Barrow on 4 July 1905 by HIH Princess Arisugawa. Subsequently, in 1912, the *Kongo* was launched by Mme Koike and completed in 1913. These Barrow-built vessels were the last of the major battleships built for Japan in Britain. By 1914, the emerging Japanese shipyards were implementing the lessons learned from such firms as Armstrong's and Vickers and putting their new-found skills to the test. While technology-transfer from Britain to

Japan did not suddenly come to an end with the cessation of orders, the nature of the exchange was to alter in 1914 along with Japan's industrial profile.

Armstrong's and Vickers-Maxim maintained their link with the Japan Steel Works for some time. By 1917, a new agreement had superseded the original contract, appointing the Japan Steel Works as sole agents in Japan for both the armaments and commercial products of Vickers and Armstrong Whitworth. In 1919 the company's capital reached £4,000,000 with Vickers and Armstrong's share of the overall assets reduced to 25 per cent.[24] The joint-venture was to eventually founder in the aftermath of the Washington Naval Conference (1921) and the demise of the Anglo-Japanese Alliance.

The fortunes of the two rival firms, linked through this Japanese business venture and various other enterprises over the years, were to become permanently intertwined. Financial difficulties precipitated a forced merger between Armstrong Whitworth and Vickers in 1927. While Vickers-Armstrong Ltd, as it became known, retained the original shipbuilding and armaments interests of both competing companies, the market-place was changing and a restructuring of the industry had been called for to accommodate its changing circumstances.

For both Armstrong's and Vickers, Japan had provided important custom in the heyday of Victorian and Edwardian industrial supremacy. British shipbuilders, in particular, amassed their fortunes through lucrative foreign orders which were assiduously pursued both at home and abroad. For the Japanese, these firms had supplied the technology so crucial to naval modernization and to the long-held ambition of catching up with the West. Along the way, both these British shipbuilders and their Japanese customers were to learn from one another, to experience different cultures and to build personal relationships which sometimes outlasted the business transactions from which they had sprung. Armstrong's and Vickers were but two British firms who played a part in this process. In contributing essential technology to a rapidly changing Japan, each has earned its place in the history of Japan's modernization and of her early business relationship with the West.

9

The Silent Admiral:
Tōgō Heihachirō (1848–1934)
and Britain

KIYOSHI IKEDA

ADMIRAL of the Fleet Marquis Tōgō Heihachirō was for the first two decades of this century the symbol of good Anglo-Japanese relations. Trained in Britain, he came to the highest rank just as the British alliance, which was largely a naval alliance, was signed in 1902. Because of his sweeping victory over the Russians at the battle of the Japan Sea, he became the best-known Japanese in Britain at the time. By the end of the Meiji period, he was less conspicuous politically and gradually went into reticent retirement, though he was frequently consulted and was influential behind the scenes among the Satsuma group in the navy. Observers commented that, in spite of his formidable reputation, he was shy and modest in public as might be expected from a man of samurai background.

Tōgō Heihachirō (1848–1934) was born in Kajiyamachi, Kagoshima, the fourth son of Tōgō Kichizaemon and Masuko, with the childhood name of Nakagoro. Kichizaemon belonged to the lower samurai class, though he was known as a good fencer. In 1847 he was appointed as revenue collector and master of the wardrobe for the Satsuma clan. Kajiyamachi was a little town, but it already had given birth to Saigō Takamori, Ōkubo Toshimichi and others who were to take an active part in the Meiji Restoration. At the age of eight, Nakagoro began his formal studies with male tutors, who taught him subjects such as calligraphy, Confucian classics, history, Japanese literature and swordsmanship. At the age of thirteen he became a man, according to the samurai tradition of those days, and was given his permanent name of Heihachirō. He was then given a job as a copy-clerk in the clan office.

In 1862 when Hisamitsu Saburō, the father of the Satsuma prince was passing through Namamugi Village, a few miles from Yokohama on the way back to Kagoshima, four Englishmen on horseback trotted across the path of the procession. This breach of samurai etiquette by crossing a clan prince's (daimyō) procession aroused the escort of young samurai to fury; consequently they rushed upon the Englishmen, killed one of them named Richardson and severely wounded two others. When this news reached London, the British government was extremely angry and instructed its Chargé d'affaires, Lieutenant-Colonel Neale, to demand an indemnity from the Shogun's government and make strong protests against the Satsuma clan. Colonel Neale consulted Vice-Admiral Kuper, Commander of the British China Squadron, and a fleet of seven men-of-war left Yokohama for Kagoshima. On 17 August 1863, the British fleet dropped anchor off Kagoshima, demanding that those samurai who had killed the Englishman should be turned over to a court-martial and that an indemnity should be paid. The Satsuma clan refused their demands. Thus Anglo-Satsuma relations were plunged into hostilities.

The whole Satsuma clan was in turmoil. Tōgō's father, Kichizaemon, as army-inspector, was stationed at Fort Yamagawa, and his three sons, Shirobei, Shokurō, and Heihachirō, were mobilized at the headquarters of their clan-prince. On the fifth day the British fleet opened fire and the battle lasted six hours. Satsuma's old-fashioned round balls were unable to do much damage to the British fleet. On the other hand, the British shells had a long range and were of great destructive power: the streets caught fire, while the shore houses and many other buildings were burnt to the ground. Most of the Satsuma guns in the forts were put out of action. In the turbulent sea the English guns overshot their marks and set fire to the whole of the town. On the eighteenth day the British fleet left Kagoshima for Yokohama. Young Tōgō had learned the terrible aspects of modern war from this battle. He had seen the impressive might of the British fleet and could not have failed to notice the devastation brought about by the pointed projectiles of a modern navy. He reached the conclusion that the enemy which comes over the sea must be met on the sea, and finally made the decision to serve in the navy.[1] In June 1866, at the age of 18, Heihachirō began his career as a seaman entering the clan navy with his brothers Shokurō and Shirozaemon at the newly-established Naval Bureau at Kagoshima. Two years later Tōgō, by this time a gunner, fought aboard the *Kasuga* as the third officer under Captain Akazuka, in the Boshin civil war which had broken out. The *Kasuga* engaged in several sea-battles against the Tokugawa navy; on 28 January 1868, Enomoto Takeaki's ship *Kaiyo* fired at the *Kasuga* and opened hostilities off the coast of Awa, the first battle fought in Japan with foreign-style warships; in April 1869 the *Kasuga*, *Yoshun*, *Kotetsu*, *Teiun* and four transports carrying 6,500 troops left Tokyo on a punitive expedition to Hokkaido which brought about the surrender of Enomoto's rebel forces on 27 June 1869. After the civil war was over, Tōgō was able to join the newly-organized Imperial Navy in 1871.

TRAINING IN BRITAIN

Although Tōgō had served on *Kasuga* as a naval officer of the Satsuma clan and had taken part in several battles, he had to begin all over again as an apprentice when he transferred to the new Imperial Navy. Ordered by the clan-prince to study in Tokyo, Tōgō went to Yokohama and learned English, then moved to Tokyo to enter the school run by Mitsukuri Rinshō, who was noted for his knowledge of the English and French languages. There Tōgō made remarkable progress in English. In October 1870, Japan established a Naval Training School and a year later, it engaged Lieutenant Hawes of the Royal Navy to train the officers and petty officers of the warships on board the *Ryujo*. Tōgō was appointed a cadet on board that vessel. This was the first time that the name of Tōgō Heihachirō appeared in the records of the Imperial Navy. In February 1871, Tōgō and eleven others were selected to go to Britain for the further study of modern sea warfare. They arrived in April at Southampton.

The British Admiralty refused to allow these Japanese students to enter the Naval College on the ground that it was full, so the students could only study on a training ship. Tōgō was assigned to the training ship *H.M.S. Worcester* of the Thames Nautical

Training College, the students of which, if of high enough proficiency, could enter the Royal Navy as midshipmen. Cadet Tōgō studied naval subjects zealously and became noted among his companions for his conscientiousness. The other cadets called him 'Johnny Chinaman', because, in their sketchy knowledge of the remote Far East, any person from that part of the world must be a Chinaman. Captain Henderson Smith who taught at the time on the *Worcester* told some friends during the Russo-Japanese War thirty years later, that Tōgō was not what one would call smart, but he was always diligent and painstaking and, though he was slow to learn, he thoroughly mastered what he learnt.[2] Tōgō's teachers, both Japanese and English, who were later questioned about his early days never described him as brilliant; but they all commended the persistence and diligence with which he applied himself.

After two years of hard work in the study of seamanship on board the *Worcester*, Tōgō left her for the sailing ship *Hampshire* (gross tonnage 1,214). She left the Thames towards the end of February 1875, for a long voyage to Melbourne, passing the southern tip of South America and returned to England in September. During the sea trip of seven months and 30,000 miles as an ordinary seaman, Tōgō gained practical experience of the art of navigation. Tōgō left the *Hampshire* immediately upon her arrival in England and moved to Cambridge where he lived with the Reverend A.S. Capel and devoted himself to the study of mathematics.

At this time, the Japanese government entered into a contract for the construction in England of three warships to be completed in two years, namely the *Fuso* (at Poplar), the *Kongo* (at Kingston-upon-Hull) and the *Hiei* (at Pembroke), which were later to become the backbone of the Japanese Navy. This was the first time since the establishment of the Navy Department that the construction of warships was contracted abroad. The naval students in England, including Tōgō, were ordered to supervise the construction. Cadet Tōgō, therefore, transferred to Greenwich and was occupied in inspecting the *Fuso*. This was one of the tasks at which he excelled and it greatly contributed to his later career. The young naval officer, Tōgō, haunted the shipyard and asked the shipbuilders interminable questions, learning about the ship from the keel up.

In February 1878, nine of the naval students were ordered to return home on board those three warships; Tōgō's vessel being the *Hiei*. The officers and crew on the three vessels, with the exception of the Japanese naval students, were all British according to the contract drawn up between the Japanese minister in London, Ueno Kagenori, and Edward James Reed, M.P. for Pembroke. On 22 May 1878, Tōgō, full of knowledge acquired in England, returned to his native land after seven years abroad. In 1877, during his absence in Europe, the Satsuma Civil War had broken out, and all the members of Tōgō's family at home had joined Saigō's army and his elder brother Shokurō died fighting on 24 September. Though he had heard the news of the Satsuma War, Tōgō did not change his mind and remained in England in order to continue his studies.

After the Satsuma Rebellion was suppressed, Japan enjoyed a time of peace, during which Tōgō was promoted to be first lieutenant of the *Jingei* in 1878 and was then transferred to the *Amagi*. In 1882 events occurred in Korea and the Japanese minister, Hanabusa, was forced to flee. The Japanese government ordered eight warships, including *Amagi*, to Korea. Tōgō led his ship's company in landing troops at Seoul. Upon returning to Japan, he was given his first command, the ship No.2 *Teiu*, which in 1884 came under the command of *Amagi*. Though he was promoted to the rank of captain in 1886, ill health struck him in the form of rheumatism and forced him to stay in bed for nearly three years. Tōgō was not idle even while flat on his back. He read voraciously, especially poring over books on international law. He theorized that a captain at sea and far from advice had to avoid making diplomatic mistakes which could have serious consequences for himself and his country.[3]

SINO-JAPANESE WAR AND THE KOWSHING QUESTION

It was not until the outbreak of war with China in 1894 that the real ability of Captain Tōgō as a seaman became known to his countrymen and foreign observers. Tōgō had regained his health and been appointed to the command of the *Naniwa* in 1891. In Korea a lawless mob calling itself the Tong-hak (East-Learning) Party had appeared and, by 1894, its power had grown so formidable that the Korean government was unable to suppress it. On 3 June 1894, it applied to the Chinese government for assistance, and the latter, thinking it to be a good opportunity for asserting its rights, immediately despatched three divisions to Korea, at the same time informing the Japanese government of its action. In this note, however, Korea was referred to as a Chinese dependency. As this was not in keeping with the view held by the Japanese Empire, a reply was at once sent to the effect that the Japanese government did not recognize Korea as a dependency of China and that Japan also intended to despatch forces to the peninsula.

The despatch of Japanese forces to Korea immediately followed this note and the *Naniwa* was ordered to convey a fleet of transports. The two nations were not yet at war. On 25 July, Tōgō's *Naniwa* and two other cruisers under the command of Admiral Tsuboi Kōzō were heading for Asan when they met two ships, the *Chi-yuen* and the *Kwang-yi*. At this inopportune moment the *Chi-yuen*'s steering gear jammed and both ships headed straight for the Japanese squadron. Who opened fire first was a matter of some debate.

Earlier on, Admiral Itō Sukenobu of the main Japanese fleet had hoisted a signal for all to read: 'Do your utmost to enhance the reputation of the Imperial Navy'. Despite the niceties of international law, it was most probably Tōgō who decided to read into the message its fullest meaning and do his duty. It was the sea-battle off Phundo (P'ung) Island which caused international controversy and made Tōgō's name well known. *Naniwa*'s lookouts sighted two other vessels heading towards them from the west: one was the sloop *Taso-kiang* and the other a large ship flying the red ensign of the British merchant fleet. The latter which was carrying more than 1,000 Chinese soldiers bound for Korea, proved to be the *Kowshing* and continued to head towards Asan. It was a touchy business for any Japanese commander to interfere with a British vessel. But Tōgō, after firing two blank rounds, ran up a signal for her to stop immediately. The British vessel hove to as directed. Tōgō then ordered her to drop anchor. The ship obliged. Tōgō was startled to see flags indicating 'May I proceed?' run up the halyard of the British ship. To *Kowshing* which had been chartered by the Chinese government, Tōgō repeated his previous signal, which was interpreted by the English captain to mean, heave to or suffer the consequences. The *Naniwa* sailed several times around *Kowshing* menacingly while the Chinese soldiers on deck watched excitedly. Soon Tōgō halted his ship and sent a boat over to the *Kowshing*.

The English captain, T.R. Galsworthy, protested vigorously against the fact that his ship, bearing the British flag, had been stopped, and in peacetime at that. He was unaware that a war, even if not formally declared, had in effect been started two hours earlier by this same *Naniwa*. Nevertheless, he agreed under protest to follow the *Naniwa* as directed. But as soon as the *Naniwa*'s boat left the *Kowshing*, the angry Chinese took over the ship and prevented Captain Galsworthy from carrying out the orders. Tōgō had to do something without delay or risk being attacked by other Chinese ships which might be near. Tōgō was in a dilemma. The might of the British Empire, which backed the *Kowshing*'s flag, could be brought down on Japan's head by Tōgō. His actions would have serious consequences. After cautious deliberation, Tōgō dared to fire on the British flag and sank the *Kowshing*.

When the news of sinking of the *Kowshing* reached Japan, the whole nation was amazed, and, notwithstanding the explanations given by Saigō Tsugumichi, the Navy minister, the government was apprehensive of the consequences. Generally speaking, the action of Tōgō was condemned. Moreover, public opinion in England was hostile to Japan on account of this incident and Lord Kimberley, the Foreign Secretary, presented to the Japanese minister, Aoki Shūzō, a protest to the effect that the Japanese government should be held responsible for any loss or damage to life and property suffered by British subjects through any acts of Japanese naval officers. But among impartial publicists in England, there were not a few who considered Captain Tōgō's act justifiable. Dr T.E. Holland, the noted jurist of Cambridge, wrote in *The Times* an article which fully justified Tōgō's action. Dr J. Westlake, the well-known publicist, also wrote *The Times* a straightforward letter, in which he stated that Tōgō's action was just and there were nothing in it that one could find fault with.[4] Meanwhile, British public opinion gradually subsided, and before long Tōgō's attitude was praised in some quarters for its resoluteness. It may be interesting to know that Captain Galsworthy, the key figure in this dispute, had been one of the instructors of Tōgō at the *Worcester* as a young cadet.

On 1 August, the Japanese government declared war against China. On the morning of 17 September, Admiral Tsuboi's First Squadron to which *Naniwa* belonged, was cruising along in the vanguard of Admiral Itō's main fleet towards Talu Island in the Yellow Sea, when the flagship (*Yoshino*) sighted the Chinese main fleet under the command of Admiral Ting Juch'ang which was composed of twelve battleships besides torpedo boats. Itō instantly ordered the fleet to form a single line ahead in battle array. The ships all got up steam and advanced rapidly. As they approached the enemy, they saw them on the starboard bow in echelon with the wings spread out to the rear. The flagship *Ting-yuan* and the *Chen-yuan*, ships which the Chinese boasted to be without a peer in the East, occupied the centre of the line. Of the two fleets confronting each other, the Chinese was the more heavily protected with armour, but the Japanese was heavier in firepower. The Japanese also were backed up by numerous rapid-firing guns of lesser calibre. Tōgō's *Naniwa* was in the fourth position in Tsuboi's Squadron. Behind him at an interval came Admiral Itō's flagship *Matsushima* and the rest of the main fleet.

At 12.50 pm bursts were seen from the Chinese flagship *Ting-yuan's* guns. Itō held off until his rapid-firing guns could be brought into effective play. Suddenly Tōgō received the order to open fire at the close range of 3,000 yards. The time was 1.05 pm. The battle between the rapidly-manoeuvring Japanese fleet and the slow-moving Chinese fleet continued for four-and-a-half hours. The Japanese fleet attacked the enemy repeatedly with the double advantage of speed and rapid-firing guns. Scarcely two hours after the battle had started, Admiral Ting had lost four of his cruisers, two of which had been set on fire and the other two had run away from the fight. Itō, on the other hand, had lost from the line of battle only one auxiliary cruiser, a gunboat and corvette. A Chinese shell hit the Japanese flagship *Matsushima* which suffered very serious damage. Tōgō's *Naniwa* had also suffered nine direct hits but, surprisingly, no one on board was killed or injured. Admiral Ting withdrew, with his two big ships and finally reached Port Arthur and safety; but he had few vessels left. Thus Japan had won control of the Yellow Sea in a few short hours. Her army in Korea was assured of supplies. The war was to last six months more, but the battle in the Yellow Sea (off the Yalu River) had been the decisive one. On 22 November, Port Arthur was taken by land; then on 13 February 1895, Ting, losing most of his fleet from the attack of Japanese torpedo flotillas at Weihaiwei, sent a letter of surrender to Itō who accepted it. Ting, then, committed suicide by swallowing poison. After the battle Tōgō wrote a letter to a friend: 'Admiral Ting Juch'ang has died, admired by us all'.[5] On 17 April a Treaty of Peace was signed between Japan and China. In the final stages of the war, on 16 February, Captain Tōgō was promoted to rear-admiral and appointed commander of the Standing Squadron.

On 23 April, just after the treaty of peace, Russia, with the aid of France and Germany, forced Japan to return to China the Liaotung Peninsula which had been ceded to Japan by the treaty; but soon after Russia extorted the peninsula from China under a lease. From that day Port Arthur became Russia's base from which she intended to carry out her ambitions in Manchuria. Russia, moreover, in 1900 took advantage of the Boxer trouble in China to send large forces to the Far East and occupied important parts of Manchuria. Russian troops covered the plains of Manchuria and threatened China while at the same time a policy of intimidation was adopted towards Korea.

The Japanese began to feel sure that Russia would extend her encroachment and threaten the independence of Japan herself by penetrating into the Korean peninsula. They instinctively felt that their next potential enemy was to be Russia. Thus the Japanese government hastened its war preparations, and from the viewpoint of diplomatic strategy the Anglo-Japanese Alliance was concluded in 1902 to be ranged against the Franco-Russian Alliance. On the side of the Imperial Navy, under the Naval Minister Yamamoto Gombei, several modern warships including *Mikasa*, the future flagship of Admiral Tōgō, were ordered to be built or bought abroad. By the outbreak of the Russo-Japanese war in February 1904, the Japanese Navy could assemble a main force which was composed of six battleships, six first-class cruisers, in addition to twelve second- or third-class cruisers, and many destroyers, with a total tonnage of 233,200.[6] Russia, however, was a formidable enemy to Japan since she had at this time the world's third largest fleet in number of ships and fourth largest in tonnage.

After the Sino-Japanese War Tōgō was recalled to Tokyo and spent the next four years on shore. In 1896 he took up the assignment of bringing to new perfection the Advanced Naval College. In 1898 after promotion to vice-admiral, he took command of the Sasebo Naval Station. At the turn of the century

Tōgō was sent back to sea and became the commander-in-chief of the Standing Squadron, which took part in the allied operation against the Boxers. On 1 October he was appointed the commander-in-chief of Maizuru Naval Station on the Japan Sea coast. In those days, many people who knew Tōgō (by this time aged 55) guessed that his naval career was approaching its end. Surprisingly to them, Tōgō was summoned to naval headquarters in Tokyo in October 1903, and informed officially that it was expected there soon would be a war with Russia. On the advice of Navy Minister Yamamoto, Tōgō was appointed as the supreme commander of the fleet, instead of Admiral Hidaka Sonojo, an unobservant though brave officer, who was then commander-in-chief of the Standing Squadron. Yamamoto preferred Tōgō's composed and obedient character suitable for the role of the supreme commander.[7]

RUSSO-JAPANESE WAR

On 10 February 1904, Japan declared war against Russia, and the Treaty of Peace was signed on 5 October 1905. It is not the purpose of this essay to describe the details of every sea battle during the war. It might be enough to trace the general aspects leading to the last and decisive sea battle, that is, the Battle of the Japan Sea which took place on 27–8 May 1905. Generally speaking, Admiral Tōgō's principal strategy was to defeat the Russian Pacific fleet based on Port Arthur first, then to wait and destroy completely the Russian fleet coming from European waters and the Black Sea.

The war began with Tōgō's first surprise assault on Port Arthur on 11 February, and the attacks were repeated eight times until 14 April. Meanwhile, he tried on several times to blockade the entrance of Port Arthur by planting mines and sinking cargo-vessels. But most of the attacks and the blockade was unsuccessful. The Russian fleet under the command of Admiral S.O. Makaroff would not come out of Port Arthur except on scouting manoeuvres until the end of July. The Second Pacific Fleet was formed in Russia, Vice-Admiral P.Z. Rozhestvenskii was appointed as commander-in-chief of it and prepared it for its long journey to the East, while Tōgō's fleet suffered considerable damage losing *Yoshino*, *Hatsuse*, *Yashima* and *Akatsuki* which struck mines which the Russians had planted and sank.

With a part of his fleet away at Vladivostok and with his losses through accidents, Tōgō's fleet was far smaller than it had previously been. On 23 June Admiral Witgeft came out of Port Arthur with six battleships and five cruisers. Tōgō with his guns at maximum elevation chased after him. Then, just as the battle was about to commence, the Russian turned and raced back towards port.

At daybreak on 10 August the Port Arthur Squadron again came out of harbour. Unknown to Tōgō, the Tsar had ordered it to fight its way out to Vladivostok. The battle was about to begin. To meet the Russian fleet of six battleships and three cruisers, Tōgō had four battleships and the two new first-class cruisers. His biggest worry was that the Russian fleet would sneak back to base, so he had to hold back in order to encourage it to come out. Tōgō gave orders to open fire at 1.15 pm, and the enemy instantly replied. The *Tsezarevitch*'s steering gear was damaged at 6.37 pm and, unable to steer, she ran into her own line. Witgeft was killed and Admiral Ukhtomskii of the *Peresviet* took over the command, ordering his fleet to change course for port, not wanting to fall into Tōgō's trap. Tōgō ordered his fleet into a turn in succession, which had serious consequences. It cost the Japanese time during which the Russian fleet gained a lead in escaping from Tōgō's trap. The Russian fleet took flight and again returned to Port Arthur. Eventually, the Russian Vladivostok Squadron was caught and defeated by the Japanese Second Squadron on 14 August: the *Rurik* was sunk, while the *Rossia* and *Gromoboi* returned, seriously damaged, to Vladivostok.

It was not until the middle of December that most of the Russian First Pacific Fleet in Port Arthur was destroyed or sunk by the Japanese Navy's big guns, after the assault on land by General Nogi Maresuke's Third Army had occupied the Russian fortress. Port Arthur surrendered on 1 January 1905. On the other hand, the Second Pacific Fleet under the command of Rozhestvenskii left Libau Naval Station on 15 October 1904, followed by the Third Squadron on 15 February 1905, and they joined up on 9 May 1905 after a long, boring voyage. On 14 May they left Wanfrong in Cam Ranh Bay with the auxiliary Fourth Squadron. The Russian fleet totalled fifty ships; including eight battleships; three first-class cruisers; six second-class cruisers; nine destroyers. They steered northwards to the Tsushima Strait.

Early on the morning of 26 May, Commander Nagigawa on patrol aboard the auxiliary cruiser, *Shinanomaru*, sighted the advancing Russian fleet through the mists. By 5.05 am, Tōgō had a signal from *Shinanomaru* in his hand. He ordered the whole of his fleet anchored at Chin-hei Bay on the south coast of Korea, to come out to intercept the enemy. At 6.05 am, Tōgō's flagship *Mikasa* weighed anchor and left the channel, followed by over forty warships.

At 1.39 pm, Tōgō sighted the Russians through a break in the haze. He had to get ahead of the Russians in order to cut them off in their dash for Vladivostok. The two fleets were heading towards each other, but in opposite directions. Tōgō, therefore, decided upon a dangerous turn, the famous 'T turn', in succession. At 2.05 pm, the Japanese First and Second Squadron advanced first directly and aslant upon the enemy. Three minutes later Rozhestvenskii on the bridge of his flagship *Suvorov* ordered his guns to open fire at 8,000 metres, while the Japanese guns were silent. But, as soon as the *Mikasa* was heading in parallel with the Russian fleet, she opened fire. The other Japanese ships commenced firing as each came out. The Battle of the Japan Sea, off Tsushima island, began. The Japanese victory was settled within the first thirty minutes; soon the *Oslyabya* was severely damaged; the *Suvorov*'s hull was wrapped in flames and Rozhestvenskii seriously wounded; the *Alexander III* and *Sisoi Veliki* left the line; and the *Oslyabya* sank. The *Borodino* led the line and tried to escape but failed.

The Japanese suffered little more than 100 dead and 500 wounded. As darkness fell, Tōgō set his course due north with others to rendezvous the next morning at Ullon-do Islands, while the Second Destroyer Flotilla opened a night attack, followed by four other destroyer flotillas and six torpedo-boat flotillas; the *Navarin* sank and the *Sisoi Veliki*, the *Nakhimov*, and the *Monomakh* were disabled; and three Japanese torpedo-boats were sunk. At 10.34 pm on the 28th the Japanese fleet re-opened fire; and nine minutes later the flag of the *Nikolai I* under the command of Admiral Nebogatov came down and up went the signal in international code, 'XGH', which meant 'We ask to negotiate'. Tōgō quietly ordered 'Cease Fire'. He had destroyed the Russian fleet as a fighting force, while he had lost only three torpedo-boats. Of the 36 Russian warships that went into action, 22 were sunk, six were captured, six were interned in neutral ports and only three escaped to Vladivostok.[8] This decisive naval success in the Japan Sea assured victory on land. President Theodore Roosevelt was asked to mediate, and the peace treaty was signed at Portsmouth, New Hampshire, on 5 September 1905.

Needless to say the brilliant Japanese victory in the Japan Sea owed much to the skill of Tōgō's command. But we must also set a high value on the backstage war preparation which Japan had made; the Anglo-Japanese Alliance to counter-balance the Franco-Russian Alliance, especially on its naval side by intelligence, technology, coal-supply etc.; Navy Minister Yamamoto's reshuffle of personnel including Tōgō; scrupulous arrangements – warships, vessels, coal-stocks; Japanese excellent arms – wireless, gunpowder etc. Above all, the extremely high morale of the crews was backed by the passionate patriotism of the Japanese as a whole. On the other hand, the formidable Russian fleet, despite its size, had many weaknesses. Many units were obsolete; equipment did not work; most of the warships and other vessels operated at far below their expected speeds. Moreover, her crews lacked training and were not always backed up by the whole Russian nation, which was shown on board the *Potemkin* in the Black Sea Mutiny of June 1905.

Just after the Russo-Japanese war Tōgō was made Chief of the Naval Staff in March 1906 and a count in September 1907. When the Connaught Mission visited Japan early in 1906 to confer the Order of the Garter on the Emperor Meiji, Admiral Tōgō accompanied the visitors as a member of the Japanese suite throughout the journey and received the Order of Merit, along with Generals Yamagata and Ōyama. At the end of 1909 he was relieved of the post of Chief of the Naval Staff and was appointed a member of the High Military Council. It was in this capacity that Tōgō left Yokohama with General Nogi Maresuke in the suite of Prince and Princess Higashi-Fushimi, who were to represent the Imperial Family at the coronation of King George V. During his stay in Britain, Tōgō, who was by this time the only survivor of the group of fourteen who had been sent to the United Kingdom in 1871, revisited the *Worcester*. He took the opportunity to visit sites relevant to the Japanese Navy, calling at Barrow (10 July), Glasgow (13 July), Newcastle (20 July) and Sheffield (22 July). It would appear that Admiral Tōgō was regarded both in Britain and Japan as a symbol of goodwill between the two countries and of the Anglo-Japanese Alliance in particular.

On 21 April 1913 Tōgō became Admiral of the Fleet, an appointment until death, and was made a member of the Council of Marshals and Admirals of the Fleet. In April of the following year, the Office of Tuition for the Crown Prince Hirohito (later to be the Emperor Shōwa) was established and Tōgō was appointed its president. The Crown Prince received his higher education under a group of private tutors headed by Tōgō. When the office was closed in 1921, Tōgō who had completed his task as imperial tutor was freed from responsibilities and strain, and retired to his private residence with no other duties. He was then seventy-five years old.

INFLUENCE IN RETIREMENT

After the Washington Naval Conference (1921) Admiral Tōgō assumed a rather anti-American attitude but he still remained loyal to Britain on the whole. As Tōgō achieved fame among the nations, being called 'Hero' or 'The Nelson of the Orient' and his prestige and informal influence inside the Imperial Navy increased, his position was naturally exploited by his earnest admirers and followers. The trouble over the London Naval Conference of 1930 is a most interesting illustration of this. The Imperial Navy was divided as to whether Japan should conclude the treaty or not: on the one hand, the fleet faction headed by Admiral Katō Kanji, Chief of the Naval Staff, rejected it, while, on the other, the treaty faction headed by Admiral Takarabe Takeshi, the Navy minister and a plenipotentiary to the conference, hoped to accept it. The former severely criticized the treaty based on the American proposals, that is, a 5:5:3 ratio for heavy cruisers and the reduction of total submarine tonnage from 78,000 to 52,000 from the view of Japan's national security. The latter advocated it because of the state of the national economy and the need for cooperation with USA and Britain in keeping the peace in the Pacific. Prince Fushimi and Tōgō initially supported the treaty; but, under the personal influence of Tōgō's closest associate, Viscount Ogasawara Nagayo (a retired Vice-Admiral who was also to become the main biographer of Tōgō) they soon became disenchanted. Ogasawara, the would-be adjutant to Tōgō, had close relations with Admiral Katō

Kanji, the protagonist of the turmoil. Katō visited Tōgō several times to encourage him to resist the conclusion of the treaty and put pressure on the plenipotentiaries in London.[9] Tōgō was moved deeply by Katō and Ogasawara but, in view of the Emperor's hope to conclude the treaty as explained by the acting Navy Minister Hamaguchi Osachi, he refrained from further resistance. On 1 April when Vice-minister Yamanashi Katsunoshin told Tōgō of the Government's wish to accept the treaty, Tōgō replied: 'Once the government has decided the matter, we must obey its decision. No more now, we must try to build up the unity of the navy'.[10] Behind the turmoil surrounding the treaty, there seemed to be some personal dissatisfaction with Navy Minister Takarabe who was accompanied by his wife to London. To Tōgō, an old samurai at the age of 84, negotiation was a kind of warfare, too serious a business for a negotiator to be accompanied by his wife!

On 30 May 1934, Admiral of the Fleet Tōgō passed away in his sleep, suffering from throat cancer. The cabinet held a special meeting and decided to hold a state funeral for the late admiral, which took place at Hibiya Park on 5 June. When the news of Tōgō's death was circulated, thousands of telegrams of condolence were delivered at his residence from various parts of the world, including one from Sir Bolton Eyres-Monsell, First Lord of the Admiralty. *The Times* in its leading article, praised Tōgō's excellent character and distinguished service, saying: 'The British Navy recall with pride that the Admiral of the Fleet carried out some of his early sea training in this country, and feel that they may be allowed to have a share with the Japanese Navy in the undying memory of his great achievements'.[11] Moreover, before Tōgō's state funeral, an impressive memorial service in honour of him was held on 2 June on board the training ship *Worcester* at Greenhithe, where he had been a student sixty years earlier, attended by a large number of prominent officers of the Royal Navy and the graduates of the College.[12]

10

Japan's Adoption of the Gold Standard and the London Money Market 1881–1903: Matsukata, Nakai and Takahashi

COUNT MATSUKATA MASAYOSHI (1835–1924) who is the key figure in this essay, was Japan's leading financial expert in the early period of Meiji. Since Britain was the world's banker at that time, it was vital for Matsukata as minister to cultivate the goodwill of British governments and bankers and ensure their confidence in Japan. From 1881 when Matsukata took over the position of finance minister, he recognised that his greatest ambition should be to obtain the recognition of the Western powers, and Britain in particular, for Japan's standing as a financially prudent state and that, in realizing this ambition, he should get Japan to adhere to the gold standard. Matsukata's vision would have remained unattainable, had it not been that, following China's defeat in the Sino-Japanese War (1894–5), she was required to pay a huge indemnity which Japan insisted should be paid through the London money market. The handling of the moneys extracted from China was a transaction over which Matsukata's personality brooded. The dream of attaining the gold standard thus became a reality. And through the various efforts of the two bankers discussed in this essay, Nakai Yoshigusu and Takahashi Korekiyo, Japan came by the end of the nineteenth century to be respected in financial circles in London.

COUNT MATSUKATA IN BRITAIN, 1902 '

Matsukata did not have the occasion to visit Britain before the early summer of 1902.[1] He arrived in London on 28 April to the kind of warm welcome only accorded to a foreign leader of remarkable distinction. The portrait of Matsukata which *The Banker's Magazine* printed in its issue of May 1902 was impressive for, although he was indeed the 'financial wizard' who had manipulated Japanese money and banking throughout the last two decades of the nineteenth century, he was almost unknown in the West. *The Times* noted that 'Confined as his role has been mainly to the sphere of internal administration, its results have not brought Count Matsugata (sic) into the degree of prominence,'[2] , while *The Bankers' Magazine* commented that 'his services to his country, and the world in general, are less appreciated by statesmen and financiers in this country'.[3] Both *The Times* and *The Bankers' Magazine* produced brief, but accurate, accounts of Matsukata's career while *The Bankers' Magazine* honoured him by referring to him as 'A Financier of the First Order'.

The Times strongly recommended that '. . . the reception accorded to Count Matsugata (sic!) will not be lacking in any of the cordiality and respect which characterized that of the Marquis Ito', who had, several months before Matsukata's arrival, visited London.[4] On 30 April Matsukata was the guest-of-honour at a banquet given by Lord Lansdowne, the foreign secretary, while on 2 May, perhaps the highlight of his visit, he was received by King Edward VII at Buckingham Palace. On 6 May he was entertained by the Rothschilds at their residence and two days later on 8 May he attended the 11th Annual Japan Society Dinner, at the Hotel Metropole, presided over by Viscount Hayashi Tadasu, the Japanese minister to the Court of St James's. On this occasion the Japanese National Anthem was sung.[5] Late that evening he travelled north to Glasgow visiting various Clydebank shipbuilders, moving south-eastwards to Newcastle where he inspected the Armstrong works and then coming south to Sheffield where he looked at the Vickers works. At all these places he met Japanese engineering apprentices.[6] Arriving back in London, Matsukata was banqueted again by the foreign secretary on 13 May, joined by his cabinet colleagues including the colonial secretary. On 14 May at the Hotel Metropole, the

Institute of Bankers hosted a banquet attended by more than 160 gentlemen including the Lord Chancellor and the officials of the Bank of England. There were several complimentary speeches to which Matsukata cordially replied, in Japanese.[7]

Two days later, on 16 May, the Earl of Sandwich received Matsukata, accompanied by Minister Hayashi at Huntingdon. Next day, Matsukata in the company of the Earl visited Cambridge, where he had talks with Herbert Somerton Foxwell (1849–1936)[8] and Alfred Marshall (1842–1924)[9] at St John's College, with whom he had luncheon. He also met the Provost of King's College, who took him around the old Colleges.

Earlier on 5 May, Japanese businessmen in London, including those of the Yokohama Specie Bank, Mitsui Bussan and Nihon Yūsen, held a banquet for Matsukata. Towards the end of his stay in London, Matsukata enjoyed a boat trip on the Thames organized by the Specie Bank. Then last but not least, on 20 May, Matsukata was entertained at the Savoy Hotel by Ōtani Kozui, brother-in-law of the Crown Prince (later the Taishō Emperor) and successor to the influential Otani faction in Kyoto of *Jōdoshinshū*, an important Buddhist sect, who incidentally commemorated the anniversary of their founder.[10] On 24 May when Matsukata left Britain to continue his continental tour, a *Times* correspondent accompanied him. Before returning to Japan, Matsukata again visited Britain and was received at All Souls College, Oxford. Next day, on 24 June, the Vice-Chancellor conferred on him and Minister Hayashi the honorary degree of the Doctor of Civil Law.[11]

Why was Matsukata so well received? There are two possible reasons. On 30 January 1902, the Alliance Treaty between Britain and Japan had been signed by the Japanese minister and the British foreign secretary in London. The Alliance brought about an end to the isolation of both island empires giving both parties assurance of the support against any aggression shown, say, by Russia. This was the fundamental fact that stirred up enthusiasm among the British in welcoming any distinguished visitors from Japan. Another reason was probably Matsukata's own skill in leading Japan to financial stability. Matsukata clearly had another, and crucial, mission for he was searching for an opportunity of tapping the London money market in the event of Japan going to war, say, against Russia.[12] Although his 'financial wizardry' had been well publicized in *The Times* and

The Bankers' Magazine, would all this publicity convince the British bankers of Japanese creditworthiness?

MATSUKATA'S DREAM OF THE GOLD STANDARD

In the wake of the turbulent years of transition from the collapsing Shogunate to the rising Meiji regime, Matsukata, holding offices concurrently in the ministries of finance and of the interior, undertook important reforms. He was commissioned in the early 1870s directly by the cabinet to convert the tax system from payment in kind, in rice, to payment in money. After this demanding task was completed, Matsukata was asked to head the Japanese delegation to the Great Exhibition in Paris in 1878. This European journey was to prove a crucial educational experience. At the suggestion of the French finance minister, Leon Say, in Paris, Matsukata examined the newly-founded National Bank of Belgium, which became in effect the model for the Bank of Japan, founded in 1882. Matsukata also witnessed the collapse of the bimetallic Latin Monetary Union led by the French. From this date he was suspicious of bimetallism, that is the double gold-and-silver standard. And, perhaps most significantly, while in Europe, Matsukata learnt that the Germans had successfully based their gold standard upon the French indemnity paid in the aftermath of the Franco-German War. It was no surprise, therefore, that from this date Matsukata started to dream of putting Japan on the gold standard.[13]

In October 1881 Matsukata assumed the office of finance minister, which he retained for almost two decades. His first task was to support the Yokohama Specie Bank, the first Japanese international bank, which had been founded in February 1880 by his rival, Ōkuma Shigenobu (1838–1922), in direct opposition to Western banking. Domestic financing of Japanese exporters was urgently needed in Yokohama where all financial business had in the past been conducted by Western bankers and merchants. The primary role of the Specie Bank was to compete with the Westerners and to earn foreign currency and specie. The specie thus collected would eventually enable the Bank of Japan to issue silver-convertible bank notes.[14] Thanks to the work of the Yokohama Specie Bank, the Bank of Japan in May 1885 launched silver-convertible banknotes thus successfully halting the rampant inflation dominant during the 1870s. Matsukata's deflationary policies caused substantial hardship, especially for the farmers.

Although Matsukata was successful with his money and banking policies and keen to encourage change, he could not, in the climate then prevailing in Japan, publicly endorse gold as the sole standard for Japan. When, however, in the early 1890s India, the largest silver-standard country in Asia, deserted that metal, he took the opportunity to appoint a monetary commission (October 1893). Matsukata was fortunate in being able to ensure that three of his nominees served on the commission.[15] As had been anticipated, the commission was, in general, opposed to the gold standard preferring either a silver or bimetallic standard, that is, the *status quo*.[16] In the meantime the Sino-Japanese War broke out in July 1894 and ended, with a Japanese victory, in March 1895. When the Treaty of Shimonoseki was signed in April, it stipulated that Japan should receive an indemnity from China of ¥360 million, equivalent to approximately £38 million.

On 17 March Matsukata was asked by the Meiji Emperor himself, in Hiroshima, where the Emperor had been attending the meetings of the chiefs-of-staff during the war, to advise on the collection of the Chinese indemnity. In May Matsukata submitted to the cabinet a proposal for the procedure for receiving and remitting the Chinese indemnity money and its management. He was strongly opposed to the money being paid in silver, as the treaty stipulated, and recommended that the Japanese should receive the money in gold in London.[17] From May onwards, Matsukata and his men on the commission manoeuvred so that they succeeded by the end of June in passing a resolution, by the narrowest of margins, that there should be a modification of the silver standard. Almost immediately, Matsukata resigned as finance minister because of divisions among the cabinet members regarding his plan for the management of the indemnity money.

A year later, in September 1896, when the second Itō cabinet tendered its resignation on account of political as well as financial problems, Matsukata succeeded Itō as premier, taking concurrently the office of finance minister. With the whole administration under his control, the Monetary Act, stipulating the adoption of the gold standard, passed the Diet in March 1897 to take effect from October 1897. And so Matsukata's dream of the gold standard came true.

THE YOKOHAMA SPECIE BANK IN LONDON, 1881–1903

In January 1881, an officer of the Yokohama Specie Bank had arrived in London to work at a desk inside the Japanese legation, in Bishopsgate, London. In December 1884, the office was elevated to independent branch status at 84 Bishopsgate, the sole monetary agent of the Japanese government in London. The Oriental Bank which had hitherto carried out business in London for the Japanese government, went into liquidation in 1884.[18] The Yokohama Specie Bank, London branch, urgently needed direct London contacts in the capital and, through an old friend of Japan, Alexander Allan Shand (1844–1930) successfully negotiated with the Alliance Bank, the London Joint-Stock Bank, the Union Bank of London and Lloyds Bank until 1886.[19]

What was the Yokohama Specie Bank's business in London? The Specie Bank discounted foreign bills of exchange for the Japanese exporters, mainly silk merchants, by using paper currency lent to it by the government. The bills were then sent to London, New York, or Lyons, for the collection of the proceeds. This was effected by the Specie Bank officials based in the Japanese legations. The proceeds were in due course remitted by wire back to the Yokohama headquarters of the Bank, which then finalized the process through the repayment to the government of lent paper currency in specie, or foreign hard currency, such as pounds sterling. This was the system adopted at the suggestion of Matsukata in June 1880 and, indeed, became the governmental method of financing export trade. In this business, the Yokohama Specie Bank, London branch, was most crucial, because the London money market was the financial centre of the world.[20]

The autumn of 1889 witnessed an exceptionally bad harvest of rice which forced the Japanese for the first time in their history to import extra rice. The situation developed into a monetary crisis in the spring of 1890 when the Yokohama Specie Bank felt it necessary to strengthen its position in London. Between November 1889 and June 1890, an exchange fund was installed in the Specie Bank, London branch, totalling 1.1 million pounds sterling. Further, in the summer of 1890, the United States Congress passed a bill for the free purchase of silver, which caused serious difficulty for the Specie Bank as well as the Japanese economy, because of the sudden rise of the silver price.

Learning from these successive crises, the Yokohama Specie Bank reviewed and then revised its conduct of business. Firstly, because it was operating effectively on a bimetallic basis, the Bank resolved to allocate the silver business to Yokohama and the gold business to London. Secondly, the top management was changed. One of the senior Japanese consular officers in London and the acting manager of the Specie Bank, London branch, were called back to Japan to assume the presidency of the Bank and the assistant managership at the head office respectively.[21] Koizumi Nobukichi (1849–1894) at the Bank of Japan was transferred to the Specie Bank as head office manager.[22] Nakai Yoshigusu (1853–1903), chief of the foreign exchange department at head office in Yokohama, became manager in London.

Nakai Yoshigusu,[23] accompanied by his wife Ryu, arrived in London at the beginning of 1891 and the Nakais soon became well known in the Japanese community. Number '84 Bishopsgate', where the Yokohama Specie Bank, London branch, was accommodated, was important because most Japanese had to go there to collect their money remitted from Japan. 'Streatham Hill', where Nakai Yoshigusu and Ryu resided, became, because of the generous hospitality of the Nakais, a favourite Japanese meeting place.[24] Nakai as chairman of *Nihonjinkai* (otherwise known as the Nippon Club) in London without doubt entertained Matsukata on his visit to London.[25]

The burden of the negotiations regarding the Chinese indemnity business fell inevitably upon Nakai's shoulders. The Japanese government wished to receive the money in London. The Chinese government agreed. The magnitude of the transfer, equivalent to 28 per cent of the 1895 national income of Japan, obliged Nakai and the Japanese government to request that the Bank of England open an account for the Specie Bank. This had previously been denied. The Bank of England agreed to open an account for the Yokohama Specie Bank in October 1895 when the first instalment of the indemnity was due. This account was the first official formal connection between British and Japanese banking.

CHINESE INDEMNITY PAYMENTS, 1895–1903

For the payment of the first instalment, the Chinese government decided to issue bonds in Paris, which French and Russian banks underwrote. The proceeds were then transferred in the form of French treasury bills to the Bank of England, where on 31 October 1895, at 11.00 am at a formal ceremony held in the presence of the chief cashier of the Bank of England, the first moneys were received. The receipt reads:

> The undersigned hereby acknowledges in the name of His Imperial Japanese Majesty's Government, the receipt from his Excellency King, His Imperial Chinese Majesty's Envoy Extraordinary and Minister Plenipotentiary to the Court of St James's, the sum of eight million two hundred, twenty five thousand, two hundred and forty five pounds sterling and one shilling, ten pence and three farthings (£8,225,245-1s-10 3/4d) which is the agreed equivalent of fifty million (50,000,000) Kuping Taels, as the first instalment of the war-indemnity of two hundred million (200,000,000) Kuping Taels which the Chinese Government is to pay to the Japanese Government in accordance with Art.4 of the Treaty of Shimonoseki.[26]

The receipt was signed by two persons, 'Kato, His Imperial Japanese Majesty's Envoy Extraordinary and Minister Plenipotentiary to the Court of St James's' and H.G. Bowen, the chief cashier of the Bank of England. Together with the first instalment, the 'pecuniary compensation for the retrocession of the Southern Portion of the province of Fengtien' amounting to £4.9 million (30 million Kuping Taels) was paid.[27] In January 1896, the full mandate was given to Nakai of the Yokohama Specie Bank and a representative of the Bank of Japan.

Although all payments were made in pounds sterling as the Japanese requested, the Chinese in the months of May 1896 and 1898 had twice to rely on the Germans because of the delicacy of the bond issuing market. To this the Japanese agreed. The Chinese were assisted in Berlin by the Imperial Bank of Germany, Discont Gesellschaft and another German bank. From London, the Hong Kong & Shanghai Banking Corporation and Deutsch-Asiatische Bank also supported the issues.[28] Between October 1895 and May 1898, the Chinese paid the whole sum of £38 million to Japan, £33 million in London and £5 million in Berlin. Witnessing the payment of the last instalment, *The Bankers' Magazine* observed that 'The cheque of £11,008,855.16s.9d. paid on the 7th ulto. was by far the biggest ever drawn upon by the Bank of England.'[29] Indeed, this was one of the rare cases in which the Bank of England required to act carefully in partnership with a private customer in order to avoid market disturbances.[30]

The next formidable question facing Matsukata and Nakai was how to remit these moneys back to Japan. The matter was complicated because the Japanese government had already issued bonds once in 1897 and was to do so again in 1899 for some £13 million. The proceeds of these transactions would also have to be transferred to Japan. According to Matsukata's instructions, the procedures were carefully arranged between the London branch manager, Nakai, and the head office manager in Tokyo, Takahashi Korekiyo (1854–1936).[31] There were only two methods by which to remit the indemnity money from London to Yokohama, that is, the purchase and shipment of gold itself, and the purchase of foreign bills of exchange payable in pounds sterling or dollars at Yokohama or elsewhere in Japan. The gold market in London was thought to be so sensitive to the scale of the purchase that it was specially instructed to proceed with caution and to buy in silver specie if necessary to produce the counter-effect, thus stabilizing gold prices.[32]

The safer and more reliable method was the purchase of bills of exchange, but that too was risky. Bills of exchange payable in Japan involved both export and import bills for the Japanese. When import bills were purchased in excess of exports, it would inevitably lead to an increased deficit in the trade balance which had constantly plagued the Japanese financial authorities even before 1895. In order to avoid this danger, the Yokohama Specie Bank quietly purchased bills on New York, San Francisco, Bombay, Hong Kong and Shanghai, where the Bank again bought in bills on Japan so that demands in London on the bills payable in Japan would not seem so high. Simultaneously the Specie Bank reduced the discounting of import bills as much as possible. Otherwise the trade balance deficits would be swollen unmanageably.[33]

Between the end of 1895 and the spring of 1903, the Yokohama Specie Bank in London remitted some £49 million, of which 66 per cent was sent in the form of bills of exchange, 28 per cent in gold specie, including British crown coins, and 6 per cent in silver. The operation was executed despite the fact that the Japanese were suffering from trade deficits of ¥53 million in 1896, ¥56 million in 1897, ¥111 million in 1898 and ¥5 million in 1899. Notwithstanding the size of both the remittance and the trade deficits, no visible disturbances were felt according to the Japanese consulate reports sent from overseas financial centres.[34] *The Bankers' Magazine* also observed that the whole operation was 'not likely to have any specially hardening effect upon the money market'.[35] It should be added that part of the amount sent back to Japan consisted of reserves for the banknotes issued on the basis of the newly-adopted gold standard. The London branch of the Yokohama Specie Bank continued to hold some ¥11 million in the account of the Bank of Japan, which was to be called 'specie abroad' and became a barometer for the well-being of the Japanese economy as well as Japan's monetary system.

THE END OF AN ERA, 1903

The Yokohama Specie Bank's operation of the Chinese indemnity receipt and remittance attracted the attention of London bankers. Nakai Yoshigusu made his *debut*, with an article and a portrait, in *The Bankers' Magazine* in January 1896, the first Japanese to be so honoured. Later, in the March issue of 1903, the same magazine acknowledged Nakai's accomplishment in an obituary assessment:

> 'Mr Yoshigusu Nakai, whose untimely death took place at Tokyo on February 8. - - - Throughout that time he had to meet with all the difficulties which beset the path of a bank working in a city to which it was a stranger. When the office was first opened, it was treated as of little account by other Eastern exchange banks, but, by dint of the persevering labours and judicious management of its chief, the Yokohama Specie Bank worked its way into a place of prominence among those institutions having connection with Oriental countries.

The Bankers' Magazine's acknowledgement in 1896 was followed by two successive honours in Japan for Nakai. In March 1899 he was promoted to be a member of the board of directors of the Specie Bank. In October of that year, he was awarded the Fifth Order of Merit by the Meiji Emperor. Such an award to a person like Nakai, who had neither distinguished governmental nor military service, was remarkable. Why then has Nakai Yoshigusu subsequently been forgotten, or ignored, by banking historians in Japan?

Takahashi Korekiyo, of far humbler samurai stock than Nakai, had a chequered career before his appointment as head of the construction department (Kenchiku Shunin) at the Bank of Japan, Tokyo, in the early 1890s. His successful career started when he was brought from the Shimonoseki branch of the Bank of Japan to the headquarters at Tokyo. Later, in August 1895, he became the head office manager of the Specie Bank, an office which Koizumi had held until his untimely death in December 1894. Takahashi became the vice-president of the Specie Bank in 1897. Concurrently with this, he also assumed the deputy governorship of the Bank of Japan in 1899. His rapid promotion was related to the successful management of the Chinese indemnity at the Japanese end and also undoubtedly to his 'secret aggressiveness'.

Matsukata retired in 1900 from active service after twenty years at the forefront of Japanese financial management. The end of the 'Matsukata era' gave Takahashi his chance. Once Nakai had left London and died soon afterwards, it was only Takahashi at the Yokohama end that knew exactly how difficult the Chinese indemnity business had been. Takahashi left a *Jiden* (autobiography) on which many banking historians have relied for information about the politics and financial history of Japan. Notwithstanding all this, there can be no doubt that Takahashi saw things from his own point of view. For example, he chose to play up his own role in the indemnity issue and overlook the contribution of Nakai Yoshigusu mentioning him, by name, only twice. Takahashi's suppression of the details of Nakai's career has detracted from Nakai's accomplishments.[36] Is it possible that Takahashi's achievements, before 1903, have been exaggerated? There seems to be no doubt that he was an extremely talented man.

In February 1903 Matsukata Masayoshi in Japan received the honorary Grand Cross of the Order of St Michael and St George for his distinguished services to finance.[37] In the same month Nakai Yoshigusu who for more than a decade had served Matsukata in London so faithfully, died in Tokyo. The year 1903 indeed marked the end of an era during which the Japanese banking system became visible for the first time to the London money market through the adoption of the gold standard. Matsukata and Nakai had in their different ways laid the foundations for the important loan operations which were to be undertaken during the Russo-Japanese War (1904–5). Japan was to send Takahashi Korekiyo, the vice-president of the Bank of Japan, to the United States and London to raise foreign loans on 24 February, within two weeks of the war breaking out. After his return to Tokyo to report back on his mission, he was sent on a second mission as financial expert on special government assignment (*seifu tokuha zaimu iin*) between February 1905 and February 1906 to Britain and a number of other countries. In this way he managed to raise war loans reckoned at £82 million. The confidence which had been carefully built up in earlier years in banking circles in Tokyo and London had proved invaluable in Japan's time of emergency.

11

Sir Claude and Lady Ethel MacDonald

IAN NISH

MACDONALD'S claim to fame rests with the long period of twelve years he spent as head of the British diplomatic mission in Japan. He went there first as minister from 1900 to 1905 and then became the first ambassador (when the two countries agreed to raise the status of their missions to embassies), and occupied that position till his retirement in 1912. The MacDonalds presided over the British embassy in the halcyon days of the Anglo-Japanese alliance, at a time when relations between the countries were closer than they have ever historically been.

Claude Maxwell MacDonald (1852–1915) was educated at Uppingham and Sandhurst and joined the army in 1872. As an officer in the Highland Light Infantry, he was posted as the War Office's representative at the British agency in Cairo during the Egyptian campaign of 1882. He was highly commended by Sir Evelyn Baring (Lord Cromer). He then occupied the position of consul-general, Zanzibar, in 1887–8 and went on to become consul-general of the Oil Rivers (later the Niger Coast) Protectorate, thought to be the most unhealthy and uncomfortable posting in the British Empire.[1] He was knighted by the Conservative government of Lord Salisbury in 1892, the year in which he married Ethel MacDonald (1857–1941). When Salisbury came back to power as prime minister and foreign secretary in 1895, he had to find a replacement for the minister at Peking. He chose MacDonald who had retired from the army and occupied the post from 1896 to 1900. It is often asked how MacDonald who had no experience of the East was chosen for this sensitive position. It appears that he had the strong

133

recommendation of Cromer and had, by his activities in Africa, acquired the confidence of Salisbury. These years proved to be stormy ones for Britain, both from the Chinese and from the other powers: they were the years of high imperialism. It may be that Salisbury reckoned that MacDonald, as soldier and avowed imperialist, was not ill-suited to the post. But, as contemporaries wrote, he was appointed '. . . to the indignation of the rest of the service.'[2]

In spite of this, his years in Peking were agreeable and congenial for those immediately around him. He and his wife looked the part of Britain's representatives. MacDonald was tall, mustachioed and had the craggy good looks of a highlander. Lady MacDonald who was Anglo-Irish was also tall, good-looking, and tactful. They together established a tradition of hospitality at the legation which they were to continue in Tokyo. On the debit side, some have criticized his handling of his staff. The minister at Peking had the responsibility for the large number of members of Her Majesty's China Consular Service who were scattered around the treaty ports on China's coast and rivers. One author writes that MacDonald '. . . left China again without so much as clapping eyes on most of the consular officers whose careers and well-being lay in [his] hands.'[3] This criticism, if true, does seem to be an important one, even if it would hardly have been possible for him to have visited all the outlying consular posts. For those on the compound of legation or embassy, whether Peking or Tokyo, MacDonald was, however, the perfect family man, always solicitous about the 'bairns' of his juniors.

In the summer of 1900 the Legation Quarter in Peking was besieged by the Boxers. MacDonald and his wife were deemed lost. Obituaries were published and arrangements for the funeral were put in train. In fact, MacDonald survived. Because of his military background, he was asked to assume command of the community of the besieged, while Lady MacDonald was fully occupied, attending to the sick and arranging for food supplies. Shiba Gōrō, an artillery major in the Japanese legation, was the chief staff officer and most effective collaborator of Claude MacDonald. He helped to establish a good relation between the two nations which he records in his account of the siege. The resistance of the defenders and the success of the allied expeditionary force, to which the Japanese contributed the second largest army, in pushing through to Peking and breaking the siege owed much to the cooperation of the Anglophile Shiba and MacDonald.[4]

MOVE TO JAPAN

The post of British minister to Tokyo was under consideration at the time. Sir Ernest Satow, the present incumbent, had completed five years in Japan and was then on leave in London. When the Peking siege began and MacDonald's life was in peril, Salisbury began to contemplate the despatch of Satow to Peking in order to supervise the peace settlement. There had earlier been a thought that MacDonald might move on to Tokyo. In succeeding telegrams of 16–17 September, Salisbury expressed his gratitude but invited MacDonald to return to England for recuperation. MacDonald, however, replied on 24 September:

> '. . . the solicitude of Her Majesty and your Lordship with regard to my health calls for my deep gratitude. The anxieties and hardships of the siege do not, however, appear in any way to have caused my health to suffer. Under these circumstances, I feel that I should not be altogether justified in returning to England. I propose, therefore, that [sic] when my affairs are settled, say in three weeks from now, to leave for Tokio, and to arrange with Sir Ernest Satow to meet him en route, and confer with him.'[5]

MacDonald described himself as a soldier-outsider in the diplomatic world. But there was something appropriate in a soldier being posted to Japan where in the Katsura government and among the Genro (elder statesmen) the power of the military was considerable. He may have lacked diplomatic finesse and been criticized for this by career diplomats but he was on the whole a sound and energetic British representative. Perhaps he was not unduly tested because the 1900s were a time of good Anglo-Japanese relations. But he had been tested in China and not found wanting. For the historian, too, he was interesting. He was a copious letter-writer. These were not intellectual letters, carefully balanced in judgement and cautious like those of Ernest Satow. They were chatty letters crammed with little bits of gossip, written in a firm hand and (if the historian may be permitted to fantasize) scribbled just in time to make the boat as it left from Yokohama pier. Unlike Satow, he did not think his private diplomatic letters needed to be copied so there are no 'MacDonald papers'. But his letters are scattered in the public record and in the private collections of his friends and contemporaries.[6]

ANGLO-JAPANESE ALLIANCE

MacDonald was very much the diplomat of the Anglo-Japanese alliance. It is on that aspect that we shall concentrate here. By an odd coincidence he was in Tokyo for the negotiation of the first alliance, the second alliance in 1905 and the third alliance in 1911. In each case the prime negotiations took place in London; and, in Britain's case, it was global issues and imperial considerations which dictated the policy rather than the regional issues of East Asia. This meant that MacDonald and the staff of the Tokyo embassy had a reactive role. Their function was to maintain liaison with the Japanese government while most of the negotiations were channelled through the Japanese legation in London.

Anglo-Japanese discussions of a fairly imprecise kind took place in London from the spring of 1901. Lord Lansdowne, the new foreign secretary, discussed possibilities with Hayashi Tadasu, the new Japanese minister. Before they embarked on more formal discussions, MacDonald was recalled for consultations and set off from Tokyo on 28 May. The degree of consultation was concealed since he was in any case overdue for leave. As we saw, he had gone directly to his new post in Japan the previous October without taking up the offer of convalescent leave in Britain after his ordeal at Peking. It was plausible, therefore, for Whitehall to state in public that he was visiting Britain to rest and recuperate and receive honours for his efforts in Peking without arousing suspicions about secret diplomacy. But there is evidence that he was fairly frequently consulted during the three months of his return.[7]

In his letters, MacDonald claims to have spoken to the king, to several members of the royal family and the Duke of Cambridge. Perhaps more significant, he travelled to Hatfield to discuss an Anglo-Japanese alliance with the prime minister, Lord Salisbury. MacDonald wrote: '(En parenthèse he was rather against the alliance)'.[8] Since Salisbury was later to be the member of the cabinet most resistant to a Japanese alliance, the visitor from Tokyo did not make a convert on this occasion. But it is nonetheless significant that MacDonald who owed his preferment in the diplomatic profession to Salisbury as foreign secretary, should have been assigned to talk things over at Hatfield after serving barely eight months in his new post. He also had several talks with Minister Hayashi who reported to Tokyo his distinct impression that MacDonald's object was to pave the way for serious negotiations. He was therefore seen in Japan as the mouthpiece of the British government and establishment and in the role, familiar to Japanese, of go-between. More formal negotiations began on 31 July. There was, however, something of a hiatus in August while the British ministers repaired to their summer retreats in the hills.

MacDonald himself had taken a holiday in the Scottish highlands and on the continent but his time for return to Japan was at hand. This delay worried Hayashi who was the pace-setter and begged an interview with MacDonald to which he was only too pleased to agree. In this farewell conversation on 30 August, Hayashi confessed that he sensed that Britain was reluctant to make the first move over 'the understanding'. He therefore beseeched MacDonald, when he returned to Tokyo to try to persuade the Japanese leaders, Itō and Komura, to take the initiative. His anxiety was in fact unnecessary because Komura Jutarō who had only taken over as foreign minister in September was not slow to study the papers and make the next move. He made this overture on 16 October which was a week before MacDonald returned to his post. But MacDonald was of course able to provide the Japanese leadership with some local colour about Britain's thinking at the time.

The alliance negotiations were carried through in spite of delays caused paradoxically by the senior statesmen on both sides. For Japan, Itō was reluctant to see a British alliance, though he finally agreed to come to London to put his seal of approval on it.[9] For Britain, Prime Minister Salisbury was also reluctant to take on such a risky commitment as an entanglement with Japan, though he was a minority voice in his own cabinet. The alliance was signed on 30 January 1902 and published on 12 February. As MacDonald reported, the British treaty was enthusiastically welcomed by the Japanese people.

For the rest of MacDonald's stay in Japan the alliance dinners were to be an important anniversary in the diplomatic calendar. It was an important anniversary for the Japanese and an occasion which MacDonald with his gregarious personality relished. Whether in the British embassy compound or at the villas at the mountain resort of Chuzenji, he and Lady MacDonald were generous hosts.

The alliance was soon followed by Russo-Japanese disputes which eventually led to war in February 1904. During the run-up to the war MacDonald had a subtle role to play: he had to restrain Japan and, while avoiding any charge of interfering, advise her statesmen to consider carefully Japan's military strength. Probably this advice was not needed because the foreign minister and the elder statesmen had cool heads and delayed the final decision. Britain's selfish worry was to avoid being drawn into any war which arose. In the event the alliance never came into play. Britain remained neutral, though this did not preclude her from giving financial aid through the London money market after the war began and making coaling and repair hard for the Russian Baltic fleet as it made its way painfully to the East. The British embassy in Tokyo reflected the feeling in Britain herself: Japan was a popular victor. Lady MacDonald was prominent in her work for the Japanese Red Cross and for charities for soldiers and sailors' families.[10]

THE ALLIANCE IS STRENGTHENED

In the negotiation of the second alliance which was concluded on 12 August 1905, it was again Hayashi, and not MacDonald, who bore the brunt of the negotiations. The foreign ministers, Lansdowne and Komura, were the same as before; but there was no suggestion that the talks would be carried on in Tokyo. The original alliance was due to continue until 1907; but there were reasons why both sides found advantages in carrying out the revisions – which were substantial – earlier. Unlike 1901 MacDonald was not recalled to London for consultation. The new alliance was made in London and took account of Britain's perceived imperial weakness. It was to stay in existence for ten years.

Following Japan's victory against Russia and the conclusion of the new alliance, the Conservative government decided to raise the status of its mission in Tokyo to that of an embassy. The

Japanese were honoured and reciprocated. The result was that the existing incumbents, MacDonald and Hayashi, attained the rank of ambassador. There was, of course, the view that MacDonald had already served five years and was due for replacement. But, unlike Hayashi who was shortly instructed to return to Tokyo, MacDonald was allowed (by the new Liberal government) to stay in his post for another contract.

This desire to cement the alliance relationship symbolically led Britain to confer on the Emperor Meiji the Order of the Garter. Edward VII appointed Prince Arthur of Connaught to lead a Garter mission which conferred the decoration in Tokyo on 20 February 1906.[11] MacDonald was, needless to say, much involved. Personal decorations were also exchanged with great liberality. Ambassador Hayashi was given the KCVO, while MacDonald was presented with the GCVO and sworn as a member of the Privy Council in 1906 and also became Dean of the Diplomatic Corps in Tokyo.

MacDonald took a long-deferred leave in the spring of 1907. He was able to fit into the London scene without difficulty. Thus he reports on a dinner party where seated '. . . between John Morley and Jack Fisher last night I received much instruction'.[12] He was able to clear up some commercial matters, dealing with perpetual leases and possible British contracts in the South Manchurian Railway zone. He was able to take part in the early sessions of the army and navy talks in May to work out the strategic implications of the second alliance in the presence of Admiral Yamamoto Gombei for the navy and General Nishi Kanjirō for the army. Sir Claude probably made some contribution to the occasion with the benefit of his local knowledge. He returned to Tokyo by the weekly international train on the Trans-Siberian railway. Lady MacDonald lost all her baggage as was the hazard of that route.[13]

MacDonald enjoyed a period of leave in 1909 when the Chargé d'affaires was Horace Rumbold. While he was on good terms with his Chief, Rumbold records in his diary that 'Our Government did not trust their man here to be sufficiently energetic in his language and think he looks at things too much from the Japanese point of view'.[14] There were times when the minutes of the officials in Whitehall showed impatience, if not exasperation, with MacDonald who was very often suspected of not passing on their complaints with adequate forcefulness. He was a proud ambassador of long experience and felt that he had a feel for the ways of Tokyo. There is often a state of creative tension between Whitehall and a post abroad. That certainly came to exist with MacDonald. But George Sansom who was his private secretary writes of him with affection and understanding. It was an exceptional time for the British embassy when Japanese cabinet members used to visit it frequently, admirals and generals called in to play billiards, and the Japanese social élite enjoyed embassy parties greatly. In view of the role of the military in Japanese political life after the Russo-Japanese war, MacDonald was an appropriate figure who was able to speak to the leaders on the same wavelength.[15]

Apart from Whitehall impatience there was also a growing dissatisfaction in commercial circles. Ambassador d'Anethan, a shrewd observer of the Tokyo scene, wrote that MacDonald '. . . has lately been very much attacked in financial circles . . . for not defending English interests with enough energy'.[16] Writers under commercial influence like Putnam Weale (B. Lennox Simpson) were hostile to him. It is doubtful what substance there was in these complaints. British interests had not made much progress as a result of the alliance and of the support given to Japan during the war; but that was scarcely the fault of MacDonald who, if he was Japanophile, was still intrepid in taking up with the Japanese matters of British national interest. Whitehall appears to have recognized this because it granted him an extension of his appointment in 1910 for two years.

PROBLEMS WITH WHITEHALL

In 1911 the underlying tensions between MacDonald and Whitehall came to a head. Japan, fearing that the alliance might not be renewed when it came to its completion date in 1915, asked for its renewal to be advanced. The British cabinet at its meeting on 29 March decided to propose that it be renewed straightaway till 1921, that is for ten years. On 3 April Japan and Britain entered into a new commercial treaty which finally gave Japan tariff autonomy on terms not unfavourable to Britain. In both cases, the decision had been taken in London with only limited consultation with the Tokyo embassy. MacDonald was clearly put out. Understandably MacDonald was indignant that he had not been asked for his views. On 5 April he sent off an urgent telegram:

'Next few years, particularly those during which the alliance has still to run, are of vital importance to Japan; and her policy in Corea, Manchuria and China generally during those years will be valuable indication to us whether we should renew alliance at its expiration or not . . . If we do not renew until alliance expires four years hence we can pretty well rely on tariff not being denounced before then and in other ways the uncertainty of renewal would be useful lever and also check to any unnecessarily forward policy.'[17]

In reply MacDonald was told that the value of an American arbitration treaty must 'outweigh those urged by you on other side'. By implication he was being told that he was taking too narrow a view of the transaction. He did not give up the fight, however, arguing:

'. . . though a modification of the Agreement might with great advantage be made now, its definite extension at the present juncture should if possible be avoided.'

Grey concluded that 'to modify without extending would create a most undesirable impression.'[18] The Tokyo embassy had been outpointed. Soon after MacDonald left by sea for Britain to attend the coronation of King George V. He was able to see the correspondence while he was in London and discussed the issue with Grey. But the consultations took place after the basic decision had been made.

On 13 July the third alliance treaty was signed in London in a more subdued atmosphere than greeted the earlier treaties.[19] It took account especially of Japan's annexation of Korea the previous year and omitted the clause dealing with Korean independence. This was the focal point of the treaty and of the ambassador's final tour. Not long after MacDonald returned to Japan in July, he launched himself on an energetic tour of northeast Asia. It was appropriate in the circumstances that he should visit Korea and the Kuantung Leased Territory where Britain had problems to resolve with Japan and examine the situation for himself. Sidney and Beatrice Webb happened to meet the embassy party while they were on their way from Japan to China and recorded on 22 October:

'On [crossing] over the Yalu River into Manchuria, we ran

across the British Ambassador, Sir Claude MacDonald who was journeying in state through Manchuria and Korea, as the guest of the South Manchurian Railway administration. . . . Although we had brought introductions, both official and personal, to the MacDonalds and to two of the attachés, they had not managed to see us. When we did meet at Antung, they were extremely desirous to be civil and they were, I think, [conscious] that they had not "played up" sufficiently.'[20]

While this reveals much about the Webbs, it reveals something also about the MacDonalds. Although normally gregarious, they ran a mile from intellectuals, especially those suspected of having leanings towards international socialism.

1912 was a traumatic year for the Japanese. The Emperor Meiji died on 30 July and was buried in September in the presence of dignitaries from around the world, Britain being represented by Prince Arthur of Connaught. The ceremony was evidence that the new and modern Japan had been internationally recognized. General Nogi, one of the heroes of the Russo-Japanese war, and his wife took their own lives the same day as the burial. This showed that the ancient Shinto traditions and values of Japan were clearly still alive also. There was general recognition that it was the end of an era.

MacDonald had to address the question of whether the demise of the Meiji emperor would bring instability to the most stable and successful nation in Asia. He informed London what was known to inner circles in Japan:

'Intellectually [the Taisho emperor] is generally supposed to be somewhat wanting, and that is certainly the opinion the casual observer would arrive at after some moments' conversation.'[21]

Sir Claude's view was that for stability to be achieved, he stood in need of a man of strength and knowledge of the ways of the world. He saw it as a role for Prince Katsura who had resigned as prime minister earlier in the year and was in St Petersburgh when the Meiji emperor's illness became serious. He immediately returned, reaching Tokyo nine days after the emperor's death. He was then appointed to the post of Grand Chamberlain (*Nai Daijin*) and Lord Keeper of the Privy Seal.

Against this background of uncertainty MacDonald made his exit from Japan at the beginning of November. The Japanese press, never wholly predictable in its attitudes to the alliance, was united in expressing Japan's affection and appreciation of his efforts on behalf of Anglo-Japanese understanding.[22] His immediate successor, Chargé d'affaires Horace Rumbold, thought that he had served Britain's objects well, most notably by restraining Japan.[23] MacDonald, while he never became chairman of the Japan Society of London, did lecture to it in 1913 on the subject of his experiences – and those of Major Shiba – during the Seige of Peking Legations, a topic which he clearly regarded as one of the high-points of his adventure-laden life.[24] Sir Claude was not permitted to enjoy a long retirement and died in September 1915, much lamented.

Lady Ethel MacDonald had shared her husband's life in Tokyo and, like him, had enjoyed her long sojourn in Japan. Her role is described thus:

> 'Lady MacDonald was a model Ambassadress – very good-looking with a fine presence, clever and tactful: she entertained largely, and her kind nature and sympathy endeared her to all the English in Japan, especially the large colony in Yokohama.'[25]

Lady MacDonald was renowned for her wit. When General Horatio Herbert Kitchener visited Japan in the summer of 1909, he acquired the reputation among the British community for meanness: for taking all he could get in the way of presents and giving nothing in return. 'Lady M.', (as she was widely known) commented, '. . . he would take a piece of sugar out of a bird's cage'[26] – a remark which, needless to say, travelled like greased lightning round the embassy compound. After her return to England, she lived for twenty-five years at Royal Cottage, Kew, which was allocated to her by King George V. For two decades she led an active life for charity, being especially active for the Overseas Nursing Association. In 1935 she was made a Dame of the British Empire in her own right. She died in 1941 at the great age of 84, after seven years of illness.[27]

CONCLUSION

There can be no doubt that the MacDonalds presided over a special Anglo-Japanese relationship and may in the decade of their residence have contributed to that relationship. They were fortunate in having good access to Japanese ministers, bureaucrats, sailors and soldiers. One of the most baffling things for those in Whitehall was to understand the power structure in Japan, especially the role of the emperor and the elder statesmen. Unusually among diplomats, Claude MacDonald was able to throw some light on this, as when he attended a banquet on the occasion of the visit of the Royal Navy squadron to Tokyo in the autumn of 1905. In one of his private letters which did not betray many marks of Eton and Balliol, he wrote:

> 'His Majesty [the Meiji emperor] chatted most amicably with everybody around. The Imperial Princes, Arisugawa and Kanin, who sat on either side, treated him with marked deference but Marquis Ito and Count Inouye (the latter sat next to me) seemed to speak on absolute terms of equality and cracked jokes which made this direct descendant of the Sun roar with laughter. It was a great revelation to me and one which pleased me very much for though a Mikado he seems very human.'[28]

The same inside knowledge of the Japanese scene suffuses MacDonald's Annual Reports which he wrote for the years 1907 to 1911. The Tokyo embassy was close to the Japan bureaucracy which was inclined to disclose matters on which it might be secretive in other respects. Not least valuable in these reports are MacDonald's views on the personalities of the Japanese leaders which bear the stamp of his own authorship. He had been intimately involved with the Japanese scene for a decade, and earlier at Peking for another four. Although he had no knowledge of the Japanese language and did not try to acquire any, he was something of a Japanese expert by sheer length of service.[29]

MacDonald had been Britain's representative in Japan for twelve years and had therefore as minister and ambassador been the longest-serving Chief in the British embassy ever. He had presided over a decade of cordiality in relations (1900–11). At the time of his departure the relationships had entered into a decade of suspicion, though the alliance continued. Even Sir Claude, who was generally regarded as Japanophile, was aware of this deterioration. He had reservations about Japan's continental policy as we saw in 1911. In spite of this, he survived – partly, one feels, because the ministers in London liked his simple approach to foreign affairs; but partly also because MacDonald was the symbol of the alliance. To relieve him of his duties would have meant cutting the knot of Anglo-Japanese cordiality.

In the month before their departure, Sir Claude and Lady MacDonald made the gastronomic sacrifices which the British expect of their diplomats. They were entertained by the French embassy (16 October), the Russian embassy (17 October), Marquis Nabeshima (18 October), the Cambridge Club (18 October), the Swedish legation (23 October), the British Club (Eikoku kyokai, 25 October), Prince Tokugawa (29 October) and the Tokyo Club (1 November). Such were the friends of the British ambassador in 1912. Long suffering and exhausted, the MacDonalds slumped in their seats on the 8.30 am train on 4 November from Shimbashi, bidding farewell to Tokyo for ever.[30]

The Japan-British Exhibition of 1910: The Japanese Organizers

AYAKO HOTTA-LISTER

THE JAPAN-BRITISH Exhibition was held at the White City, Shepherds Bush, London, from 14 May to 29 October 1910. The official opening was delayed because of the sudden death of King Edward VII on 6 May. The Exhibition was the result of a British initiative but was soon taken up by the Japanese with an enthusiasm much greater than the British were to show.

The benefits of participating in international exhibitions were recognized at an early stage by the new Meiji Government. Between the first such exhibition hosted by Britain in 1851 and the Shepherds Bush exhibition of 1910, about seventy major international exhibitions had been held. Britain had hosted about a dozen of them. While Japan had never held one herself, she had taken part in about thirty-six, starting with the Exposition Universelle in Paris in 1867. This was due partly to influential men like Fukuzawa Yukichi, who had seen the International Exhibition of 1862 in London and stressed the benefits of such exhibitions in his *Seiyō Jijō* (The Condition of the West), and Shibusawa Eiichi, who had been one of the delegates sent by the Tokugawa Bakufu to the Paris Exhibition in 1867. During their tours in the West, both men were dazzled by Western civilization and its advanced technology, and they were undeniably impressed by the scale and complexity of the international exhibitions they had experienced; these impressions were to inspire them later and had some influence on their ideals.

The frequent appearance of Japanese exhibits at these

international exhibitions from almost the beginning of the era was bound to be conspicuous. As time passed, the attitudes of the visitors towards Japan and her exhibits were, in general, slowly changing, reflecting changes in Japan's position in the world: at first, the main reactions were curiosity and a delight in novelty; after the Sino-Japanese war of 1894–5 a certain enthusiasm was added; during and immediately after the Russo-Japanese war of 1904–5 reactions of curiosity, sympathy and admiration seem to have been generated. By the time of the Japan-British Exhibition, the general public in Britain seems to have shown a mixture of curiosity, admiration of Japan's achievements and traditional arts, suspicion and apprehension of Japan's conduct in East Asia, and friendliness towards an allied country. The overall impression of the Japan-British Exhibition on the British public seems to have been favourable.

Around the turn of the century, these exhibitions had begun to appeal to the masses by offering popular forms of entertainment with spectacular amusements and extravaganza. There was a notably imperial theme in exhibitions in Britain, France and the USA, in particular. Private entrepreneurs sprang up to make a profitable business from these events. In most countries, governments in the earlier period had not been too much concerned with exhibitions making a loss so long as the country had been successfully promoted and host cities had been given an impetus to modernize, leaving to posterity the proud museums and elaborate buildings erected for those exhibitions. Governments still continued to be deeply involved in international exhibitions in the twentieth century, including the provision of funds. But a man such as Imre Kiralfy in Britain emerged as one of the most prominent private exhibition organizers; Kiralfy had accumulated vast experience in this field and realized the potential of international exhibitions, accommodating them to his business interests. Political or diplomatic developments, too, were certainly amongst the reasons inspiring Imre Kiralfy to hold the Franco-British Exhibition and the Japan-British Exhibition, honouring the Entente Cordiale of 1904 and the Anglo-Japanese Alliance of 1905 respectively. The Japan-British Exhibition was arranged during the great age of international exhibitions with all the pomp and circumstance of a still confident Edwardian grandeur.

HOW THE JAPAN-BRITISH EXHIBITION CAME ABOUT

The proposal to hold this exhibition was first put forward as early as 1906 by Imre Kiralfy to Mutsu Hirokichi, the son of the influential Mutsu Munemitsu and the First Secretary at the Japanese embassy in London. However, at that time, the Japanese Government had itself been planning to host a great international exhibition for the first time in 1912 in Tokyo. Japan was emerging as a world power, particularly after the Russo-Japanese war, and had aspirations to be regarded as such: hosting an international exhibition was one of the manifestations of great power status in those days, and the idea came naturally to the Japanese leaders. As might be expected, this exhibition was to be on the most lavish scale for Japan, and there was an air of great enthusiasm among the organizers, who were already busy with the preparations.

Official invitations for the Grand Japanese Exhibition of 1912 were sent out early in 1907 to various countries including Britain and the United States which was so enthusiastic that it voted a substantial amount for the exhibition and sent a group of delegates to undertake a preliminary study. The Grand Japanese Exhibition Committee, set up in 1907, elected prominent people to its ranks, including as chairman Kaneko Kentarō who had earned great respect in the United States during the Russo-Japanese war. Despite this, Kiralfy's plan was not entirely abandoned, as Komura Jutarō, the ambassador in London from August 1906 to July 1908, recommended Foreign Minister Hayashi Tadasu, early in 1908 to hold a Japan-British Exhibition in order to provide an opportunity for consolidating friendship between the two countries, stressing the benefits which would arise from such an exhibition, and referring as an example to the forthcoming Franco-British Exhibition. Komura also thought it would serve as a good place to advertise the proposed Japanese Exhibition of 1912. But, after some consideration in Tokyo, Hayashi informed Komura that it was not the right time to hold a joint exhibition in London.

This situation changed early in 1908 when the Japanese Government decided to postpone its Grand Exhibition to 1917 because of financial difficulties. This, of course, provided an opportunity for Kiralfy to resume his efforts with the Japanese

Government. In July, Komura was invited to attend the Franco-British Exhibition at the 'White City' where Kiralfy proposed again to him that a joint exhibition between Britain and Japan along similar lines should be arranged. Komura seems to have been deeply impressed by the exhibition, and pledged to Kiralfy that he would raise the matter seriously on his return to Japan.

Upon taking up his second assignment as foreign minister in August 1908 in the second Katsura Cabinet, Komura officially proposed to the cabinet the idea of having such an exhibition. It was duly decided, after a series of discussions, that it would be a great opportunity for Japan to share such an event solely with her ally, Britain, but that it should be held in 1910, not 1909 as suggested by Kiralfy. Two government officials, Wada Hikojirō and Beppu Ushitarō, were subsequently sent to London to prepare a feasibility study, often meeting the British organizers including Kiralfy, inspecting the exhibition sites, and carrying out other relevant investigations. Upon their return, thorough studies, discussions, and exchanges of ideas took place to pave the way for the final decision to go ahead with the exhibition. On 31 March 1909, after the Diet had unanimously voted funds, amounting to ¥1,800,000 – a stupendous sum for the time – an agreement for holding a joint exhibition with Britain in 1910 was officially signed by three parties, Imre Kiralfy, his Shepherd Bush Exhibition Company, and Katō Takaaki, the new Japanese ambassador in London, representing the Japanese Government.

While the Japanese Government had approached the exhibition as a national undertaking, the British Government, though giving moral support to the exhibition, did not provide any financial assistance to the British exhibitors. This was normal British practice, whether or not Britain was hosting an exhibition. From the spring of 1909 preparations for the exhibition started with great enthusiasm on both sides, with the formation of the British and Japanese Committees headed by prominent dignitaries and leaders. Selection of the exhibits also started; these included a great number of rare art works, some of which had never been publicly shown before and had been generously loaned by prominent people and institutions, such as Inoue Kaoru, Suematsu Kenchō, Iwasaki Koyata, and Kōzanji Temple, Chionji Temple, and Tōfukuji Temple in Kyōto. Most British newspapers paid a great deal of attention to the exhibition even before the opening and gave it favourable reviews. During

149

the six months the Japan-British Exhibition was open at the 'White City', over six million visitors attended. It is therefore regarded as one of the most popular international exhibitions before the First World War.

KOMURA JUTARŌ, THE JAPANESE INITIATOR

The main Japanese initiator of the Japan-British Exhibition was Komura Jutarō, who was from Obi, a small clan in southern Kyūshū. After studying law at Harvard, he was picked by Mutsu Munemitsu, Foreign Minister in the 1890s, from a mundane office job in the Foreign Office for a more distinguished career, serving briefly in Korea, Peking, Washington, and St Petersburg; he is said to have studiously researched each country where he was posted, and this knowledge became a great asset for him later. In January 1901 he represented Japan at the Peking International Conference after the Boxer Rebellion, during which time he earned great respect among the Western powers as a prominent Japanese leader. In September that year, he was appointed as Foreign Minister for the first Katsura Cabinet. One of his first priorities was to conclude the Anglo-Japanese alliance, which was signed on 30 January 1902 after much political consideration. It is believed that Komura had enjoyed the special patronage of Yamagata and had a close relationship with Katsura, and that Komura's contacts among the military and his association with right-wing groups had been the source of his hard-line policy towards Russia and tough-mindedness towards Asia.[1] Thus, he is believed to have been one of the advocates of a war against Russia and of Japanese expansion on the Asian continent.

His policy during his first foreign ministership was based, it is thought, on firstly tackling domestic diplomacy (*naikō*), that is dealing with the *Genrō*, before dealing with foreign policy; one such case is illustrated by the long series of events, involving Itō and Inoue, leading to the conclusion of the Anglo-Japanese alliance.[2]. He steered a difficult course with much skill around the time of the Russo-Japanese war and at the Portsmouth Conference in particular when he represented his country as chief delegate.

In his last months as foreign minister, Komura did not uphold the 'Open Door' policy in Manchuria, the main cause of the war against Russia, a cause which had been supported by Britain and the United States, and he also disregarded the pledge that Japan had then made publicly to the powers. While Komura was ambassador in London between August 1906 and July 1908, he was strongly opposed to the railway building project proposed in Manchuria by a British firm, which would have competed with the existing Japanese managed line, and protested to Sir Edward Grey, the Foreign Secretary. who eventually supported him by declining to promote the scheme. This became one of the sources of suspicion towards Japan at this time and aggravated the tension already existing between Japan and Britain.

While Komura was ambassador in London, he was well aware that the popularity of the Anglo-Japanese alliance was in decline and that anti-Japanese feelings were on the increase in Britain, because of Japan's conduct in Manchuria. Upon his return to Tokyo as Foreign Minister in August 1908, his main foreign policy was therefore very cautious; stressing that Japan's continental expansion policy should be carried out within the limits permitted by the Western powers and within a framework of international harmony. He presented to the cabinet in September 1908 a statement of the new government's foreign policy. In it, he declared the Anglo-Japanese alliance to be 'the backbone of Japan's foreign policy'.[3] Keeping a friendly relationship with Britain was of the utmost importance to Komura. He also set up and chaired an official Committee for Tariff Revision to prepare the negotiations which were due to start in July 1910, when he intended to end the existing tariff structure.

The importance Komura attached to maintaining a good relationship with Britain as part of his overall foreign policy can be seen in the appointment of Katō Takaaki as his successor in London and in the proposal to hold the Japan-British Exhibition. Though Komura and Katō had not been personally on good terms in the past, Komura saw in Katō the qualities needed at that point to carry out important tasks in London which would have been lacking in other candidates. Katō, strongly pro-British, had earlier served as minister in London and foreign minister, and possessed a wide and deep knowledge of Britain and of the world economic situation. Komura thought that Katō would maintain a good relationship with Britain. But Komura took the precaution of checking Katō's extreme pro-British leanings, which, he thought, might not represent Japan's true interest: Komura took the unprecedented step of leaving in London his confidant, Yamaza Enjirō, whom he had taken with him when he went to London in 1906.[4]

As Komura had earlier promised to Kiralfy, he presented his arguments to the cabinet in October in favour of holding the Japan-British Exhibition in 1910 for reasons of international diplomacy and on grounds of developing trade. He also succeeded in persuading the Diet to vote generous funds, spread over three years, together with some funds to cover Taiwan's exhibits.[5] It seems to have been common knowledge among the leaders at that time (there were a few references to it) that another power had applied to Kiralfy to hold an exhibition jointly with Britain, but that it had been rejected as Kiralfy had favoured the Japanese exhibition. Though there was no evidence which country that could have been, it was speculated that it was the United States. Komura was even accused of using the exhibition to gain some advantage over the United States: the Japanese editor of the *London Shimpō*, Katō Satori, a London resident, attacked Komura vigorously, saying: 'The diplomatic game in the Japan-British Exhibition is therefore solely to have some effect upon Uncle Sam' (*sic*). Komura does not seem to have taken any notice of these remarks, since he had been warned by Mutsu earlier of Kato's rather notorious character.[6]

SOME OTHER JAPANESE ORGANIZERS

Japan took up the idea of an exhibition mainly for political and diplomatic purposes. But, once it became an official government undertaking, the Department of Agriculture and Commerce took charge, and formed the Japanese Committee for the Japan-British Exhibition, which appointed, or elected, or employed a great number of people, working on different duties at different times. These numbered just over a hundred at the time of the opening of the exhibition, among which about forty were sent to London to undertake various tasks. The Commission was headed by Baron Ōura Kanetake, Minister of the Agriculture and Commerce Department, who was to be in charge of the whole project. Ōura was formerly governor of several prefectures, Commissioner of Metropolitan Police and Minister of Communications. He was one of the leaders of the political party known as the *Daidō* Club for a long time, and was one of Yamagata's trusted followers. As president to the exhibition, he is believed to have personally visited the heads of old *daimyō* ('clan') families and others in possession of treasures, many of which had never been on display for generations, and successfully persuaded them to loan their treasures to the exhibition for the sake of the nation.[7] Ōura had worked with Komura closely before the final decision to hold the exhibition was made and later visited London at an early stage of the exhibition to deliver speeches at various meetings, confirming the goodwill existing between the two countries.

Prince Fushimi was honorary president to the exhibition. His counterpart on the British side was Prince Arthur of Connaught, who had visited Japan on behalf of King Edward VII to confer the Order of the Garter in 1906 on the Emperor Meiji. The prince in turn made a reciprocal visit to London in 1907 on behalf of the Emperor. On that occasion Komura, who has sometimes been accused of being an unsociable ambassador to London, made a strenuous effort to strengthen the diplomatic ties with Britain by giving lavish parties for prominent dignitaries including members of the royal family, and organizing other functions for the prince. Prince Fushimi's eldest son also went to London to study early in 1910. On hearing of King Edward VII's death, Prince Fushimi, who was due to have arrived in London by then, showed respect to the late king by declining to land in London and remained in Paris until the funeral. King George V's consideration in not delaying the opening of the exhibition more than was necessary was appreciated by the Japanese officials, who had of course invested much time and effort in the enterprise. A close friendly relationship between the royal families in Japan and Britain played an important role during the exhibition in sustaining high morale among the organizers in both countries.[8]

Other members of the Japanese Commission to the exhibition included Matsudaira Masanao, vice-president of the exhibition, and chief commissioner Wada Hikojirō and commissioner Beppu Ushitarō, both of whom were bureaucrats working under Ōura in the Ministry of Agriculture and Commerce. Wada and Beppu made preliminary investigations in London prior to the signing of the official contract and organized the actual overall preparations. Matsudaira and Wada had worked in a similar capacity at the St Louis Exposition in the United States in

1904, and they, together with Beppu, had also been put in charge of the Grand Japanese Exhibition which was first postponed till 1917 and later cancelled and had been working on the project for some time. Their experiences in international exhibitions were indispensable to the smooth and coherent organization of the London exhibition.

Smooth arrangements could not have been achieved without the existence of a body which would oversee and organize the actual exhibits to be transported and displayed, and supervise exhibitors at the exhibition. This was the Exhibitors' Association which was formed in April 1909 under the auspices of the government, which sanctioned the sum of ¥300,000 for the association. Hirayama Seishin was duly elected as the president of the association. An expert in this field, Hirayama had witnessed the Vienna International Exhibitions of 1873, when the Meiji Government first participated in such an exhibition, and had since been engaged in helping the government over the exhibits to be selected, shipped, and displayed at international exhibitions, and finally arranging for them to be returned home safely. In May 1909, he emphasized the existing trade imbalance with Britain and encouraged the would-be exhibitors with prospects of increasing their exports to Britain, but warned them that, in order to achieve long-term benefits from the exhibition, they would need to observe high business standards and send only high quality goods for display. He also recalled that on earlier occasions the benefits of such exhibitions had been so poorly appreciated by the private sector that the government had had to purchase all the goods to be exhibited from them. Hirayama also recalled in his memoir an episode during the Vienna Exhibition of 1873, when Cunliff P. Owen, the Japanophile British commissioner for the exhibition and the head of the South Kensington Museum, had advised a Japanese commissioner that Japan should try to exhibit at these exhibitions authentic goods of her own rather than inferior Western imitations – sound advice, as the latter kind of exhibit seems to have become more common at such exhibitions and drew considerable criticism.[9]

A similar contribution was made by the London embassy staff, who worked in close association with those who had been sent from Japan and their counterparts in the British section. This group was headed by Ambassador Katō Takaaki, Yamaza Enjirō, and Mutsu Hirokichi, Katō, as has been briefly mentioned earlier, had been one of the foremost advocates of maintaining strong ties with Britain. He regarded the Anglo-Japanese alliance as an important instrument which had assisted in the rise of Japan's status to that of a world power. Connected to the Iwasaki family through his wife he had served as minister in London between March 1895 and April 1899, and had been appointed as Foreign Minister under Itō between October 1900 and June 1901. After he left the Foreign Ministry, he went into journalism as the proprietor of the *Nichi Nichi Shimbun* for some time. He was again appointed as Foreign Minister under Saionji in January 1906, only to resign in March as he was opposed to the nationalization of the railways, though another school of thought regarded his resignation as a protest against the military occupation of Manchuria.

Katō, who was now an influential political figure, was appointed as ambassador to London in succession to Komura in February 1909 and served until February 1913. Katō became one of the strongest promoters of the exhibition which he thought would form a strong bond between the two countries and he enthusiastically informed Grey in April 1909 of the exhibition proposal. At this meeting, in response to the foreign secretary's idea that the aim of the exhibition was to increase Japanese exports to Britain since the Department of Agriculture and Commerce was in charge of the exhibition, Katō stressed that the aim of keeping friendly relations between the allies was the main driving force behind the exhibition, though improving trade was equally important.[10]

As the man on the spot, Katō had been well aware of the anti-Japanese feeling prevalent in certain circles in Britain, and he was very sensitive to the reactions of the British public to Japanese conduct. He seems to have been disconcerted to find out from an article in *The Times* that among the Japanese exhibits would be a model of a Chinese tower from the Kuantung Government, models of some Chinese people delivering soybeans in Manchuria, and displays of some products from South Manchuria. Katō immediately wrote a letter to Komura, pointing out the insensitivity of such exhibits featuring areas not officially recognized as being Japanese possessions, and citing a similar case in Osaka in 1903 at a Japanese domestic exhibition, which had resulted in numerous protests by Chinese students in Japan. Katō warned that this would only aggravate the tensions already existing between Japan and Britain, China and the United States, damaging the main purpose of the exhibition, but his plea did not seem to be effective.[11] As ambassador, he tried to do his best by delivering friendly speeches at various functions in relation to the exhibition, mediating tactfully between Japan and Britain at difficult, but important, times, particularly during the start of the negotiations for the new Japanese tariff, and at the time of Japan's annexation of Korea in August, and later, at the time of the negotiations for the revision of the alliance, which had started in the autumn of 1910 and was to be concluded in July 1911. All of these occurred during the exhibition and affected the atmosphere.

One of the officials under Katō who took charge of the exhibition was Mutsu Hirokichi, briefly mentioned earlier. He was the eldest son of the late Count Mutsu Munemitsu, had studied in England for several years from 1887, and returned to Japan as a barrister. After passing a diplomatic examination, Mutsu worked as third secretary in the United States, as second secretary at Rome and was transferred to be first secretary at the Japanese embassy in London in 1904. He was very fluent in English and had an English wife who showed 'a disposition to keep in the background'. He was appointed as commissioner to the exhibition, and was deeply involved with the actual preparations, liaising between Japan and Britain, sending out prospectuses of the exhibition to interested firms in Britain, arranging meetings, banquets, making speeches on the relationships between the two countries, and carrying out other tasks. He had been suffering from asthma, with consumptive tendencies for some time which greatly concerned Katō. Mutsu had to return to Japan for convalescence in October 1910, around the time of the end of the exhibition, and did not take another appointment until 1914 when he was appointed to Brussels.[12]

It is interesting that the first Japanese to receive a Doctorate of Economic Science in Britain, Uehara Etsujirō, a graduate of the LSE, was also hired by Mutsu as an interpreter to Kiralfy in order to pay for his passage back to Japan. His research paper, 'Political Development of Japan, 1868–1910', received praise from *The Times* and gained the Adam Smith Award. His task at the exhibition was to soothe Kiralfy which was much appreciated by his fellow Japanese staff, as Kiralfy was reputed to be rather stringent and demanding.[13]

Another prominent organizer was Yamaza Enjirō. Though he was not appointed a commissioner for the exhibition, he took charge of the London Embassy as chargé d'affaires between August 1908 and February 1909 before Katō's arrival. It was during this time that feasibility studies for the exhibition were being made by the Japanese Government: it was he, together with Mutsu and Wada, who paved the way for the exhibition. Yamaza is believed to have been one of Japan's ablest career diplomats, probably second only to Komura. He had been posted to London with Komura in 1906 and remained there until August 1912 – an exceptionally long period. Yamaza was reputed to be an indispensable diplomat and a gifted drafter of official documents, for which many, particularly Komura, had a high regard.

JAPANESE PRESS SUPPORT

The contribution made by Japanese newspapers was also important. It provided the Japanese public with the latest information about the exhibition on a regular basis in order to raise enthusiasm and to gain the moral support of the Japanese public, particularly as it was being held at the other side of the globe. Hasegawa Nyozenkan, a journalist from the *Osaka Asahi Shimbun*, a large liberal newspaper, had been sent to London specifically to report his observations and views on the exhibition, which were published regularly in the *Asahi Shimbun*. Hasegawa, a distinguished journalist widely known as Nyozekan, was well-fitted for this work; his teachers, such as Tsubouchi Shoyo, had given him a good grounding in English literature, he had studied Samuel Smiles' *Self-Help*, and he was greatly influenced by British liberal and democratic ideas. Throughout his life he was known as 'a thinker and journalist of the English school'. Yet, he respected his Japanese cultural heritage. He had a great admiration of Eastern culture including Chinese philosophy and *Manyōshū* and *Kojiki*, and he published a number of works, among them, *The Japanese Character*.[14]

A considerable number of Japanese visited the exhibition for various purposes. Apart from those who were engaged in working for the exhibition, government and municipal officials made the trip to get new ideas and businessmen made special efforts to establish contacts for the future. The *Asahi Shimbun* also organized a special tour for people from different fields, and Japanese residents in Britain and Europe, too, had a natural interest in seeing what it would be like, as well as in giving moral support to the Japanese participants.

The Japan–British Exhibition differed from earlier ones in that the initiative on the Japanese side had been taken by Komura Jutarō, one of the ablest foreign ministers Japan had ever had. After persistent persuasion by the British exhibition organizer, Kiralfy, Komura thought it was a timely opportunity for Japan to hold the exhibition for political and diplomatic reasons, despite the fact that Japan's financial position was not really strong enough to allow it to take on such a venture. As in other exhibitions, economic factors, such as expanding Japan's export trade, were very important considerations, and there were educational aims. As the government accepted it as a national undertaking, prominent and experienced people cooperated to make the exhibition successful. Politically and diplomatically, therefore, the Japan–British Exhibition was one of the most important events before the First World War in the relationship between Britain and Japan. Although Japan's exports to Britain increased slightly as a result and Japanese goods were given an impetus to expand, the exhibition could not reverse the existing trade imbalance in favour of Britain. But there is no doubt that the British visitors to the exhibition were, in varying degrees, impressed about Japan by the Japanese exhibits, demonstrations, accompanying books, newspaper articles, journals, and some other means. If the success of an international exhibition can be measured in terms of self-advertisement, the Japan–British Exhibition was undoubtedly successful for Japan.

'In One Day Have I Lived Many Lives': Frank Ashton-Gwatkin, Novelist and Diplomat, 1889–1976

IAN NISH

FRANK TRELAWNY ARTHUR ASHTON-GWATKIN was an expert in Anglo-Japanese relations. His long career in the Foreign Office was concerned with the political aspects of the problem, particularly in the years between 1913 and 1935. At the same time, the four novels which he published mainly in the 1920s were generally preoccupied with the personal relationships between Japanese and British people It could be said that he was merely responding to the British readers' appetite for accounts of quaint oriental societies and inter-cultural dissimilarities; but his novels show a penetrating understanding of Japan and a sympathy for her people.

Ashton-Gwatkin was born in 1889 and received his education at Eton College and Balliol College, Oxford. He won the Newdigate prize for a poem on Michelangelo. This showed early evidence of the literary flair of which he was self-depreciatingly proud in later life. After graduation he took the entrance examination for the Foreign Office and was accepted in 1913 and posted to Japan as a student interpreter to learn the Japanese language. When Gwatkin came ashore in Kobe in April to join Britain's Consular Service in Japan, he was following in the footsteps of (Sir) Edward Crowe and (Sir) George Sansom. As Gwatkin later wrote, these were to become his life-long friends.[1] When he had taken his interpreting qualification, he was posted for three years as consular assistant in Yokohama, becoming deputy consul in 1917. But Major-general Sir Dudley Ridout, C. in C., British troops in the Straits Settlements, wrote to the ambassador in Tokyo expressing his anxiety about Japanese activities in his area during the war and asking for someone with Japanese language qualifications to monitor the situation. Gwatkin was chosen for this intelligence work, since others had already departed for similar assignments in South-East Asia. In April 1918 he sailed from Yokohama for Singapore where for over a year he worked as attaché in charge of Japanese affairs at army headquarters, not knowing whether it would lead to permanent employment. In 1919 he was given home leave after spending six years overseas.[2]

In London he met Dr George Ernest Morrison on whom he had earlier called while taking a vacation in China. Morrison who had been *The Times'* correspondent in Peking and later one of the Political Advisers to the Chinese Republic, asked Gwatkin ironically whether he proposed to spend his life moving between Shimonoseki and Moji and between Moji and Shimonoseki, and planted the seeds of dissatisfaction over a career in the consular service. Knowing that Gwatkin had experience as a journalist, working in a voluntary capacity for the *New East*, a propaganda journal for the British government, published in Tokyo during the war by John Robertson-Scott, Morrison suggested that he should try to get a post as Far Eastern correspondent with *The Times*.[3] That fell through and he was employed temporarily in the political intelligence department of the Foreign Office. He soon resigned but withdrew his resignation when he was appointed to the diplomatic service with the rank of second secretary. Such a transfer had been relatively rare in the past and was only made possible by the reforms in the Foreign Office which took place after the war. In his new capacity Gwatkin, now a married man, was able to settle in London, and become for most of the 1920s one of Britain's specialists on Far Eastern affairs.

ANGLO-JAPANESE ALLIANCE

Gwatkin was much involved in one of the most vexing aspects of British policy at the time: the renewal of the Anglo-Japanese alliance which was due to end in 1921 but was given a one-year extension of existence. Opinion in Britain and the British Empire was seriously divided on the issue. Those in the Foreign Office secretariat saw arguments both for renewing and for ending the alliance which had lasted two decades. In a minute of 23 March 1920, which followed the disturbances in Tokyo and the dissolution of the Diet, Gwatkin set forth his views:

> '. . . a "democratization" of Japanese institutions would modify the aggressive character of the country's foreign policy. Leaders of the intellectuals have openly condemned the bullying of China and Korea, and have declared that "military diplomacy" must be abolished . . . The present juncture, therefore, suggests the following considerations with regard to the renewal of the Anglo-Japanese Alliance:
>
> 1. That the present time of unsettled conditions in Japan, when the tendency of Japanese policy at home and abroad is doubtful, is unpropitious for the renewal of so binding an agreement as the Anglo-Japanese Alliance in its present form . . .'[4]

Of course, a junior official of thirty years of age was not in a position to sway Britain's policy on this many-sided issue, but he did at least focus attention on the domestic political weaknesses of Japan. The debate continued into 1921 when the initiative was grasped by the United States which proposed to call a conference at Washington in order to deliberate on Eastern and naval matters, including Britain's alliance with Japan.

Gwatkin and Miles Lampson (who did not know the Japanese language) were deputed as 'officials who know Japan' to be responsible for the visit to the United Kingdom of the Crown Prince during the summer. They accompanied him on his busy schedule and found him to be an able ambassador for his country.[5] In the autumn Gwatkin was lucky enough to be appointed as a member of the British team to go to Washington to attend the conference. Among his papers is a letter from his former boss in Tokyo, Sir Conyngham Greene, now in retirement:

> 'I am so glad to hear that you are attached to the Washington mission, and I hope it will mean another advance in your career. It will, as you say, be a most interesting experience, but I confess that I am rather bewildered as to what our line of policy is to be. We have been compassed by such a cloud of witnesses in the last few months, many of them not recommending the same courses of action, that it is not easy to know what we mean. I suppose in the end it will resolve itself into the traditional

"wait and see" attitude, and I dare say that will be the best in the end.'[6]

This assessment was fairly accurate: Britain's delegates went to Washington without a firm policy line, prepared to be reactive.

In place of Jordan who had to return home early, Ashton-Gwatkin had special responsibility to sit in with Lampson as an observer on the Sino-Japanese discussions dealing with the Shantung question. It involved him in many fraught meetings outside the conference itself and, though close-fought to the bitter end, finished with an agreement of settlement. The Chinese delegates, Alfred Sze and Dr Wellington Koo, expressed their thanks to Gwatkin in a letter of 27 February:

'Your collaboration as Mr Balfour's representative in the conversations between the Chinese and Japanese Delegations, which led to the conclusion of the Shantung Treaty here in Washington was of invaluable help. Your intimate knowledge of the problem and friendly interest all contributed to facilitate the agreement.'[7]

It is doubtful whether Gwatkin and Lampson moved far from their positions as 'observers' on this sensitive issue; but the Chinese delegates were not initially displeased with the outcome and grateful for a foreign presence which probably had its effect on both parties. The above letter was obviously written in the euphoria of Washington and, when the reaction in China proved to be less favourable, they may have become less sanguine.

Gwatkin was too junior to have much influence on the proceedings or on British policy-making. But he had a clear recollection of the standpoint of the policy-makers at least on the issue of the future of the Japanese alliance. Two quotations will indicate his perception of the line-up:

'The Department [Far East] was opposed to renewal, but they knew that the Prime Minister, Lloyd George, was in favour and that the Foreign Minister, Lord Curzon, was hesitant.'[8]

Behind the views of the department was the influence of Sir John Jordan, the British minister at Peking from 1906 to 1920, who had retired after a long career in the East in April 1920. Like many others in Britain, Jordan was hopeful of the creation of a new China and a Chinese revival. Gwatkin commented:

'Jordan and Wellesley and Miles Lampson were the pilots of
the Far Eastern policy at that time – away from the Japanese
Alliance. Our misgivings regarding Japan were justified; our
hopes for China were not.'[9]

This judgement which was made much later suggested that
Gwatkin regarded himself as still too young to venture his own
opinion.

The Four-Power Treaty replacing the Anglo-Japanese alliance
(the so-called 'Quadruple Pact') was signed on 13 December
1931. Gwatkin had some role in the wording of the
'Supplementary Treaty to the Quadruple Pact' which was
eventually signed on 6 February 1922. Its effect was to exclude
from the purview of the treaty the main islands of Japan. Japan's
anxiety was that, if the phrase 'the insular possessions in the
region of the Pacific Ocean' was deemed to include Japan's
home islands, the other signatories would have cause to interfere
in her domestic affairs. The amendment made clear that it
applied only to mandated territories.[10]

LITERARY VENTURES

Gwatkin's presence in Washington was because of his
professional expertise. It also had the effect of taking him out
of London at an embarrassing time. He had long had an
enthusiasm for writing. He had savoured that in Tokyo by his
writings for the *New East*, when, thanks to Robertson-Scott, he
had moved in Japanese literary circles. When Gwatkin left
Yokohama in April 1918 for Singapore, he had '. . . half the
typescript of my first novel in my box and unbounded self-
confidence'.[11] While he was returning from Singapore to the
United Kingdom on board the SS *André Lebon* in the following
year, he completed the manuscript. On arrival in London, he
offered this novel about Japanese life, to which he gave the name
Kimono, to six publishers before it was finally accepted by
Collins. But there was the proviso that it should be heavily
reduced in size. On the advice of Ernest Morrison, he offered
what was to have been the first chapter to Dr George Prothero,
the editor of the *Quarterly Review*, who accepted it with alacrity
as an article on Japanese politics. It appeared anonymously in the
October issue for 1920 under the title 'Japan and the War'. A
brief extract will show how one Britisher perceived the changed

position in East Asia brought on by Japanese's wartime progress:

> 'During 1918 [Japan] exported about ten times her average annual pre-war value of goods to British India, the Dutch Indies, Australia, New Zealand, South America, Egypt and Cape Colony. Much of this trade may be abnormal, but much will be retained. Thanks to her geographical position, to the energy and intelligence of her people, and to the unremitting support and guidance of her Government, this profiteer among nations has, during the days of Europe's calamity, won an incalculably vast reward . . . "The responsibility for the maintenance of security in the Far East rests entirely upon Japan", declared the Minister for Foreign Affairs, Viscount Motono, when the Russian Empire had collapsed . . . And indeed, until the entry of the United States into the war, Japan had actually realized her ambition of becoming the mistress of the Pacific and paramount power in Eastern Asia.'[12]

It was opportune that Gwatkin whose views on Japan's conduct during the war were so sour should not go back to Japan in an official capacity.

In the summer of 1921, shortly after the departure from Britain of the Crown Prince, the novel *Kimono* was published by 'John Paris', the pseudonym adopted by Gwatkin. It is a tale of a well-to-do Englishman, Captain Geoffrey Barrington, who has met in London and married a charming, Western-educated Japanese girl. They decide to spend their honeymoon in Japan. There, a Eurasian girl takes a fancy to Geoffrey and, when she is rejected by him, turns against him by announcing that his wife's substantial fortune comes from the brothel quarters of the Yoshiwara. Simultaneously with this, the wife is being induced to return to the bosom of her family. Disillusioned, Geoffrey alone returns home and joins his regiment in the war. The wife who stays on in Japan is sexually assaulted by the family lawyer and is rescued by her attendant who kills the assailant with a knife which he leaves as he takes to flight. The wife is therefore incriminated and is incarcerated on suspicion of having been the murderer. Her plight comes to the ears of an ex-ambassador to Britain, Count Saitō, who arranges her release. She then returns to Britain and joins her husband who has in the interim been elevated to the peerage as Lord Brandon.

The publication caused a storm of protest in Japan. The far-fetched tale did not show the Japanese male in a particularly good light. Yet it had all the marks of plausibility for the foreign reader. It was the reference to the sensitive subject of the Yoshiwara which seems to have been at the root of the protests. It seemed to be a reflection on the state of Japan's civilization — as indeed it was. And the Japanese were understandably ashamed of the issue being raised internationally.

The fact that it was the work of a member of the British diplomatic service was known only within privileged circles. It added to the piquancy of the issue. Let Gwatkin tell of the consequences in his own words:

> 'The Japanese Government protested against it. It was rumoured to have been banned in Japan — a great help to the sales . . . I believe that the charming Ambassador [in London], Baron Hayashi Gonsuke, thought that his government were making themselves ridiculous, but to appease them I had to promise that I would not part with the film rights of "Kimono". Baron Hayashi with whom I was on friendly terms, used to tease me about my books, and I used to reply that he must not talk about them, that it was tactless to do so, for were they not my bastard children — *shiseiji?*'[13]

Naturally also the ire of Japan was not without its effect on the future prospects of Gwatkin's career.

> '. . . when I applied to be sent as Counsellor to Peking, I was told, "No, impossible — because those books had given such offense to the Japanese". And some years after, when a friend in Tokyo asked the same Baron Hayashi how the Japanese would take it if Gwatkin were posted in the embassy there, he received the oracular reply: "He would get a very warm reception".'[14]

The Japanese ambassador, Hayashi (1920–5), was relatively broad-minded but he says nothing of this strange episode in his autobiography. This view was not shared by his seniors in Tokyo.[15]

Japanese officials were apparently affronted by the novel. They protested against its unfair exposure of Japan, while those in the know were doubtless doubly perturbed by the knowledge of the identity of 'John Paris'. Nevertheless they offered Gwatkin in 1924 the Japanese decoration of the Order of the Sacred Treasure (4th class) for services in connection with the Crown

Prince's visit to Britain. The award of the decoration was, however, slightly delayed compared to that of others involved in making the arrangements for the 1921 visit.

The Foreign Office seems to have observed the discomfiture of the Japanese with *sang froid*. Instead of transferring Gwatkin to a different department as might have been expected, it retained him at the Far East affairs desk in Whitehall where his expertise lay. He continued with the work of the department though in 1925 he became secretary of the (British) Boxer Indemnity Committee.

Gwatkin thought that much of his work in the Foreign Office was drab routine. Certainly Japan in the 1920s represented many drab problems. The Kantō earthquake of 1923 caused devastation in Tokyo and Yokohama. Then legislation was passed in the United States to exclude Japanese immigrants. Then a relatively strong government was created in Canton and staged two northern expeditions – one to the Yangtse area, the other subsequently to the capital of Peking. The Tokyo cabinet of General Tanaka despatched troops to protect the interests Japan had had in Shantung province for a decade. It was at this juncture in July 1928 that Tanaka proposed Anglo-Japanese cooperation in China, even an alliance. It was for Gwatkin to give guidance to his Foreign Office chiefs. He wrote:

> 'This talk of an "alliance regarding China" is as vague as it is dangerous. The only occasion for alliance would be if British and Japanese interests were openly and forcibly attacked by China. This might compel the two countries to take joint action in self-defence; but the events of 1927 (Hankow and Nanking) are not encouraging for this kind of cooperation even in those extreme cases. Japan refused to help us at Shanghai and was hesitating in her support even after Nanking.'[16]

Nothing came of the alliance parleys, though it was still possible in the 1920s to speak of collaboration.

Gwatkin wrote with fondness of his contacts with the Japanese community in London. He was evidently closest to the cream of the diplomatic establishment then to be found in London:

> 'All the Embassy were friends of ours in those days: Nagai, the counsellor, Saburi (poor Saburi, who killed himself in despair of his country's policies), Hiroshi Saito, Shigeru Yoshida, Iyemasa Tokugawa (whose father, the old Prince,

was an outspoken admirer of John Paris' works) and, dearest of all, Isaburo Yoshida, who was afterwards Ambassador in Turkey.'[17]

So he was surrounded by influential Japanese friends and, if rather frustrated by promotion prospects, still took comfort from their company.

John Paris meanwhile tried to capitalize on the success of *Kimono*. He next published *Sayonara – Goodbye*, a story of missionary life in Japan (1924) and *Banzai*, a semi-biography of an adventurous Japanese youth based on conversations with one who after a life as a *ronin* had landed up in dire straits in London (1925). This trilogy (with *Kimono*) was re-published in an omnibus volume under the title of *Japanese Revealed* (1927). One cannot avoid the suspicion that Gwatkin's sin in the eyes of the Japanese authorities was in revealing too much. His line was inconsistent with the line taken in the works of the official image-builders like Nitobe Inazō and Okakura Kakuzō, who were emphasizing the aesthetic elements of *bushido* and the tea ceremony.[18]

Collins had meanwhile published a poem entitled *A Japanese Don Juan: Narihira at the Temple* (1926). There was a further novel entitled *The Island Beyond Japan* which appeared in 1929, at a time when the world had perhaps lost the appetite for things oriental. Another called *Matsu* was published in 1932. But this was the end of the canon. They had supplied something of the colour and flavour of Japan in the Taisho period.

Despite these distractions of 'John Paris', Gwatkin was not seduced to a literary career. He was, of course, tempted to resign from the Foreign Office and become a full-time writer for which he certainly had the talent. But with the poor returns from novel-writing as he put it, '. . . he was well advised to stick with the Whitehall drudgery, and to use his writing as a hobby and a provider of pocket-money which was desperately needed.'[19] The drudgery of the Office was one of the recurring themes of this period; and writing was clearly one of the antidotes to this drudgery.

FOREIGN OFFICE ECONOMIC SECTION

In 1929 Gwatkin left the Far Eastern Department on his promotion to Acting Counsellor at the British embassy in

Moscow. His stay there was brief because his wife collapsed under the strain of life in the Soviet capital. He was back in the Foreign Office in April 1930 and acted as secretary to the Anglo-Soviet Debts and Claims Committee for two years. But he was moving gradually towards a new avenue of work: the economic side of the Foreign Office. It was innovative for the Office and new for Gwatkin who took it with remarkable enthusiasm and (at least to my layman's eye) analytical skill.

Of the past Gwatkin wrote: '. . . my long connection with the Far Eastern Department of the Foreign Office came to an end – for ever. I was tired of it; it had lasted too long'.[20] This was largely true. But there is an odd twist to his remark. The fact was that Japan had become too large a subject to be dealt with merely by the Far Eastern department. Japan was spilling over into other areas of diplomacy. Because of this it was still to be in the limelight for Gwatkin for a few more years.

He was initially attached to the League of Nations and Western department of the Office. For a long period of eighteen months after the Mukden incident of September 1931 the Manchurian crisis was a major preoccupation of this department while the subject was receiving the regular attention of the Council and the Assembly of the League of Nations. Gwatkin, although he was not a prime actor in this crisis, held strong views on the controversial question of sanctions as the following minute shows:

> 'The danger of trying to block the expansion of this vigorous country [Japan] which is armed to the teeth, by "economic sanctions", whether for political or commercial reasons, is obvious.'[21]

Gwatkin does not seem to have committed himself on paper over other aspects of the Manchurian crisis. But he spoke very forcefully to the author on one aspect of British policy. This related to the decision of the League of Nations to send a Commission of Enquiry to Manchuria. He strongly criticized the British government's folly in allowing Lord Lytton, its nominee on the Commission, to act as chairman of the Commission and lend his name to what came to be known as the 'Lytton Report'. He felt that this conveyed the idea to Japanese public opinion that Britain was dominating the commission and was responsible for the anti-Japanese elements in its reports. This was, in his view, a completely false impression and unnecessarily created bad feeling which the Foreign Office had been trying to avoid in the 1920s. How widespread this view was among Foreign Office staff is hard to say.[22] But it does seem that Lytton was indeed the member of the commission most critical of Japan and was only with difficulty persuaded from not tabling a minority report on some aspects. This fact was known to the Japanese who assumed, wrongly, that Lytton was not acting on his own responsibility but reflecting the attitudes of the British government.

In 1930 the Foreign Office recognized that it was indispensable to adjust to the increasingly economic aspect of diplomacy since the world-wide depression. It was decided to set up a politico-economic department within the Office. In February 1931 Gwatkin's name was first mentioned in connection with the economic section; and increasingly the groundwork for it was being laid by him. In September he became Foreign Office representative on the Economic Advisory Council.

Why was Gwatkin given this appointment? He was a scholar, novelist and poet but no economist. We can only guess at the answer. But he had at least two allies with commercial credentials. One was (Sir) Edward Crowe (1877–1960) who had been a language officer with special experience in Yokohama and had by this stage left the Japan consular service. He had become commercial attaché in 1906 and commercial counsellor in 1918. From 1919 he was attached in Tokyo to the Department of Overseas Trade, which had been set up at the end of the war under the joint control of the Foreign Office and the Board of Trade. In 1924 he was recalled to London to serve in the department and four years later became the head of that office as Comptroller-General, a post he held for a decade. In the early 1930s he was increasingly engaged in patching up an arrangement between Lancashire interests and Japanese cotton-goods exporters.

Gwatkin's other ally was (Sir) George Sansom whom he described as a loyal, life-long friend.[23] Sansom had by this time a very high reputation as one of the world's experts in international trade. Yet he had chosen to stay in Japan rather than seek promotion in the hurly-burly of Whitehall. It was useful for him to have in the Office a man like Gwatkin who, in a time of anti-Japanese animus, shared at least some of Sansom's balanced views on Japan as a trading nation. Whether Gwatkin's preferment was due to the intervention of these two, the result was that he was entrusted with the setting up of an economic section within the Foreign Office with links to the Board of Trade. His first annual report – for 1932 – appeared in January 1933.[24] Gwatkin had to steer through the proposals; select the staff and arrange the supply of information from abroad. This all involved the study of methods employed by other foreign ministries around the world and by the League of Nations itself. It also involved foreign appointments. Thus, he served as one of Britain's delegates to the Imperial Conference at Ottawa in the summer of 1932 and as Foreign Office representative on the British delegation to the World Economic Conference in London in June of the following year.

Gwatkin's view in the summer of 1933 was that the economic situation in East Asia was among the most serious that he had to tackle. He felt that it was leading to the growth of '. . . an independent economic area and the determination of Japan to control that area. Our own Ottawa policy and the failure of the [1933] Economic Conference are likely to increase this tendency.'[25]

At the end of 1933 Gwatkin produced a memorandum on the economic position of Japan. It was one of a series prepared by the Far Eastern department, Gwatkin and the American department in connection with a new study of Britain's Far Eastern policy.[26] Gwatkin's assessment was as follows:

'In 1932, raw silk exports were for the first time passed by textile exports (as a group) as the principal export of Japan . . . In contrast to raw silk [which primarily went to the United States], the market for Japanese textiles is distributed all over the world. Japan's principal markets for textiles, viz., British India, Egypt, the Netherlands East Indies, are developing their own textile industries; and clearly intend to exclude Japanese imports in their own domestic interests. The maintenance of her textile markets is therefore a vital concern to Japan – a national interest as important as the retention of her hold on Manchuria.

The China market, which used to be the mainstay of this trade, is now (in part) permanently lost. Compensation has to be found in Manchukuo and in other foreign markets. Hence, the sudden Japanese commercial offensive which began in 1932. The invaded markets are (some of them) preparing for self-defence; and the first great battle has begun in British India – which is the most important of Japan's foreign markets . . .

The recent revival of the Japanese export trade did not begin until about August 1933, eight months after the reimposition of the gold order. In that month (owing to the "boomlet" in America) the price of raw silk shot up by over 50% above the preceding month; and from that time onward begins the intensive development of Japanese exports, which has led to increasing misgiving in foreign countries, especially in the British Empire.'[27]

If Gwatkin's analysis was alarming for Britain, it was objective and measured, when compared with the effusions of chambers of commerce and journalists. With these views the Foreign Office tried to moderate the tempestuous reactions of other ministries. Gwatkin was reestablished in his career, being made CMG in 1933 and becoming Counsellor in the following year.

The direct contact between Gwatkin and Japan probably ended in 1935. His work gradually came to concentrate on the affairs of central Europe. With the outbreak of war in 1939, his section was absorbed within the newly-created Ministry of Economic Warfare where his responsibility tended to be with wartime France. With the fall of France, however, he returned to the Foreign Office to become Principal Establishment and Finance Officer, succeeding in resurrecting for that office the title of 'Chief Clerk'. In this capacity, he was responsible for the post-war reorganization of the diplomatic service. On his return to London in 1919 he had published (anonymously) an essay on the need for some amalgamation of the consular with the diplomatic service. Now he had the opportunity to bring to fruition these earlier ideas in the wartime White Paper on Foreign Office reform.[28] He was also involved in the deliberations of the Scarbrough Committee, which, created in the last years of the war, reported to the government on the future of Oriental and African studies in 1947. This committee made seminal recommendations which led to the expansion of Japanese (among others) studies in British universities.

In 1944 Gwatkin was promoted to Senior Inspector of Diplomatic Missions with the rank of minister and later achieved the rank of assistant under-secretary.

POSTLUDE

After retirement in 1947 Ashton-Gwatkin devoted himself to Chatham House where he worked in conjunction with Arnold Toynbee and also spent time lecturing abroad, often on the fraught subject of appeasement in the 1930s. In that connection he published in 1949 a book on the British Foreign Service.[29] His link with Japan relied on a slender thread, the Japan Society of London. When the society was reconstituted in 1949, he became a foundation member of the council. At the special general meeting Sir Robert Craigie took over as chairman; and it was the task of Gwatkin to pay tribute to his predecessor, Sir Francis Lindley.

In the manner of Gwatkin's novels themselves, his life-long connection with Japan has a strange twist at the end. In 1971 the Emperor Hirohito paid a state visit to Britain on the fiftieth anniversary of his earlier visit to these islands. Gwatkin recounts the incident thus:

> 'And I was disinterred. Someone had discovered that I was still alive, the last survivor from the Emperor's last visit as Crown Prince in 1921. I like to think that this second journey was his own choosing, because he had liked our country then and wanted to see it once more and to show it to his Empress – a treat well-deserved after the appalling strains and stresses of his reign.'[30]

He had a special audience of the Emperor at Hampton Court Palace.

On the occasion of the Emperor's golden wedding anniversary, Gwatkin received an invitation to re-visit Japan. By the kindness of Japan Air Lines, *Yomiuri Shimbun* and Japan Travel Bureau he was able to return to haunts in Tokyo, Kamakura, Yokohama and Kyoto, that he had last seen fifty-five years earlier. His impressions are best expressed in his own words:

> 'I saw Tokyo (population now 10 million compared with 1 million in my day) where the geographical configuration is still the same – like an enormous spider's web spun round the central mystery of the Emperor's moated palace. All the rest of the city had been refashioned on quasi-American lines (the Coca-Cola period of Japanese architecture) with roadways and subways interwoven in tier over tier, impressive in its way and redeemed by the beauty of the

Japanese script. A city teeming like an anthill; and buzzing with taxis and private cars and lorries and omnibuses (the rickshaws and the clanking trams of my day have vanished). Very few men wear *kimono* now although they put them on with relief when they go home; but the women (of whom far more are now in circulation) have not entirely discarded their gracious national dress.'[31]

As this extract shows, Gwatkin was a witty writer and a born lecturer with a gift for the right phrase and the vivid image.

Gwatkin gave the Japan Society an account of his impressions under the title 'Japan Revisited' on 8 April 1975. He called it self-deprecatingly his 'fireside chat'.[32] It also proved to be his swansong. He died on 30 January 1976 at the age of 86.

Britain's Japanese experts come in many differing forms. The career of Frank Ashton-Gwatkin stands in interesting contrast to that of Sir George Sansom. Sansom managed to spend most of his working-life in Japan; Gwatkin only a fraction. Sansom became an eminent Japanologist; Gwatkin, in spite of his early immersion in the Japanese language, cannot claim to be a Japanologist but can lay claim to an expertise which came from his closeness to the centre of British decision-making on Japan for a long period. Although often critical of Japan, both have to be described as Japanophiles, that is, sympathetic to the Japanese people. As for Ashton-Gwatkin, if we may interpret some of the remarks of his poem, *A Japanese Don Juan*, as having an autobiographical content, he was able to identify with the Japanese:

> *Life is not measured by tale of days*
> *Or months or years, but by the experience*
> *We garner from our opportunities.*
> *For in one day have I lived many lives;*
> *And there are men – old, self-important men –*
> *Whose lives are not one day.*
> *Then farewell, Life!*
> *We have had good times together and rare sport;*
> *We have tasted pleasure, poetry and love;*
> *We have seen the beauty of the world, and feared*
> *Nothing – not even death. For we have chosen*
> *Our own way, and have won no small renown.*[33]

14

Yoshio Markino, 1869–1956

CARMEN BLACKER

PAINTER, writer, *anima candida*, philosopher in the true sense of the word, Makino Yoshio (1869–1956) lived in London for nearly half a century from 1897 to 1942. He painted misty and mysterious views of Edwardian London. He wrote four books of memoirs and philosophy in his own special style of English. He made friends with people from every walk of life. He was a Suffragette, ardently supporting the cause of Votes for Women. He fell in love, idealistically and platonically, with several English women. He would never have left England had it not been for the outbreak of the Second World War, and he was always hoping, however vainly, to come back.[1]

For years he suffered undeserved neglect. His paintings, once so admired, were forgotten, and his books, once so praised, were relegated to the shilling shelves of second-hand bookshops. But in the odd way that synchronicities assert themselves, interest in his work revived, suddenly and simultaneously, in both Britain and Japan. In Japan in 1990 a splendid exhibition of his work was mounted in Toyota city. Large crowds of people hitherto ignorant of his name and his work were enchanted by the beauty of his views of London, Oxford, Rome and Paris, which so vividly evoked the vanished atmosphere of the beginning of the century. In Britain his books have been reprinted, and a permanent gallery of his work established in London. He has been rediscovered after some seventy years as a painter and a personality of rare spiritual genius.[2]

Let me introduce him as I saw him in 1953, by a lucky chance, climbing slowly up the stone steps leading to Tokei-ji in

Kitakamakura. An old man in a battered panama hat, a shirt covered in smears of blue and green paint, and long white hair curling down to his shoulders, an unusual sight at that time. He carried a sketchbook in his hand, and frequently paused for breath as he climbed. At the top I caught him up and greeted him. In very nearly perfect English he told me that he had lived in England for forty-six years, and that his name was Yoshio Markino. I was able to tell him that I had seen one of his paintings, in General Piggott's house in Ewhurst, and one of his books.

From that moment the old man continued to talk torrentially for three-and-a-half hours, now in English, now in Japanese. He would rush at full speed up more steep flights of steps to look at the famous graves in Tokei-ji, and then to be too intent on what he was saying to notice who was buried there. He told me how happy he had been in London, and that he had never wanted to leave. He had had so many friends, and was never tired of sketching the people and painting the mists. He talked of Plato, and Captain Scott, and of his parents, who had married for love. This was why he always had such a romantic view of women. He was always in love. He had been a keen supporter of the Suffragettes too, at the beginning of the century, and Miss Christabel Pankhurst had given him her prisoner's dress. This prisoner's dress had been one of his treasures, but unfortunately he had had to leave it behind in a suitcase in the Japanese embassy in London when he was repatriated in 1942 after the outbreak of the war. In fact, he had had a little room in the embassy for two years, and during the bombing of London in 1940 he had climbed on to the embassy roof to watch the wonderful colours of the fires and exploding bombs, red and green and blue. Most people shut their eyes when a bomb exploded, but that was a pity.

Eventually, as it was getting dark, I escorted him home. He had a room in a little house just behind Kitakamakura station, a chaos of tubes of paint, brushes, odd pages of manuscript, an overturned basket of charcoal. The trains whistled piercingly as they passed the house.

I visited him there on several more occasions before returning to England as my studentship had expired. He would clap his hands when he saw me, and launch into further reminiscences and philosophizing. He was writing another volume of autobiography,[3] and asked me to look up certain points of information after I got back to England so that he could be sure of getting his facts and dates right. Would I find out the name of the Danish Consul in Rome in 1910? And would I enquire at the Foreign Office after the suitcase he had left behind in the Japanese embassy, and which had contained Christabel Pankhurst's prisoner's dress?[4] And finally, would I enquire after his best friend during his last years in London, Miss Betty Shephard?

I enquired at the Foreign Office, to be told that everything left behind in the Japanese embassy had been put up for auction, and that the suitcase had vanished without trace. But Betty Shephard was alive and living in London. She subsequently became one of my best friends, and her memories of Heiji, as he liked his friends to call him, fill a gap during a period for which there would otherwise be scant record.

BETTY SHEPHARD'S MEMORIES

Betty had first met him in 1928, at an exhibition of his watercolours at the Cottars Studio Gallery in Kensington, opened by the poet John Drinkwater. Heiji had come into the gallery beaming with smiles, with a paper bag in his hand full of slices of ham. These he ate in the gallery with immense pleasure, as though the ham was the most beautiful and delicious thing he had ever seen and tasted in his life. The visitors to the gallery were all very conventional, wearing their best clothes and even white gloves. But to Betty's amazement they were immediately won over by Heiji. He made them all laugh with him, and he made them see, as he did, that the slices of ham were just as interesting as the pictures. It was as though he had released something in all of them which was usually tightly buttoned up, and Betty herself perceived in him '. . . an absolutely calm feeling of security, and a capacity for being able to react to any situation with absolute truth'.[5] Their friendship had begun from that moment.

But his heyday, she told me, was during the early years of the century, when he had been a well-known figure in Edwardian London. He was invited to parties and 'At Homes', and to speak at clubs and to write articles in magazines, and of course to paint, to sketch and to illustrate books on the London scene. All this he had described in his book, *A Japanese Artist in London*, 1910, and this I lost no time in reading. In his own inimitable and special English he had a tale to tell first of abject poverty, then of sudden glamorous success in Edwardian London.

MAKINO IN LONDON

He arrived in England in 1897 after four miserable years in America. After America, he wrote, England seemed like paradise. Newhaven seemed like New Heaven. People were polite and friendly to him. They did not mock and jeer, or throw stones at him, or spit at him, or smash his paintbox, as they had done in San Francisco. He did not have to become a domestic slave to a tyrannous housewife in order to earn a pittance to take him to an art school. He did not wash dishes or windows, or make false teeth for dentists, or live off the hunks of bread the art school provided for charcoal drawing. No one seemed to swear, and when he sat down next to ladies in buses, they did not at once move to another seat.[6]

In London he got a job in the office of the Japanese Naval Attaché, who was busy with the warships that Japan had ordered to be built in British shipyards. For a while he was in clover, with enough money to take him to an art school in the evenings, and Japanese friends such as Yone Noguchi with whom he could discuss literature and art, and a kind landlord in Greenwich called Mr Watson, with '. . . such a benevolent-looking face, like that famous picture of Sir John Millais' "Victory, O Lord" '.[7]

But soon all the warships that Japan had ordered from Britain were finished, and he found himself out of a job. His friends warned him that he would have a hard time earning his living as an artist in London, but he was determined after a sleepless night to reject the comfortable life. He was in for another period of poverty verging on pennilessness. 'From that moment,' he wrote, 'I did not laugh heartily for eight long years.'[8]

He moved his lodgings several times to cheaper and humbler addresses and there are no more touching passages in this endearing book than those which record the kindness of his poor landladies. They brushed his clothes and tidied his drawers and mended his socks. When he had not even a penny to buy food, they let him share their own. When he had no money to pay the rent, they said, 'Pay us when you are more prosperous'. Some

177

even lent him money from their own savings boxes. They were always scrupulously repaid whenever he managed to earn a few shillings.

One of his landlords was a blacksmith in Kensal Rise, who had to keep a wife and four children on £2 a week. 'They had such a sweet home, if poor,' he wrote. 'Many rich peoples ought to be ashamed before them if they saw such sweet harmony in their devotion to each other.'[9]

He engaged a very small room in this house for three shillings and sixpence a week, a sum which was intended to include both lunch and supper. But when his last penny was gone and he could not afford to pay the rent, he could not bear to go back and eat their food. On such days he had no more for lunch or supper than a drink of water from the street fountains.

With no money for a tram, he would walk from Kensal Rise to the City to try to sell his sketches. But no editor wanted them. Every evening his landlady was eager to hear 'happy news', and it cut him to the heart to have to report failures to her day after day.

'She often showed me her tears and said, "Never mind about your debts to us, but I am sorry for your hard life".' And, 'Mr Markino, please take this tea, as a pleasure to me. I cannot bear to see you working so hard without tea.' And they both said to him: 'We have never seen a man so honest and diligent. God bless you. Believe us you will be all right some day soon.'[10]

Another friend was Mr Bax, a tailor in Milner Street, whom for five years he could not pay for the suit he had ordered during his prosperous legation days. Fred, Bax's son, meeting him again after five years, was shocked to see how ragged and seedy his clothes had become, and despite the five-year debt, offered to make him another suit.

'No, my dear Fred, my debts to you have already been a heavy burden on my heart. How could I double my debt to you?' he cried. Fred, with remarkable tact and kindness, suggested that they make him a suit in exchange for some pictures, and went to consult his father. In an hour he came back 'with such a bright expression' and said: 'My father wants three pictures of yours. For these we shall cancel our £5 debt against you. Besides that we shall make one lounge suit and overcoat, and here I bring you the cash of £2 to make the balance for all.' The extra £2 he gave to his landlady, who after long discussion agreed to accept one pound and fifteen shillings.

'Nowadays,' he added in 1910, 'when I go to his shop to order some clothes I always look at those three pictures hanged on his room and I recollect his kindness to me when I was so poor.'[11]

For three weeks he got a job as a model wearing Japanese costume at the Goldsmith Institute, an art school. Then he made designs for tombstones at a workshop near Norwood cemetery. But customers complained that his angels looked too much like ballet girls, so he lost this job after only three months.[12]

Then, one magic day, just as he was on the verge of suicide, his luck turned. He called at the offices of the *Magazine of Art*, where to his amazement the editor, kind Mr M.H. Spielmann, accepted his drawings, paid him handsomely, encouraged him to draw, to paint and write, and proceeded to introduce him to a wide circle of literary and influential friends.

Spielmann himself described the encounter some years later:

'A few years ago there appeared in the doorway of my room a young Japanese with a portfolio under his arm. He looked tired and pale, but as he smiled and bowed . . . I was struck with his quiet dignity, his air of self-respect, his lustrous intelligent eyes. Would I look at his drawings of London? Yes, willingly. Opening his portfolio he showed me a bright and luminous drawing of the exterior of Marylebone Church on a warm moist day, the buildings and the atmospheric effect altogether admirable, the figures . . . so simple in a manner as to suggest a Japanese colour print. I was charmed with the combination so artlessly and sincerely evolved, and I looked at others . . . I promised him I would have them published in the *Magazine of Art*, and I bought one or two. His eyes danced, but no other sign of pleasure did he give, his natural dignity seeming to forbid any marked demonstration of satisfaction . . . Yet at the time, as he told me afterwards, he was in the direst straits as regards ways and means.'[13]

It was this gentle and kind art critic who rescued him from penury and suicide, and launched him into a world which eagerly acclaimed his painting and loved him for the childlike honesty of his personality.

One of the influential friends to whom Spielmann introduced him was Douglas Sladen, the author of *Queer Things about Japan*, and the editor of *Who's Who*. Sladen was a master of that civilized, yet unaccountably vanished, occasion, the literary 'At

Home'. He gave huge tea parties in his large Kensington house, to which he invited a galaxy of writers, poets and painters. Makino was a great success at such gatherings, and lost no opportunity of sketching the guests. With several of these sketches Douglas Sladen illustrated his book of reminiscences. We see here lightning portraits of Conan Doyle, Jerome K. Jerome and Israel Zangwill. Also watercolour impressions of Sladen's luxurious house, which boasted a Moorish Room and even a Japanese Room decorated with a strange clutter of jars, lanterns and miniature *torii*.[14]

Douglas Sladen also gave him an entry in *Who's Who*, alongside the distinguished and great in the land. His name appeared in *Who's Who* for thirty-three years, from 1916 until 1949, a privilege he claimed to share only with the Emperor and the Japanese ambassador. His books are duly listed, and his recreation stated to be 'Reading the ancient Chinese, Latin and Greek Classics in order to forget the modern civilization.'

WRITINGS AND SKETCHES

Commissions now began to flow in. He was invited to illustrate W.J. Loftie's *The Colour of London* (1907), and to contribute an introductory essay. Later commissions followed for similar picture books on Paris, Rome and Oxford.[15] Spielmann encouraged him to write his life story, and the result was the enchanting *Japanese Artist in London* (1910). Next came the story of his childhood in Japan, *When I was a Child* (1912), which includes an account of his unhappy years in America. The following year another book, entitled *My Idealed John Bullesses* described his romantic feelings for Edwardian women.

The Colour of London and the *Japanese Artist* contain some of his famous misty views of London. For it was mist or even fog, which by lending mystery to a scene, by giving a sense of something hidden and secret yet close, specially appealed to him. 'I went into the study of London mists,' he wrote. 'One evening I started from my place about 9 o'clock and enjoyed myself in fogs until I felt my feet so tired that I came to my conscience. The more I observed the mists the more I fell in love . . .'[16] So much in love with mist was he that he succeeded triumphantly in transforming, as Whistler put it, '. . . warehouses, shot towers and factory chimneys into castles, palaces and campanili'.

His pictures always started as quick sketches in the London streets. He would rush about, running after cabs to see how the horses' legs moved, and so intent that he would knock into lamp posts and people. These sketches he would bring home, and there ruminate on them until the ideal picture presented itself to his mind, a scene in which mist and mystery were intriguingly combined with the clear crisp brightness of an *ukiyoe*.

In *The Colour of London* it is clear that he was prepared to go and look anywhere, high or low, for the beauty he sought to capture. Here, for example, we see a scene of Tea on the Terrace of the House of Commons; an elegant company, the gentlemen in black, the ladies in white or pale yellow, with a misty Westminster Bridge in the background against a rose and yellow sky. Here on the other hand is a different group, of people in a street dancing boisterously to the music of a barrel organ. Here again is Piccadilly Circus, with flower-sellers sitting on the steps of the Eros statue behind wicker-baskets and clumps of red flowers. Here is the *Inaba Maru* in the Albert Docks. Here is the Elephant at the Zoo, standing in a pale unearthly brightness wearing a red saddle and surrounded by white children. Here the Chelsea Power Works is transformed into a group of castellate towers reflected in a rose and grey river. And here the steps of the Albert Memorial become a scene from a legend, in which small figures climb white marble steps towards a frieze of statues that seem to stand on some high and barely accessible eminence. It was said that he had the ability to put 'air' into his pictures. One critic, indeed, compared him to Turner in the success with which he filled his water colour pictures with air.

In the book about the John Bullesses, we have examples of the quick sketches with which he always began his pictures, like notes for a book. Again it is clear that he was prepared to go anywhere, that he dared to penetrate any fastness, to observe these goddesses and transfer them to paper. He caught them outside theatres, elegantly dressed in silken 'wraps' with enormous fur collars, being handed out of carriages by men in top hats and white ties. He caught them playing hockey or croquet or golf; or walking in the driving rain; or punting on the Thames under willow trees. He even dared to go into a fashionable milliner's shop to observe them trying on the huge hats of the period in front of a mirror. Other women, less fashionable, he caught with equal felicity washing piles of dishes, ironing clothes, or queuing for stewed eels.

He was full of sympathy for the Suffragettes, and published an article in the *English Review* saying how odd it was that Englishmen should open doors for ladies, hand them out of carriages, pick up their handkerchiefs, give their seats to them on trams – and yet deny them the vote simply because they were women, and underpay them so much that men were done out of a job.[17] He sat on the platform in the Albert Hall at Suffragette meetings alongside Mrs Pankhurst and her two redoubtable daughters, and observed their 'picturesque and poetic procession', with bands and floats, through London on 27 June 1911. He sketched them endlessly, slim determined figures in the hobble skirts of 1911 and 1912, the huge hats worn with a dash which he brilliantly conveys, and the diagonal sash bearing the legend *Votes for Women*.

His fourth book, *My Recollections and Reflections* (1913), is a miscellany of thoughts on art and philosophy, spiritual wisdom and reminiscence. He writes of dreams and ghosts, of actors and friends, and moonlight at Wedhampton near Salisbury Plain. Also of his old schoolmaster, Mr Iinuma, who once said to him:

> 'This world is false. I am afraid you shall be disappointed with it. But in this false world there exists the Truth, almost like the miracles. You shall be lucky if you can find it out, for it will make your whole life perfectly happy.'[18]

He writes also of his own remarkable visual memory. He could call up in his mind's eye the pages of books he read as a boy so vividly that he could 'read them off' from the visual image.[19] He could also hold in his mind's eye a clear and distinct image of a landscape until he got home and was able to transfer the image to paper. To hold the details of the scene in his mind's eye, Betty Shephard told me, he would sometimes cover his face with his hands. On one occasion, indeed, he was on his way home in a bus after beholding such a scene that he wanted to retain. The lady sitting next to him thought he must have toothache and commiserated with him. 'Oh no,' he replied, 'I am just "holding in" my picture.'

The reviewers were, one and all, kind to his books. They said he had shown us beauty and colour in corners of London which normally we would never have noticed. He had succeeded

Lafcadio Hearn as the chief interpreter of Japan to the Anglo-Saxon nations. But he was better than Hearn because as a Japanese he could unveil mysteries necessarily hidden from a foreigner like Hearn. He had shown us that simplicity and profundity were closely akin, and he made us feel on almost every page that our own experiences had been enriched.

They praised his soft opalescent lights, his '. . . grey tones with muffled undertones of rose and yellow, vivid impressions of flying moments of rare beauty transferred straight from the soul to the canvas'. They praised his delicate and truthful brushwork, and the sense of wonder he imparted to familiar scenes.

His special English, too, won many admirers. It was praised for its 'curious freshness of phrase', for its 'wonderfully effective secret all of its own', which conveyed with seeming artlessness truths we had forgotten or neglected. 'We hope,' *The Times* remarked in 1912, 'that Mr Markino's English will never get better; for as it gets better it will certainly get worse.'

Indeed, there is an undeniably special quality about his use of English. Translate or transpose it into conventional language and it goes dead-pan, its character gone. How inimitable, for example, is the pathos with which he describes his friend Yone Noguchi's departure from London: 'I went to see him off at Paddington Station and I saw that his eyes were much inflammated with tears.'

This happy heyday in the high Edwardian period ended abruptly with the outbreak of the First World War. Among the million men that England lost in that holocaust were many of Makino's friends. He found himself no longer able to sketch in the London streets, because anyone seen sketching was suspected of being a German spy. The Suffragettes all became nurses and munition workers. So he retired to his lodgings and learned Greek, living on rice and Bovril, and 'wearing out' two Greek dictionaries. By the end of the war he had learned enough Greek to read Plato, whom he always held in special reverence as a bridge between East and West.[20]

In the changed scene which dawned with the 1920s he found that he was barely remembered, and that his paintings were no longer appreciated. Once again, therefore, he was poor, living from hand to mouth. But he was always confident that he would never starve. He told Betty Shephard that he was like a bird which, when it was hungry, would simply sit stock still with its mouth wide open. Very soon, sure enough, insects would fly inside.

FRIENDSHIPS

He continued to idealize women, so that it is surprising to find that in the spring of 1922 he went so far as to get married. A French girl, whose name seems to have been Marie Byron, wrote to him to say that she had read his book *A Japanese Artist in London*, that she was in great trouble from an unkind stepmother, and felt that Makino was the one person who could help her. He wrote telling her to call if she liked, but that he would not have much time to devote to her as he was very busy on a picture. She came and poured out her troubles for a couple of hours, during which he continued to paint his picture. At length he said to her, 'You see that I am too busy with this picture to have much time to help you, but I'll marry you if you think that would do any good.' She went away to consider the proposal, and the next day came back to say, yes, she would like to marry him very much.[21]

So, marry they did, in London on 16 April 1922. But Heiji was too idealistic, too platonic and too spiritual in his view of women to make a very good husband. The union was apparently a *marriage blanc*. But, when he went to America the following year, she accompanied him, and there apparently found a more suitable partner. A perfectly harmonious divorce was arranged in 1927.

Betty Shephard believed that he was always looking for the perfect woman, with whom his soul could accomplish a perfect union. The body was much less important. And he was always imagining that he had found this perfect woman, from whom he could draw the inspiration and energy necessary for his work.

She recalled that in the late 1930s, when Heiji was in his late 60s, he believed that he had found this ideal woman in the person of a quite, demure Italian girl whose father kept a café in Duke Street, much frequented by taxi drivers and sellers of newspapers. He christened her Divina, and would spend hours every day in the café writing at one of the tables, so that he could look up at any time and see his adored Divina carrying cups of tea and sandwiches to the taxi drivers. Often he would lecture the taxi drivers about art and philosophy, especially about Ruskin's *Stones of Venice*. It did not worry him at all that they understood almost nothing of it. Every Saturday evening he would scrub the café floor, by way of humble service to Divina.[22]

Divina wrote to him after the war, and he wrote back in February 1947 a letter which still carries his old artless pathos:

> 'How often I have dreamed about you all, sometime very happy jolly sometime sad. In my dream I often said to myself "This time it could not be a dream but must be reality", and how disappointed I was when I found myself in bed in Japan. Even now I often said "This is Oxford Street. It could not be a dream!" Well let us hope the reality will come soon in future.'[23]

His other great friend during this period was Shigemitsu Mamoru, the Japanese ambassador in London from 1938 until almost the outbreak of war. Their friendship dated back to earlier days when Shige had been a young attaché, and they had met at an eel restaurant in London. Shige was wonderfully kind to him, giving him a small room in the Japanese embassy after the war with Germany started in 1939, and the air raids and bombing of London began. Into this room Heiji moved with his cat, his paints and his books, and Betty recalled how often all three of them would have Sunday lunch together, or supper of an evening, joined sometimes by the painter Edmund Dulac or the novelist Charles Morgan.

Shige also gave Heiji £300 to open an account at the Yokohama Specie Bank, advising him to buy himself some new clothing. He bought himself no less than forty pairs of socks, because the shop said they were a bargain, and a black velvet suit from Horne Brothers, with a black velvet hat to match, reminiscent of the one Rembrandt wears in his self-portraits. The beauty of this suit was soon marred, alas, by a layer of cigarette ash which reduced the rich black to a pale grey.

He had another unusual accomplishment; he was a master of the *I Ching*. Little or nothing was known outside sinological circles of this ancient classic at the time; neither Richard Wilhelm's translation nor John Blofeld's book had yet appeared, and it was only when Jung came to London and lectured on the *I Ching* that Betty realized that the work was known to others except Heiji and herself. Heiji spent many evenings transmitting his entire knowledge to her, one hexagram at a time which she was to memorize, with the happy outcome that for the rest of her life she found herself able to give wise guidance through this means to friends in trouble or perplexity.

Heiji eventually committed some of his knowledge to writing, in the form of a letter of nearly a hundred pages of faded blue typing. He is as usual most eloquent on matters of Love and Marriage. For hexagram 31, for example, Mountain under Lake, he says of the prospects for love:

> 'Here when the whole loves the whole they become Non-Ego, what I always call "Dipping in God". Just sit in silence, whose happiness is greater than partial excitement . . . But suppose it changes to Mountain under Heaven, it means although you are now holding Love with your mountain, it would be evaporated or leaked, then your mountain will turn into a baren monastry (sic) or convent.'[24]

Another of his gifts, Betty recalled, was a close sympathy and communion with trees. If a problem arose he would say: 'I'll go and ask the trees.' The trees would give him the 'feel' of the way things should go. Sometimes he would say: 'Yes, the trees are happy today; it will be all right.' And at others he could see from the sad and 'shrivelled' look that the trees conveyed to him that some disaster had taken place in nature, perhaps many miles away.

Heiji was repatriated to Japan in 1942 with other Japanese nationals and it was not until after the war that anything was heard of him again in England. Then Betty Shephard had a long letter entitled 'My news to Betty, Divina and all the families of you both'. He wrote of the wonderful kindness of Shigemitsu, who had taken him to Nanking for seven months, and also to Peking, and of his shock at the sight of the Japanese army in China.

> 'So many ugliest Japanese soldiers were marching over the town so haughtily and arrogantly . . . These soldiers are the Oceanic cannibals. There were no Chinese girls in Nanking because this army had chopped off 6000 Chinese citizens, binding them with wire and dragging them to the shore of the Yangtse River etc etc.'

He added a revealing sketch of the face of one such soldier. In London he had never believed the reports of Japanese atrocities.

'Now I must apologize to you that all the English papers said was absolutely true . . .'

Shigemitsu had subsequently taken Heiji into his house in Tokyo, where they escaped a terrible bombing raid by taking refuge in the moat surrounding the Imperial Palace. He wrote:

> 'The oil bombs fell down all over our house. I sent Mrs and Miss Shigemitsu away to a safe place, and Atsushi and I stayed in the house till the last moment. Then 15 fierce bombs came down at once and we had such a narrow escape rushing out through the fire and coming down the burning staircases. On that night we stayed on the bank of the foss around the Imperial Palace which burned down too.'[25]

POSTWAR YEARS

The Shigemitsu family had then taken Heiji to their house in Kamakura. But in 1948 Shigemitsu, at the insistence of the Russians, was condemned as a war criminal and imprisoned in Sugamo Gaol. In 1949 Heiji wrote to say that to some extent he was lucky, for at least he was given three meals a day and some heating in winter, whereas the Shigemitsu family and himself were virtually starving, with next to no food and no fuel in winter. In February 1947 he wrote to Divina:

> 'The ration for me is one slice of toasted bread for breakfast two pieces for luncheon and one small boal of rice and a litle vegetable for supper. I have become ever so thin and look old. Never mind, as soon as I get enough fat of meat I shall rejuvinate myself at once . . . Just now it is very cold, 7 degrees below zero, with no fire whatever. I wear three suits of wool underwears and three jumpers and coat and two pairs of trousers. I feel quite warm. Only my hand is freezing, but the spring is coming to warm me up. Please forgive my pencil as it is very difficult to get ink.'[26]

Betty thereupon exerted herself, and wrote innumerable letters to high placed persons. One of these, addressed to Frank Ashton-Gwatkin, eventually came to the eyes of Joseph Grew, the former American ambassador in Tokyo. With great and imaginative generosity, he wrote to say that he was distressed to hear of the destitution of the Shigemitsu family, and that he would arrange for some of the money due to him as royalties from the Japanese edition of his book *Ten Years in Japan* to be used for the support of the family and Heiji. Their plight thereafter became less distressing.

In 1950 Shigemitsu was released on parole by General MacArthur; but he was still 'purged', which meant that he continued to be deprived of civil rights and unable to earn a living. He was not 'depurged' until March 1952.

Meanwhile Heiji had vanished from the Shigemitsu house in Kamakura, and for some time none of his friends knew what had become of him. Shigemitsu wrote to Betty in April 1952 that, to their great disappointment, Heiji had left to stay with a 'Japanese family with no good reputation' for several months. 'His behaviour has not been altogether respectable'.[27]

But in December 1955 a short article appeared in the *Asahi* newspaper by the novelist Takami Jun, which reported that the painter Makino Yoshio, or *Kiri-no-Heiji* as he was nicknamed owing to his affection for mists, had at last been discovered after being for three years *yukue-fumei*, whereabouts unknown. All the time, unbeknown to anyone, he had been living close by in Kitakamakura, presumably in the house where I visited him in 1953. The reason that his whereabouts were now known was that the poor old man had collapsed through poverty, malnutrition and weakness, and that the neighbours had put him into hospital. Contributions towards his welfare and hospital expenses came pouring in, and he seems to have made a brief recovery. But it was to be a brief one only, and in October 1956 he died in the Akizuki hospital in Kamakura.

Betty Shephard used to say of him that he saw the world with always new eyes, as a child sees something for the first time and finds it marvellously exciting and beautiful. Every experience that came to him he lived with these new eyes, in which ordinary humdrum things became wonderful. At the same time he had a courtesy and dignity of personality all his own. He was a spiritually free person, free of the attachments to things which are most people's prison.

One of the marks of spiritually-free persons is that they have no *persona*, that face or mask which we present to the world and which we wish the world to believe is our real nature. The *persona* is never real. It is always a mask, hiding aspects of ourselves of which we are not aware, and least of all would like the world to know about. When we meet someone with no *persona* we instantly recognize in him a quality of genuineness, of immediate warmth and sympathy which evokes love and affection as a natural reaction. Heiji had no mask, and that may be part of the reason why everyone loved him.

It is good after so many years of neglect his genius has once more come to the recognition it deserves. It is deserved not only for his work, but for himself, and for the qualities I have tried to describe which made him such a rare and blithe spirit.

15

The Mingei Movement and Bernard Leach

SIR HUGH CORTAZZI

THE MINGEI MOVEMENT was founded in Japan at a meeting on Koya-san in 1926 by Yanagi Sōetsu (1889–1961, also known as Muneyoshi, the *kun* reading of Sōetsu), Hamada Shōji (1894–1978) and Kawai Kanjirō (1890–1966). The main practical result of this decision was the establishment of the Mingeikan (The Folk Art Museum) at Komaba in Tokyo and the publication of a monthly magazine devoted to mingei called *Kōgei*. Bernard Leach (1887–1976) was in England at that time and was not directly involved in the decision to start the movement, but he was a close friend of all three founders and his influence especially on Yanagi and Hamada was significant. He can accordingly be regarded as one of the inspirers of the Mingei movement and played an important role in its development of Japan, in Britain and elsewhere. His work as an artist-craftsman was also of major significance in reviving the art of hand-made pottery in Western countries. In recognition of this, he was given the Japan Foundation award for 1974.

Mingei is short for *minshuteki kōgei* which may be translated as popular craft. Yanagi Sōetsu defined mingei in the following way:

> 'Mingei is a new word . . . Etymologically, it has the sense of "the art of the common classes". In fact, I conceive it in opposition to the art of the aristocracy. The functional objects that common people use in everyday life are called *mingeihin*, which can be abbreviated to *minki* (utensils of the people). Objects of daily life – clothes, furniture, tableware,

and writing implements – fall into this category . . . Mingei consequently have two characteristics: the first is functionality, and the second is ordinariness. In other words, objects that are luxurious, expensive, and made in very small numbers do not belong to this category. The makers of mingei objects are not famous people but anonymous craftspeople.'[1]

Yanagi had rummaged through the antique markets of Kyoto collecting what were termed *getemono* (literally, simple ware or folk ware) which might now be called bric-à-brac items made by hand. These items would in future be called *mingeihin*.

Yanagi Sōetsu was the philosopher and aesthetic interpreter of the movement. Hamada Shōji and Kawai Kanjirō were above all potters of outstanding merit. Yanagi's philosophy can most easily be studied by the reader of English through Bernard Leach's translation of Yanagi's writings contained in *The Unknown Craftsman: A Japanese Insight into Beauty*.[2]

Yanagi's philosophy is concerned with art as he saw it. It is not always wholly consistent or logical in the Western sense. It is an amalgam of ideas derived from oriental and Western sources adapted and expanded by Yanagi himself to explain his advocacy of mingei. He believed that 'beauty' was a moral quality. He asked: '. . . might not beauty, and the love of the beautiful, perhaps bring peace and harmony?'[3] He asserted that '. . . an object is truly beautiful because it belongs to the Eternal Now. All art movements tend to the pursuit of novelty, but the true essence of beauty can exist only where the distinction between the old and the new has been eliminated. The Sung dynasty pottery of China reveals a beauty that is forever new, that is still alive today.'[4] He also believed that the Mingei movement was a '. . . spiritual movement . . . The Folk Craft Movement cannot be said to exist without its ethical and spiritual aspects . . . A craftsman is first and foremost a human being, and as a human being his life has to be founded on spirituality . . . Beauty cannot exist unless it contains elements of truth, goodness and holiness.'[5]

For Yanagi (as for William Morris – see below) objects must be useful. When he was asked what was the particular kind of beauty in crafts, Yanagi's response was: 'Beauty that is identified with use. It is beauty born of use. Apart from use there is no beauty of craft.'[6]

Mingei objects were essentially the product of anonymous

craftsmen. Yanagi pointed out: 'Once we realize that a piece of Sung pottery is not the product of some individual genius but rather of the non-individualist power of tradition, we understand that its beauty is not personal and there is no need, therefore, to question who its maker was.'[7] This suggested that he denied the importance of personality in crafts. Yanagi rejected this saying: 'To negate personality is an error; however, to remain satisfied with personality is yet a greater error. There is a beauty that emerges from individual art, but it is not the purest. In the case of a really great individual, the greatness lies in his having gone beyond his individualism . . . Stress on individualism is totally unsatisfactory; on the other hand, where do we find beauty without individualism? Having no individuality and transcending it – these two issues must not be confused. The virtue of folkcrafts is that one feels no obtruding personality in them. The thing shines, not the maker. Consider Persian rugs; one feels their beauty before any question arises as to who made them.'[8] There are, he noted, '. . . individual artists who dismiss as unimportant traditional crafts and craftsmen. I wonder why their own work is so poor. If they had the eyes to see with and the will to ponder over what they saw, instead of exhibiting arrogance or mere learning, the situation would be different.'[9] Humility was in his view an essential quality in a great artist.

Yanagi stressed that: 'The beauty of folkcraft is the kind that comes from dependence on the Other Power.'[10] The word for other-power *tariki* is contrasted with *jiriki* or self-power. *Tariki* is a Buddhist concept but has something of the meaning of the Christian term 'grace'.

Another essential element in Yanagi's aesthetic was his attachment to the concept of innocence and his rejection of intellectualism and artificiality. 'In works created by primitive peoples many are tremendously vital, reflecting the primitive power of man. It follows, therefore, that even if a man lacks high intelligence or advanced technique, he can still produce objects that are beautiful although they may at the same time be unskilled. The reason such objects so very often deserve our love is that in them the maker's inherent Buddhahood is revealed to the observer. It is noteworthy that both Jesus and Laotze adored the innocence of children.'[11]

Yanagi had to a very high degree that quality which the Japanese call *mekiki* which may perhaps be translated as 'the seeing eye' i.e. an intuitive ability to recognize the good from the bad, the beautiful from the ugly. Not everyone has this quality but Yanagi believed that it could be acquired if only with difficulty:

'When I am asked for a Buddhist explanation of the perception of beauty, my answer is a simple one: "one must discard one's self". But, of course the process is not easily accomplished; grasping the reality of beauty is no easier. In looking at objects, a man makes sure of this intelligence; he evaluates on the basis of his own conceptions, he passes judgement on the basis of his own experience. In so doing, "I" become the master pronouncing on the "object", which I regard as my guest. Since one's self does not disappear in this process, "I" and "it" remain two different entities; no union between the two occurs.'

He believed that: 'To be unable to *see* beauty properly is to lack the basic foundation for any aesthetic understanding'.[12] 'Beauty is a kind of mystery, which is why it cannot be grasped adequately by the intellect.'

Another important element in Yanagi's aesthetic philosophy was his emphasis on the *shibui*. The nearest English adjectives for shibui are '. . . "austere", "subdued" and "restrained" but to the Japanese the word is more complex, suggesting quietness, depth, simplicity, and purity. The beauty it describes is introversive, the beauty of the inner radiance.'[13] The Japanese preference for the *shibui* is not, of course, confined to mingei but is a part of a long Japanese tradition in art and literature.

Yanagi also saw great attraction and beauty in the imperfect or the irregular. He wrote:

'The precise and perfect carries no overtones, admits of no freedom; the perfect is static and regulated, cold and hard. We in our own human imperfections are repelled by the perfect, since everything is apparent from the start and there is no suggestion of the infinite.'[14]

Yanagi was fascinated by patterns. He considered that: 'A good pattern is pregnant with beauty. The maker of a pattern draws the essence of the thing seen with his own heartbeat, life to life. . . Pattern is not realistic depiction. It is a "vision" of what is reflected by the institution. It is a product of the imagination.' 'Since pattern is a portrayal of essence, all non-essentials must be stripped away; the pattern is what remains . . . Good patterns are simple; if they are cluttered they are not yet patterns. The kind of pattern I am speaking of is not primarily decorative; it comes of Zen emptiness, of *mu* "void", of "thusness". The more the significance contained in a pattern, the more its vitality. In its placidity there must be movement.'[15] Leach in his book *Beyond East and West*[16] has commented that:

> 'Pattern – in the old sense of folk dance, or melody, a few sounds, or movements, or colours reduced to an ultimate simplicity or related and evocative elements – has almost vanished with the weakening of the vitality and close-to-nature country life. Now we have become so intellectualized that this stream of common beauty has dried up.'

The oriental influence on Yanagi's philosophy is at once obvious. His writings contain much about Buddhism. For instance in the chapter on 'The Buddhist Idea of Beauty' in *The Unknown Craftsman*[17] Yanagi points out that: 'from the Buddhist's point of view, the "beauty" that simply stands opposed to ugliness is not true beauty. It is no more than a relativistic, dualistic idea . . . In the *Muryōju-kyō* ("Sutra of Eternal Life"), the following statement is attributed to the Buddha: "If in the land of the Buddha there remains the distinction between the beautiful and the ugly, I do not desire to be a Buddha of such a land." '

Dr Suzuki Daisetsu (1870–1966), the famous interpreter of Zen Buddhism to the Western world, was a close friend of both Yanagi and Leach. Yanagi had also been a pupil of Suzuki at the Gakushūin (Peers School). Suzuki was not, however, solely an exponent of Zen. He also supported the beliefs of the followers of Jōdo-Shinshū Buddhism. Leach[18] wrote of Suzuki's teaching:

> 'Of Buddhism, he said to me, the objective was the state of mind which lies beyond dualism, but which can employ either approach without attachment. Of Zen and Shin [i.e. Shinshū], representing the way of individual endeavour and the humble road of self-forgetting, respectively, he remarked that the apparently different ways meet at the top of the hill. The narrow way of individualism of the genius, and usually the artist, is full of pitfalls and self-deception, he said, whereas the broad path of humility and reliance on "other Power" (*Tariki Do* in Japanese), reliance on "Amida", or on "Oya Sama" (the nearest Buddhist

equivalent to our concept of God), shed our self-bound propensity proportionately to the giving. Yanagi carries this idea to the modern craftsman.'

Like most Japanese thinkers Yanagi was eclectic and absorbed Confucian, Taoist and Shinto ideas. But Buddhism and, in particular, Zen were the predominant oriental elements in this thinking. Zen led him to the tea ceremony (*Cha-no-yu*). In the chapter entitled 'The Way of Tea' in *The Unknown Craftsman* Yanagi wrote:[19]

'Everything that concerns Tea, to say nothing of the utensils in particular, is related to craftsmanship . . . Isolated from craftsmanship, Tea cannot maintain its way. To apprehend beauty in crafts and crafts in beauty that is the characteristic of Tea . . . The way of Tea is the aestheticism of craftsmanship.'

Later in the same chapter he wrote:[20] 'Harmony, reverence, purity, and the serenity are the inculcated traditional principles of Tea . . . *Tea is a religion of beauty.*'

Yanagi's aestheticism was not based, however, simply on the philosophies of Buddhism and Tea. He was a collector of beautiful things. In particular he loved the pots of the Yi dynasty in Korea and '. . . had a great sympathy for Korea, its people and its arts.'[21] Yanagi went to Korea many times and Leach recorded[22] that:

'After the occupation of Korea, the heavy hand of Japanese militarism fell upon The Land of Morning Calm. It became unsafe to raise a voice in protest, but Yanagi, an anti-militarist, went to Seoul and started a small museum in one of the old palace buildings, where Japanese and Koreans could meet in the common enjoyment of Korean art, leaving politics aside and thereby avoiding possible offence to the government.'

Leach[23] said of Korean pots that they were '. . . naive . . . in the good sense of the word.' He compared a Korean pot made for rice and costing 'less than a penny' with one of his own with a market value of 'about seventy-five dollars':

'Mine is quite pretty, and I do not think it is bad, but the Korean one was born; mine has been made . . . When I compare the Korean pot with mine I say that the Korean pot is better: it has warmth. That warmth is there because there is no ego: we do not feel any egotism on the part of the maker.'

Chinese wares, especially Sung pots, were another source of inspiration to Yanagi. He explained[24] that: 'The beauty of China's Sung pottery, then, is an instance of the goal attained by following the Easy Way, the way of reliance on grace.' He noted that: 'Sung ware is not a manifestation of the individual personality of the maker: that lies submerged beneath the surface, while the article itself stands out. Sung potters were working in a world where identity is not of importance.' The fact that 'much Sung ware is decorated with superbly drawn pictures' did not mean that they were drawn by great artists; '. . . the job was performed by boys around the age of ten, children of poor families, many of whom no doubt disliked the work and had to be forced by their parents to do it.' 'To the craftsman tradition is both the saviour and the benefactor.'

YANAGI AND LEACH

Oriental influences and inspiration such as have been described above were matched by much that Yanagi absorbed from the West, to a considerable extent with the help of Bernard Leach. Leach recalled[25] that he first met Yanagi in the spring of 1910 at a Tokyo exhibition mainly of German art, arranged by the Shirakaba (silver birch) society of which Yanagi had been a founding member[26] and became the editor of the society journal. At first Leach took a dislike to Yanagi's enthusiasm for German art which was, he felt, at the expense of the French Impressionists. Then one night at a gathering in Yanagi's house they opened a parcel of large and fine German colour reproductions of paintings by Cezanne and van Gogh:

> '. . . the first to reach Japan. Amazement was followed by excited talk. From that room and the pages of *Shirakaba* enthusiasm spread all over Japan. I, English and in my early twenties, was enthralled by the classicism of the one and the burning romanticism of the other.'

Leach noted[27] that Yanagi and his fellow enthusiasts on the Shirakaba:

> '. . . searched the horizons of Western Art and thought, ancient and modern. Progressively educated, but tradition-

ally Oriental, they selected and reappraised our artists and authors from, let us say, Giotto as an artist and Meister Eckhart as a mystic, through the High Renaissance, into all the movements in art and literature up to the present day . . . Yanagi said to me of Cezanne, "He is a doorway between East and West", and of Rembrandt, "He is one of our artists." '

Leach also introduced Yanagi to the work of Augustus John who in 1912 wrote to Yanagi about sending one of his works for exhibition in Tokyo.[28]

The friendship between Yanagi and Leach blossomed and lasted until Yanagi died. Yanagi visited Leach in Peking in 1916 and stayed with him for a month. They viewed together the old imperial collections of pots and developed their appreciation of Sung wares. Leach was not happy in Peking and Yanagi invited him back to Japan where Leach had earlier studied pottery under the sixth Kenzan. His former master sold him his kiln for re-erection on Yanagi's land at Abiko near Tokyo. In 1919 Leach was preparing for an exhibition in Tokyo when his kiln with all his notes, books, tools and designs was burnt down. Yanagi consoled him in his despair, Leach was then allowed to put up a new kiln in Tokyo on land belonging to Viscount Kuroda.

Leach returned to England in 1920 to set up his own pottery at St Ives in Cornwall but he kept in touch with Yanagi by correspondence. Leach re-visited Japan in 1934/5 and spent much time with Yanagi. After the Second World War his first visit to Japan was in 1953. Yanagi and Hamada had come to the 1952 World Craft Conference at Dartington and together they went on via the United States to Japan, lecturing, demonstrating and discussing the problems of crafts with audiences up and down the United States.

When Yanagi died in 1961, Leach summed up his feelings in these words:[29]

'A great man has gone, the father of the Japanese Craft Movement and founder and director of the incomparable Folk-Museums of Japan. The loss is not only theirs but ours too, for Soetsu Yanagi during his life was the thinker and guide who provided the aesthetic philosophy for the craftsmen of the Orient, corresponding to some extent with that provided by Morris and Ruskin almost a century earlier for England and the Occident. It is not the same message, though it is akin. Yanagi's Buddhist aesthetic is deeply concerned with that aspect of truth and beauty described by such words as nakedness, humility and holy poverty, in the sense of St Francis of Assisi. Non-egoistic art was his concern – there he spoke to the West as an antithetical Oriental.'

One important influence which Leach introduced to Yanagi was that of William Blake (1757–1827) who became a major source of inspiration to Yanagi. In 1914 Yanagi had produced a substantial volume on Blake. In 1915 (8 November) Yanagi wrote to Leach of his deep interest '. . . in Christian mysticism, partly from my own nature, partly from studying Blake'.[30] He went on in this letter to discuss Christian mysticism and Zen. In a letter of 24 November 1915,[31] he commented:

'My critics attack Blake because they think his visional spirituality to be pathological rather than normal – he was called a "madman". Man's perception is not bounded by organs of perception; he perceives more than sense can discover. He who sees the infinite in all things sees God.'

William Blake's appeal to Yanagi lay not only in his mysticism. Blake loved nature but he knew that it was not possible to copy nature. He emphasized rather the importance of copying imagination. To Blake: 'Knowledge of Ideal Beauty is Not to be Acquired. It is Born with us. Innate Ideas are in Every man. Born with him; they are truly Himself.'[32] As Kathleen Raine points out:[33] 'For Blake all is human, since in this world man is central, "made in the image of God", as the microcosm:

> . . . Each grain of Sand,
> Every Stone on the Land,
> Each rock @ each hill,
> Each fountain @ rill,
> Each herb @ each tree,
> Mountain, hill, earth @ sea,
> Cloud, Meteor @ Star,
> Are Men Seen Afar.'

Blake had other qualities which appealed to Yanagi. He had the quality of 'innocence'. He loathed 'mechanistic rationalism'. He was tirelessly industrious. Blake led Yanagi to Walt Whitman (1818–1892) and Yanagi published for a time a magazine devoted to Blake and Whitman.

Another important source of inspiration for Yanagi was William Morris (1834–1896). Morris advocated the medieval ideal of craftsmanship. He was convinced '. . . that the enjoyment of art, far from being esoteric or rarefied, was part of man's birthright and as such part of everyday life'.[34] He saw the Renaissance as '. . . the root of all evil in modern civilization paving the way for mechanization and ultimately the slavishly, imitative, lifeless and vulgarly philistine art of the Victorian era'.[35] This sentiment was echoed by Yanagi[36] who, when asked about the effect of industry on crafts, replied that it was at present exceedingly bad: 'As things are, the desire for a world of normal beauty, once more, is unlikely to arise. Although there can be a kind of beauty in things made mechanically, yet nothing so made has surpassed the beauties of the age of handwork.'

Morris believed that a designer must absorb himself thoroughly in his medium and familiarize himself with the materials and production techniques it required. One of his greatest convictions was that nothing could be a true work of art unless it was useful. His celebrated maxim, 'Have nothing in your houses that you do not know to be useful, or believe to be beautiful' was a sentiment which Yanagi shared. Morris in his turn owed much to John Ruskin who had taught him that '. . . art is the expression of man's pleasure in his labour'.[37]

Morris, however, did not know or understand Japan. In his Arts and Crafts essay on 'Textiles' (1889), he remarked with astonishing ignorance that 'The Japanese have no architectural, and therefore no decorative, instinct'. While he admired the brilliance of Japanese craftsmanship, he saw Japanese works of art as '. . . mere wonderful toys . . . outside the pale of the evolution of art . . . which . . . cannot be carried on without the architectural sense that connects it with the history of mankind'.[38]

Though Blake and Morris were probably the most significant Western influences on Yanagi, he found many other sources of inspiration. Leach recorded[39] that Yanagi

'. . . stood long and silent before the great facade of Chartres [cathedral]; he said, "That is what you have lost. You need a new gospel". Implying any man for everyman, he meant the totality of belief in all mankind. The French built stone upon carved stone visible for thirty miles, lit through coloured glass painted with their dreams and faith –

clear-cut as their belief. All men for all men, life for Life
Itself. Our disbelief is for lack of wholeness.'

Among the many Christian writers quoted or cited by Yanagi
were Sir Thomas Browne, the author of *Religio Medici*,[40] St
Thomas Aquinas,[41] St Francis of Assisi[42] and St John.[43]

Leach brought an essentially English element to the Mingei
movement, namely the shapes, techniques and designs of
medieval English slipware. When Yanagi died some fifty
thirteenth-century English medieval pots were on their way to
Japan for exhibition from the Guildhall Museum in London.
Hamada wrote to Leach: 'Nothing else could truly make better
for the repose of his soul than your personal call with the
Guildhall pots he had, with great excitement, so looked forward
to seeing.'[44]

HAMADA AND LEACH

Leach first met Hamada when he was working at Abiko on
Yanagi's land in 1919. Hamada had been studying pottery
techniques in Kyoto where he had heard of Yanagi and Leach.
Having seen some pots by Leach and by Tomimoto Kenkichi, he
asked if he might call. Leach recorded:[45] 'Hamada and I struck
up an immediate friendship. He knew the chemistry, I the day-
to-day workshop practice, also I had the advantage of art-school
education. For two days on end we talked and then he returned
to Kyoto.' Later, when Hamada heard that Leach had been
invited to start a pottery in Cornwall, he asked if he might come
to England with Leach. When they started work at St Ives, they
were '. . . more or less bounded by conditions of craftsmanship
in Japan' and[46] based their 'economics on the studio'. They
founded an oriental-style climbing stoneware kiln. Hamada had a
room off the pottery workshop and looked after himself. He
quickly made friends and spoke 'of the following three years with
nostalgic gratitude'.[47] Leach and Hamada remained close friends
for the rest of their lives.

Leach greatly admired Hamada's pots. In *The Potter's
Challenge*[48] Leach noted that Hamada had been using the same
'design' for thirty years:

'It is a stem-leaf motif that was originally based on a growth
of sugar-cane he saw that had been blown askew by a
typhoon. When asked why he always repeats himself his

answer is: "It is not a repeat. It is never the same twice, all different. Even if I tried to repeat, the pigment, brush, my arm and the thought would be different." When we look at Hamada's pots we see the truth of this. We recognize the same motif, but each application has fresh vitality and is appropriate to the pot it decorates.'

Leach's admiration was returned. Hamada wrote of Leach's work:[49]

'Whether he works in the East or the West he preserves a simple and straightforward approach. The focus of his work is the most concentrated and personally expressive. The quality in his work has been apparent for over fifty years. The feeling in his pots comes from a high inspiration that defeats both weakened traditions and the violence of modern motivation I have mentioned. He draws his strength from the soil of his own nature and life experience. This is spring water. I feel the difference between this inspiration and that of others very strongly. His stance between East and West is a true balance, not a measured middle.'

Leach was also a good friend of Kawai Kanjirō, but there was never the same empathy between them as between Leach and Hamada. In July 1934 Leach[50] went to Kyoto to work at Kawai's. He made a number of pieces there, '. . . mostly in porcelain, many of them pressed from beautiful moulds made for me by his assistants'. Leach recorded:[51]

'Despite the fact that I seldom liked his pots, I did admire the man. It was impossible to hide my reservations about this work,[52] but he never allowed this to interfere with our long friendship, although I could see that it hurt his loyal wife. Many years later, when he was dying and no longer able to speak, I sat by his bedside for a quarter of an hour holding his hand; finally I stood up and raised mine in farewell; he lifted both of his as I walked out of the hospital room in silence.'

Leach was also a friend of the Japanese potter Tomimoto Kenkichi (1886–1963) who had studied at Goldsmith's college in London. They first met in 1910. Leach recorded[53] that between 1910 and 1920 they were '. . . like good brothers – we shared everything. We were of an age; young, enthusiastic, open-minded, and gave and received without reserve because we trusted each other's characters'. They were both draughtsmen. They walked and bicycled through the countryside of Nara prefecture where Tomimoto's family had lived for generations. Tomimoto acted as interpreter when Leach was introduced to the sixth Kenzan who was to become Leach's master. When Leach had his own workshop he persuaded Tomimoto to '. . . come and throw his very first pot'. Tomimoto managed more or less to centre the clay on the wheel and he decorated his first pot with plum blossoms and a popular spring song. He later gave this pot to Leach and it is now in the Victoria and Albert Museum in London. Tomimoto and Leach both admired greatly the first Kenzan; and Leach eventually wrote his book entitled *Kenzan and his Tradition* to help Westerners to understand Kenzan's achievements. Leach considered Tomimoto '. . . a fine craftsman and good colourist'.[54] 'He employed and expanded the repertoire of over-glaze enamels on porcelain, and introduced the use of platinum, together with gold and silver, as no potter has done before. But I would add that on a potter's wheel he was always a bit of an amateur as I am myself.' To Leach Tomimoto was '. . . a rare maker of patterns, an originator. All his work was fine and sharp'. He had '. . . a fine discriminating sense of form'.

At first Yanagi and Tomimoto[55] '. . . got on fairly well, but later when Yanagi's ideas of craftsmanship took form in museums and craft shops, a gradual divergence began to develop, partly due to differences of personality'. Yanagi asked Leach to try to bridge the gap. He tried but failed. 'Tomimoto was impatient: his very sharp perceptive eyes did not always echo Yanagi's verdict, nor did he approve of much in the craft shops claiming to be folk-craft. My friend Tomimoto had a courtly kind of finesse, while Yanagi had a religious breadth of outlook.' Perhaps as a result of the estrangement from Yanagi, although Leach and Tomimoto remained friends until the latter died, they were not as close in later years as they had been in the first years Leach had been in Japan. Tomimoto was an artist and decorator of pots. He may have thought that Yanagi went too far in looking down on the individual artist and in his preference for the *shibui* and the imperfect. Leach was, of course, also a decorator and a great admirer of the decorative works of the first Kenzan and his contemporaries but there was much more of a *shibui* element in Leach's approach and he had a natural sense of kinship with the craftsmen of the Mingei movement.

Hamada was not the only Japanese potter to study and work with Leach. Among other Japanese potters Leach got to know three generations of the Funaki family who worked at the long-established Fujina kiln in Shimane prefecture which lies on a promontory on Lake Shinji outside Matsue. Hamada and Yanagi thought that Leach could help the Funakis with the techniques of lead-glazed English earthenware.[56] Funaki Michitada became a friend of Leach during the latter's stay in Japan in 1934/5 and his son Kenji came to England for a year and worked with Leach's son David at his pottery at Bovey Tracy in Devon. There Funaki Kenji concentrated on medieval lead-glazed earthenware.

During his visits to Japan Leach travelled extensively visiting and working at traditional Japanese kiln sites. Sometimes he was accompanied by Hamada. Onda in Kyushu was a village which invited Leach to come and stay during his visit to Japan in 1954. Yanagi told Leach of his first visit to Onda after hours of walking over mountain tracks and described the simple unspoiled life of the potters who worked there and the good pots which they made.[57] On this visit Leach was accompanied by both Hamada and Kawai. Leach stayed on after they had left. Leach recorded:[58]

> 'I don't think any European craftsmen can have had such an experience as these weeks with these delightful, unspoiled hill-potters in the remote mountains of Kyushu, have given me . . . What impresses me most is the spontaneous community action with its basic unity of heart.'

Leach as a friend of Yanagi naturally supported the latter's efforts to develop the ideas of mingei into areas other than pottery. One of these was furniture and in Matsumoto he met a furniture-maker called Ikeda,[59] an enthusiast for English rural furniture. Another exponent of mingei known to Leach was Serizawa Keisuke (born 1895) whom he described as '. . . the best dyer and stencil printer, definitely an artist-craftsman'.[60] A third was the great print artist Munakata Shikō (1903–1975) whom Leach described as '. . . one of the best artists in Japan'.[61] But neither Serizawa nor Munakata were close friends in the same way as Yanagi and Hamada were.

LEACH IN BRITAIN

Although Leach made many visits to Japan in his later years his main work was inevitably in Britain and especially at his pottery in St Ives. In his book *Beyond East and West* Leach traced the development there. For many decades this was largely managed by his son David, a fine potter in his own right. After Leach's marriage to Janet (née Darnell), who has continued the Leach tradition and took over the running of the St Ives pottery, David Leach established his own pottery at Bovey Tracy in Devonshire.

Many of the outstanding modern British potters worked and studied with Leach. Michael Cardew joined Leach from Oxford in 1923. Leach said of him: 'I do not believe anyone in this country has made such warm, honest, more or less traditional English slipware, and with so much life.'[62] Kathleen Pleydell-Bouverie was the next arrival in 1924: 'an aristocrat, she had a very telling and communicative laugh like the neigh of a horse, especially if she disagreed.'[63] She wrote in 1960 an article of appreciation in which she said:

> 'I shall always be grateful to Bernard for letting me be at St Ives that year. It was a great experience and he was very kind, ungrudgingly generous with information and suggestions. He did not know the meaning of the words "trade secret", and I have never known any one who would give his name and attention so completely to another person's problems.'[64]

David Leach brought to the St Ives pottery William Marshall. Leach wrote of him[65] in 1978:

> 'William Marshall is still with us after 36 years . . . Without further education or private money, and with little travel, he has through contact with various students, learnt not only first-rate skill as a craftsman, especially as a thrower on the potter's wheel, but has gradually become quite an expressive potter – one of the best in the country.'

Leach met his near contemporary the potter, William Staite Murray, at his first London exhibition: 'We stalked each other round a show-case in the middle of the room before making acquaintance. Eventually the friendship broke up – we were doomed to be rivals.'[66]

Leach got to know Lucy Rie, another great British potter, in the years before the war:

> 'She did not become a student of mine in the ordinary sense and her pots do not show any of my influence, although she says I slaughtered her at Dartington where she came to meet me just before we entered the war, and that I changed her course.'[67]

In the post-war years Leach travelled widely in Europe, Australia and New Zealand but especially in the United States to promote his views on pottery and mingei. Leach, Yanagi and Hamada were disappointed by most of the works of American potters which they saw. They were, however, impressed by some of the Indian crafts which they discovered in New Mexico and Leach was particularly struck by an Indian potter called Maria who '. . . made coils of clay rolled between her palms to the thinness of her little finger'.[68]

Yanagi's admiration for Leach and his work was genuine. In the Introduction to Leach's *A Potter's Book*,[69] Yanagi wrote:

'Enchanted by the memories of his childhood in the East, and fascinated by the magic of Lafcadio Hearn's prose, Leach came to Japan at the age of twenty-one, full of dreams and wonder . . . Fortunately his love of Japan was not the sentimental one so often met with, but an honest one, informed by the insight and imagination of an artist. It would seem that art is always the best highway for mutual understanding between different peoples . . . His taste, as I understand him, is rather for the austere Gothic than the sweet Greek. In this sense he is the true descendant of William Blake, whom he admires above any other British artist . . . Above all, the outstanding character of his work is the union of East and West. All his ideas, life and endeavour seem to have been focussed on this one point . . . We in Japan feel him to be a brother, not a stranger at all.'

Yanagi ended with this Buddhist quatrain:

'Really there is no East, no West,
Where then is the South and the North?
Illusion makes the world close in,
Enlightenment opens it on every side.'

Matsudaira Tsuneo, Diplomat and Courtier (1877–1949)

IAN NISH

MATSUDAIRA TSUNEO was the longest-serving Japanese ambassador to the Court of St James. He presided over the London embassy from 13 February 1929 to the end of May 1935. This was a total of six-and-a-half years and slightly exceeds the period spent by Ambassador Hayashi (1900–06).[1] Matsudaira gave continuity to Anglo-Japanese relations during a time of political instability in Japan: he was ambassador under eight prime ministers. Moreover, relations with Britain were always tense; and he had to make the best of a deteriorating situation. The Manchurian and Shanghai crises of 1931–33 destroyed many British illusions about Japan; and it was the task of the ambassador to present his country's case in Britain and in the wider forum of the League of Nations in liberal terms in order to forge a *modus vivendi* with European statesmen. When he left London in 1935, he took up an appointment close to the Emperor and from this obscure position was still engaged in the exercise of damage limitation. His exploits did not prevent war but they were one strand in the complex tapestry which was being woven in the years before 1941.

Matsudaira Tsuneo (1877–1949) who was related to Matsudaira Sadanobu, a leading Tokugawa statesman, was educated at Gakushūin and Tokyo Imperial University where he studied law and politics. He entered the Foreign Ministry by examination in 1902 and was sent to London for training in the following year. The tension with Russia and the war which followed strained the legation staff of six. He married in 1906 the daughter of Marquis Nabeshima of the Saga clan. They left London with their two children in June 1911 after a happy period. Matsudaira was posted to the treaty revision section and rose steadily in the ranks of the Gaimushō. After a period in China, he became head of its Europe–American section (Ō-Bei kyokuchō), in which capacity he served on the Japanese delegation to the all-important Washington Conference (1921–22) where he made valuable international contacts. When the Yamamoto cabinet took over in 1923 with Ijuin Hikokichi as foreign minister, he became vice-minister, a post he retained under the short-lived Kiyoura cabinet in 1924.[2]

On 18 December 1924 Matsudaira was deservedly promoted to the key post of ambassador to Washington. Relations had deteriorated because of the anti-Japanese immigration legislation introduced in 1923; and it was to be his role to continue the task which had already absorbed him as vice-minister to work for improved relations with the United States. He was warmly welcomed by the Japan Society in San Francisco and in Washington. Among the diplomatic issues taken up during his tenure in Washington, the most significant were the arrangements for the Geneva Naval Conference of 1927 and the treaty for the Renunciation of War, sometimes referred to as the Kellogg–Briand pact. The first initiative came to nothing, while the second came to maturity after Matsudaira's return to Tokyo on leave in June 1928.[3]

A month after he reached home, it was announced that he would succeed Baron Matsui Keishiro as ambassador to Britain. This was followed in September by the marriage between his daughter Setsuko and Prince Chichibu, the younger brother of the Shōwa Emperor. After the long sea journey, Matsudaira reached London in February of the following year. In the climate of the twenties London was not just a centre for sorting out bilateral issues but also a focal point for sorting out multi-national issues. The ambassadors at London and Paris were expected to represent Japan at the international conferences of the day. Matsudaira was immediately engaged on behalf of the Tanaka government in working out the preliminary details of the London Naval Conference which eventually began early in 1930. The purpose was to control and limit the extent of naval armament. Matsudaira was plenipotentiary along with Wakatsuki Reijirō, and Admiral Takarabe Takeshi, the vice-minister of the navy who travelled from Japan with Admiral Baron Abō Kiyokazu, vice-chief of the naval general staff (kaigun gunreibu jichō). It was a triangular conference, taking in Japan, Britain and the United States.

When the conference opened on 21 January, the Japanese delegates announced that they did not wish to accept the Washington ratio of 60 per cent overall applied in the case of cruisers, as the American plenipotentiaries wanted. But, by reason of Matsudaira's frankness and patient diplomacy, cordial discussions took place on this fraught issue. Compromise was difficult because Admiral Takarabe was confronted by opposition from his accompanying technical staff whom he was unable to win over. In order to prevent deadlock, Matsudaira met for a long series of sessions with Senator David Reed, one of the American delegates. Eventually on 13 March, a formula was reached whereby Japan should have 69–75 per cent in overall tonnage and 60.02 per cent in respect of heavy cruisers. This 'Reed–Matsudaira compromise' preserved the Washington formula of 10-10-6 while allowing Japan in practice a ratio of 10-10-7.

The navalists argued that Matsudaira had not pressed the case as he should.[4] Wakatsuki, the head of the delegation, defended him and urged his government to accept the formula in order to avoid causing the breakdown of the talks. But the naval objections in London were as nothing compared to those raised in Tokyo. Nonetheless, the government, acting through the vice-minister for the navy, agreed to go ahead with the treaty on 10 April and instructions were sent to London accordingly. But Admiral Katō Kanji, chief of the naval general staff, sought an interview with the Emperor and announced his resignation. Though the treaty was signed on 22 April, there was a lengthy ratification process; but eventually the ratification procedures were completed and the treaty came into force in October.[5]

The American and British leaders extended their thanks to Wakatsuki and Matsudaira. In London much had been left to the diplomacy of civilians; and Matsudaira and Reed had had to bear the brunt of finding a solution to a prickly and emotional issue. Given the high expectations in Japan, Matsudaira tried to negotiate a formula which would ensure the continuation of arms limitation while saving the face of the navy. It may be that the result was a fudge, but it was a fudge skilfully arrived at.

MATSUDAIRA AND MANCHURIA

Hardly had the crisis over the naval treaty passed than a new international crisis over 'Manchuria' developed. On 18 September 1931 the Kuantung army moved out of its Leased Territory and occupied the key cities of south and central Manchuria. The Chinese reported the dispute to the League of Nations which for two months tried to get the parties to withdraw their troops without success. The sessions of the League Council and the League Assembly in Geneva and Paris greatly increased Matsudaira's work-load as he had to travel over to the continent and coordinate policy with the ambassador to France, Yoshizawa Kenkichi, and the ambassador to Rome, Yoshida Shigeru. It is impossible to cover the vast canvas of the Manchurian crisis in this essay: we shall confine ourselves to sketching the importance of Matsudaira's role. He was important because of his wide experience at Washington and London and his relationship with the new British foreign secretary, Sir John Simon, because Britain was still assumed to have more of a role in settling the crisis than the other pillar of the League, France.

After two months of embarrassing diplomatic failure, Matsudaira met Simon in Paris on 17 November and presented a memorandum. Under point 2 of the note, the Japanese offered to propose that the League should send a 'Study Commission' to examine the whole question of Sino-Japanese relations and, in particular, the relations of those two countries in Manchuria. Sugimura Yōtarō, an assistant secretary at the League, told the director-general: '. . . Mr Matsudaira was being extremely courageous in making these proposals. He would simply announce to Tokyo that he had put them forward to Sir John Simon and to General Dawes. If Tokyo refused to accept them, he would then resign, but his personal position was such that he did not believe Tokyo would take this step.'[6] Since the League Commission that emerged from this proposal was the nearest that the League came to solving the Sino-Japanese dispute, it is historically important to know how far Matsudaira was the author of the proposal.

The proposal of an enquiry committee sent by the League to China (*chōsadan*) which had been mooted by Matsudaira and Dr Sugimura on 17 November, was then presented to the Gaimushō in their reports and through the efforts of Frank

Walters, a senior official of the League secretariat, who happened to be in the Far East at the time. He was travelling as secretary of the League mission of educational experts, investigating the school system throughout China.[7] He had moved to Tokyo and was in touch with Shidehara and 'high officials' [kōkan] of the Ministry. It was simultaneously taken up by Matsudaira with Ambassador Dawes, Sir John Simon and Sir Eric Drummond, the League secretary-general, who had all moved to Paris for the meetings of the League Council. It was conditional on the delegates (shisatsuin) visiting China proper as well as Manchuria in order to investigate the anti-Japanese movement.[8] After discussion it seems to have received the endorsement of all three parties in Paris and Simon conveyed this to Matsudaira on 19 November. At the Tokyo end, Shidehara was understandably vigilant but was probably more responsive than many other Japanese leaders. So Matsudaira did not lose his job.

As the League Council drew up the mandate for the new commission, there were three weeks of bitter recriminations between Japan and China. But it was finally proposed on the motion of the Japanese delegate that a commission of five members should study on the spot and report on circumstances which had disturbed the peace in China. This was approved on 10 December with the understanding that one of the five would be from the United States.[9] So the League Commission which took shape in January 1932 was in effect the result of Matsudaira's bold initiative.

It is important to remember that Japan took the initiative to propose an international commission. It appears from Japanese documents that Matsudaira was the moving spirit. Yoshizawa and Japan's other League delegates played their part, as did Dr Sugimura of the secretariat. But it was evidently Matsudaira who carried the clout to have it adopted in Tokyo. When a similar proposal had been raised in October, Japan had disapproved of sending inspectors from Peking into Manchuria to report to the League. Now it passed because it broke the stalemate.

Foreign Minister Shidehara felt that the new private initiative (shian) of Matsudaira was worth a try, partly because the Chinese were threatening to ask for the dispute to be examined under Clause 15 of the covenant, partly because Japanese opinion was becoming increasingly extremist (kyokutanka) and needed to be held in check. I have argued elsewhere that there was also an element of party politics in Japan which entered into Shidehara's calculations because the cabinet was at that moment in disarray;[10] it would suit the Wakatsuki ministry to have a League enquiry commission (chōsadan) which, being lengthy, would permit a cooling of opinion. If international opinion could be wooed away from support of China in this way, it would redound to the credit of the more moderate elements in the ministry and in the country at large. So Shidehara was able to give the proposal his blessing, even if another foreign minister might not have been inclined to do so. Hence Yoshizawa was able to report on 20 November that the Council was already considering drafts of the resolution which the representative of Japan was proposing.[11]

The League commission, generally known as 'the Lytton commission', in due time reported from the East to Geneva. While it was away, Japan had been fighting a backs-to-the-wall struggle at Geneva. Sawada Setsuzō, one of the Japanese delegates and head of Japan's League secretariat, explained his perspective on events:

'When the Manchurian crisis arose, Geneva became the heart of international affairs. Even Japan seems to have focussed her overseas activities there. Hence our delegation gradually increased and was at one time 170–80 strong.'[12]

Over Manchuria – and over the Disarmament Conference which was being held simultaneously – Matsudaira was playing a full part. When, however, the Lytton report appeared in late summer 1932, Tokyo sent to Geneva Matsuoka Yōsuke to head the delegation. This was an implied criticism of Matsudaira and his fellow negotiators who protested politely. They did not think it was necessary for Japan to recognize Manchukuo (as she had done in September) and questioned Matsuoka's commitment to the League.[13] From November the focus was no longer on Matsudaira. In due course the vote was taken on 24 February 1933 on the resolution to approve a report based on the Commission's recommendations. Japan alone opposed. Matsuoka beckoned to the Japanese delegates to withdraw from the floor of the Assembly. There is reason, however, to believe that Matsudaira was not in favour of such a flamboyant gesture.

The final act of the crisis was the decision of the cabinet in Tokyo to give notice of withdrawal from the League at the end of March. This was made without consultation with senior ambassadors overseas and there is every reason to believe that Matsudaira, if he had been approached, would have advised Japan to stay within the League. But it was not to be. The resignation did not take effect until 1935 and Japan was able for the time being to continue to take part in League-inspired events. Thus, at the World Economic Conference held in London in June 1933, Matsudaira was one of Japan's chief delegates. Matsudaira did not like the strategy of leaving the League and '. . . sighed from the bottom of his heart about the climate of the times, saying that Japan should build up her strength quietly and thus recover her international position'.[14]

AMBASSADOR IN A DIVIDED BRITAIN

It is not the purpose of this essay to offer a ball-by-ball commentary on the second half of Matsudaira's embassy to London. Anglo-Japanese relations were not so cordial after the Manchurian incident of 1931–33 and Japan's departure from the League as they had been before. It was hard for Matsudaira who was conscious of British opinion being generally favourable to China. It was progressively less easy for the ambassador to operate through the Foreign Office which seemed to reflect these pro-Chinese sentiments. Naturally, therefore, Matsudaira gave encouragement to a Japanophile group which came into existence in 1934 around Sir Warren Fisher, the permanent secretary to the Treasury, with Neville Chamberlain as his accessory.[15] Its avowed object was to repair 'the relation of friendship and mutual respect' with Japan. In this way, Matsudaira knew of the disagreements among British policy-makers and learnt to exploit them.

As part of his desire to broaden the range of Japan's friends in Britain, Matsudaira promoted the mission organized by the Federation of British Industries which went out in the summer of 1934 to visit Japan and Manchukuo. In Britain's perception, this so-called Barnby mission was an unofficial group which did not have the backing of the Foreign Office and was playing with fire by visiting Manchukuo. Matsudaira reported to Tokyo that it was superficially 'an industrial mission' in search of contracts but had in fact the political aim of promoting friendly relations.[16] As the result of his strong recommendation, it was given a royal reception in Japan and special treatment when it ventured on to

Manchukuo. That no contracts for British industry resulted from their efforts was due to the reluctance of the nominally independent Manchukuo authorities to open their market to Britain, not to the absence of support on the part of the London ambassador.

On 14 May 1935 Matsudaira was permitted to return home on leave. There was a host of hastily improvized functions in his honour. Most prominent was the special dinner at Claridges given on 19 June by the Japan Society. The then foreign secretary, Sir Samuel Hoare, offered a eulogy of Matsudaira as president of the Society in these words:

'He has in fact been one of the most distinguished members of the Corps Diplomatique. No one can better interpret the views of Japan to England and those of England to Japan. His Excellency has entered into all our interests and activities. He is as well known on the golf course as he is in Whitehall. He has taken a prominent part in all social functions and with Madame Matsudaira has made friends whose number is quite uncountable.'

Matsudaira replied in a moving way, saying that his absence from his country for such a long period as six years was not necessarily desirable:

'Especially in the Far East there have occurred in recent years several serious events and political and economic conditions there have altered so rapidly that I ought to have returned home before this to see them, as well as to report to my Government in person all I have seen abroad.'[17]

He then set off *via* Canada and reached Japan at the beginning of August. It should be observed that Matsudaira seems genuinely to have been under the impression that he would be returning to Britain and was only going temporarily on leave. He wrote to correspondents that this was his intention. If he had returned, it would have been in contradiction to the normal practices of the Foreign Ministry: for an ambassador who stayed longer than four years in one post was almost unknown. But there was nothing to be gained by dissembling and every reason to believe that Matsudaira genuinely felt that his mission was unfulfilled and that he would return.[18]

The autumn was filled with family events. At the end of October his second daughter Masako was married to the eldest son of Tokugawa Yoshitomo, a scion of the Tokugawa house. Later on 28 December, his eldest son Ichirō, married the eldest daughter of Tokugawa Iemasa, Japan's ambassador to Turkey. Matsudaira's aristocratic connections had been confirmed by marriage.

Despite this, matters of grave political urgency were looming. The second London Naval Conference was due to open in January. Britain as host was anxious about Japan's representation and took the bold step of suggesting to Kasumigaseki that '. . .it may prove convenient if your Government were to be represented by your Ambassador in London'.[19] London wanted Matsudaira back but, for personal reasons, this was next to impossible. It is, however, indicative of the confidence that the British authorities felt in him.

Mention should also be made of the mission of Sir Frederick Leith-Ross. The proposal to send a mission to Japan arose from China's proposal that Britain should give her a substantial loan and Britain's response that this should only be done after consultation with the United States and Japan. Leith-Ross, the chief economic adviser to the British government, by-passed Washington and reached Japan in September 1935. He knew many Japanese because of the World Economic Conference held in London in 1933. But he had a special relationship with Matsudaira, now back in Tokyo, whose cousin, Viscount Matsudaira Keimin, had been known to him at Oxford University. Leith-Ross records his meetings with the ambassador thus:

'[Matsudaira] before he left London had been very optimistic about the political situation in Japan, and had expressed the view that the military faction . . . had now lost influence and were under the control of the Civil Government. Since his return to Japan I found that he had completely changed his opinion. He was evidently very nervous about the attitude of the Army to my mission.'[20]

All that Matsudaira said was abundantly confirmed by Leith-Ross's Tokyo experiences. After six months of investigation in China, the question of Leith-Ross making a return journey to Japan was raised in London. The Treasury was very much in favour, while the Foreign Office reiterated its view that the China loan scheme should be dropped and he should not re-visit

Tokyo.

The political climate of Japan altered after the military mutiny of 26 February 1936. A new cabinet had been set up, but it was clear that the army still had much power because they managed to veto the appointment of Yoshida Shigeru as foreign minister. It is interesting that Matsudaira who had entered the Foreign Ministry four years ahead of Yoshida in 1906, was not considered for that office. But the Lord Keeper of the Privy Seal had been murdered by the troops and Yuasa Kurahei, the Imperial Household Minister, moved over to the take that job. Matsudaira agreed on 6 March to take over from Yuasa as Kunai Daijin, as soon as he had given notice of leaving the Foreign Ministry. He had assumed an office which made him one of the mediators between the cabinet and the court and a figure of some indefinable influence in Japanese society. Matsudaira wrote to the Japan Society on 9 March that he found himself unable to return to England because of his appointment to this new post. The Society replied with congratulations upon this high office '. . . giving pleasure to innumerable friends and inspiring renewed confidence in all who cherish good relations between our two Empires'.[21]

This affected the debate over Leith-Ross in London. Eventually, disagreements were resolved and Leith-Ross was authorized to pay a short visit to Tokyo in June in order to assess (among other things) '. . . to what extent Japanese policy is guided by those (e.g. Mr Matsudaira) who sincerely desire a rapprochement with Britain'.[22] Leith-Ross's talks with Matsudaira took priority but he had to record that '. . . Matsudaira and the Ministry of Foreign Affairs were anxious to maintain good relations with Britain and America and to find some solution of their difficulties with China, but I sensed that many of the younger Foreign Office officials whom I met were in full sympathy with the programme of the military'.[23] It would appear from these quotations that, both in Britain and in British circles in Japan, Matsudaira was regarded as an important leader who was regarded as favourable and sympathetic towards Britain. Indeed, he was a prominent member of the Ei-Beiha, though he was as a member of the court precluded from taking too conspicuous a role in leadership.

It is difficult to assess Matsudaira's role as Imperial Household Minister which he held until June 1945. The secrecy in which the office was shrouded does not permit many insights. It is probable that the court, like the Elder Statesman, was 'marginalized' after 1936 and did not have much influence on the direction which affairs were following. Matsudaira's name is not to be found in the newspapers of the day. But, if we may judge from the experiences of Leith-Ross, he was still able to pull a few strings.[24] His internationalism was resented by the organizers of the anti-British movement of 1939 when an assasination attempt on Matsudaira failed.

RETIREMENT JAPANESE-STYLE

After the war the Matsudairas lived in their private house in straitened circumstances. Sir George Sansom, who as a member of the Far East Commission visited Tokyo in January 1946, recalled that:

> 'The Matsudairas had lost everything and he himself [Tsuneo] was wearing his son's tidy suit, which they wear in turns.'[25]

But he still had wide international interests and certain court connections. In June 1946 he was appointed to the privy council (*sumitsu komonkan*). In the first general election in April of the following year he was elected to the House of Councillors (*sangiin*) and became its president. But his illnesses increased and he died in Tokyo on 14 November 1949 at the age of 72. Sansom's account shows that Matsudaira was more than an uninvolved private citizen. He still had access to the Emperor and was clearly given assignments by the latter to act as intermediary with foreigners.

As General Piggott wrote in his obituary in the Japan Society *Bulletin*, Matsudaira came of ancient lineage but was a commoner: 'The innate conservatism of his race was blended with a streak of modern liberalism that he had acquired from the West'. He was, wrote Piggott, '. . . the physical embodiment of sound, solid commonsense'.[26] He was neither brilliant nor intellectual. He was sociable, even gregarious, and made friends, both Japanese and foreign, fairly readily. As a senior diplomat, he had the reputation for using 'golf diplomacy'. He tells how Sir John Simon would phone up to say that there were some troublesome points facing him in the Office and ask him whether he would take some exercise at Walton Heath or Combe Hill. As ambassador, he acquired a taste for Old Parr whisky; and it was as a connoisseur that he was affectionately remembered by his juniors in the London embassy. Like his companion in the Manchurian diplomacy, Dr Sugimura, he was rather over-weight but this gave him a reputation for bonhomie.[27]

Matsudaira had a career which went from strength to strength. Passing into the diplomatic profession in 1902, he was promoted steadily until he reached London at the summit of his career. Given his aristocratic background, it was a natural progression for him to become Imperial Household Minister. Though he was criticized after the war by opponents of the *Tennōsei*,[28] his election as speaker of the Upper House was a mark of the respect which he had earned from the majority of Japanese.

His connection with Britain was a thread running through his diplomatic career. His long first stint gave him a taste for the British way of life. The postings he had were mainly in the English-speaking section of the ministry. To end up with long stays in Washington and London was indeed good fortune. Even in the straitened circumstances of the allied occupation of Japan, he was still interested in Things British and quizzed Sansom when they met in 1946. Yet, if he was Anglophile he was also a Japanese patriot. It is not easy to assess the advice he was giving his home government from London. But there is good evidence that, at critical points in his career, he was prepared to put his career on the line and stand up to his government. Matsudaira Tsuneo, the longest-serving ambassador to the Court of St James, seems to have accomplished that most difficult of conjuring tricks: advising his government and representing his country, while at the same time sympathizing with the country to which he was accredited and presenting its case to Tokyo. He was, in the assessment of Sir John Tilley, 'a most successful ambassador in London'.[29]

17

Gordon Munro: Ventures in Japanese Archaeology and Anthropology

JANE WILKINSON

DR NEIL GORDON MUNRO (1863–1942), a Scottish doctor who received his MD at Edinburgh University, lived in Japan for most of his life. He was neither professional archaeologist nor anthropologist; but his curiosity about the human race kept him abreast of the leading theories of the day and in contact with many leading scholars in these disciplines. His interests in archaeology led him to discover evidence of the prehistoric people of Japan in 1905/6 during his excavation of the Mitsusawa shell-mound. Munro found human skeletons which he was sure belonged to the ancestors of the Ainu, an indigenous race living in Hokkaido, Japan's northernmost island.

In 1898 Munro first visited the Ainu and became concerned about their disappearing life-style. He was at that time employed as the medical director of the Yokohama Hospital but kept in contact with the people he met in Hokkaido until he moved there in 1930. He opened a clinic in Nibutani to treat the Ainu and record the richness and diversity of a dying culture for posterity.

However, the various contributions Munro made to Japanese Studies are not commonly appreciated. The general reader is more likely to have come across the names of the American scholar, Edward S. Morse (1838–1925) connected with Japanese archaeology or John Batchelor (1854–1944) where studies of the ancient Japanese race, the Ainu, are concerned. Morse was an American biologist who was appointed Professor of Zoology at the Imperial University of Tokyo. He was interested in shell-mounds and on noticing shells, at the side of the railway cutting at Omori on his first trip up to Tokyo from Yokohama, Morse wished the area to be fully investigated. He led the first fully-reported excavation of a shell-mound in Japan.[1]

The Reverend John Batchelor was a missionary who lived in Hokkaido, Japan's northernmost island, for most of his life. His main concern with the Ainu was to convert them to the Christian faith and he received grants from the church for this purpose. He wrote a Japanese/English/Ainu dictionary and an Ainu Grammar and used his knowledge of the language to translate some passages of the bible into Ainu. The dictionary, though full of mistakes, was the first of its kind. He also wrote about Ainu folklore but his main concern was to educate the Ainu to the Western way of life and thought.

In 1891 Munro arrived in Japan, having long been interested in archaeology. His book *Prehistoric Japan*, published in Yokohama in 1908,[2] was written mainly for a Western audience though it was translated into Japanese. It remained the main reference work on Japanese archaeology published in English until the 1950s when G.J. Groot and J.E. Kidder wrote books on the subject. Munro's work, though wordy and at times difficult to follow, is still a useful source of information based on the observations of a man concerned with detail, and of comment arising out of an insatiable curiosity.

Munro later became directly involved with the Ainu, who in turn appreciated his concern and trusted him, enabling him to make detailed notes about their past culture and way of life. Batchelor was a missionary, amateur linguist and folklorist whereas Munro was a doctor, amateur archaeologist and anthropologist. Batchelor adopted an Ainu daughter and had her educated in England. He is remembered by the British and Japanese, but Munro is remembered by the Ainu. In each of Munro's main fields of interest, therefore, others had arrived in Japan before him and even today remain better known in the West for their contributions to the study of Japan, than does Munro. It is hoped that this account of Gordon Munro's life and Ainu studies will redress the balance.

Neil Gordon Munro was born at Woodbine cottage, Lochee, Dundee in Scotland on 16 June 1863. His father, Robert Munro, was a surgeon and married Margaret Pringle in June 1861. Neil Gordon Munro was the second eldest of a family of eight children but as the eldest boy he was named after his grandfather, Neil Munro, a market gardener. Although his family called him Neil he was to favour the name Gordon when he lived in Japan. When a copy of his book, *Coins of Japan*, which was published in Yokohama (1904),[3] was acquired by the library at the Royal Museum of Scotland, Edinburgh, it was found to be inscribed: 'To Mother, with best wishes for Christmas from Neil'. But the letters written to the museum between 1908 and 1929 are signed 'N. Gordon Munro'.

Educated at Scottish schools, Gordon Munro chose his father's profession and studied medicine at Edinburgh University, graduating as Bachelor of Medicine in 1888. Through illness he had to take a year off studying and failed to get his Master of Surgery qualification. He spent some of his time convalescing in Italy and Tunisia which gave him a taste for travel and a warmer climate. During university vacations it is likely that he took part in archaeological digs.

Instead of returning to Edinburgh, Munro got a job as ship's doctor. He boarded ship at Southampton bound for Hong Kong via India. The ship was mainly for cargo but there were a few passengers. Its route took him to Gibraltar, Port Said, through the Suez Canal and on to Aden. He had plenty of time to read and think, the crew only occasionally needing his services for stomach upsets, colds, and the occasional bout of seasickness. The most difficult thing he had to do was to operate for appendicitis at sea. He travelled and excavated in India but there is no report of where or with whom. He was reported to be very upset about the poverty in India which was much worse than he had expected. The Indian monsoons, however, and the hot weather suited him no better than the cold Edinburgh air. He became ill and was quite weak when he reached Hong Kong.

MUNRO IN YOKOHAMA

Munro thought that the milder climate of Japan might suit him, particularly the fact that there would be four marked seasons. In 1891 he arrived in Japan, still a very sick man. He took a rest cure at Yokohama General Hospital and was helped greatly by the medical director there. This man was transferred to a government post in 1893, and Munro was invited to replace him as medical director at the hospital which had first admitted him as a patient.

He accepted the offer as he thought a settled life would suit him better than being a ships' doctor and he held this post for the next thirty years.

He was finally awarded his MD in Surgery at Edinburgh University in 1909. His thesis 'Cancer in Japan' is mainly a statistical statement about the occurrence of this disease in Japan from 1900 to 1905. Although the disease was less widespread in Japan than England and Wales, Munro noted that the rate of deaths caused by cancer was increasing faster in Japan. He also compared the deaths caused by tuberculosis, a disease in which he maintained a life-long interest, to those caused by cancer. It is a said irony that Munro himself was to die from cancer in 1942. He was not in Edinburgh to receive the degree at the graduation ceremony on 23 July 1909 and the MD was awarded to him in absentia, according to University records.

It is easy to imagine that Munro's wide interests had been stimulated by visits to the Museum of Science and Art in Edinburgh, which was next door to the university buildings where he was a student. The present museum is known as the Royal Museum of Scotland and is part of the National Museums of Scotland. The original collections at this museum included material acquired in the seventeenth and eighteenth century by the University of Edinburgh, when the exploration of the New World had stimulated interest in the environment at home and a general curiosity about the natural world in all its forms. In the mid nineteenth century the Victorian thirst for knowledge and the need to expand education and promote information about manufacturing industries followed the Great Exhibition of 1851. The museum of Science and Art was founded in 1854 and opened in 1861 to help fulfil these aims. This museum combined Edinburgh University's Natural History collections which included ethnographical specimens and newly acquired indus-trial and artistic objects from all over the world.

Later, Munro was to add valuable material to the museum collections. Between the years 1909 and 1914 fourteen crates containing over 2,000 Japanese antiquities arrived at the newly-titled Royal Scottish Museum. The collection falls into three main categories. The first and largest contains archaeological specimens dating from the Jomon period to the eighth century BC. The second is a small collection of nineteenth-century objects, including some good quality musical instruments, and the third group contains Ainu objects collected on visits to Hokkaido.

This material illustrates Munro's two main concerns and it stimulated the interest of the present curator of the collections and author of this chapter in this remarkable man. Even the musical instruments relate to one of Munro's hobbies. He had played the violin from the age of three. Though not a performer of great ability, he did play in an amateur orchestra in Yokohama for fun!

It was not unnatural that Munro who already had a medical background should on arriving in Japan in 1891 engage in the study of the physiognomy of a people new to him. He was also interested in the evidence of the past found by the study of archaeology. He explored the Japanese countryside, at first mainly around the Tokyo area, turning over stones with his stick and examining them for evidence of use. He was particularly interested in finding evidence of the Palaeolithic period. There has been much difficulty in matching the stones from the Hayakawa river area, illustrated in his book *Prehistoric Japan* with actual specimens.[4] It was thought that they may be amongst the collections at the National Museums of Scotland or lost in the 1923 earthquake when Munro suffered the destruction of his home in Yokohama. He lost many of his notes, specimens and photographs in the ensuing fire.

Kuwahara Chiyoko in her biography of Munro, *Waga Manrō-den* (1984)[5] suggests that the stones illustrated in his book may be the ones which had been given to Doshisha University, which she was shown there by a Professor Mori. He describes them as being wrapped in English newspapers of the end of the Meiji period and pages from the Yokohama General Hospital notebooks, the story being that these specimens had been moved to Karuizawa and so missed the earthquake. They had finally been given to a doctor, Saeki Riichirō, of Kyoto Maternity Hospital by Chiyoko Munro after Munro's death and Saeki's bereaved family had in turn presented them to the university.

It is still difficult to tell whether these are the original specimens or whether they may be found amongst those at this museum. However, in 1907 Munro did report finding Palaeolithic evidence beneath the volcanic formations of red earth along the Hayakawa and Sakawagawa rivers in Kanagawa prefecture. Although it is difficult to see evidence of working on the stones in the photographs, he wrote that his specimens suggested the presence of Palaeolithic people. Specialist archaeologists have yet to examine all the stones and hopefully find the ones shown, before deciding whether they show signs of use.

PREHISTORIC JAPAN

Gordon Munro's main contribution to the study of Japan was his book, *Prehistoric Japan*. He had spent many years excavating prehistoric sites all over Japan and this comprehensive study and his papers to the Asiatic Society of Japan portray him as a keen observer. He had earlier published *Coins of Japan* in Yokohama (1904) which remains a useful reference work in English on this subject. When it was published in Yokohama in 1908, Munro's book on Japanese prehistory was hailed by Japanese as well as by the expatriate community. *Shigaku Zazzhi*, the senior journal in the historical field, asserted:

> 'Its value consists . . . in its contents, which are not a mere recapitulation of old opinions but an admirable exposition of its own. His investigation of ancient sites, his study of ancient relics and his acknowledgement of other work, prove his ability and the sincerity of his scientific investigation.'[6]

Meanwhile, the *Yorozu Chōhō* ventured an assessment of Munro himself, saying that he was '. . . in the same rank as Chamberlain, Aston, Satow and Murdoch: he produced some time ago an excellent book on the *Coins of Japan*: now he has published this great work, supplying invaluable materials for the study of archaeology in Japan'.[7]

The expatriate press of the Japanese treaty ports, not always the most charitable of judges, agreed with this assessment. Thus, the *Japan Times* wrote:

> 'To the names of Morse, Milne, Siebold, Batchelor and the not overlong list of foreign scholars contributing to the archaeology of Japan is now to be added that of Neil Gordon Munro, author of a valuable work on *Coins of Japan*, who now earns the gratitude of the public by giving it a more comprehensive work on the early races of Japan, under the title of *Prehistoric Japan*.'[8]

The *Daily Advertiser* tried to set Munro's work in the context of the research done by foreigners in the Meiji period:

'Since the earlier years of the modern life of Japan when such men as Satow, Brinkley and Chamberlain entered and adorned the field of research here, there has been no work done in that field evincing such scholarly ability or such careful investigation and mastery of its subject as the recently published *Pre-Historic Japan* by Neil Gordon Munro.'[9]

The archaeological collection donated to the National Museums of Scotland by Munro consists of about two thousand objects. The material dates from Jomon to Nara Japan, 10,000 BC to AD 794, though archaeologists have yet to ascertain whether any material from the early Jomon period is present. The collection comprises objects of stone, shell, flint, earthenware and metal. These were mostly excavated in the old provinces of Musashi, Mutsu, Kotsuke and Hokkaido. At least twenty per cent comes from the Mitsusawa Shell-mound, Musashi Province. Another large group of material is less definitively provenanced in northern Japan.

The Mitsusawa shell-mound was excavated by Munro in 1905/6. In 1905 Munro married a Japanese, Takahata Toku, and took out Japanese citizenship. As his work at the Yokohama Hospital took him away from the site during the week, his new wife helped by directing the excavation when he was not there and also probably as an interpreter when he was.

Munro continued the excavation below the shell debris so finding evidence of 'pit-dwellings' of what has since been called the Horinouchi-phase, Late Jomon period. Associated with these dwellings were the burials of five adults and a child. This was the first time that an excavation had continued below the limits of the shell-mound itself and Munro had been richly rewarded for his curiosity. Takahata Toku stayed at the site on the day the burials were discovered, probably to ensure their safety, until Munro and an archaeologist, Yagi Shōzaburō, who had been helping him with the excavation, arrived.

The discovery of skeletal remains in the Mitsusawa shell-mound fired Munro's interest in the origins of the Japanese race and the birthright of the Ainu. Munro suspected from some of the characteristics of these skeletons that the prehistoric inhabitants of Mitsusawa could be related to the modern Ainu living in Hokkaido. He consulted Professor Koganei Yoshikiyo at the Anatomy Department of Tokyo University. Koganei was an authority on Ainu skeletons and agreed with Munro. The cranial indices and many other features had similarities with those of the modern Ainu living in Hokkaido. However, Munro unwittingly found himself at the centre of controversy. His opinion was not popular.

It was possible that this was exacerbated by the fact that he as a foreigner was putting forward theories which would bring the divinity of the Emperor into question. The Imperial family was thought to be descended from the sun goddess, Amaterasu. The study of archaeology and physical anthropology, both introduced from the West, were likely to bring these beliefs into disrepute. It should be noted that it was thought by physical anthropologists at this period that racial characteristics could readily be identified from skulls, a theory that has since been discredited.

Koganei had long been in disagreement with Professor Tsuboi Shōgorō, about the nature of the people of Prehistoric Japan. Tsuboi was an influential figure. He had spent some time in Britain and founded the Anthropology Society of Tokyo in 1886. He later established the Anthropological Institute of Tokyo University. Tsuboi favoured 'the theory of koropok-guru'. Koropokguru was an Ainu term meaning persons dwelling below. These dwarf-like creatures were supposed to be cannibals and the prehistoric inhabitants of Japan. Tsuboi also suggested that they were akin to the Eskimo.

Morse recorded that he found evidence for cannibalism in the Omori shell-mound. Munro was always prepared to question prevailing theories and in *Prehistoric Japan*, he states: 'A careful examination of the human bones from excavations has led to results at variance with those of Professor Morse, so much so indeed, that I feel obliged to dissent from his verdict of prevailing cannibalism.'[10] Morse's theory has been abandoned by modern scholars but Munro was the first Westerner to disagree with it.

Munro published an explanation of his discovery of the skeletons at the Mitsusawa shell-mound in an essay 'The skeletons of Stone Age natives of Japan', where he opposes the theories of Adachi Montarō who suggested that the Stone Age peoples were a mixture of southern and northern peoples. Although Munro discusses his findings in *Prehistoric Japan*, caution prevented him from publishing all his evidence concerning the origins of the Japanese until he had a cast-iron case and political circumstances were more favourable. However, as previously stated, all his notes, specimens, photographs and detailed measurements of eighty Ainu people from visits to Hokkaido were destroyed in the Great Earthquake of 1923.

Today, it is generally accepted that Japan was subject to several migrations from both north and south and that the Japanese race resulted from the mixture of these peoples. It is likely that the Ainu inhabited a much larger part of Japan than Hokkaido at one time and were later driven north by the expanding populations of peoples practising cultivation. The Ainu living in the north of Japan enter the annals of Japanese history at regular intervals as various generals are sent north to quell them.

Munro thought the Ainu probably originated from a branch of an ancient people living in Western Asia. He favoured Turkestan between latitude 40 and 50 North. He assumed one branch penetrated Europe whilst another migrated eastwards following the mammoth and reindeer in their retreat north, dictated by the shrinking glaciers at the end of the last period of glaciation 35,000 years ago. He cites the Ainu use of aconite poison, the religious association with trees of cold and temperate climates and the similarity of the construction of an Ainu roof with a tent drawn on the outline of a mammoth in Bernifal cave from the Aurignacean era, as evidence for this view.

He observed the similarity between facial marks on the clay figurines of the Jomon period and the tattooing found on Ainu women. The enormous eyes on some of these figurines suggested to Munro that they might represent the dead deified, the large closed eyes open to inner spirit vision. He also noted the occurrence on these figures of the commonest patterns used on Ainu ceremonial dress. He suggested that the hair dressing often found on these early figures is referred to in oral tradition, though not part of Ainu culture as he knew it in the 1930s.

He was particularly interested in the similarity between the patterns found on prehistoric Jomon pottery and those carved on Ainu woodwork and it was this which led him initially to investigate the possibilities of a link between the two cultures. Many of the potsherds he excavated show reserved panels of design derived from textile impressions, surrounded by moulded coils. These are echoed in the curved and scrolled borders reserved in relief against intaglio panels filled with hatched designs found carved into wooden artefacts by Ainu craftsmen. The handles of several knives in the Ainu collection at the National Museums of Scotland illustrate this type of decoration and are representative of Ainu design.

The Hakodate Museum, Hokkaido, has examples of Esan and Ebetsu, both types of Zoku Jomon pottery, c. 200–600 AD, found in Hokkaido. The Jomon period lasted much longer in the far north. The designs on these pots are also similar to Ainu design. However, these characteristics are not found on the artefacts of the intervening Satsumon period, c. 600–1300 AD. Much research still needs to be carried out on Ainu prehistory and the parallels between Zoku Jomon and Ainu culture. Comparative studies of research carried out by Japanese anthropologists, archaeologists and historians may help to solve the many problems in this area. Are the bears found on spoons and as handles to pots of the Esan period evidence of an ancient bear cult related to that of the Ainu?

These early discoveries of Munro are finally being recognized in Japan. On April 7 1982 *Prehistoric Japan* was reprinted by Daiichi Shoburu with a commentary by Makoto Saitō, Professor Emeritus of Tokyo University. In his commentary the professor quotes the review of *Shigaku Zasshi*, an historical society magazine, as saying that Munro's book was the most important work among a number of books on Japanese archaeology because of the broad scope and complete study given to the subject. It also points out that this was achieved by an assiduous foreigner and thanks Munro for his study of 'our ancestors' and for stimulating Japanese scholars.

Munro's main contribution to Japanese archaeology was to provide information and comparative material for Westerners through his book and the collections sent to the Royal Scottish Museum in Edinburgh. In Japan he is now recognized as one of the first to dig statigraphically and to reveal 'pit-dwellings' by extending excavation below a shell-midden. It is also possible that he was the first to suggest the presence of Palaeolithic people in Japan.

RESIDENCE IN KARUIZAWA AND HOKKAIDO

In 1921 Munro founded the International Hospital, then known as the Home Sanatorium, at Karuizawa, a hill-station north of Tokyo, where the coolness of the summer attracted those who could afford it away from the heat of the Kanto plain. He was medical director there during the summer months. On 1 September 1923 when the great earthquake hit the Tokyo area, Munro was in Karuizawa. He immediately left for Yokohama and helped the injured in a temporary hospital tent, set up for the purpose as the General Hospital had not survived the earthquake. It was rebuilt by December, but Munro was sixty years of age and decided to retire and move to Karuizawa permanently.

The following March he fell in love with the chief matron of the Home Sanatorium, Kimura Chiyo, who had been transferred from Kobe in 1921. She became his constant companion. Munro had first married in 1895, when he was thirty-two. His wife was German and they had their first child in 1896. Unfortunately, this baby, Robert, died when he was two years old. They had their second son, Ian, in 1990. In 1905 Munro was naturalized and in March he obtained a divorce in order to marry a Japanese, Takahata Toku, in May of that year. They had a daughter in December, Iris, but the marriage lasted no longer than a few years and they were divorced in 1909.

Munro married his third wife in 1914. She was a Swiss woman, named Adele. After falling in love with Chiyo Kimura in 1924, however, Munro separated from Adele. Since he did not hear from her for five years, it was difficult to obtain a divorce. He was finally able to marry Chiyo in 1937. Looking back at his previous marriages in a letter written to a friend during the last years of his life, Munro suggests that he may have been a little unreasonable in the way he treated his earlier wives. He writes that he was always busy following up his research and perhaps did not give enough time to his family. In these last letters he constantly praises the patience and loyalty of his last wife.

In 1928 Munro retired from his post as medical director at Karuizawa Home Sanatorium, though he was appointed to an honorary post. In the following year he met Professor Charles Seligman, a renowned ethnologist, who was distressed to hear of his losses in the earthquake. As Munro could no longer support his Ainu studies at his own expense, Seligman resolved to help him.[11] Funds were secured from the Rockefeller Foundation but unfortunately Munro was not able to use them as they were only applicable to British citizens and Munro had been naturalized in 1905.

Munro moved to Nibutani in the Saru river area of Hokkaido in 1930 on hearing of the likelihood of the grant. After his experience of the earthquake, he wanted a fire-proof library and study. Before these were completed, disaster struck again. One early December morning in 1932 Munro woke to the smell of smoke. For the second time in his life he lost everything.

Although nearly seventy years old Munro did not give up. With the support of friends and further grants he was able to start again. With the help of John Batchelor's *Ainu English Japanese Dictionary and Grammar* (1905) he translated a large number of songs, legends and invocations for the treatment of various ailments. He filmed and photographed many rites and ceremonies and recorded Ainu music and stories. He mentions these in letters to Seligman. His film, *The Bear Ceremony*, an interesting series of photographs and ten chapters of his book *Ainu Past and Present* reached Britain before Japan's entry into the Second World War in 1941. Munro's book, abridged and edited by Brenda Seligman, and entitled *Ainu Creed and Cult* was published posthumously in 1962. The original manuscript and his papers were placed at the Royal Anthropological Institute, London.

Munro established a permanent residence in Nibutani with his companion Kimura Chiyoko. With her help, he gave free medical advice and treatment to those Ainu who wanted it. Having gained their confidence, he kept open house and the villagers gathered at his home to tell stories, sing songs and talk of old times. His letters to Professor Seligman during the 1930s mention a weekly concert with tea and home-made cakes and note '. . . the popularity of Chiyoko who treated the Ainu as honoured guests'. Munro thus became friendly with several elderly men and women who were still well versed in Ainu lore which was fast disappearing under growing Japanese influence. Grateful patients and their relatives were also a useful source of information.

GIRDLES OF AINU WOMEN

It was in this way that he discovered evidence of matrilineal descent. Whilst enquiring about a form of bullroarer which was used to still a tempest or repel demons of pestilence, Munro was told about the secret girdle which women wore under their clothes. He was informed that they could use the power of their girdles to stamp out pestilence, repel a storm and hold back a fire. He remembered seeing a group of women standing at a discreet distance from his house during the fire of 1932, waving their arms and probably gyrating their bodies. He only realized the significance of what they had been doing subsequently.

Investigating the girdles was a delicate matter as they were secret and should not be seen or talked of by men. However, several women were grateful to Munro for the medical care he had given to their relatives. Munro used Scottish tartans and heraldic crests to illustrate his interest in signs of kinship. With the help of his wife, he was able to persuade these women to make copies of their girdles for him and explain their significance. These copies are now in the British Museum. They employ string made from the bast of the elm rather than the more generally used hemp produced from nettle fibres. This substitution, it was hoped, would mitigate the impropriety of the task they had performed for a man and a foreigner. Munro was later able to secure two original examples and these were also given to the British Museum.

It is important to emphasize the special relationship Munro had with these women. They would not have divulged the information about these girdles if they had not felt in great debt to Munro for his treatment of their close relatives. Thus he was able to elicit information that was not available to other researchers. He was also carrying out his investigations in the 1930s when some of the informants were very old and many Ainu traditions were still living beliefs.

The girdles are referred to as *upshoro tush*, bosom cord, which aptly describes the plaited cord of eight strings from which it is made up. More politely it was called *upshoro kut*, bosom girdle, and in ancient tradition it is referred to as *a-eshimukep*. 'A' is an honorific corresponding to the Japanese 'O' and *eshimukep* means 'most hidden thing'.

Altogether Munro discovered eight types of *kut* associated with various deities within the Ainu Pantheon. Most of these were theriomorphic such as the bear, fox, eagle, wolf, badger and grampus or salt-water deity. The specific manufacture and design of each girdle was supposed to have been taught to each deity by the fire goddess *Kanui Fuchi* referred to by Munro as the great ancestress, supreme over the ancestral cult. Each deity was then thought to have assumed human form to mate with an Ainu and pass on the secret lore to her daughter. There appear to be girdles associated directly with *Kamui Fuchi* but Brenda Seligman suggests that, as all women believed themselves to be allied to the fire goddess, who gave instructions for making the girdles, the possibility of these specimens being associated with theriomorphic deities as well should not be excluded.

The matrilineal group of four generations provided a bond of kinship in all crises such as childbirth, illness and funerals. Although it included the sons and brothers of the women involved it was mainly the women who gave each other help and comfort. A girl's maternal uncle also had some say in whom she married.

Itoppa are found on the ends of the upper surface, or underneath some *pasuy* or libation sticks, used when praying to the gods. These marks exist on various ritual items such as *inau* or offerings, and *tsuki*, the cup and saucer, often made of lacquer, used when making libations to the gods. These marks often represent one of the Ainu theriomorphic gods. Munro describes these as patrilineal ancestor signs. He was told their use was restricted to one *pasuy* in each household and that this was taken on hunting expeditions partly for protection and partly for identification in case of death. Munro was also told that special methods of securing *inau* to their poles, for offering at the *nusa* (family altar), were passed down from father to son. In this way the deity was able to identify who had made the offering. *Inau* are offerings made to the gods, which often act as an intermediary. *Itoppa* have many different forms for one deity and Fosco Maraini[12] illustrates ninety-seven forms which could be derived from a simple shape of the whale.

Munro found that ancestors could be recalled for two generations on average. A few elders could go back between five and ten generations, there was one exceptional case of an elder recalling fifteen generations. Often women were better at remembering their matrilineal ancestors, most being able to recall at least the four generations which comprised the matrilineal group.

MISCELLANEOUS RESEARCHES

In his original manuscript Munro described Ainu textile traditions in detail, both weaving and the making of mats. He also describes hunting activities, building a house, the exorcising of evil spirits and many other Ainu traditions not all of which were transferred to *Ainu Creed and Cult*.

The special relationship Munro had with his patients gave them the confidence to divulge sensitive information about aspects of their culture, such as the secret girdles worn by women discussed above. He was able to elicit information that was not available to other researchers. The problem does not appear to be that Munro was given false information; rather that some of the information is now incomplete. In the case of the girdles their design was probably a form of *itoppa* and evidence of matrilineal descent.

Munro also sent the Royal Scottish Museum over 150 objects between 1908 and 1914, a period long before he lived in Nibutani. However, it is probable that most of the collection comes from the Saru river area as he is likely to have had contacts there many years before he settled at Nibutani in the 1930s. The greater part of the collection has ritual significance, there being 117 of this nature. This reflects one of Munro's prime interests as illustrated in his book *Ainu Creed and Cult* (1962).[13] Of these objects twenty-three are associated with iomande (the bear festival), a ceremony which Munro recorded on film and wished to preserve. In this view he was totally opposed to Dr John Batchelor who described it as a 'very degrading and cruel spectacle'. Munro notes that it was unfortunate that Batchelor's theological bias prevented him from sympathizing with the beliefs which had 'sustained Ainu hearts'. Munro wrote to Batchelor, who advised the Hokkaido government on the Ainu, suggesting that, if he wished to preserve the Ainu, he should move more slowly in altering their religious outlook. Batchelor's reply contained a tacit admission that he was opposing Munro's investigation.

Of fifty *pasuy* (libation sticks used in prayer) in the collection, seven are *kike* (those which have shavings cut on them and are used at the bear festival) and a further fourteen have *itoppa* (a mark identifying village of lineage). Many of these are typical of the Saru river area. The six *inau* in the collection have no *itoppa*, indicating their provenance as Saru river. The rest of the ritual material includes seven robes, one of attush, and six of cotton, various other articles of dress, *shintoko* (treasures), *ikayup* (quivers), arrows used in the bear festival, again mainly from the Saru river, and fifteen *ikayup ikoro*.

The *ikayup ikoro*, small model quivers, are of special interest as they reflect Munro's concern with medicine. One of their uses was to ensure good health in Ainu children. When a child was asleep, the *ikayup ikoro* was slipped under the pillow. The belief was that it would enhance the qualities desired of children and ensure their good health. They were also used when a child was sick in the belief that they would drive away the evil spirit. Munro was careful not to interfere with traditional forms of medicine, only treating Ainu who asked him for help and then respecting traditional methods where practical. Hunting methods are represented mainly by bow and arrow. There are both carrying and spring arrows, some parts of a spring bow trap and various quivers.

Gordon Munro was also interested in the domestic skills of the Ainu, particularly weaving. The collection has eleven pieces of weaving equipment including an *obita* (loom) incorporating a roll of woven attush and a ball of fibre with heddle, warp spacer and separator. Other items include *attushpera* (beaters), *shunkana* (shuttle), two more *wosa* (warp spacers) a *kamakap* (warp separator) of the headrest type, a girdle which is attached to the roller for the woven material and fits round the weaver's back enabling her to provide the loom's tension, and a *nuitsayep* (thread winder). There are several examples of weaving amongst the clothing in the collection. Munro also observed methods of weaving, mat-making and measuring thread.

MUNRO'S ACHIEVEMENT

In trying to assess Munro's contribution to the study of the Ainu, it is paramount to consider the time at which he was carrying out his investigations. Munro made his first visit to Hokkaido in 1898 when he was thirty-five. After many subsequent visits he settled in Nibutani in 1930 when he was sixty-seven, living there until his death in 1942. He was carrying out his research when many Ainu traditions were still being practised and their rituals expressed living beliefs. This would account for some of the differences of opinion between his view of certain religious beliefs and those of his successors.

To take one example: there is some disagreement between Munro's interpretation of the spiritual essence of vegetation and that of Watanabe Hitoshi, a research member of the Tokyo Joint Research Committee on the Ainu. Munro was told that the essence (*ramat*) of the god of vegetation (Shiramba Kamui) was distributed throughout plant life so it was present in the trees that provided houses, domestic utensils, tools and firewood. It was particularly strong in oak and especially potent in aconite, which was used as poison, but resided in all types of vegetation.

Watanabe stated that every plant is the 'incarnation of a spirit' and that sacred objects made of vegetable matter derive their virtue from the spirit of the individual plant from which they are made, not from Shiramba Kamui. It has been suggested that when the Tokyo Committee were carrying out their investigations in the 1950s, religious ideas may have been remembered as theological doctrine rather than as living belief.

Munro had a special relationship with many of his informants. Often they were in debt to him for medical services and grateful for the opportunity to help him in his studies. Many of them were very old and well versed in Ainu lore. Both Munro and his wife Chiyoko were popular amongst the Ainu. They respected Ainu traditions and did not want to encourage them to become Christian as did the missionaries such as John Batchelor. The Munros wished to preserve the Bear festival, not ban it.

The Ainu had been a life-long concern of Munro's. He wished to record for posterity the richness and diversity of a disappearing culture with no written language. He wished to contradict the ideas propagated by A.S. Landor who wrote: 'I wish my reader clearly to understand that their intelligence does not go much further than that of an intelligent monkey, though of course the Ainu have the advantage over beasts of being able to talk.'[14]

Munro published books on diverse subjects apart from his two main areas of interest. *Coins of Japan* (1904) has already been mentioned. He wrote a philosophical book, *The Soul in Being* (1918). His musings even included an essay, *The Riddle of Mentality and Einstein* (1922) which he presented to Einstein when he met him at the Tokyo Imperial Hotel in 1927. He was still concerned with philosophy when he was seventy-two and wrote an essay entitled *Life and Truth, Riddle of Existence* (1935).

Even at the end of his life Munro was still abreast of current affairs and was meeting important contemporaries such as Helen Keller at Sapporo in 1937. When he died in 1942 Fosco Maraini, who remembers him well, wrote his obituary in the *Japan Times*. Maraini, who was then a student studying for his PhD but has since been honoured for his many contributions to fostering an understanding of Japan in the West, describes Munro as a man of catholic tastes. He goes on to discuss Munro's philosophical work *Soul in Being*, as revealing '. . . the author's uncommonly deep and well focused knowledge of what were then the latest developments in chemistry, physics, biology, psychology and epistemology, together with a profuse cropping up of quotations from Shakespeare, Bacon, or from classical and Indian writers'. Maraini sees this as a natural result of Munro's '. . . untiring wanderings in every field where man's soul exerts its capacities'.

Maraini greatly admired Munro for his humanity and unaffectedness. He found his conversation, somewhat one-sided but never pompous. He certainly had his fixed ideas and recurring subjects but never gave the impression he was lecturing. 'He would never stick to a subject if the subject would not stick to itself . . .' and like many old men Munro had his recurring jokes which Maraini 'soon learned by heart' but this, he says, '. . . only made him more human and loveable'.

Two anecdotes from the obituary will help us to fill out the picture a little. Maraini describes walking in the village of Nibutani with Munro: '. . . he would march along with his youthful gait, with his pipe in his mouth and a stick in his hand, pushing aside a stone . . . "This wasn't here last Tuesday" . . . pointing out some feature of the landscape . . . "Old Shirabeno's wife died some days ago. He's put up a remarkable row of inau beyond his hut".' Inau were offerings to the gods.

'The Ainu all knew him: and all loved him. For nearly ten years he had been constantly ready to visit them in their illnesses, to give them medicine, to console them, to encourage them. During his last illness, while he could hardly speak, a poor woman from a village very far away brought a child with a serious case of poliomyelitis to the "good doctor". He saw the child and faintly, slowly, gave the mother all the advice such a case would need. Afterwards, exhausted he fell again on his pillow unable to utter a word for many hours.'[15]

Another admirer was (Sir) George Sansom who worked at the British embassy from the 1900s. His biographer records that Munro was '. . . a Scot who possessed the passion for learning of his educated countrymen . . . [Sansom] used to stay in the doctor's nursing home near Karuizawa, enjoying his learned talk and entertained by his stringent speech and somewhat eccentric personality'.[16]

Sansom respected the painstaking research which Munro gave to the background and provenance of the Ainu people:

> 'Munro collected their skills, and at one time drew upon himself vague suspicions and doubts. It was even said that he came near to being expelled from the country. But one thinks his medical skills must have come to his rescue. Not to exclude his Scottish stubbornness – a difficult man to get rid of'.[17]

In assessing Munro's contribution to Japanese studies, it is important to consider the prevailing politics of the period when he was carrying out his research in Japan. Japan's seclusion during the exploration of ideas and the industrial revolution in Europe meant that there had to be periods of adjustment to ideas and disciplines which had been formed in the West over a longer period.

Some of these disciplines such as the study of the human species and its origins were going to be politically sensitive in a country which had just reaffirmed its loyalty to a divine Emperor. This reaffirmation was central to overthrowing a military dictator who was related to the Tokugawa shoguns. This family had united Japan in 1600 and closed the country to all foreigners except a carefully controlled number with trading concessions in Nagasaki.

Munro was neither professional archaeologist nor anthropologist in an academic sense, but he was a pioneer in both disciplines. He used the genealogical method, taught to him by Seligman, to help him elucidate the social organization of the Ainu. He was also very well read in both subjects and familiar with the leading theories and scholars of the day. Above all, he recorded what he saw and heard in detail and had the possible advantage of not having to fit it all into pre-conceived and rigid structures of academic discipline. As Fosco Maraini said of him,

Munro was '. . . a typical representative of the modern thinker who not only speculates but observes'.

18

Sir Robert Craigie as Ambassador to Japan 1937–1941

ANTONY BEST

THE REPUTATION of Sir Robert Craigie (1883–1959) as ambassador to Japan in the years 1937–41 is one of more controversial subjects in the history of inter-war Anglo-Japanese relations. Two schools of thought have appeared in an effort to assess his impact; one has portrayed Craigie as a man inexperienced in Japanese affairs and thus too easily given to unwarranted acts of appeasement in an attempt to win over the nebulous Japanese 'moderates'.[1] The other school has in contrast drawn a picture of a realist all too aware of Britain's weakness in East Asia and determined to use his substantial skills as a negotiator to prevent the outbreak of a potentially disastrous war for Britain.[2] In attempting to present a portrait of Craigie, both schools have focused primarily on the various crises with which he had to contend, such as Tientsin in 1939, the *Asama Maru* and Burma Road incidents in 1940, and the final path to war in 1941. In addition, there has been much debate over his contentious Final Report in 1943, in which he criticized the Churchill government for not having done enough to try to prevent war from breaking out. There is, however, a danger in concentrating simply on these crises because, although they are important, they do not necessarily lead one to see the broader motives behind his thinking: to get a real understanding of Craigie's attitude towards his role as ambassador one first has to look at his career in the years immediately preceding his appointment.

One of the most important things to note is that before he

reached Yokohama on 3 September 1937 Craigie had never held a position within the Far Eastern Department at the Foreign Office or been posted to East Asia, and does not even appear to have had any substantial links with the Japanophile lobby in Britain. He instead emerged as a figure of some prominence in the field of Anglo-Japanese relations due to his role as Britain's chief negotiator in the naval limitation talks of 1934–36. This was significant for two reasons; first, because it helps to explain why many of his later contemporaries in Japan treated his observations on Japanese politics with disdain, and second, because Craigie's experience in the naval talks left him with a deep-rooted personal belief in how Japan should be perceived relative to Britain's global interests. It was this resolutely 'power political' approach, rather than one of espousing a sentimental *rapprochement* at any price', which was to be the main influence on his diplomatic efforts in Tokyo, and which was to make his position different from the Japanophiles in British circles.

Fundamental to Craigie's assessment of his responsibilities in Japan was the belief that he should do all in his power to neutralize that country in terms of the global struggle for influence with Germany and that, in particular, he should counter Ribbentrop's efforts to win over Japan. As early as January 1936 Craigie was indicating his fear of the consequences of a German–Japanese understanding, and in December of that year, after the signing of the Anti-Comintern Pact, he wrote in response to a criticism of the Eden–Yoshida talks from the then British ambassador to Japan, Sir Robert Clive, that:

> '. . . to rebuff our friends in Japan just at the moment when there much searching of the Japanese heart as to the wisdom of the recent agreement with Germany would be to play the German game.'[3]

This assessment of a potential two-front threat to British interests led Craigie to believe that Britain should be circumspect in its treatment of Japan and, while deploring in private Japan's unprincipled expansionism, avoid any moralistic outbursts which would only have the effect of antagonizing the Japan policy-makers. The logical consequence of this attitude was a distinct tendency to play down Britain's regional interests in East Asia for the sake of the larger goal of keeping Japan placid on the global scale.

The most obvious example of this came with Craigie's contention that Britain should adhere strictly to a policy of neutrality in the Sino-Japanese war, on the grounds that Japan was bound to win and that to support the Chinese in any way would antagonize the Japanese needlessly. This was not a popular line to take, as it seemed to ignore the general sentiment that China was deserving of support and the feeling that a Japanese victory would mark the collapse of Britain's considerable economic stake in East Asia. In July 1938 *The Times'* journalist Peter Fleming noted in this respect that:

> 'His line seems to be to drift in a dignified way into a position where, in a haze of benevolence, we shall be presented by the Japanese with the jackal's share in China (which the poor sap believes will be worth having) . . . [T]hough he may be following what is nowadays often called by the English a "realistic" policy, he almost entirely fails to apprehend the realities in Eastern Asia, however alive he may be to the realities in Europe.'[4]

In this analysis Fleming missed the point of Craigie's case, which was that the potential danger of a German-Japanese military alliance meant that the 'realities in Europe' were of vital importance to the formulation of Britain's East Asia policy, and that to concentrate upon defending every aspect of Britain's interests in China would only create grave dangers. The clearest expression of Craigie's views on this subject came in a telegram to the Foreign Office at the height of the Tientsin Crisis, in which he noted caustically:

> 'There has been an open partisanship about our policy which in the circumstances of today does more credit to our heart than to our head. . . . I feel bound to emphasise deadly dangers to which we are heading if we cannot get back to a position of stricter neutrality.'[5]

Another example of Craigie's emphasis on the need to take cognizance of the global consequences of Britain's policy towards Japan was his reaction to the debate in Whitehall in 1939–40 over war-time relations with Japan. With the start of the European war it became even more necessary than ever to isolate Japan as a threat, and Craigie felt that Britain could best achieve this by taking the opportunity provided by Germany and Japan's falling out over the Nazi–Soviet Pact to improve relations with

Tokyo. On 16 November he wrote forthrightly to the Foreign Office:

> '. . . I assume it to be of vital importance that Japan should not become an adversary in the present conflict and, however improbable this may appear at the moment, we must try to arrest at the start any trend in policy leading to that direction.'[6]

He saw the potential for increasing mutual understanding in a number of spheres, and argued in particular for a quick solution to the continuing controversy over Tientsin and for Britain to take a lenient attitude towards Japan over problems arising from the policy of economic warfare against Germany.

The height of his efforts to pursue this policy came, however, in July 1940 when, in reaction to the latest crisis in Anglo-Japanese relations over the Burma Road, he argued not simply for a solution to that particular issue but for an altogether wider settlement. He began a telegram on 14 July by arguing:

> 'In general I agree with the underlying ideas; Powers having possessions in East Asia should be prepared to make concessions to Japan as a means of purchasing a generous peace for China.'[7]

He then proceeded to set out Japan's grievances against the West, and came to the conclusion that the most effective way in which Britain and the United States could satisfy Japan's sense of being discriminated against was to allow her much easier access to raw materials, which he held to be more important to Japan than territorial aggrandizement. This was a penetrating analysis of Japan's motives for trying to revise the international system, and can be contrasted usefully with Craigie's comments in 1936 about the idea of a colonial deal with Germany, when he had stated: 'What puts us wrong not only with Germany but with the whole world is the slogan, when applied to mandates, of "what we have we hold".'[8] This type of analysis was a logical extension of his fears of the consequences of imperial over-commitment and showed that Craigie's thinking was capable of moving beyond the short-term, day-to-day defence of British interests to a broader understanding that a rigid and inflexible defence of the *status quo* might create the very challenge which one wanted to avoid.

To state that Craigie's aim was to avoid war by tailoring

British policy to eschew confrontation does, of course, suggest that his policy was tantamount to appeasement and that, in terms of his attitude towards China, it involved all the sacrifice of another nation's interests and moral pejoration that the word implies. This view can also be supported by reference to the common claim that Craigie was a 'Chamberlain man', and the widely held but unsubstantiated suggestion that Chamberlain had been responsible for his appointment.[9] In addition, one can point to Craigie's reaction in an embassy memorandum to the Munich Agreement, which was to praise it for its realism and laud it as a check to Hitler's ambitions.[10] In taking such a moralist view, however, one has to be careful, for Craigie's advice by no means always stressed conciliation over confrontation; there was an important element in his thinking of making it clear to Japan that Britain was willing to agree to a reasonable settlement of Anglo-Japanese rivalries but that, if pushed, it was equally willing to see escalation. To choose but one example, during the early days of the Tientsin Crisis, while engaging in efforts to get the Japanese government to accept talks, Craigie was also urging the Foreign Office to set up the necessary apparatus to oversee the initiation of economic sanctions.[11]

There were indeed occasions when Craigie went further than espousing a 'carrot-and-stick' policy, and instead came down strongly in favour of the need for harsh action to be taken against Japan. One example of this can be seen in January 1939 when, following Japan's unilateral abrogation of the Nine Power Treaty and amid rumours of Japanese negotiations with Germany and Italy about a military alliance, Craigie wrote a strident letter to Sir Alexander Cadogan, the permanent under-secretary at the Foreign Office, in which he observed:

> '. . . I advocated a policy of conciliation here as long as I felt there was any hope of the Japanese people playing fair with us; but the prolongation of this trouble, the military successes and the eclipse (temporarily I hope) of more reasonable elements from Japanese political life have necessitated a change of method on our part until such time as the situation here changes for the better.'[12]

This sense of disillusionment caused Craigie to propose that Britain should urge strongly on the United States, which had just requested an exchange of views with the Foreign Office on the subject of economic reprisals against Japan, a policy of refusing to purchase gold from Japanese banks.[13] However, the interest of Washington in pursuing a tougher line towards Japan was not to last long, and Craigie was forced to return to his usual cautious stance.

The above incident is significant because it helps to illustrate that Craigie's attitude towards Japan was not constant and that, in particular, it was influenced by two transient factors; first, the position in Japanese political life of a group of policy-makers who were seen by Craigie as moderates and, second, the continuing debate in Washington over whether or not the Roosevelt administration should take a more active role in East Asia and throw off the shackles of isolationism. Of these two factors it is the influence on Craigie of the Japanese 'moderates' which has been the most controversial. As the comment made by Craigie to Cadogan illustrates, the ambassador was convinced that there did exist in Japan a group of politicians and others who were broadly sympathetic to the idea of closer Anglo-Japanese relations, but this was by no means a view shared by many of his British and American contemporaries. The most significant of these critics in this area of debate was the commercial counsellor at the British embassy in Tokyo, Sir George Sansom who, with his long experience in Japan, felt that the 'moderates', if they did exist, only differed in terms of method rather than aim from the 'radicals', and that they were anyway small in number and not very influential.[14] This view was shared by the Far Eastern Department in the Foreign Office and also by Stanley Hornbeck, the adviser on Far Eastern Affairs to the State Department in Washington.[15]

To Craigie this dismissal of the Japanese 'moderates' was overly cynical and lacking in an understanding of the subtleties of the situation. His reaction to one particular episode, in which Hornbeck told Lord Lothian, the British ambassador to the United States, that he entirely discounted the influence of the 'moderates', was to note to the Foreign Office:

'Though every Japanese naturally desires the advancement of his country's fortunes, distinction must be made between moderates who favour gradual economic expansion through the control of vital raw materials and the development of overseas markets as the solution for Japan's organic economic ills, and extremists who, impelled by mystical fanaticism, aspire to world domination.'[16]

His belief in the existence and significance of a 'moderate' group can be seen as having its origins in two factors, first the fact that the majority of the Japanese contacts that Craigie had made before his appointment to Tokyo, such as Matsudaira Tsuneo, Rear Admiral Yamamoto Isoroku, Yoshida Shigeru and Nagai Matsuzō, favoured a broadly pro-Western foreign policy and, second, the influence of the military attaché he had inherited in Japan, Major-General F.S.G. Piggott.[17]

IN PURSUIT OF JAPAN'S 'MODERATES'

Piggott's acquaintance with Japan was almost as long as that of Sansom, but his conclusions about the direction of Japanese policy in 1937, when Craigie arrived in Japan, were very different from those of the commercial counsellor. Where Sansom saw only a cause for pessimism, Piggott felt that, if sufficient patience and understanding was shown by both sides, then some sort of *rapprochement* was possible. This attitude, unsurprisingly perhaps, appealed to Craigie more than that of Sansom, for Piggott's thinking seemed to be in line with his desire to counter Germany's influence in Tokyo, and also offered a greater prospect for a personal diplomatic triumph. The result was that Piggott was soon able to develop a close relationship with Craigie, introducing him to Anglophile Japanese and stressing what the 'moderates' could achieve if only given the chance. The ambassador's seeming reliance on the military attaché was anathema to the Far Eastern Department, and indeed to a number of the junior members of the embassy staff, and only helped to underline the impression that Craigie was naive when it came to understanding Japan.

To argue that Craigie's belief in the 'moderates' rested only on the above two factors would, however, be to do him a disservice, and in particular it is too easy to blame his enthusiasms on Piggott. The fact of the matter was that, in the main, it was Craigie's experience of diplomacy in Japan that led him to believe that there was a moderate branch of opinion in the Japanese government. In negotiation after negotiation Craigie found that there were figures, particularly in the Gaimushō, who favoured an amelioration of tensions. His talks with General

Ugaki Kazushige in the late summer of 1938, and his meetings with Araki Hachirō over Tientsin in July and August 1939 and over the *Asama Maru* in January and February 1940, seemed to show that with the right sort of approach common ground could be found to overcome even the most difficult of crises.

The inference from these experiences was that, when he was allowed to engage in real diplomacy, progress could be made, but that he was only allowed to negotiate when the Foreign Office had dug themselves in to a new crisis. Even in these circumstances Craigie was only allowed to operate on a very short leash and the Far Eastern Department remained as a constant immovable obstacle to any attempt to strike a more general deal with his Japanese counterparts. The result was a growing sense of exasperation on the ambassador's part, which sometimes boiled over into waspish attacks on the Foreign Office; for example, during the Tientsin Crisis, when Piggott was criticized by the department over his informal meetings with Japanese army officers, Craigie wrote back to London:

> 'I am left here with the feeling that such efforts as we are able to make here to prevent the state of our relations with Japan from going from bad to worse are viewed with suspicion and misgiving by the Far Eastern Department and that only when we are engaged in our normal duty of protesting and recriminating can you really sleep comfortably in your beds.'[18]

However, as noted above, there were times when it appeared clear to Craigie that the influence of the 'moderates' had been eclipsed temporarily and that Japan under the 'extremists' was bent on confrontation. In these circumstances his usual policy was to urge the Foreign Office to follow a more coercive line in the hope that pressure on the Japanese government might lead to a revival of moderate fortunes, or at the very least deter them from escalating tensions further.

It is noticeable that on these occasions Craigie's espousal of a tougher policy was frequently influenced by the simultaneous possibility of Britain receiving diplomatic support from the United States but, even when he seemingly was swept away with enthusiasm at the chances of Anglo-American co-operation, he retained a somewhat jaundiced view of Washington. In understanding Craigie's thinking on America, it is again important to see him as heavily influenced by his diplomatic experience prior to his arrival in Tokyo. His role in the naval talks and his years from 1928 to 1934 as head of the American Department in the Foreign Office had led him to construct his own views on the reliability of the United States, which are best summed up in a letter he wrote to Lord Simon in July 1940:

> '. . . the Americans are for ever inciting us to assume an attitude of utmost firmness towards Japan, only to tell us, when the inevitable crisis comes, that they are of course not in a position to use force. I have been aware of this tendency from the start but the Far Eastern Department of the Foreign Office have been less wary – or perhaps less well-acquainted with American methods – than I have been.'[19]

This cynical assessment helped in general to cement even further his belief that Britain should pursue a cautious policy towards Japan, for he felt that, if Britain should confront Japan, there was little chance that America would do more than support Britain with high-sounding rhetoric. This is not to deny that there were various episodes during his time in Tokyo when the United States did appear to be on the verge of collaborating with Britain against Japan, for example in January 1938 and January 1939, but even in these circumstances, when pressed to commit itself, Washington backed down.

In arguing that Craigie's actions as ambassador must be seen against the background of Britain's global security problems, the reluctance of the United States to commit itself to Britain's aid in East Asia, and the complications caused by the factionalism in the Japanese polity, it is possible to see his preferred policy not so much as one of abject appeasement but rather as a practical response to a complex and potentially explosive situation. There may have been occasionally a streak of naïvety in his optimism about the good intentions of the Japanese 'moderates', but in the end his view that, as Britain already had enough enemies in the world, it would be foolish to alienate another power needlessly, was fundamentally sound. In the years 1937–40 this was a sensible attitude to take, and Craigie's long-term vision and skill in negotiations acted as a useful counter to a Far Eastern Department which at times seemed hell-bent on propelling Britain into desperately dangerous crises over relatively trivial issues, the most obvious case being Tientsin.

FINAL MONTHS OF PEACE

It is, however, arguable whether Craigie's attitude towards the events of 1941 was as sound as his advice had been in previous years. Before looking at his role in the final months of peace, it is worth noting that from August 1940 Craigie took an increasingly tough line towards Japan. The initial catalyst for this change appears to have been the widespread arrests of British civilians in Japan in late July and early August and the suicide in Japanese custody of the Reuters' correspondent, Melville Cox. Following on from this, the Japanese occupation of north Indo-China and Japan's accession to the Tripartite Pact with Germany and Italy seem to have confirmed in Craigie's mind that the 'moderates' had been swept away by the new Konoe cabinet. In addition, these events caused the Roosevelt administration to conclude that Japan must be resisted, and the subsequent galvanization of America's resources and will seemed to suggest that Britain could afford to take a tougher stance itself. The result was that by 11 October 1940 Craigie was reporting to the Foreign Office:

> 'The pro-British faction has been driven . . . to ground . . . and is now powerless to exert any influence whatsoever. Japanese foreign policy will continue to be dominated by the extremists until such a time as the Axis powers meet with a decisive reverse in Europe or until the period of an unwanted war with the United States becomes so great that a decisive change in popular opinion begins to make itself felt.'[20]

Craigie's pessimism manifested itself in the autumn and winter of 1940–41 in his urging on the Foreign Office the introduction of economic sanctions against Japan, the reinforcement of Britain's military position in South-East Asia, and increased defence collaboration with the Americans; the emphasis was now squarely on containment rather than conciliation.

His backing for the expansion of sanctions, however, began to become more conditional in the spring of 1941, when he feared that restrictions on the sale of foodstuffs to Japan, such as Canadian wheat and copra from north Borneo, might, instead of deterring Japan, drive her into further aggression.[21] On 21 May his fears in this field led him to warn that:

> 'To extend restrictions on Japanese imports to an extent that would force Japan to draw on her reserves on any

considerable scale would at present be liable to produce those very actions we wish to avoid.'[22]

This he saw as the worst possible outcome for a Britain which was still fighting for its very survival against Germany, and he took it as read that Britain should do all in its power to prevent a war in South-East Asia. In general, it can be taken from this that he saw the object of sanctions as hurting Japan and making her rethink her present path, but not as a means of inducing surrender.

Despite these reservations about the direction of British policy, Craigie did not, however, raise any objections to the Anglo-American-Dutch introduction of a far more comprehensive sanctions policy in late July 1941 following the Japanese occupation of south Indo-China. In the light of the nature of the provocation he saw this as a just chastisement of Japan, and this fits in with the pattern of his support in previous crises for the use of the 'stick' as well as the 'carrot'. Even with the benefit of hindsight he noted in his Final Report that this action:

'. . . had the merit of removing from the minds of the more responsible Japanese leaders the lingering hope that any further southward advance could be made without the virtual certainty of war with the United States.'[23]

He did, though, begin to express doubts when it became clear in September that this policy of coercion was not to be balanced by one of rewarding concessions by Japan unless those concessions bordered on a complete surrender of all the material advantages Japan had gained since 1935. His view of this apparent lack of desire for a compromise in Washington, which he shared with the American ambassador in Tokyo, Joseph Grew, was that it would not deter war but only make it more likely.[24] On 9 September he noted to the Foreign Office:

'Neither my United States colleague or I are (sic!) suggesting any relaxation at this stage of measures our two countries have taken against Japan: but it stands to reason that in a confused situation such as exists today in Japan the more clearly we can bring home to the Japanese public the advantages of a break with Matsuoka's policy the better.'[25]

Faced with the resolute refusal of Washington over the next two months to take a more positive attitude towards negotiations, Craigie could only hope to remedy the situation by pressing the Foreign Office to intervene in the Hull–Nomura talks, but here, too, there was firm opposition to even the faintest glimmer of compromise. It is over this issue that Craigie's reputation has become most controversial, for in his Final Report it is Britain's failure to try to influence thinking in Washington that comes in for the greatest criticism. In analyzing this episode, it is crucial to understand that Craigie was as convinced as ever that his mission was to prevent Britain from being faced with a second front that would turn the European war into a global conflict that would fatally overstretch Britain's limited resources. What he failed to see was that Britain's priorities had now changed; by this stage of the war Britain had reached full wartime production levels but was still unable to challenge German domination of Europe, and in Eastern Europe the Soviet Union in late November 1941 looked to be on the verge of defeat. The result was that it had become increasingly clear in London that the war could only be won if America not only committed its economic might to the allied cause, but also became a full combatant.[26]

The necessity for the United States to fight alongside the British was so vital to Churchill and his advisers that it outweighed any risks arising from a possible Japanese entry, although of course this perception of relative worth was influenced by the gross underestimation of Japanese military potential. This line of thinking influenced the Foreign Office into arguing that the most dangerous thing they could do in autumn 1941 was to advise the State Department to compromise in its Pacific policy, for such action would raise the spectre of appeasement and perhaps have unfortunate consequences in Congress and on American public opinion.[27]

It can therefore be said that, though Craigie's criticisms of American policy were arguably valid, in that a more flexible policy might have led to war being averted, this cannot be said of his attacks on the Churchill cabinet, as the latter were pursuing the only policy that seemed at that time to offer the prospect of victory, namely, the concerted wooing of the United States. It might be held that, in hindsight, Britain's apparent acquiescence to the path of war proved to be disastrous with the loss of Malaya and Burma and the shaming defeat at Singapore, but even this analysis can be balanced by Churchill's comment on Craigie's Final Report in which he observed:

'It was . . . a blessing that Japan attacked the United States and thus brought the United States into the war. Greater good fortune has rarely happened to the British Empire than this event which has revealed our friends and foes in their true light . . .'[28]

It is difficult to escape the conclusion that in 1941 Craigie's previous innate sense of what policy would best serve Britain's global interests deserted him. In a sense this is not surprising; he was after all many miles away from the main theatre of war, and had not returned to London since his first appointment in 1937. In his isolation he adhered to his original orders to keep Japan out of the war at all costs, not realizing that such a policy was now considered expendable.

Craigie was detained after Pearl Harbor and returned to England in the diplomatic repatriation ship in 1942. He went into retirement at the age of 58, but served as UK representative to the UN War Crimes Commission (1945–8) and to the Geneva Conference for the protection of the victims of war (1949).

Craigie's period in Tokyo is thus not an easy one to assess in terms of whether he proved to be a good ambassador or not, and the task is not made any simpler by the continuing partisan debate over the morality of Britain's appeasement policy in the late 1930s. It is important in putting Craigie in context to get away from the idea that he was merely a 'Chamberlain man' with all the connotations that that implies, and instead judge him on his own records and words. The picture that emerges is of a man trapped in one of the most difficult diplomatic missions imaginable; he was set the task of keeping Japan mollified so that there would be no chance of an alliance between Tokyo and Berlin, but at the same time was supposed to do all he could to protect Britain's interests in East Asia, where virtually insoluble differences naturally led to rising Anglo-Japanese antagonism. In these circumstances it seemed logical to Craigie to try to play down the regional rivalry and instead to concentrate on a low-key, practically-based policy of conciliation; in this he was encouraged by his belief in the Japanese moderates and his lack of trust in the Americans. In the end, however, with the defeat of France and the arrival of a war Britain could not win without American support, Craigie's policy became unsustainable. As American-Japanese antagonism steadily escalated towards war

Craigie's line that Britain could take a third position as a mediator was simply not practical; events had passed him by.

19

R.H. Blyth, 1898–1964

ADRIAN PINNINGTON

SINCE THE Meiji Period, Japan has been fortunate enough to attract to the study of its literature and culture, not only a number of profound scholars, but also a series of gifted amateurs. If the scholars – and here one thinks of such figures as W.G. Aston, B.H. Chamberlain and Sir George Sansom – laid the foundations for the modern Western academic study of Japan, it was often the amateurs – such people as Lafcadio Hearn, Ernest Fenollosa, Ezra Pound or Paul Claudel – who did more to attract the interest of non-specialists and to influence Japan's image among the general public.

Such amateurs did not see traditional Japanese culture as an object of recondite study, but rather as something with a living relevance for the modern West. The subject of this essay, R.H. Blyth, should perhaps be seen as the last of such gifted Japanophiles. He shared their conviction that Japan has something important to teach the West, and his writings have had an enormous influence, direct and indirect, upon popular Western understanding both of Zen Buddhism and of that quintessentially Japanese poetic form, the *haiku*.

At the same time, Blyth's unique position in the immediate post-Second World War period allowed him to play an unusually large role in establishing the character of the contemporary Japanese monarchy. Despite all this, very little has so far been written about this fascinating figure; in 1984, however, a close friend and colleague of his, Shinki Shōnosuke, gathered together and published in Japanese a volume of memoirs written by many of those who had known him in

Japan.[1] Most of the biographical information in what follows has been drawn from this volume.

Blyth was born on 3 December 1898, in Ilford. His father worked for the Great Eastern Railway, and in later years Blyth more than once remarked upon the poverty of his home. The first sign of Blyth's strong-minded individualism came when he left school in 1916 and was called up for active service. The eighteen-year-old Blyth refused and was sent instead of Wormwood Scrubs, where he stayed, doing heavy labour, until 1919. He seems to have referred little to this experience in later life, although one colleague recalled him as saying that he refused to fight, not out of any fear of death, but because of a horror at the thought of killing another human being. (It seems to have been at this time that Blyth became the strict vegetarian which he remained throughout his life.) It was, presumably, the First World War which gave him his extreme scepticism about modern politics, which is reflected in his later comment that '. . . slaves to some definition of (life), men die for Freedom, kill themselves for Honour, slaughter millions in the name of Democracy or Communism'.[2]

After his release from prison, he worked for six months as a teacher at his old primary school and then entered University College, London, to take a degree in English literature. In 1923 he graduated with First Class Honours. Indeed, Blyth seems to have been a brilliantly talented youth; he was not only a keen sportsman, but also a very talented amateur musician, able to play the organ, piano, violin, oboe and other instruments, as well as a hard-working and gifted linguist. Blyth's American protégé, the Zen *rōshi* Robert Aitken, tells us that Blyth more than once remarked that as a youth his great inspiration had been Matthew Arnold and that under his influence he had determined to develop himself to the full, to become the best linguist, musician, artist and scholar possible. Traces of both Arnold's writings and this powerful ambition are everywhere evident in Blyth's later work.

It was during his final year that Blyth met and became friendly with a young Japanese scholar studying at London University, Fujii Akio. Fujii had been sent by the Japanese government before taking up a post in the Preparatory Department of Keijō Teikoku Daigaku, the Imperial University established by the Japanese in Seoul. Fujii had been asked to look for an

Englishman who might work in the same department; when, one day, he casually suggested to Blyth that he might take the job, he was surprised to find that his friend agreed on the spot. Fujii and his wife were to become Blyth's closest friends during his long stay in Korea, and it was Fujii's wife who first taught Blyth how to read haiku. With characteristic industry, Blyth not only gained his teaching licence before leaving for his new post, but also married Anna Bercovitch, a friend from university, about whom very little is known. In August 1924, the young couple arrived in Kobe, and in the following month Blyth began teaching at the new university. He was to continue there until 1940.

BLYTH IN KOREA

Blyth's mentor, Suzuki Daisetsu, claimed later that Blyth had taught as a young man in India, and that his revulsion at the attitude of his compatriots to their colonial subjects had led him to move to Korea. This story, which has been repeated elsewhere, seems to have no foundation;[3] but it contains a certain irony, apparently overlooked by Suzuki. For Blyth did indeed find himself working for a colonial government, that established in Korea by the Japanese themselves. It is unclear what Blyth thought of Japanese policy in Korea; on a personal level, he obviously felt compassion for many of his Korean students and did his best to help them. He instructed the university office to set aside a certain amount of his salary, which was very generous by Japanese standards, to help worthy but needy Korean students, and, when he discovered that many of the members of his music circle could not afford violins, he bought up second-hand ones, repaired them and sold them to the students for a minimal sum. Moreover, he more or less adopted one of his students, paying for his education both in Korea and later at London University. (This student met a tragic fate; returning to Korea after the War, he became a university teacher in Seoul, only to be captured by the North Korean army upon the outbreak of the Korean War. He was forced by the North to employ his English skills in broadcasting to US troops. After the end of the War, when he returned to the South, he was promptly shot as a traitor by the South Korean army.)

Yet, despite this personal kindness, Blyth's later comments

upon Korean culture strike one as rather negative, with an emphasis upon the violence and cruelty of the Korean character. In his book *Oriental Humour* (1959), he remarks in the Preface: 'I am afraid my Korean friends will be displeased, but I thought that something (on the subject of Korean humour) was better than nothing to express my gratitude for all that I learned in their land.' When we turn to the section on Korean humour, we find the Korean national character described as a mixture of 'placidity and vehemence': '. . . the latter involves the power to act, to go to the extremes of kindness and cruelty, the former to be a spectator and have the power to see the latter as a form of unbalance. Add to this, a toughness, not exceeded by the Chinese, which does not flinch at any kind of grossness or sadism . . .' (p. 165) and he adds: 'It was (before the War) quite a common thing for all the village children to gather under the trees to watch a man slowly beating his dog to death suspended by the nose' (p. 167). Given Blyth's sensitivity to, and love of, animals, especially dogs, one can see why he would be out of sympathy with aspects of Korean culture. His remarks on the nature of Korean Confucianism are also extremely negative.

Yet, while there can be no doubt that Blyth found Japanese culture more attractive than either Chinese or Korean culture, it is equally true that his sense of Japanese culture was very different to the militarism and nationalism which he must have encountered in the 1930s, and that it was what he called the 'real, unmilitary, poetical power and glory of Japan'[4] which attracted him. In a revealing aside, in his *Haiku, Volume I* (1952), he remarks: 'With Shinto and its boring and repulsive mythology, haiku has little to do, directly or indirectly, but primitive or crude Shinto, which still exists throughout Japan, both expresses the national character and affects it' (p. 158). He later commented that, if the Japanese had loved haiku and senryū more, then the War would never have happened.

Blyth built himself a two-storey Western-style house on a hill near the campus and lived there together with his wife and various animals. His life seems to have continued placidly enough until 1934, when his wife left for England without him. A year later, Blyth himself also suddenly left, saying he was unsure whether he would return. While he was away, the couple were in fact divorced and he returned alone in 1936. From this point on he increasingly seems to have adopted a Japanese way of life, renting a Japanese-style house in Seoul, and in 1937 marrying the twenty-two year old Kishima Tomiko, the daughter of the Japanese owner of a local construction company. He was never to return to Britain.

Although Blyth had read, and been deeply impressed by, Suzuki's first volume of *Essays in Zen Buddhism* in 1927 – in typical fashion he compared its effect to that of, among other things, reading *Robinson Crusoe* as a boy[5] – it was not until 1938 that he began to practise Zen meditation himself. In this year he began to attend meditation sessions and classes in the classics of Zen Buddhism under Kayama Taigi of Myōshinji Betsuin, a Rinzai Zen temple near Seoul which trained both monks and missionaries. Kayama Taigi himself was a graduate of Tokyo Imperial University and a particularly learned rōshi. It was at this time that Blyth began to study Chinese and Japanese classical writings as well as at times to stay in the temple, sharing the arduous lives of the monks.

WAR-TIME EXPERIENCES

In 1939, however, with the outbreak of the war in Europe, things began to grow more uncomfortable for Blyth, and one of his teaching contracts was suddenly dissolved. This was followed, in 1940, by the far greater shock of the sudden death of Fujii Akio at the early age of forty-two. As the likelihood of war between Japan and the allies grew, the Blyths decided to move to Japan. At first they spent three months in Tomiko's hometown in Yamaguchi Prefecture, and then they moved to Tokyo, where Blyth contacted Suzuki as well as Fujii's own teacher, Saitō Takeshi. With Saitō's aid, he managed to obtain a post at Kanazawa Daiyon Kōtō Gakkō and he started teaching there in November. In April 1941, he applied for Japanese citizenship, presumably fearing deportation if war broke out, and concerned as to what might happen to his young wife. (His application was never processed and the papers were returned to him after the War.) When, on 8 December, the Pacific War began, he was promptly taken into custody by the Ishikawa Prefectural Police and kept in Kanazawa Police Station until March 1942, when he was transferred to an internment camp in Kobe. His first daughter, Harumi, had been born in February, and wife and daughter took up residence in Kobe, where they were allowed to visit the interned Blyth once a week. It was in December of this year that, strangely, Blyth's first book, *Zen in English Literature and Oriental Classics*, was published by Hokuseidō in Tokyo.

In 1944 the scattered groups of enemy aliens were brought together in one camp near Kobe; it was here that Blyth met the young American, Robert Aitken, who had been taken by the Japanese in Guam. Aitken had been given a copy of Blyth's book by a guard in his first camp, who had been a student of Blyth in Kanazawa, and he had read it countless times during his confinement. Blyth then helped Aitken begin the study of Japanese and Zen, and thereby set the course of the latter's life. Aitken himself has left a vivid portrait of Blyth in the camp.[6] Blyth shared a room with six others, and would sit all day on his bed surrounded by Japanese and Chinese texts and dictionaries, taking quotations and making notes. It was here that he worked on what would eventually become the four volumes of his *Haiku*. In the evenings the internees, who included many specialists on Japan, would gather and argue about Japan and the war across a smoke-filled atmosphere.

With Japan's surrender in August 1945, all of the internees were immediately released; at first Blyth and his family stayed with Lewis Bush in Kobe. From here Blyth wrote to Suzuki, who immediately wrote back offering to find him a post at Otani University. On the strength of this, Blyth moved to Tokyo in October to begin the most hectic and exciting phase of his life. Here he met Suzuki again and also Saitō Takeshi. The latter in turn introduced Blyth to Yamanashi Katsunoshin, the President of Gakushūin (the Peers' School), who was also intimate with Suzuki, as well as being a trusted adviser of the Emperor.[7] Blyth also visited SCAP in search of employment and was there introduced to H.G. Henderson, an expert in Japanese culture who had been appointed head of the Education Division of SCAP. In his *Zen in English Literature*, Blyth had described Henderson's pioneering work on haiku, *The Bamboo Broom* (1933), as 'a little masterpiece' but although each knew the other's work, this was the first time they actually met. Henderson introduced Blyth to his superior, Brigadier General Dyke, who did in fact offer him a job in the Civil Information and Education Section of SCAP. A week or so later, however, Blyth returned with the news that he had found a post at Gakushūin, and had been asked to tutor the Crown Prince in English and also to act as an informal liaison between the Imperial Household and the Occupation. Dyke agreed that this would be beneficial for both sides.

Blyth now found himself in a unique position. On the one hand, his Japanese friends and patrons knew of both his profound belief in, and commitment to, Japanese culture, and his application for Japanese citizenship, for which Suzuki had written a reference. His American contacts, on the other hand, knew him as an Englishman who had spent the war in captivity in Japan. There must have been few other figures at the time able to gain to such a degree the trust of both sides. It was evidently this unique position which led Yoshida Shigeru, at this time foreign minister, to ask Blyth to act as a liaison between the two sides.

BLYTH AND THE IMPERIAL RESCRIPT, 1946

Undoubtedly the most important event in which Blyth was involved was the Emperor's 'Ningen Sengen' or Declaration of Humanity, which was published on 1 January 1946, and which is often held to have secured the survival of the Imperial system in Japan. Much about the precise generation of this declaration remains a mystery or a matter of hearsay, partly for the obvious (and very Japanese) reason that it was important that it not be identified too closely with any one person or group, and yet had the backing of all concerned. In what follows I have chiefly followed the detailed account given by William P. Woodard, who personally interviewed many of those concerned.[8]

Blyth began to visit Henderson once or twice a week, arriving in a government car, in order to discuss problems connected with the Japanese education system. Indeed, it appears that the primary motive for Blyth to act as liaison was a desire to secure the future of Gakushūin itself, which at this time still belonged to the Imperial Household. The Occupation were clearly determined to abolish the peerage and to transfer the Emperor's assets to the nation. Thus it was feared that Gakushūin itself might be abolished. Some favoured making it a state institution, but Yamanashi, Blyth and others felt that the best solution would be for it to become private. This is indeed what eventually happened, in April 1947, and those involved at Gakushūin itself believed that the chief credit for this went to Blyth and his influence at SCAP.[9] At this time, however, Henderson and Blyth were chiefly engaged on discussing the future of the Emperor Meiji's Rescript on Education.

One day, early in December, Blyth arrived in a state of high excitement, saying that he had heard from Imperial Household Minister Ishiwata that the Emperor wished to renounce his divinity so as to ensure that his position could never be misused again. (It is interesting that Ishiwata himself later recalled that the whole business began with a hint from Blyth himself![10]) Blyth then asked Henderson what form he thought such a declaration should take. Henderson, greatly surprised, told Blyth that he could give no answer for a day or two as his superior, General Dyke, was absent. Blyth urged that there was no time to be lost and pressed Henderson for some 'personal, unofficial suggestions' of his own. As it was lunchtime, Henderson retired to his hotel room and wrote a few lines on his usual yellow notepaper: 'The ties between Us and Our people have always stood upon mutual trust and affection. They do not depend on mere legend and myths. They are not predicated on the false conception that the Emperor is divine, and that the Japanese are superior to other races and fated to rule the world.' This he handed to Blyth who took it to Yamanashi.

The following day Blyth composed a longer English statement, including Henderson's words, which he brought to Henderson. Henderson then gave this to Dyke who in turn showed it to MacArthur. MacArthur declared himself delighted and returned it to Blyth. Blyth thereupon asked Henderson to burn his original yellow note in front of him, which Henderson promptly did. This was the last any at SCAP heard of the matter until they saw the Declaration itself on New Year's Day.

The Emperor himself then gave Blyth and Henderson's composite English draft to Prime Minister Shidehara, asking him to improve it. (Unfortunately Blyth's own draft, which survived until 1962, was burnt by accident with other waste paper!) Shidehara's expanded English draft was then translated into Japanese by a secretary, the Japanese text being reworked by a number of cabinet ministers before being shown to the Emperor on the 24 December. The Emperor then asked that the Meiji Emperor's Charter oath be included. After more reworking, the final text was released to the newspapers on 31 December 1945 and published on 1 January 1946.

Yamanashi later insisted that it was important that the Declaration be seen as the Emperor's own words while at the same time gaining the approval of GHQ; in true Zen style, when William Woodard interviewed him, he clapped his hands and asked 'Which hand made the sound?'. Although the Declaration was probably Yamanashi's idea (the idea itself had been floated by a variety of people, both American and Japanese, from the closing days of the war), only someone in Blyth's unique position could have successfully brought together the two hands. (More negatively, it may be said that the very ambiguity of Blyth's position led both sides to think that he was representing the other; at any rate, it seems likely that Blyth's draft was thought of by the Imperial Household as representing the views of SCAP, and that it was not realized that Blyth was acting independently or as Yamanashi's agent.)

Blyth himself believed that he affected the Emperor's decisions in some other ways; for example, he claimed later to Shinki that it was he who had urged that an American tutor be found for the Crown Prince, so as to mollify American feelings. (Elizabeth Vining, the American Quaker eventually chosen for the task, remembered Blyth at this time as '. . . a charming and scholarly man of middle age, a devotee of Zen Buddhism, with a wide knowledge of Japanese life and culture'.[11] Blyth also presented a book on the activities of the British royal family during the war to the Emperor, and he believed that it was this book which inspired the Emperor to make his unprecedented tour among the ordinary people.

POST-WAR TEACHING AND WRITING

Blyth began teaching at Gakushūin in December 1945. The following April the Crown Prince entered the middle school and Blyth became his tutor in English. Although the classes later took the form of lectures, Blyth continued in this capacity right up until his death; as he liked to joke, the Crown Prince became his 'oldest pupil'. Meanwhile, Blyth began to take on more and more teaching jobs; in the same April he began to teach part-time at the Foreign Ministry, at Tokyo University and at Nihon University. In 1947 his second daughter, Nana, was born, and he began to teach at Tokyo University of Education. In the following year he began teaching part-time at Jissen Women's

University and Waseda University. Not content with this Herculean teaching load, Blyth also began to produce a steady flow of works on Zen and Japanese literature which continued until his death. In 1949 the first volume of his *Haiku, Eastern Culture*, was published. This volume was dedicated to '. . . Sakuo Hashimoto through whose patriotic generosity the publication of these volumes was made possible'. Blyth later more than once remarked that it was Yoshida Shigeru who had put up the money for *Haiku* to be published; presumably this was in recognition of his services after the war, and Sakamoto and Ichimada Naoto, the dedicatee of the last two volumes, were used as fronts by Yoshida. In the same year, *Senryu: Japanese Satirical Verses* was also issued.

The second volume of *Haiku, Spring*, followed in 1950, and the third and fourth volumes, *Summer–Autumn* and *Autumn–Winter* in 1952. In 1954, Blyth was awarded a doctorate in literature by Tokyo University for *Zen in English Literature* and the four volumes of *Haiku*. In this year, too, Blyth evidently contemplated a visit to England. Unfortunately, he was not able to gain enough foreign currency to make the trip, and when an official hinted that he should try the black market, Blyth gave up his plans. In 1957 he published his *Japanese Humour* and this was followed in 1959 by *Oriental Humour*. In this year, Blyth, with the aid of Yamanashi, finally built his own house, in Oiso.

In the following year, 1960, Blyth published the first volume of the series *Zen and Zen Classics*, the major project which was to occupy him until his death. In 1961 both *Japanese Life and Character in Senryu* and *Edo Satirical Verses* were published. In 1962 came *Zen and Zen Classics, Volume V*, in 1963 *A History of Haiku, Volume I*, and in 1964, the year of Blyth's death, *A History of Haiku, Volume II*, and *Zen and Zen Classics, Volume II*, were issued. The remaining two volumes of *Zen and Zen Classics* were published posthumously, in 1966 and 1970. In fact in a relatively short time Blyth managed to produce some seventeen books, a very substantial body of work.[12] What are we to make of these books on Japanese literature and culture today? Why were they so influential? Clearly, in a short essay such as this, detailed comment in impossible, but I think various points can be made.

The first of these is that Blyth, despite his extremely wide reading in both Western and Eastern literature, is not primarily a scholar or a historian. Rather he is a critic, in the special sense which he explains in his *Senryu, Japanese Satirical Verses* (1949): 'The principle of selection for the senryu translated is the one given by Hazlitt: "That which interests is interesting". Using the word "interests" in its largest and most profound sense, this is the one and only principle of all criticism' (Preface). Although Blyth does incidentally reveal quite substantial knowledge of an historical or scholarly kind, as in his discussion of renga, one always feels that his heart is not really in it, that he is impatient with information for information's sake.[13]

Indeed, despite their different titles, Blyth's books can in a sense all be read as part of one great work. This is so for two reasons. The first is that his books are all essentially anthologies of texts together with discussions designed to elucidate the spiritual meaning or value of these texts. (In the case of *Haiku*, this approach happened to coincide with the approach of the traditional seasonal haiku anthology, the *saijiki*, and indeed Blyth's books have much in common with the kind of chatty haiku anthologies so frequently produced by well-known haiku poets.[14]) The second reason, which is linked to the first, is that all of his books reflect his own peculiar set of interests, so well summed up in the title *Zen in English Literature and Oriental Classics*. Whatever the ostensible subject, they all revolve around the attempt to convey the indefinable quality of Zen and reflect his belief that this quality, while especially evident in haiku and Japanese culture in general, is actually present in all literatures in the world.

This anthology-like character reflects, I think, Blyth's own manner of working. His friend Shinki recalls that, when he visited Blyth at home in Korea, he noticed a reading schedule pinned to the wall, which ran: 'Mon. Cervantes: Don Quixote/ Wed. Dante: Divina Commedia/Fri. Goethe: Faust'. On the desk were the original texts, English translations, and notebooks in which quotations and comments had been written in. Here we surely see both the influence of Arnold and his idea of culture as '. . . the best which has been thought and said in the world', and the origin of Blyth's *Zen in English Literature*, with its extensive quotations in Latin, French, Italian, Spanish, German, Chinese and Japanese. Blyth's manner of working in the internment camp in Kobe was evidently the same. When we add to this the fact that it appears that Hokuseidō simply printed his manuscripts as they arrived, with no editing, we begin to understand just how Blyth managed to produce so much.[15]

In one sense this 'anthology' quality gives the books far greater value than is often realized, simply as a treasure-trove of translations. In the first volume of *Haiku*, for example, one section on Zen consists largely of translations from the *Zenrinkushū*, while that on Confucianism is made up mainly of translations from the *Saikontan (Ts'ai-ken t'an)*, both as far as I know unavailable elsewhere.[17] This value is further enhanced by Blyth's inclusion of the original texts. By the same token, however, this 'anthology' character is also related to the books' obvious faults, for they tend to be rambling, undisciplined, repetitious and contradictory; indeed, like other anthologies, they are better sampled than read straight through.

At the same time, this anthology-like character is surely also deeply related to Blyth's view that Zen is something which can never be defined abstractly, but only pointed to, a mysterious insight which is continually in danger of being lost. It is this which gives Blyth that love of paradox which is perhaps the chief feature of his style. The greatest influence on Blyth's under-standing of Zen was clearly Suzuki, whom Blyth himself called his 'godfather' and to whom many of the later books are dedicated.[16] If contemporary scholars are inclined to see Suzuki as an eclectic and anachronistic writer,[17] it must be said that Blyth himself made eclecticism and anachronism the guiding principles of his thought. Indeed, especially in *Zen in English Literature*, Blyth is quite capable of criticizing Suzuki for being overly abstract and logic-chopping, and he has harsh things to say concerning his understanding of haiku and poetry in general (pp. 244–6). (Suzuki himself was gracious enough to include some generous quotations from Blyth in his essay on haiku in *Zen and Japanese Culture*.[18])

As Blyth himself states, he in fact uses the word Zen in two rather different ways; one meaning is: '. . . the state of mind in which we are not separated from other things, indeed, are identical with them, and yet retain our own individualities and personal peculiarities'. The other is: '. . . a body of experience and practice begun by Daruma'.[19] It is the first, general meaning which is far more important to Blyth, and this seems to have just as deep roots in Western Romanticism as in Eastern thought. In fact, one might say that Blyth is so successful at pointing to examples of Zen in European literature, that he brings out the extent to which modern Zen thought, even in the case of the Kyoto school, is something created by reading traditional Buddhist texts in the light of modern European preoccupations. In Blyth's case, this is further emphasized by the degree to which he is steeped in Christian literature; while he rejects Christian theology as childish, he nevertheless insists that there is more Zen in Christianity than in Buddhism and continually cites both the Bible and Christian poets.[20]

In the same way, Blyth's understanding of haiku as the record of a moment of '*satori*', which was to prove so influential in the United States, while inspired in the first place by the writings of Suzuki, also has deep roots in English Romanticism, and in the poetry of Wordsworth in particular: 'Haiku record what Wordsworth calls those "spots of time", those moments which for some quite mysterious reason have a peculiar significance. There is a unique quality about the poet's state of feeling on these occasions . . .'.[21] What is striking here is the way in which Blyth completely assimilates the haiku to the European lyric; although he is quite aware of the complex web of rules and conventions which controlled *haikai no renga*, he regards this as mere scaffolding, which at times allowed some Japanese poets to reach the same destination as some English poets, albeit by a different route. As he remarks elsewhere: 'Haiku is at its best when it is simply Wordsworthian, that is Wordsworth at his most simple, "a sort of thought in sense". It is at this point that haiku and English nature poetry coincide'.[22] To object, as (for example) Hiroaki Satō has objected,[23] that most haiku have little to do with Zen, is to miss the point; indeed, Blyth himself argued that it was very unlikely that Bashō's study of Zen had influenced his haiku.[24] The point is rather that what Blyth values in any poetry, Eastern or Western, is the moment of insight into the life of things which he calls Zen.

This conception of haiku in turn influences Blyth's approach to their translation – and it is his translations which above all have influenced Western understanding of haiku. Blyth himself described his translations as '. . . as literal as the English language will bear',[25] and certainly his decision to avoid rhyme, which had been used by Henderson, as well as the elaboration and archaisms of much earlier English-language translations, resulted in poems which were strikingly similar to minimalist Modernist poetry, such as that of William Carlos

Williams. (The few surviving original poems by Blyth indicate that this similarity was largely accidental, his own style being something of a blend of Arnold and Lawrence;[26] it is significant that he never refers to Eliot, Pound or other Modernists in his work.) While this literalism reflects his emphasis upon the objectivity of haiku, his actual approach to translation is rather more complex than this suggests. In his work, Henderson had remarked that the chief difficulty which faces the translator of haiku is whether 'to follow the strict grammatical form or the order of thought'.[27] Most translators of Japanese poetry seem automatically to follow the order of the images, frequently ignoring the grammar of the original. Blyth, by contrast, is very willing to change the order of the images, and to alter the grammar of the original, because his translations have a further aim, that of creating a certain poetic effect in English:

(ume ga ka ni notto hi no deru yamaji kana)

Along the mountain path,
    The scent of the plum-blossoms, –
        And, on a sudden, the rising sun!

(furuike ya kawazu tobikomu mizu no oto)

        The old pond.
        A frog jumps in –
        Plop!

(ochizama ni mizu koboshikeri hanatsubaki)

        A flower of the camellia-tree
Fell,
        Spilling its water.

(ushi mo mo to kiri kara detarikeri)

        The cow comes
Moo! Moo!
        Out of the mist.

The relationship between the original and the translation here varies, but in each case the haiku has been recast so as to create a poem in English which mimics a psychological event, a sudden moment of realization. In Haiku, Volume I, Blyth commented:

'We may note in passing that Japanese readers will all have slightly different translations and meanings to give most of these verses. This is both the power and the weakness of haiku. It is a weakness in that we are not quite sure of the meaning of the writer. It is a power in that haiku demand the free poetic life of the reader in parallel with that of the poet. This "freedom" is not that of wild irresponsibility and arbitrary interpretation, but that of the creation of a similar poetic experience to which the haiku points' (p. xi).

It is this creation of a poetic experience which Blyth attempts in his translations, and which give them such vitality. It also, incidentally, laid the foundations for English haiku, which, whether Zen-inspired or not, tend overwhelmingly towards the concrete expression of similar moments of discovery. Indeed, by reading haiku in this way, Blyth unconsciously brings it very close to a kind of poetry which was independently being generated in Europe. Much of what seems most Japanese about haiku – the sense of a shared culture and shared attitude towards nature – disappears from view, replaced by an emphasis upon the unique moment of insight.

BLYTH'S INFLUENCE

Blyth's chief influence has naturally been on the writers of English haiku, whether those such as Eric W. Amann and J.W. Hackett who explicitly linked haiku to Zen, or others with a more purely literary approach. In the 1950s and 1960s, however, he also exerted a wider influence on more mainstream English literature, especially on the Beats and the San Francisco Renaissance. In Jack Kerouac's influential *The Dharma Bums* (1958), we find one of the characters, Japhy Ryder (based on Gary Snyder), reading '. . . the complete works of D.T. Suzuki and a fine quadruple-edition of Japanese haikus' and writing haiku himself. Again in Allen Ginsberg's *Journals* he records a number of haiku written in 1955 while reading Blyth's four volumes of *Haiku*.[28] The black writer, Richard Wright, also spent the last part of his life writing haiku, after borrowing Blyth's books from a friend.[29] A less-discussed case is that of J.D. Salinger, who quotes Blyth in one story of 1955, and who, in *Raise High the Roofbeam Carpenters* (1959), has his narrator remark: 'The best short Japanese poems – particularly haiku, but senryu, too – can be read with special satisfaction when R.H. Blyth has been at them. Blyth is sometimes perilous, naturally, since he's a high-handed old poem himself, but he's also sublime – and who goes to poetry for safety anyway?'[30] Indeed, I think a strong case can be made for saying that Salinger's understanding not only of Zen, but of mysticism in general, is directly derived from Blyth's writings.

There is a sense, then, in which Blyth, for all the eccentricity of his writing, domesticates the haiku. Like earlier Japanophiles, he manages to make traditional Japanese culture seem excitingly modern. Such an approach obviously will not satisfy academic scholars, and it has been said that Blyth's influence actually served to inhibit the academic study of haiku in the West, giving the subject an aura of fashionableness or frivolity. Yet it is also surely true that one of the peculiar strengths of the haiku of Bashō, Buson, Issa and others is the multiplicity of ways in which they can be read; the survival of haiku in Japan itself depended upon Shiki's radical rereading of the traditional form. In this sense we must surely see Blyth himself as one of history's 'strong' readers, a person who has given an unexpected new and international lease of life to a traditional poetic form. Indeed, by virtue of what seems a very English eccentricity and individuality, Blyth contributed profoundly in both practical and spiritual ways to the life of his adopted country, Japan.

20

Otome and Frank Daniels

RONALD DORE

IT WAS AN ODD and unlikely pair one saw walking down Malet Street to the School of Oriental and African Studies on those wartime mornings. Frank James Daniels (1900–83), with the bulging briefcase full of things he had thought he might get round to the night before; tall, bearded, chin slightly raised, gaze directed just above the heads of passers-by, a gaze in which, when one called it down and saw the sometimes hesitant smile of recognition, one could sense the sternness of conscience with which he would protest against any sloppy or publicity-seeking deviation from scholarly rectitude, and see why Sadao Oba, writing years later about war-time Japanese language teaching, should have called him 'the shy and single-minded scholar'.[1] Otome, about a head shorter, too plump of cheek to be called a typical Japanese beauty, a not quite symmetrical mouth clearly capable of a wide range of expressive smiles and pouts, eyes animated even when they were modestly cast down, a walk which betrayed that this was a *modaan-gaaru* who had spent more of her life in skirts than in kimono – an impression which, back at home, her cigarette holder would confirm.

The war-time Japanese language courses in which they were both involved were the crucial prelude to Daniels' lasting achievement, the building of Britain's first centre of modern Japanese studies at the School of Oriental and African Studies (SOAS). It was a future which, for the first twenty-eight years of his life, he is unlikely ever to have contemplated. A grocer's son, product of Kentish village schools in Sissinghurst and Brooklands, and Cranbrook Boys Grammar School, perhaps he worked in a lawyer's office when he left school. At any rate, he ended the First World War, still only eighteen, in training with a bicycle corps in a London regiment recruited from the Inns of Court.

Demobilized, he became a clerk at the Admiralty and embarked on the long haul of a part-time evening-course degree at the London School of Economics (1923–7) with Sociology as his special subject. By the mid-1920s he was a Bachelor of Science in Economics, confiding in his sister that he was restless and wanted to see something of the rest of the world. His first attempt, to get a posting to Latin America, was thwarted. Instead, in 1928, he was offered the chance to transfer to the office of the Naval Attaché in Tokyo. He must have been there through all the excitements of the London Naval Conference of 1930, the reactions to which helped to seal Japan's choice of path that made the Pacific War inevitable. But I do not recall hearing him talk about it, and to my knowledge he wrote nothing about contemporary Japanese history. Instead, from the moment of his first arrival in Japan, his curiosity about the world around him focused on the task of mastering the Japanese language. It was hard work; it was only later when he had a group of seventeen-year-olds to teach that he realized the disadvantage of being already twenty-nine; but he persisted; fluency or nothing; and he succeeded. In this he was greatly helped by his marriage to Otome. When this happened and how they met is not clear, though I have a vague memory of some story about Otome losing a *geta* while rushing across a closing level crossing, and Frank gallantly and doubtless at romantic risk to life, retrieving it.

At any rate, they were married by 1933 when Frank returned to Britain to introduce his bride to his family and to hand in his resignation to the Admiralty. The introduction obviously went well. Daniels' sister still treasures a letter Otome wrote to their mother in the summer of 1940 from which the warmth of her anxiety about her adopted family in a Britain about to be invaded by Hitler shines through. He was resigning from the Admiralty because he had got a better job – as teacher of English at Otaru Commercial High School.

Whether he got the job from some connection of Otome's I have no idea, but Otaru was her birthplace. The Nishide family must have been quite well-to-do. The photograph of her father which she kept in her little *butsudan* in London shows him with the same handsome and confident look as Fukuzawa in that ubiquitous photograph of his youth. He was almost certainly old enough to have gone to the fief school in pre-Restoration Kanazawa, perhaps already to have become head of the family – a lower-samurai Kaga retainer family – at the time of its migration to Hokkaido. He was certainly far from young when Otome was born. She used to tell the story that her mother was somewhat ashamed to have borne her; having a child in one's mid? late? forties showed a certain disreputable frivolity. Father was by this time a 'net-owner' – merchant organizer of the fishing trade – and the family was well enough off for Otome to be brought up almost entirely by her *baya* nanny. Her parents always remained somewhat distant remote figures. Her eight-year-old sister was her only centre of family affection after the death of her *baya*.

When that sister died in the early 1990s her great-nephew located a copy of the family registers and discovered a curious fact. Otome, of course, is the ancient and poetic word for 'maiden'. Otome used a variant, writing the *me* with the character for 'princess' rather than the character for 'woman'. She was registered, however, plain katakana *tome* which means 'Stop!'. O could be prefixed to any two-syllable woman's name, so Otome would probably always have been the name by which she was called, but the naming intention seems to have been, like *sue* in boys' names, to say 'Thank you, fertility gods. That's enough!' – which confirms the story of the advanced age of her mother at Otome's birth.

What terrible scandal she was involved in, I never did hear, but she used to say that she was 'disowned' by her parents – actually subject to *kando*, being removed from the parental family register and registered in solitary disgrace on a separate page. There is no obvious trace of that in the Nishide register but it does show her disappearing off the books to become, at the age of twenty, the adopted daughter of a married elder sister, fourteen years older than herself. Did elder sister take pity on her and adopt her to soften the consequences of parental wrath, or was she, at thirty-three, already despairing of having an heir of her own?

Whatever it was that Daniels rescued her from, it probably was not boredom. She was accomplished in several womanly arts, *saganishiki*, embroidery, *kamakura-bori*, wood carving, the writing – both the composing, and the calligraphically elegant recording – of *waka* poems, but above all the making of miniature tray landscapes, a pursuit for which her 'school' had granted her a teacher's licence. It was a stock of material for the last which she brought to Britain in 1941: it remained a hobby she returned to from time to time until her death.

MEETING WITH C.K. OGDEN

That visit to London in 1933 was instrumental in changing the course of Daniels' interests. Perhaps in deliberate preparation for his new teaching assignment, Daniels came to know C.K. Ogden, the polymath founder of Basic English. He may already have known Ogden through the influential book he wrote with I.A. Richards, *The Meaning of Meaning*. It was, at any rate, a book he justly admired. I remember his telling me soon after I graduated with a degree in Japanese language and literature, that now I could begin my education and there could be no better foundation than reading Ogden and Richards. I found that he was not far wrong.

There was a missionary air about all those proposals for an international language in those days, and Daniels became a convert. Exercising the ingenuity to express every subtlety of human meaning with 850 words, only sixteen of them verbs, was his lifelong substitute for crosswords (though he did allow himself the *Observer*'s on Sunday), and the Japanese–Basic English dictionary became his major preoccupation, occupying a central place in his life for over thirty years. As convert, he was a bit of a fundamentalist, too. Richards, the celebrated critic, was teaching at Harvard when the Daniels came through on their way back to England in 1941 and he and his wife Dorothy obviously made a deep impression on them. Later, Richards, as part inventor of Basic English, took it upon himself to suggest some amendments, some dilution of the pure basicness of Basic. Schism developed, and Frank, though with some regret and embarrassment, unhesitatingly threw in his lot with Ogden.

The attraction of Basic was not only in its intellectual ingenuity. Daniels had all the decent instincts best summed up at the time I first knew him as 'New Statesman-reader views', and they included anti-chauvinist internationalism. Basic had the advantage that it was almost as difficult for native English-speakers to learn to stick to its rules as for foreigners to learn it from scratch, which removed, or at least reduced, the unfair advantage they got from having colonized the world with the English language. Transferral the other way, however, was easy. Mastering Basic English was thus a good first step towards transition to normal English, an aid to learning. It appears, however, according to accounts collected from former pupils by Oba, that his enthusiasm for Basic English did not make him entirely popular with the authorities in Otaru who wanted proper King's English, though how far he actually found scope for inserting his ideas into his teaching practice is not clear. He was remembered as a careful and conscientious teacher who let lessons over-run in order to be sure that every member of his large classes had been called on for a piece of oral performance.

Whether it was for this or for climatic reasons, Daniels resigned after his first contract and moved, in 1937, to Shizuoka High School. There he began work on his Basic-Japanese dictionary, and later received a Rockefeller grant to hire Japanese assistants to work on it full time. They moved to Zushi, then part fishing village, part peaceful summer-resort for the Tokyo middle class. But everybody could see – and the circumspection with which an Englishman had to behave anywhere near the naval base of Yokosuka constantly brought it home – that this idyllic existence was threatened. In 1941 Daniels landed a senior lectureship in Japanese at SOAS in the University of London. They crossed the Pacific at the beginning of the summer before Pearl Harbor, spent a while at Harvard, finding out how Serge Elisseeff and Edwin Reischauer taught Japanese, and were convoyed hazardously but safely across the Atlantic. According to Oba, Otome later joked that, whenever the submarine warning sirens came on, Frank was more concerned to find out where his dictionary was than where she was. It was carefully packaged in a waterproof petrol can; a second copy left with a friend in Tokyo.

LONDON AND SOAS

And so, very soon, to the excitement of organizing the first 'intensive' course in Japanese for war-time purposes. How soon after Pearl Harbor the need for interpreters and translators sank into Whitehall consciousness I do not know, but the recruitment notices went out to the schools in February and thirty bright-eyed seventeen- and eighteen-year-olds (most of whom had not made Japanese their first choice of 'Oriental language to be learned for military purposes') appeared in Malet Street on May Day 1942. I do not know whether the army, navy and airforce organizers had ever objected when the SOAS told them that, of course, universities taught only for three ten-week terms a year, nor whether the two-hours-a-day tuition for five days a week was thought to be the most that future officers and gentlemen could be expected to put up with, but in retrospect it does seem a somewhat unserious approach to a rather serious war. At the time, though, it did seem perfectly natural and to us – for I was one of the thirty – rather good fun and a splendid way of escaping the looming threat of the Higher School Certificate examination.

Daniels was clear about what learning a language entailed. If you were going to be fluent, reflexes had to be automatic. Good accents could only come from constant repetition, correction, repetition. Drill, drill, drill. Simple sentences to be endlessly repeated with minor variations. It was only the innocence and charm of Otome, our appointed drill sergeant, the transparent and single-minded earnestness of her desire to make sure that 'the boys' did things properly, that made the enterprise viable.

The pace hotted up as there came new intakes of older students, already conscripted and under military discipline. Teaching days extended to six contact hours. Rationalized production set in; the 'interrogators' learned to speak and were shielded from the knowledge that Japanese was not written in roman script; the 'translators' learned characters and grammar and were not expected to have to utter a word of Japanese. Teachers were recruited: a former Japanese newspaper correspondent released from the Isle of Man, a ship's engineer stranded in hospital, recovering from appendicitis when his ship left Liverpool, members of the Soho lampshade manufacturing community, *issei* from the Canadian army, and the ravishing Mrs Clark (apart from Yanada, the newspaperman, the only possessor of a true Tokyo accent). Mrs Clark divided her time between SOAS and the BBC and later became the heroine of one of her pupils' post-war novels and, reverting to her maiden name as Ito Aiko, editor of the Asahi's *Japan's Quarterly*. Though very different in temperament, the two women became good friends. Unlike today, Japanese was a pretty safely impenetrable anti-eavesdropper code for use in Lyons Corner Houses. They would enjoy their immunity, taking tea together, Aiko's bold appraisals of the sexual potential of the men around them sending Otome (and she thought *she* was a *moga*, a *modaan-gaaru*) into fits of shocked and envious giggles.

The instructors made up a motley crew, but one that served both the warring nations well. They taught us the language, but they also taught us that there were Japanese people for whom one could feel unqualified affection, and achievements of Japanese people for which one could feel unqualified admiration. I somewhat doubt whether the scene, filtered through who knows how many memories and recorded by Oba, ever took place in quite the tear-jerking way he describes it, but *se non e vero e ben trovato*. A farewell party for our first batch – they are off to interrogate prisoners in Burma. The wine flows; students sing the Japanese war-time marching songs they have learned from the feature films and records which formed part of the curriculum. The time comes for departure. Students all bow in grateful thanks to the husband and wife *sensei*. '*Nagai aida o-sewa ni narimashita. De wa itte mairimasu.*' (It is time to take our leave, after being so much in your debt for so long.) Otome, too, bows as tears glisten in her eyes, thinking of the wounded and unconscious Japanese soldiers, the only ones they are likely to capture: 'Don't be too hard on my countrymen.'

POST-WAR YEARS

Inertia made for a slow finish, as well as a slow start for the war-time courses. National Servicemen were still being trained for duties in Japan with the British army of occupation until 1947. By then, however, Daniels was preoccupied with turning a Berlitz operation into a genuine centre of scholarship. The stable-door exercise in planning to ensure that Britain never again lacked the means to create and sustain a core of expertise on the Far East – what became known as the Scarbrough exercise and was to lead to a big increase in UGC funds for SOAS – had begun work in 1944.

It was Daniels who drew up the plans which came to be partially implemented in the next half-decade. As he described it later in his inaugural lecture[2] '. . . there were to be ten posts in Language and Literature, two in History, two in Religion and Folklore (i.e., one in Buddhism and one in Shinto and other popular cults), and one each in Economic Institutions, Social Institutions and Law'. It did not quite happen that way, but the idea of a department which might include social scientists as well as representatives of the humanities counted then, at SOAS, as boldness indeed.

In the event, after five posts were created in language and literature and one in history, the sixth was announced to be a lectureship in Japanese institutions. Social and economic were rolled into one which meant that no London University social scientist took it upon himself to insist that the incumbent should actually have some disciplinary qualification. Of that vagueness I was the beneficiary. And benefice was almost what it was; as head of department, claiming expertise in language and literature though qualified only in economics, Daniels looked kindly on autodidacts and was prepared to encourage almost any individual bent, provided it was the product of genuine curiosity. After I left the post in the mid 1950s, it was not refilled; by then the Rise of the Social Sciences was beginning to affect SOAS as a whole, and the creation within the School of Departments of Economics and Politics and of Anthropology and Sociology, superseded notions of all-inclusive area departments.

Daniels' other major achievement in those years was in piloting through the arcane labyrinth of London University committees the syllabus for a new degree in *Modern* Japanese Language and Literature. It was, after all, only a few decades since it came to be accepted at Oxbridge, which as everyone knows was the only final arbiter in these things, that modern *European* languages could be admitted as possible objects of scholarly contemplation. And that was only permitted provided there were enough extant texts in genuinely *ancient* forms of the language to suggest that somehow they might be assimilated to that unique basic paradigm of true scholarship, the study of the Greek and Roman classics. The intellectual and cultural content of those texts was not so important; after all, outsiders on the university committees could not be judges of that, could they? But antiquity they could inquire about and anybody who could count could understand what it meant, so antiquity came to be the chief criterion of scholarly value. (The hangover effects are to be found in the British Academy today, where an archaeologist has a probability of election twenty or thirty times that of a student of modern English literature or politics.)

Egyptology, another splendidly gentlemanly antiquarian pursuit, opened the door to the concept of Oriental Studies, and that led to the possibility of Chinese studies which in antiquity could actually rival Greece and Rome. Japanese studies were obviously harder to justify, but somehow Yoshitake, the solitary Japanese lecturer at SOAS before the war, had managed to do so, and a degree in Classical Japanese, guaranteed to protect the student from anything written in the last century, was created.

Bringing scholarship into the modern world could not be done all at once. After all, even students of English literature had to struggle through Beowulf. Daniels was able to create a degree structure which put the emphasis on the ability to read – and write – modern Japanese, and provide, in a history paper, and even a paper on Japanese institutions, something of the *joshiki* – the 'common sense, common knowledge' of contemporary Japanese who had been through a Japanese schooling. But there still had to be a sizeable chunk of the classical language, taught largely through the medium of unedifying set texts like the fairy-story *Taketori Monogatari*.

PUBLICATION OF 'THE DICTIONARY'

As things settled down, the first war-inspired batch of degree students left, and student numbers dwindled to their 1950s' trickle, there was more time for scholarship. Work resumed on the dictionary. For years, his day at SOAS finished, Daniels would move on to a cubby hole near Bedford Square for more work on his dictionary, getting home for a latish supper with two or three phrases to try out on Otome, his arbiter of normal Japanese usage. It seemed to go on for ever. There were frequent going-back-to-the-beginning revisions in the conventions employed. Those conventions were indicated by an ever-expanding language of hieroglyphs which had to be mastered before one could make sense of the entries. Otome seemed loyally to share his faith that the work would one day be finished, but friends suspected that the perfectionism might have a pathological element, and that, anyway, the meticulous complexity of the entries would make the dictionary unusable.

They were proved wrong on both counts. In 1969, two years after Frank's retirement, Hokuseido published it as *Eibun wo kaku tame no jisho* – a 'dictionary for writing Japanese'. It was an enormous success, is still be found in practically every bookshop on Kanda, brought him more money in royalties than he had any desire to spend, and presumably continues to swell the coffers of the Basic English Foundation to which he willed his estate. Only slapdash impatient Englishmen would think the hieroglyphs too complex to be bothered learning; not Japanese students. The Japan Society of London wrote of the dictionary:[3]

> 'Although it makes no claim to be a full dictionary (with slightly less than 12,000 head words) it has every right to be called a dictionary of usage which can work both ways to benefit the Japanese student and the native English speaker who is learning and particularly translating Japanese. Almost every entry is followed not by a single equivalent but by a most generous group of illustrations of use in both languages, all of them plainly derived from everyday experience. The English is pure Basic which must have put a heavy burden on Professor Daniels' ingenuity and verbal dexterity but which ensures that all the illustrations are well within the comprehension of most Japanese students. Conversely, the "foreign" student of Japanese can find a great many examples of Japanese words and phrases in action – the common verb *suru*, for instance, is given more than five pages and even the humble onomatopoeic is given its picturesque view. As a final piece of practicality, the whole vocabulary of Basic English printed in easily read capitals appears inside both front and back covers together with the few very simple rules for composition and word change.'

Two other interests dominated his research. One was the study of Japanese phonetic structures, particularly the notion of *akusento* as developed by Japanese scholars. For many years he wrestled with the difference between accent, pitch and intonation, and published a few articles, but eventually electronics, oscillographs and other modern wonders overtook those who, like Daniels, did not have the resources to play this game except by ear. His other consuming interest – folklore – came to dominate. Over the years, and especially in the nearly two decades of his retirement, he built up the most formidable analytical index of folk tales from all over Japan. He loved to trace similarities and speculate to what extent they were the product of symbolic or psychoanalytic parallelism, or diffusion.

He treated them and their authors with respect; he would never have been happy in a Mediterranean society where clever intellectuals use *folklorico* as an adjective for the backward, quaint and corrupt.

He did not publish much; it *did* take a lot to overcome his perfectionist streak. In fact, Otome beat him in the publication stakes with her guide to Japanese handwriting, the *Dictionary of Sosho Forms* which came out in 1947, ahead of Frank's *Modern Japanese Prose*. Her dictionary is a testimony to the elegance of her hand, and to the patience with which she spent hours writing and rewriting till she got the shapes exactly right, and more hours pasting up the products to make a photo-ready page. She also derived a useful system of indexing elements of characters. Unfortunately, it was not ready in time for those whose need to read captured diaries in Burma had inspired it.

The Daniels enjoyed their retirement years, especially those which were enlivened by trips to Japan, notably the visit they made as honoured guests when Frank received the Japan Foundation Prize in 1978, and Otome had a last chance to spend days at a hot spring resort with her elder sister. In Otome's last weeks in hospital, the friends who gathered were astonished by the range and variety of other friends they met. Frank lived on for another five or six years, stoically surviving the loneliness, occasionally alleviated by the visits of a few friends and his sister. His colleagues in the Japan field conferred on him Honorary Membership of the European Association for Japanese Studies. He was sustained by his loyalties; loyalty to his conception of careful scholarship, loyalty to Otome's memory, loyalty to the Ogden version of Basic English, loyalty to the *New Statesman and Nation* which he continued to buy weekly through its weird transformations of the 1970s and early 1980s, loyalty to his ancient television set which it took months of persuasion to induce him to abandon in favour of one that did not require banging every ten minutes to get the picture back.

They were lives worth living, worth recording, lives many of us have reason to feel grateful for.

21

Sir Alvary Gascoigne in Japan, 1946–1951

PETER LOWE

ALVARY DOUGLAS Frederick Gascoigne (1893–1970) headed the British liaison mission (UKLIM) in Tokyo between July 1946 and February 1951. Thus his term of office coincided with the heart of the allied occupation of Japan. Gascoigne arrived less than a year after General Douglas MacArthur assumed responsibility as Supreme Commander Allied Powers (SCAP): he departed two months before President Truman's abrupt dismissal of MacArthur.

Gascoigne served in the sixth Dragoons and Coldstream Guards during the Great War and was mentioned in despatches. He joined the Foreign Office in 1919: his principal appointments before going to Japan in 1946 were as consul-general for Tangier Zone and the Spanish Protectorate of Morocco (1939–44) and as political representative in Hungary (1945–6). He married twice (his first wife, the daughter of an American general, died); he had a son and daughter by his first marriage, the son being killed in action in 1944.

Gascoigne's military experience might be expected to gain more respect than would be the case with a man of more restricted diplomatic background. As a personality Gascoigne was bluff and reasonably direct: he was in no sense an intellectual but evinced a combination of shrewdness and common sense.

It could hardly be said that Gascoigne's appointment to Tokyo was unexpected. Relatively speaking, he had a lot of East Asian diplomatic experience. He had served in China from 1923 to 1925. Later in the politically disturbed years from 1931 to 1934 he served in Japan. Then he was recalled to the Foreign Office to preside at the Far East desk between November 1934 and April 1936, which was again a significant period for Anglo-Japanese relations. Gascoigne, therefore, took up his assignment with a good deal of background experience. He was a diplomat of the old school, of a pre-war vintage.

It was essential that the head of the British mission should establish a positive relationship with MacArthur and this required a person who would be patient in listening to MacArthur and who would advance British interests effectively. At the close of the Pacific war the Foreign Office hoped that it would be feasible to achieve a prominent role for Britain in the occupation but by the time that Gascoigne reached Tokyo, it was clear that this would not occur.[1] MacArthur intended to retain as much power as he could in his own hands and the Truman administration did not envisage the allied powers playing a significant part in policy formulation.[2] Maintaining British interests, therefore, necessitated appreciable diplomatic skills combined with a realistic understanding of what could be accomplished: to press too far would antagonize MacArthur and, perhaps, Washington.

It is a measure of the successful relationship that Gascoigne established that MacArthur saw him more frequently than any other official with the sole exception of William Sebald, MacArthur's diplomatic adviser: Gascoigne and MacArthur met on 128 occasions while Sebald and MacArthur met on 138 occasions.[3] MacArthur was not the kind of man to see an official simply as a matter of courtesy. Why, then, did he see the head of the British mission with such frequency? There were two reasons: MacArthur wished to preserve regular contact with the British government in case he needed assistance in disputes with Washington and he respected Gascoigne.

For his part, Gascoigne adjusted readily to the function of listening to MacArthur's monologues, appreciating that this was axiomatic to gaining the general's trust and understanding that much information of interest could be gained in this way. The general was ready to impart his views to a diplomat from an aristocratic background. But the relationship changed dramatically with the outbreak of the Korean war in June 1950: MacArthur was so heavily involved in Korean issues that he could not see Gascoigne as he had done formerly and British criticisms of MacArthur's conduct of Korean operations inevitably affected MacArthur's relations with Gascoigne.[4]

MacArthur and the British government shared common attitudes on various aspects of the occupation while also diverging in certain areas. They were in agreement fundamentally in advocating the implementation of an early peace treaty: once the major reforms sponsored by the occupation had been applied, the United States should take an initiative in starting the process of treaty negotiations and a peace treaty should be signed as soon as practicable. MacArthur held that lengthy military occupations were counter-productive because they created unavoidable resentment among the native inhabitants of the occupied country.[5] Britain concurred and felt, in addition, that the Truman administration might succumb, if it had not done so already, to the temptation to allow the occupation to continue, since this was easier than grappling with the many problems inherent in arriving at a peace treaty. MacArthur and the British agreed that the Japanese people required a mixture of firmness and kindness exercised by a proconsular figure: the British thought sometimes that MacArthur erred on the lenient side but, in the main, endorsed his leadership.

In the first two years of the occupation MacArthur enjoyed a great deal of freedom in shaping his policies as he wished: this was the phase of sweeping, idealistic, liberal reform. The situation changed in the latter part of 1947 when he encountered the start of developing intervention from sections of the bureaucracy and big business in the United States. Criticism of MacArthur grew because of a belief that the occupation was not following a correct economic policy and that MacArthur was seized unduly with the supposed merits of radical restructuring of Japanese business. The so-called 'Japan Lobby' in Washington comprising bureaucrats, certain prominent businessmen and journalists, launched a campaign of censure aimed at SCAP.[6]

At the beginning of 1948 Gascoigne reported on speculation that MacArthur might leave Tokyo, in part because 1948 was a presidential election year and it was believed, correctly, that MacArthur was interested in securing the Republican nomination. Gascoigne wrote to Esler Dening in January 1948 that MacArthur appeared to be in good health for a man of his age (he was then 67 years old) and that MacArthur would continue his work in Tokyo unless he was nominated for the presidency.[7]

MacArthur told Gascoigne that big business was gunning for him in the USA and that he might be replaced: this was an exaggerated statement designed to elicit British support in which it succeeded. MacArthur stated that he wanted to reform the zaibatsu and to extend decentralization in the economy but this was disliked by prominent businessmen involved in the Truman administration and by Wall Street. MacArthur's observation met with British sympathy. F.S. Tomlinson of the Foreign Office remarked on the irony of MacArthur '. . . who is ultra-conservative at heart' being attacked for following '. . . what American business circles regard as left-wing policies'.[8] Tomlinson found it difficult to believe that the Truman administration would replace MacArthur who possessed such an outstanding record in Japan. Dening entirely agreed, commenting that, 'The prospect of indefinite American occupation without General MacArthur hardly bears contemplation.'[9]

BRITISH PREFERENCES

Gascoigne conversed with George Kennan in March 1948 to emphasize British preferences regarding the future evolution of Japanese industry. Kennan was involved in assessing the overall state of Japan in the context of the growth of the Cold War and his opinions were very different to those of MacArthur and the British Foreign Office.[10] Kennan wished to see the economy revived significantly, reforms cut back, and a peace treaty postponed. Gascoigne indicated that, while Britain assented broadly to the American proposals submitted to the Far Eastern Commission (FEC), Britain supported reparations and these should incorporate industrial assets, shipbuilding with concomitant restrictions on shipbuilding capacity, utilization of Japanese gold deposits and external assets. The Japanese economy should be rebuilt to some extent but it was essential to prevent a renewal of 'unfair competition': reasonable wages should be paid in Japanese factories with the eradication of 'sharp commercial practices'.[11]

The Attlee government was preoccupied with the importance of achieving a full employment economy in Britain and with stimulating British exports which would include traditional industries such as textiles and shipbuilding: Gascoigne underlined these points to MacArthur and Kennan but the former was the more sympathetic. Gascoigne believed that it was essential that MacArthur remain in Tokyo from the viewpoint of defending British interests: the appointment of someone aligned with the 'Japan Lobby' would be dangerous.

Accordingly, Gascoigne welcomed the decision of the Republican party to nominate Governor Dewey again for the presidency in June 1948. MacArthur would now remain in Tokyo – 'The General has his faults, in common with all mankind, but there are few, I think, who could have administered this country as well as he has done . . . I trust, therefore, that from the point of view of British interests, the United States Government will not find it necessary to make any change here . . . '.[12] For his part MacArthur told Gascoigne that he regarded his relationship with the British mission and British government as a 'perfect one'.[13] However, as an example in the opposite direction, Gascoigne occasionally experienced stormy meetings with MacArthur and such an occasion occurred on 1 September 1948. MacArthur was incensed at British protests concerning the National Public Service Law as envisaged and Gascoigne was the stoic recipient of MacArthur's wrath:

> 'My interview with the Supreme Commander was the most painful one which I have yet had with him during my duty in Japan. The mere mention by me of National Public Service draft legislation and of our opinion thereon caused him to shout at me without stopping for one and three-quarters hours. It seemed quite evident that he had already been reprimanded on the subject by Washington.'[14]

MacArthur conceded that all administrations made mistakes at times '. . . but to go out of his way to "side with the Kremlin" on the issue was, he thought, the greatest "betrayal of trust" which the British Commonwealth had yet perpetrated in Tokyo'.[15] MacArthur felt that some members of the Commonwealth wished to criticize him because they were jealous of his success in Japan. He made it clear that he had Australia in mind particularly, as he detested Herbert Evatt, the minister for external affairs. He repeated his strong disapproval of the British supporting the Russians in criticizing SCAP but Gascoigne stated that Britain had no intention of supporting the Soviet Union against the United States. MacArthur responded that the

Australian representative in Tokyo, Patrick Shaw, should have 'kept his mouth shut' instead of airing grievances as he had done.[16] This is an admirable instance of how MacArthur's wrath could erupt but, as Gascoigne observed, it was by far the most acrimonious encounter he had experienced since his arrival. The storm soon passed and MacArthur reverted to good humour, since he needed British support so as to defend his position against his critics in Washington.

One problem preoccupying Gascoigne at times arose from MacArthur's sensitivity to press criticism. In particular, MacArthur resented the critical tone of some of the reports written by *The Times* correspondent in Tokyo, Frank Hawley. Hawley believed that occupation policies lacked sufficient cohesion and revealed an inadequate grasp of the functioning of Japanese society. MacArthur viewed such criticism as negative and carping and voiced his feelings with characteristic trenchancy to Gascoigne. Gascoigne responded, predictably, that he could not control the press: criticism in the media was often unjust or tedious but had to be tolerated within democracies. MacArthur no doubt understood this point well enough but was not mollified thereby.[17]

ADVANCING THE RETURN OF PEACE

The Foreign Office wished to gauge how Japan would react to the conclusion of a peace treaty and resumption of sovereignty. Gascoigne was asked to give serious thought to the problem and he replied towards the end of 1948, after consulting the counsellor for information, H. Vere Redman. The Japanese wanted the occupation to end in the near future, having secured further economic gains from the USA in the intervening period; differences between the occupying powers would be exploited for Japanese ends. There would be a desire to obtain armed forces once more and the justification for acting contrary to Article 9 of the constitution would be the development of the Cold War and the advance of communism in China. The Japanese would seek to restore Japan's former commercial position, particularly in Asia. Gascoigne also accepted one of MacArthur's favourite themes that the growth of population would necessitate finding areas in which to place Japan's surplus population. Gascoigne was not sanguine regarding the long-term impact of MacArthur's endeavour to democratize Japan:

'The impact of democracy upon the Japanese mind has, as yet, been almost nil, although great play is, of course, made by the Japanese of going through the "forms" of democratic practice, because they know that during the occupation they can but obey the dictates of the Supreme Commander and that the more they please him (and through him the United States), the greater will be the bounties which will flow from Washington.'[18]

The principal priorities, as Gascoigne perceived them, were obtaining guarantees against unfair trading methods and ensuring that government was committed firmly to democracy and was well placed to prevent a swing to the 'totalitarian' right or left.[19] The Foreign Office shared Gascoigne's anxiety and doubted whether the occupation had achieved as much as MacArthur contended when it came to ensuring that Japan was wholly committed to democracy.

Gascoigne discussed the issue openly with SCAP: MacArthur was positively arguing that the benefits of democracy were so conspicuous that it was unlikely that Japan would proceed in a contrary direction when the occupation terminated. In practical terms, Japan would be compelled to rely upon the USA whether this was liked or not. MacArthur recognized the difficulty of anticipating the future but he was far more optimistic than Gascoigne.[20] Gascoigne was always alert to the negative characteristics of the Japanese, as though searching for evidence that would qualify the extent of the changes resulting from the occupation: the same was true of Dening and other British officials. This may be attributed to the cynicism not infrequently seen in world-weary British diplomats but was, arguably, also the product of Britain's exclusion from the centre of policy-making in Tokyo. Given the confusion in American policies towards China and Korea in the later 1940s, it was understandable that doubts should be entertained as to whether the United States was more successful in Japan.

The success of stability within Japan rested in part upon the newly-created institutions, in part on the calibre of political leadership, and in part on the repercussions of the Cold War. One aspect with which MacArthur was less satisfied was the quality of Japanese politicians. MacArthur liked Katayama Tetsu, prime minister in 1947–8, and regretted his loss of office. In a sense, MacArthur's respect was surprising because Katayama was a socialist; however, he was also a Christian – MacArthur saw Christianity as an enlightening influence in Japan – and MacArthur regarded him as reliable.

Gascoigne discussed the fall of the Katayama government with MacArthur in February 1948. Clearly, he regretted Katayama's resignation and MacArthur did not seem to welcome the prospect of Yoshida Shigeru returning to office. Gascoigne added, '. . . General MacArthur has assured me on several occasions, that, although he has endeavoured for the past two years to unearth a first-class politician and statesman, he has completely failed to do so'.[21] The Foreign Office tended to share MacArthur's reservations about Yoshida. He was experienced in diplomacy but less so in politics. Yoshida was an Anglophile but the British were not convinced that he was capable of dealing successfully with the considerable challenges facing him.[22] In reality, Yoshida was an astute political operator of greater ability and guile than he was credited with possessing by the British and MacArthur.[23] He served briefly as prime minister in 1946–7 and returned in 1948, retaining the premiership until 1954.

Gascoigne viewed Yoshida with more affection than did his UKLIM colleagues. He had known him since 1923 when they were both posted in China and he admired his tenacity and commitment: Yoshida's conservative inclinations no doubt complemented those of Gascoigne himself. Respect for Yoshida grew considerably so that, by the end of Gascoigne's period of office, Yoshida's continued presence as prime minister appeared indispensable.[24] Gascoigne reflected the Foreign Office's new-found interest in trade unionism, explicable through the fact that the foreign secretary, Ernest Bevin, was the greatest British trade union leader of the twentieth century, and urged the advantages of pragmatism upon Yoshida's handling of labour disputes. Gascoigne extolled British methods of conducting industrial relations and commended them for adoption in Japan.[25] Gascoigne viewed the Japan Communist Party (JCP) as a potential menace and applauded MacArthur's action in purging the central committee of the JCP in the summer of 1950.[26] Despite his liking for Yoshida, Gascoigne retained his doubts as to the future direction of Japanese government when Japan regained sovereignty.

BRITISH FRUSTRATIONS

Bevin was frustrated, in the latter part of 1949, by American vacillation over embarking on negotiations leading to a Japanese peace treaty. Dean Acheson assured him that progress would be made soon but this was blocked by the obduracy of the secretary for defence, Louis Johnson, and the Pentagon which opposed a peace treaty because of the deteriorating international situation. Gascoigne spoke to MacArthur in November 1949 when the general talked of having perused drafts sent from Washington. MacArthur told Gascoigne that opinion in the Pentagon favoured rearming Japan:

> 'For your own personal and secret information the General let slip during the conversation that some of the United States "service people in the Pentagon" "wanted to rearm Japan". He showed, however, later on that he did not think that they would win their case. He described these people as "sabre rattlers" and from the manner in which he spoke he made it clear that he was not himself of their mind . . .'[27]

British concern at the uncertainties surrounding American intentions was fuelled: Bevin sent a trenchant message to Washington on 8 December 1949 emphasizing that he would be meeting Commonwealth prime ministers in Colombo in January 1950 and it would be difficult to report the lack of progress to them – '. . . this question of security is one which very much concerns us all'.[28]

Gascoigne placed more emphasis, in his reports in 1950, on the unfortunate consequence of American failure to provide clearer signals as to where the occupation was going. Gascoigne believed that the Japanese should show due respect to the representatives of the occupying powers and he was always quick to identify examples of truculence or dissent. He reported on 12 June that he had noticed personally, in his discussions with Japanese officials, including governors of prefectures, mayors, and Ministry and Imperial Household officials, that they were prepared to express overt criticism of the prolongation of the occupation and of the absence of a long-term policy. MacArthur's action in relaxing controls in the political, social, economic, and financial spheres accentuated demands for the occupation to be ended.

The security dilemma facing Japan acted as a sobering

influence: MacArthur's past reference to Japan as a 'Switzerland of the Far East' was no longer credible and most Japanese desired American protection in an explicit form. Gascoigne believed that the crunch was approaching:

> 'As was forecast last year, the period of drift in our treatment of Japan which started some two years ago, is now reaching a critical stage, and I feel that if it should continue for much longer we may arrive at a point when either the Japanese will virtually be the masters of the occupation or the occupation will have to take very stern steps against the Japanese, which could indeed be a retrograde step . . .'[29]

Gascoigne told MacArthur of his apprehension when they met on 6 June:

> 'I thought the time had come for me to tell him that I personally felt uneasy about the manner in which the Japanese were now behaving. Public statements and incidents large and small had taken place during these past two months which would never have occurred six months ago. No doubt the Japanese Communists and fellow travellers, by their recent positive actions, roused the latent nationalistic feelings of the ordinary Japanese, who, although they might not, and, in fact, I was sure did not, agree with Communist doctrines, were nationalists at heart and were tired of the allied yoke. I further said that in my opinion the time had come when some impressive demonstration of allied might (a large parade by American forces in the air and on the ground) might well be staged.'[30]

MacArthur did not disagree and appeared to accept the force of much of what was communicated by Gascoigne.

The long period of drift over a peace treaty came to an end with the appointment by President Truman of John Foster Dulles as his emissary charged with negotiating a treaty. Dulles possessed tremendous zeal and industry: he was determined to secure rapid progress, appreciating that time should not be wasted and inspired by his own ambition to be the secretary of state in the next Republican administration. Dulles visited Tokyo just before the outbreak of the Korean war and Gascoigne spoke candidly to him:

> 'Psychologically, the effect upon the Japanese of our lack of a policy towards the future of their country was a most

unsatisfactory one, and would become more so with the passage of time. I voiced concern lest Russia should take advantage of this state of uncertainty by making a bid for the holding of a peace conference on her own terms, which would be most embarrassing to us.'[31]

Dulles questioned Gascoigne about the situation of Australia and New Zealand and how they would view strategic considerations affecting their security. Gascoigne replied that Australia and New Zealand had modified their previous approach and they favoured the conclusion of an early peace treaty with suitable security guarantees intended to defend Japan and to obviate the contingency of renewed Japanese expansion in the future. In response to a question of Dulles concerning the stationing of American troops in Japan once sovereignty was restored, Gascoigne thought that the Japanese should request assistance so that the presence of American troops on Japanese soil was not imposed overtly by the allies; Yoshida would probably react in a positive manner when approached.

As regards the nature of a peace treaty itself, Gascoigne thought that a treaty should be concise and relatively straightforward: he commented that the British would not press for too many restrictions. In this respect it should be noted that British officials were more conciliatory than members of the cabinet as the deliberations in London over a treaty in 1950–1 demonstrated.[32] Dulles emphasized his own potential antagonism to including restrictive clauses engendered by his experience of the Versailles treaty in 1919.

EFFECTS OF THE KOREAN WAR

Gascoigne's harmonious relationship with MacArthur came to an abrupt end in the last week of June 1950. The outbreak of the Korean war marked a watershed in many directions as the Cold War moved into a dangerous phase of becoming a limited 'hot' war. Certainly it was a watershed in relations between Gascoigne and MacArthur: the latter was so dominated by the new responsibilities he assumed on behalf of his own government and of the UN that he could devote only restricted time to Japan. Gascoigne resented the fact that he could not pursue his full exchanges with MacArthur as previously and the tone of Gascoigne's communications with the Foreign Office changed fundamentally. He complained to Bevin on 9 July that all was subordinated to Korean demands: he could not see MacArthur and deprecated his inability to discuss important matters with him. Gascoigne believed that MacArthur now endorsed the necessity to keep American bases in Japan.[33]

Gascoigne's pessimism regarding the future of Japan grew in the second half of 1950. He wrote to Robert Scott in the Foreign Office on 9 October that Japan was likely to move politically to the right after the close of the occupation and that undesirable Japanese practices might re-emerge.[34] Gascoigne wrote to Bevin on 18 November that MacArthur was highly autocratic: 'He certainly remains the complete Dictator and he is enjoying some strong Republican backing in the States.'[35] Gascoigne added that Truman would probably like to see MacArthur departing from his posts in Japan '. . . and there are some who think that one of Truman's main reasons for wanting an early Japanese peace is that it would bring with it MacArthur's exit from Japan'.[36]

In January 1951 Gascoigne accompanied Sir George Sansom to meet MacArthur. Sansom drafted a brief record in which he was mostly positive about MacArthur. He was unquestionably impressive, '. . . a great man, whatever his shortcomings'. MacArthur did not say anything notably original or profound but he advanced his views with vigour and conviction. He was not noted for strict adherence to the truth and he was ready to amend facts if necessary:

'His political and military views have a logical coherence and he thinks things out very carefully. He may base himself upon some mistaken premises, but it would be dangerous to dismiss his opinions as only irrational or prejudiced. He has often proved right, and I think his average is fairly high. His trouble is vanity.

He said (what he has said before) that he did not believe in occupations, and thought it was high time that the occupation of Japan came to an end. He did *not*, he said, suppose that the Japanese had become democrats. The occupation had merely provided the apparatus which the Japanese could use if they desired. He thought that there would be a good deal of change after the peace treaties were made, but he did not believe the Japanese would revert to unqualified militarism. They could not, even if they wished, so long as the Allied Powers could use economic pressure. But in any case he believed that there was, since 1945, a growth in the feeling for freedom among the Japanese people, and this was bound to play a part in domestic politics in Japan in the future.'[37]

Sansom's assessment was acute and captured accurately the positive and negative features of the enigmatic MacArthur.

Gascoigne's term in Tokyo drew to a close in February 1951 in consequence of his appointment as ambassador to Moscow. On 6 February he produced the customary reflective review of a personal nature customarily drafted by a British ambassador upon completing his mission. When he had left London in June 1946 he had been warned that MacArthur could be awkward to deal with; but he had found him to be amiable and kindly: he was welcomed as a member of SCAP's 'court'. Gascoigne reviewed the more important reforms implemented by SCAP including the encouragement given to trade unions, land reform, and educational measures. With regard to the latter he remarked that the process of revising textbooks had been protracted and demanding: he added, presciently, that: '. . . it is not at all certain even today that it has been successful'.[38]

The greatest success of the occupation was in the economic sphere. The Americans poured vast sums into restoring the basis of the economy but inflation loomed as a grave menace in 1948 to the point where MacArthur professed marked pessimism regarding Japan's future prospects. The Dodge mission (April–May 1949) combated inflation effectively through emphasizing a balanced budget, ending export subsidies and cutting import subsidies. The economy recovered substantially between 1948 and 1950 and growth was further stimulated by the Korean war. Gascoigne remarked that British commercial interests were flourishing: '. . . and the British commercial community enjoys a respect and exercises an influence quite out of proportion to its relative importance in the overall commercial and financial field'.[39] In the social sphere the chief achievement was 'the emancipation of Japanese womanhood'. The occupation sought to reform the treatment of women: SCAP aimed to impress on Japanese men the need to regard women far more favourably. Gascoigne commented that it would take considerable time to effect this fundamental reform successfully.

FUTURE PROSPECTS

When Gascoigne had arrived in the summer of 1946 he had discovered a country traumatized by defeat and willing to accept leadership from SCAP. In February 1951 he left a nation of growing self-confidence; supported economically and strategically by the USA, but critical of the extent of American dominance. Gascoigne assessed MacArthur's contribution in balanced fashion:

> 'MacArthur and his United States satellites have undoubtedly fulfilled their task of furnishing Japan with a democratic blueprint upon which the Japanese can work if, in the future, they should wish to retain the democratic way of life. But American occupation officials have spoken too long and too loudly about the concrete and positive success of their democratic campaign. In their great enthusiasm they have, many of them, made themselves believe that Japan is already firmly fixed within the democratic fold, and that the teachings which they have been at such pains to disseminate in this country for the past five years have taken firm and permanent root. The occupation has undoubtedly done extremely good work but it is patently obvious that democracy, as we know it, cannot be imposed upon a people during a time of occupation; the democratic way of life can only be attained by years of patience and practice. While I believe that there is hope that the Japanese may retain some of the principles of democracy, they are not likely, I think, to keep the Constitution as it stands. Any future liberalism which may be practised will be modelled from a Japanese pattern.'[40]

So far the Japanese had cooperated with the Americans but Gascoigne believed that once Japan regained sovereignty, a reaction would occur against Western methods and there would be a reversion to traditional Japanese principles. It was imperative that a peace settlement with Japan should be reached within the near future. It would not be feasible to stipulate a restrictive treaty and other methods would be required to exert influence in the desired direction. The question of Japanese rearmament was clearly highly contentious: the apprehension felt in Australia and New Zealand must be addressed skilfully.

Gascoigne concluded his report by reflecting on the functioning of the British liaison mission under his leadership. American influence was so all-pervasive that Gascoigne and his colleagues faced an uphill struggle in asserting British interests. Britain's cultural influence was extended through the strenuous efforts of H. Vere Redman, Gascoigne's information adviser, and by Edmund Blunden, his cultural adviser. Gascoigne and his colleagues endeavoured to foster positive relations with the Japanese people, despite the inevitable repercussions of the Pacific war. American officials did not resent the efforts to advance British cultural influence. British nationals in Japan complemented the work of the mission and Gascoigne applauded the efforts of the British community: '. . . who have impressed the Japanese by their skill, enterprise and, above all, by the assurance of the continuity of their efforts'.[41] He felt that the Japanese regarded themselves as closer to the British than to the Americans: he was optimistic on the prospects for a reasonably cordial relationship between Britain and Japan, yet governed by perceptions of mutual priorities.

The urbane tone of Gascoigne's final report was marred by a regrettable dispute over the circumstances of his departure from Haneda airport. Given the nature of the Anglo-American relationship and the length of time Gascoigne had served in Tokyo the British mission expected MacArthur and his senior colleagues to be present at the airport to bid Gascoigne farewell. George Clutton, chargé d'affaires following Gascoigne's departure, wrote to Sir William Strang, the permanent under-secretary:

'Joe Gascoigne's departure from Tokyo was marred, both for him and for us, by the absence at the airport of any American of whatever description. This absence was so painfully obvious that some of us thought that the Supreme Commander in his vindictiveness towards Joe had issued a direction that no one from General Headquarters was to see him off. I am afraid also that it has been impossible to conceal the miserable affair and there has been some indignant comment outside the Mission.'[42]

Clutton added that American ideas of courtesy and protocol were peculiar and some allowances had to be made. There was some tension in Tokyo because John Foster Dulles was arriving at Haneda as Gascoigne departed. Clutton stated that he had received an apology from William Sebald. The controversy reached the press in the form of a frank article in an Australian paper, the *Sydney Sun*: the author of the article appeared well informed and explained that the cause of the problem was that MacArthur had refused to meet Gascoigne on four occasions in order to discuss the course of the Korean conflict. Strained relations between the British mission and SCAP ensued.[43] Clutton wrote to Strang that publication of this article was not inspired by the mission and that the matter should be regarded as closed. Sir Oliver Franks, the ambassador in Washington, spoke to Freeman Matthews of the State Department who was apologetic and said he had known nothing of the circumstances of Gascoigne's departure.[44]

This episode was sad yet, in its way, appropriate for it revealed how sour relations had become between Gascoigne and MacArthur during the Korean war and it was a more accurate indication than the usual diplomatic verbiage covering strained relations. Equally it was misleading as a final note. Gascoigne enjoyed cordial relations with MacArthur from his arrival until the start of the Korean war and Gascoigne's reports of their discussions contain a great deal of importance and interest. Gascoigne discharged his role effectively until matters that he could not influence concerning the waging of war in Korea transformed the situation and destroyed his previously amicable discussions with MacArthur.

While Sir Alvary Gascoigne was not a profound thinker, he possessed an astute grasp of realities and a commonsense approach which was apposite for the kind of situation facing him in Tokyo. It is unlikely that a more forceful approach would have advanced British interests: instead Gascoigne might have experienced between 1946 and 1950 the reactions that he unfortunately encountered in 1950–1. However, between 1946 and 1950 MacArthur and the British government respected each other and were in broad agreement, a very different position to that existing in 1950–1.

22

Split Images: Occupied Japan through the Eyes of British Journalists and Authors

ROGER BUCKLEY

'WE HAVE concentrated on quality rather than quantity', reported the Foreign Office in June 1950 when preparing its defences before a parliamentary debate on Anglo-Japanese cultural diplomacy.[1] What is striking, however, in glancing at the output from British correspondents and commentators on events during the allied occupation is its sheer volume and productivity. The scale of activities is remarkable, particularly when it had been conceded shortly after the end of the Pacific War that the United States would be in the driving seat for the duration of the occupation. The British government and its advisers might be prepared to accept by December 1945 that it was to be MacArthur's proconsulate[2] but neither press editors nor publishers worked on the assumption that the public at large would no longer wish to follow events. It was certainly an American-led occupation but British interest in the occupation persisted, despite the obvious US command and the austerity of the immediate post-war years that limited press expenditure and rationed British newsprint.[3]

Japan mattered. Sufficient numbers of readers at least existed for Fleet Street and Bloomsbury to set about describing and explaining what was going on during the occupation. British correspondents in Tokyo filed regular accounts on the frenzied reforms and directives that poured out of SCAP GHQ, occasional British visitors offered their more personal version of particular events, novelists got on with their vision of war-time and post-war Japanese behaviour and poets (though outwardly disguised as cultural attachés) added yet another flavour to the feast. It might all be catering to a minority audience but the final concoction deserves attention and a degree of respect.

To date, the results have been largely overlooked for two reasons. First, there was little of the heady immediacy of, for example, John Hersey's piece on *Hiroshima* that *The New Yorker* quite rightly brought to an international audience by devoting its entire edition of 31 August 1946 to this article alone.[4] Credit here goes equally to its author and his editors, William Shawn and Harold Ross. Yet, if some British accounts carried similar messages, the second difficulty, then and now, is to track down what was a heterogeneous collection of press and published writings. The components are scattered and lack agreement on what was going on within Japan or where the nation might be going. This confusion may be good history but the sifting takes time and few in Britain in the immediate post-war years had this luxury. Coping with austerity at home had a priority that precluded all except a handful of specialists in the Foreign Office and a few within commercial and manufacturing groups from merely following what was reported.

There was certainly national agreement on the bestiality of Japan's behaviour towards PoWs but no consensus on what should happen next. The result for the brave or curious laity is nicely captured by Christmas Humphreys' preface to his travelogue *Via Tokyo* where he remarked in November 1947 that he had added a glossary: '. . . at the request of the publishers. If they, poor things, were a trifle bewildered at so many foreign terms, there may be readers in the same difficulty'.[5] Just to sow more seeds of confusion, he disarmingly adds: '. . . I am no scholar, and I may be quite wrong in my meanings . . .' and warns in his next paragraph that his book: '. . . contains no horrors, no war, no politics and no economics. The first two were deliberately avoided; of the last two I know nothing and care less'.[6] The fact remains, however, that Humphreys' work of 200 pages (almost the first half of which concerned Japan) was elegantly and expensively published by Hutchinson in 1948, helped by the author's reputation as an authority on Buddhism and as the colourful wrapper proudly announced on the spine, its ninety-four illustrations.

JOURNALISTS DURING THE OCCUPATION

The British paper that was most carefully cultivated by MacArthur's headquarters was *The Times*. Whether deserved or not, this gave undoubted advantages to the paper's controversial correspondent, Frank Hawley, in the form of a considerable number of private briefings with General MacArthur himself. It was not every journalist in Tokyo who could commence a letter to his foreign editor with the remark: 'Tonight I had a private interview, lasting over an hour-and-a-half, with General MacArthur. Speaking freely and at great length on various aspects of the occupation, he did much to clarify my ideas. I think you will be interested in a report of the interview.' Since even very senior members of GHQ SCAP (Supreme Commander Allied Powers) only met MacArthur on the rarest of occasions, this is an indication of how MacArthur viewed *The Times* and presumably, given MacArthur's penchant for publicity, the kind of dividend he expected in return.

The relationship that evolved, however, between Frank Hawley, a Japanologist with a remarkable library of Japanese books, and the occupation authorities rarely followed in the tram tracks that SCAP GHQ would have dearly liked. Despite extensive private discussions – not all taking the form of the dreaded MacArthurian monologue – Hawley was no sycophant and his writings were on occasion to become a source of discomfort to his host. Hawley, who had worked in Japan in the 1930s before being imprisoned at the start of the Pacific War, did not take kindly to being told time and again that American officialdom's every act was benevolent and correct. He was sceptical of important parts of the American edifice and said so in print.

Hawley clearly formed his opinions on the prospects for reforming Japan society at an early stage in the occupation. He reported in a confidential letter to *The Times* of May 1947 that: '. . . after some eight months of observation here . . . Democracy has barely touched the surface of Japanese life, which remains essentially feudalistic, and few Japanese desire to have democracy (as we know it) here'.[7] Hawley continued, in what was based on his recent conversation with Prime Minister Yoshida's son, Kenichi, that: 'The Japanese attitude towards foreigners remains virtually unchanged; they tend to despise

them because they consider their own culture superior; they fear
and dislike them because of their own mechanical inferiority and
of the defeat they suffered at the hands of the allies in war. Their
reaction to the whole occupation is one of well-concealed
hostility but they prefer the Americans to any other people as an
occupying force, because the Americans with their many
scientists, doctors, technicians, and experts of every kind have
so much to offer and are content to take so little away. Each time
General MacArthur insists that this or that be done for the
Japanese, i.e., each time they see their apparent recovery nearer,
their attitude stiffens, and their animosity becomes more
apparent.'[8]

Hawley does not appear to have shifted his ground in later
correspondence to this paper. If little, at least in tone, altered in
the daily press briefings from MacArthur's staff in the Dai-Ichi
Building opposite the Imperial palace, equally little change can
be seen in Hawley's observations from Tokyo. His approach was
to be both critical of the overambitious plans of the American
reformers, whether on constitutional, educational or economic
affairs, and the tactics of the Japanese establishment. In
confidential correspondence he points out his distrust of Japan's
leaders and sympathized with '. . . the common people . . .
[who] . . . have had some slight taste of freedom for the first time
in their lives'.[9] In the autumn of 1948 Hawley was still arguing in
almost identical prose that: 'Try as I could, I have been unable to
find many signs of changed thinking among the old Japanese
ruling classes, not even in the present Prime Minister, Hitoshi
Ashida, whose principal merit consists in faithfully carrying out
MacArthur's orders. In that respect he differs greatly from
Yoshida, whose tactics were to evade and procrastinate in the
hope that, in the end, he would be able to get away with doing
nothing. The common Japanese people have a glimmering of
what democracy means, but they are still largely influenced by
the old ruling classes.'[10]

Hawley's doubts left him in an uncomfortable position since
some of those conservatives attempting to influence both
MacArthur's staff and the British mission under Sir Alvary
Gascoigne were 'among my oldest friends'.[11] Hawley found it
'distasteful' to write in this manner of his pre-war contacts but he
appears to have genuinely felt that, unless the occupation
continued for many years, the prospects for democracy were

slight. This left Hawley having to criticize all and sundry from his Japanese friends to MacArthur and Gascoigne. He concluded his letter by sensing that Gascoigne was: '. . . conscious of the fragility of Japan's new democratic structure, and he has, it seems, been persuaded that the reactionary Japanese who frequent the British Embassy are again to be the rulers of Japan, and that the time has come for the British to establish good relations with them'.[12]

Hawley's position was to leave him virtually *persona non grata* by the end of the occupation. His belief that there was an anti-democratic 'invisible government' in existence within Japan severely undermined his position with the occupation authorities. Hawley's stance was an unchanging and probably impractical one from the autumn of 1948 onwards: he hoped that the US forces, however clumsy they might be in practice, would remain in Japan virtually indefinitely, since '. . . both the Communists and the reactionaries are only too keen to get rid of the American army . . .' and '. . . the common Japanese people want that army to stay in order to protect them against the struggle between the two groups. There is a widespread feeling among the Japanese people that they would be far worse off if the American army were not here'.[13] Hawley's distrust of all sides, whether within GHQ SCAP, the regrouping conservatives or on the left, ensured that he would earn little reward for his pains. He may not have helped his case by a tendency to speak his mind at official functions and by letting visiting American politicians know in forceful terms what he thought of developments in occupied Japan. It is true that his paper still outwardly supported him when he criticized American measures but his contract was not to be renewed. He lived on in Japan after the occupation ended.

Hawley's concerns were shared in part by others reporting for Fleet Street. The Australian Richard Hughes, for example, went out of his way in *The Sunday Times* to caution the West against encouraging the revival of even disguised, lightly-armed, Japanese para-military units in the shape of the National Police Reserve.[14] The ever rumbustious Hughes, who combined writing for a host of publications with a hilarious spell as a manager of the Foreign Correspondents' Club of Japan for nearly two years between 1947 and 1948, took himself and his calling less seriously than either Hawley or his rival *The Manchester*

Guardian's and *Daily Herald*'s representative, Hessell Tiltman.
Hughes in his memoirs would note how he somehow reported
for both *The Sunday Times* and *The Economist*, while running a
press club that was virtually bankrupt and in constant turmoil. It
shared, in the Hughes era at least, '. . . some of the features of the
makeshift bordello, inefficient gaming-house and black-market
centre, with the basic goodwill and bitter feuds of any press
hostelry anywhere, and the aspirations and pretensions of an
outpost of the "free world" in a defeated Oriental state'.[15]

Yet Hughes' glory years were to come later after he left Tokyo
and moved on to Hong Kong and to the still wider fame of being
a model for characters in novels by Ian Fleming and John le
Carré. During the occupation, Hughes' reporting – reflecting a
common Australian and British view of the dangers that even a
defeated and supposedly reformed Japan could well pose to the
future security of the region – was frequently sceptical in tone. In
contrast, Hessell Tiltman attempted to take a somewhat more
open stance. Tiltman, like Hawley, knew Japan in its pre-Pearl
Harbor years and would remain in Tokyo long after the
occupation had ended. He had been a prolific author on East
Asian affairs in the 1930s, most notably through his co-authored
works *Manchuria: The Cockpit of Asia*[16] and *Japan: Mistress of the
Pacific?*.[17] Tiltman's reputation with journalists in Tokyo has
remained higher than that of Hawley both because he was felt to
have taken a more balanced view in his reporting on
developments during the occupation and because he was
personally less argumentative. Unlike Hawley he served on a
number of occasions as president of the Foreign Correspondents'
Club and was decorated by the Japanese government in 1959 at
the time when he was still *The Guardian*'s correspondent in
Japan.[18] Certainly in his later years Tiltman became something of
an 'institution' in Japan, rather as Richard Hughes was able to
carve out his own more eccentric reputation in Hong Kong.
Tiltman was recognized to have had links to the Japanese
Ministry of Foreign Affairs without being seen to have
particularly compromised his independence.[19]

WRITERS AND POST-WAR JAPAN

Yet during the occupation British journalists had to share the
field with a host of their compatriots, who managed somehow to

descend on Tokyo. Japan was neither effectively isolated nor ignored. Publications by British writers like John Morris, Edmund Blunden, G.S. Fraser, Honor Tracy and Christmas Humphreys suggest that there was still (as in pre-war days) an appetite among British publishers for first-hand impressions of Japan and a readership in Britain for such publications. Similarly, the success of Richard Mason's first novel, *The Wind Cannot Read*,[20] in 1947 indicates that attitudes towards defeated Japan were rarely as clear cut as the crude line peddled by the Beaverbrook papers intended.[21] Certainly there was an obvious and understandable British suspicion of Japan in the first post-war decade that indeed persisted in many quarters until the eventual death of the Showa Emperor,[22] but there was also a more positive view on display even when memories of the bitter fighting in South-East Asia were at their harshest.

The reception accorded to Richard Mason's *The Wind Cannot Read* refutes the idea that the British reader was only prepared to accept accounts critical of its Asian enemy in the Second World War. Mason's work has a young Japanese woman – admittedly working with the British under a Chinese alias in New Delhi as a language instructor for those about to be sent to Burma – as one of its two protagonists and the tone throughout is carefully measured. The Englishman at the centre of the novel tells himself, when interviewing captured Japanese troops: '. . . to be sharing with sympathy. And I had to force myself to recall terrible pictures I had seen and stories I had heard, and to think of my brother's murder and allot to them some of the responsibility. It was not fair to do otherwise. The British guards knew it was not fair; they had come through Burma, closer to the Japs than I, and they knew what they would have done if they had had a free hand. They didn't mince matters. But they kept their boots and their bayonets in their places, and we told them: "two blacks don't make a white".'[23]

It is little wonder that such sentiments made the book a favourite of the late Louis Allen, who worked harder than most to reduce the post-war antagonisms between Britain and Japan. As a novel it is conventional in design: the dialogue can be stilted and the romance at the core of the work between one of the 'Japwallahs' and his teacher reads less convincingly than the Indian background and the brief ambush near Imphal. The very fact of its publication and the enthusiastic reception it received are testimony, however, to the complexity of British views on Japan and indicate a wish by some to avoid seeing Japanese as mere caricatures. It was no surprise that it was turned into a film.

Others also attempted in the easier medium of the travelogue to present a rounded picture of Japan. Most looked with favour on aspects of post-war Japanese society, while frequently finding it hard to put in anything beyond a perfunctory word of praise for the efforts of the United States to alter, and thereby perhaps correct, earlier Japanese behaviour. The results, with rare exceptions, are generally unsatisfactory. Most are merely impressionistic accounts based on a necessarily limited exposure to occupied Japan. The British resident journalists had both a greater freedom to observe events and far more opportunities to interview American and Japanese figures than their visiting compatriots, who depended very largely on escorted visits and standard briefings. Under the circumstances the results could hardly be expected to be penetrating or distinguished. Most British accounts disappoint through a lack of appreciation of the handicaps under which SCAP GHQ and its staff in the field operated and a singular determination to take pot shots at their military hosts.

Honor Tracy's sketches in *Kakemono* typify this easily mined vein of anti-Americanism. She announces in her foreword that the aim of the occupation was to ensure that: 'Japan was to be made over in the pattern and image of a civilization I had never been able to appreciate'[24] and rarely misses an opportunity to note the 'brutality' and 'nauseating exhibitionism' of its GIs. There are certainly moments when Tracy could indeed mint a sharp phrase as when she speaks of 'the mahogany foxholes of GHQ', but her more common ploy is to deplore each and every effort of the United States to reform Japan. Her conservatism is extraordinary and avoids taking into account any mention of Japanese imperialism abroad or exploitation at home. Tracy's sympathy for an aristocracy forced to sell its heirlooms and surrender its farmland is constant. She was, of course, staunchly in favour of the Allies' decision to maintain the Emperor,[25] thought little of MacArthur and found it easy to mock '. . . [t]he spectacle of a young and savage nation trying, hurriedly and for no clear reason, to remake one of the most civilized races on the earth to its own bizarre pattern'.[26]

Perhaps the only Irish or British figure comparable to Tracy was Compton Pakenham, the representative for *Newsweek* in Japan. Pakenham was despised by liberal elements in GHQ for his efforts to alter economic and social reform measures that were increasingly under attack by 1950 from conservative groups in Japan and the United States. General Whitney of Government Section had nothing but contempt for Pakenham, who, it has been suggested, may have connived at the forging of communications purporting to be from the Emperor in order to persuade Dulles when visiting Tokyo that in June 1950 an end to the purging of Japanese business and political leaders was called for.[27] Pakenham and Harry Kern, *Newsweek*'s foreign editor, tried with distinctly limited success to use all means at their disposal to correct what they and their supporters held to be the failings of the occupation. Their lobby organization, The American Council on Japan, probably had less effect than either Pakenham and Kern or later revisionists would have one imagine.

More successful than the one-sided pictures of Honor Tracy and *Newsweek*'s Tokyo correspondent were those accounts that were able to steer a less erratic passage through the political waters. The most impressive journalist in this category is John Morris, a former Gurkha officer and lecturer from the later 1930s at Keio University. Morris, like so many of the British correspondents and unlike most of their US counterparts, had worked in Tokyo before Pearl Harbor. Frank Hawley, then director of the British Library in Tokyo, was one of his friends and Morris wrote at length of the mistreatment Hawley received at Japanese hands after his arrest in December 1941. After his return to Britain on the repatriation ship, Morris had the additional advantage of being employed during the war in supervising the broadcasting of programmes by the BBC to South and East Asia. This led him into having some differences with George Orwell on the inappropriateness of drinking tea from a saucer in the Eastern Service canteen but more importantly permitted Morris to write an account of his pre-war Japanese experiences. His short work *Traveller from Tokyo* (London, 1943) concludes with a postscript that suggests the state that British official and semi-official thinking had reached by 1942 on considering the prospect for post-war Japan. For Morris it was essential that allied military occupation be instituted to safeguard a Japanese government '. . . with liberal ideas that is willing and anxious to cooperate with the Allied Nations. I believe that the nucleus of such a government already exists in Japan. The country has always possessed liberal-minded states-men in sufficient quantity.'[28]

Morris was fortunate to be sent to Japan in 1946 as the BBC's special correspondent to see whether his war-time predictions were near the mark. He went, the foreword to *The Phoenix Cup* informs us, to discover '. . . how the people were reacting to defeat'.[29] He wanted to learn how Japanese society was attempting to cope with '. . . the greatest disaster that had ever overtaken their country'. Morris' impressions of his six months in Japan are those of a cautious liberal who hopes that a reformed nation might emerge in time, provided that this could be the product of Japanese initiatives. *The Phoenix Cup* was put out by the Cresset Press, who were also Sir George Sansom's publishers. It is dedicated to E.M. Forster.

After the standard complaints against brash America and its incomprehensive mangling of Japanese names, Morris writes in detail of how Japan was coping with its new status. He found much that was bitterly disappointing. He hated the rampant blackmarketeering, the brothels and cynical acceptance by many Japanese of the new political order. Morris was far from certain of Japan's future. When in London during the war he had written of '. . . a peace-loving and contented Japan, an agreeable partner in international politics'[30] he clearly had not reckoned with the scale of the United States' ambitions for defeated Japan and he found it hard to accept either their necessity or the probability of their success. Morris' war-time and post-war thinking echoes the views of the Foreign Office both in being unprepared for radical change by American dictate and in sharing enormous doubts of its appropriateness for an Asian society.

Since Morris had not been able to leave Tokyo until the summer of 1942 he had retained little but contempt for the leaders of war-time Japan. In reporting after his return on the Japanese officials arraigned before the International Military Tribunal for the Far East, he could only describe them collectively as 'seedy-looking men', whose 'pathetic and inferior-looking' appearances prompted him to wonder how they had 'dared to make a bid for world domination'.[31] Yet Morris, while meeting and reporting favourably on both Yoshida and the Crown Prince, had little confidence in the depth of

Japan's new commitment to any real understanding of a liberal political order. He wrote bitterly: 'Everybody talks in terms of the new-found democracy, but I never came across a single Japanese who could give a satisfactory definition of the term'.[32] With the exception of intellectuals and students, he felt that 'most people are only acting'.

The single, if highly qualified, ground for optimism that Morris could discern for contemporary Japan involved an unlikely reassessment by the nation of its immediate post-war experiences. Morris hoped against hope that Japan might remake her political and economic arrangements herself. He, like most British observers, remained sceptical of Japan's reliance on the all-prevailing American model. He wanted both Japan and her friends abroad to ignore the 'tawdry facade' that had been thrown up by excessive Americanization; he reminded his British readers that the Japanese could still boast of 'other and better aspects of their civilization'. He proposed that British cultural links should restart as quickly as possible in the somewhat improbable wish that 'we must remain not as conquerors, but as teachers',[33] although the realities of post-war international affairs in East Asia were strongly against Morris' proposals. The best that could be anticipated was a return to some semblance of a friendship, symbolized in his discovery of a single undamaged phoenix cup among the ruins of what had once been his pre-war house in Shibuya.

Yet perhaps the British authors with least commitment to occupation politics or international prestige deserve the last word. Unlike those who sensed an opportunity to turn out a topical travelogue there were a few writers with wider concerns. For Christmas Humphreys it was an unexpected chance to observe and conduct 'a special inquiry "in Search of Buddhism".[34] Humphreys had grabbed at the opportunity to visit Asia when he was invited to join the British prosecution team assembling in Tokyo for the IMTFE under A.S. Comyns Carr and used every moment of eleven months abroad in 1946–7 to full advantage. Certainly his work *Via Tokyo* has long passages for the general reader but it also attempts to show that: 'I claimed nothing for my Western birth, nor for my membership of "allied personnel", but came as a fellow Buddhist and a would-be friend'.[35] Not surprisingly, given his long interest in Buddhism and presidency of the Buddhist society of London, Humphreys' dedicated his book to Suzuki Daisetz (Daisetsu) 'who gave to the Western world Zen Buddhism.'

Via Tokyo stands in contrast to most British writing on occupied Japan both because of the religious perspectives of Humphreys and of the generally calm tone of its remarks on the situation within Japan. It is singularly free of malice towards either the United States' intentions or the response of the Japanese public. Humphreys could appreciate the patent advantages that the American military occupation had gained in ending the 'subjection' of the past, while reckoning that it would take decades before the outcome would be clear. He held that: '. . . not even the Japanese, mercurial-minded as they are, can leap from a thousand years of feudalism to a pure democracy, and now that they have the tools for achieving freedom they must be taught how to use them'.[36] For Humphreys, required as he was through his work at the IMTFE to relive the horrors of Japanese aggression, it would take '. . . at least three generations of consistent, deliberate education to enable the Japanese to understand and use the new Constitution'. He concluded, in much the same vein as John Morris was also writing at precisely the same moment, that: '. . . only then shall we know to what extent they will have made their country a cheap imitation of the USA and how much she will be worthy of the great traditions of culture, art and philosophy of Old Japan'.

It was in order to view at first-hand as much as he possibly could of Japan's religious heritage that Humphreys had come to occupied Japan. His meetings with Suzuki Daisetz and his visits to persuade Japanese Buddhists of the need to unify their sectarian differences form the highlights of Humphreys' months in Japan. The IMTFE was merely the means by which he could pursue more serious ends. Formulating the twelve principles of Buddhism mattered far more than his work on the prosecution team in a court to which the Japanese public was largely indifferent. Humphreys claimed that their attitude: '. . . from first to last was simple and unanimous: "These men led us all into a wicked war. You won, so of course you kill them, but why take a year to do it? Is there no use for a brick wall?" '[37] Humphreys was equally unworried by some of the dubious methods of obtaining evidence for the charges. He admitted that '. . . in order to prove the complicity of the various Defendants in the overall conspiracy . . .' the prosecution sank '. . . to a standard of proof regrettably low'. Yet, as he quickly confessed: '. . . there it was, and as these were the rules of the game we played them'.[38]

On the cultural front, the impact of a few British academic figures was far more positive and out of all proportion to the very limited resources available. Edmund Blunden remains the best-known British literary figure who came to Japan in the first half of the twentieth century. He had first taught at Tokyo University in the 1920s, while his post-war visits served to cement his fame. His reputation in Japan can hardly be in doubt and recent publications have contributed to wider British awareness of his achievements in Tokyo.[39] Blunden's frantic round of public lectures and cultural diplomacy during the occupation earned him considerable praise from Japanese quarters but his very activities largely precluded him from being able to write more than occasionally for British outlets. The demands from within Japan threatened to the point of physical exhaustion to overwhelm both him and G.S. Fraser, his successor as cultural attaché to the British mission. The tasks left Blunden with neither the time nor the energy to comment on developments during the occupation or to write much beyond perfunctory poetry, though Blunden knew that the muse was already deserting him by the late 1940s.

Blunden kept up a ferocious pace throughout his period in Japan; according to one of his biographers he gave approximately 600 lectures from January 1948 to March 1950.[40] It was perhaps not so much his earlier writings on the horrors of the Western front in the First World War and his political views than his friendliness and accessibility that made him so popular with Japanese audiences. His student listeners were often more pacifist and radical than their visiting lecturer, yet many clearly appreciated a teacher with such obvious enthusiasm and willingness to explain in unencumbered language.[41] Blunden's efforts led the head of the UK liaison mission, Sir Alvary Gascoigne, to call his cultural attaché Britain's 'secret weapon' in the occupation.

Most of Blunden's writing during the occupation was confined to publication in Japan, where a succession of material based largely on lecture notes was published by Kenkyūsha in 1948 and 1949. Copies can still be readily found in any second-hand bookshop in Tokyo today but their impact was limited.[42]

Aside from a few contributions to his former employer, *The Times Literary Supplement*, and some poetry that was published by Macmillan, Blunden concentrated on his duties within Japan and the region. There was to be nothing remotely comparable to his *Undertones of War*[43] that he had completed when in Tokyo in 1924.

Between December 1947 and his farewell in May 1950 Blunden was extraordinarily busy but relatively unproductive when his literary efforts are weighed against his earlier standards. Pressed by the British mission's information minister, Vere Redman, the same punishing round of lectures and editorial deadlines was undertaken for a year by Blunden's successor, the poet and literary critic, G.S. Fraser.[44] This probably contributed to Fraser's ill health and his early return to London but it did also spur him to write what has remained a solid and frequently cited work on twentieth-century literature. Unlike Blunden's survey course material, Fraser's *The Modern Writer and His World* has lasted to be widely cited beyond Japan.[45] Coming to Tokyo had galvanized Fraser into risking that most difficult of books, the satisfactory introductory text. He admitted that '. . . I doubt whether at home I would ever have had the courage to attempt so ambitious a task'. Fraser, again following in Blunden's wake, paid tribute to his Japanese student audiences for listening to his remarks so attentively. The occupation period proved to be a rare opportunity for figures of the calibre of Blunden and Fraser to present elements of British and Western culture to a generation in Japan that had been starved of contact with the wider world. It is questionable if any comparable enthusiasm has been ignited in the years since the San Francisco peace settlements.

CONCLUSION

British perceptions of occupied Japan depended largely on the efforts of relatively few reporters and writers. These figures provided the information on which public opinion might draw to follow developments within Japan. Pride of place should go to the journalists whose task it was to explain briefly the complicated and comprehensive nature of American actions during the (nominally) allied occupation. The work of Hawley and Tiltman indicates time and again how ingrained professional scepticism reacted to the boasts of some within SCAP GHQ that Japan had been instantly and irrevocably transformed through American command and example. First-hand knowledge of Japan in the years before 1941 acted as a powerful restraint against accepting more than a small proportion of the claims frequently put out by MacArthur's publicity machine. This unfortunately left many British figures unimpressed by SCAP GHQ's considerable achievements. Hessell Tiltman, for example, would tell readers in Britain and the United States much the same story in both August 1946 and May 1950. He warned initially that there was '. . . no guarantee that if the old crowd showed up again they would not be obeyed as slavishly as MacArthur'[46] and in a lengthy analysis of the probable peace terms noted five years later that: '. . . if the British Commonwealth nations sign the treaty, it will be with mental reservations. Australians still find it difficult to accept General MacArthur's vision of Japan that has "undergone the greatest transformation recorded in modern history" '.[47] Equally, Frank Hawley could speak of his anxieties for Japan's future, though in his case this would lead to questions in the British parliament and to backbench criticism of MacArthur for reacting to what he saw to be serious inaccuracies.[48] It was probably because, as one Conservative member suggested, 'The Times was read everywhere, but most especially in Japan' [49] that Hawley was singled out for punishment.

The record of the British authors who visited occupied Japan and subsequently wrote up their impressions is decidedly mixed. Most shared doubts with British journalists as to the democratic foundations of MacArthur's new Japan but few exerted themselves to present a balanced evaluation of SCAP's handiwork. Virtually no one, for example, discussed the major contribution of General Whitney's Government Section to the occupation and few really distinguished between different political leaders. All visited Yoshida but few appear to have interviewed Socialist or Communist figures. The British commentators were equally negligent over economic and financial affairs, where, once again, the foreign correspondents based in Tokyo were far more thorough.[50]

Where a few authors excelled was in writing on subjects that the journalists were obliged to largely ignore. Christmas Humphreys' Via Tokyo is an antidote to the more wooden travelogues of some of his contemporaries, most of whom had the supposed advantage of having known pre-war Japan. Yet ironically the two books that were published by British authors with connections in Japan during the occupation years that have lasted longest in print were both silent on the events of this period. Richard Mason's novel and G.S. Fraser's examination of the modern movement in English literature achieved considerable fame in their separate fields without having anything to say on post-war Japan. Those who attempted to write of occupied Japan in the region between journalism and more serious fiction or scholarship came off the worst. Between the necessary immediacy of the press and the ambitions of the novelist or lecturer there was a void that commentators failed to fill. The lack of any guarded endorsement of the occupation's reforms was to cloud British views of Japan for the next generation and beyond.

Notes

Chapter 1 SIR HUGH CORTAZZI *Sir Harry Parkes, 1828–1885*

1. Quoted in 'The Pestilently Active Minister' by Sir Hugh Cortazzi. *Monumenta Nipponica*, Vol. XXXIX, No. 2 (1984), p. 148.
2. H. Cortazzi, *Dr Willis in Japan: British Medical Pioneer 1862–1877*, London: The Athlone Press, 1985, p. 67. (Hereafter referred to as *Willis*.)
3. Grace Fox, *Britain and Japan 1858–1883*, Oxford: Clarendon Press, 1969, p. 160. (Hereafter referred to as Fox.)
4. Isabella Bird, *Unbeaten Tracks in Japan*, London, 1880, p. 22.
5. *Willis*, p. 206.
6. *Willis*, p. 206.
7. *Willis*, p. 80.
8. S. Lane Poole and F.V. Dickins (eds.) *The Life of Sir Harry Parkes*, 2 volumes, London, 1894, Volume II, p. 357. This deals with Parkes in Japan. (Hereafter referred to as Dickins.)
9. Dickins, p. 358.
10. Dickins, p. 169.
11. Fox, p. 160.
12. Dickins, p. 169.
13. Dickins, p. 337.
14. Dickins, p. 355.
15. H. Cortazzi (ed.), *Mitford's Japan, The Memoirs and recollections of Algernon Bertram Mitford, the first Lord Redesdale*, London: The Athlone Press, 1985, p. 22. (Hereafter referred to as Mitford.)
16. *Willis*, p. 77.
17. Mitford, pp.110–12.
18. Sir Ernest Satow, *A Diplomat in Japan*, London, 1921, p. 141. (Hereafter referred to as Satow.)
19. Mitford, p. 30.
20. *Willis*, p. 68.
21. *Willis*, p. 79.
22. Satow, p. 141.
23. Satow, p. 233.
24. Mitford, p. 22.
25. *Willis*, pp.71/2.
26. Satow, p. 260.
27. Satow, p. 332.
28. Satow, p. 398.
29. Dickins, p. 354.
30. See footnote No. 67.
31. Fox, p. 596.
32. Basil Hall Chamberlain, *Things Japanese*, London and Tokyo, 1890, p.

267.
33. Mitford, pp.82–4.
34. Satow, p. 141.
35. Satow, p. 158.
36. *Willis*, p. 123.
37. Dickins, p. 354.
38. Fox, p. 161.
39. W.E. Griffis, *The Mikado's Empire*, New York, 1876, p. 577.
40. Fox, p. 176.
41. Fox, p. 214.
42. Fox, pp.224/5.
43. Fox, p. 543.
44. W.G. Beasley, 'Sir Harry Parkes and the Meiji Restoration', *Transactions of the Asiatic Society of Japan*, Third Series, Vol. 12, December 1975, p. 33.
45. Ibid, p. 35.
46. Ibid, p. 36.
47. W.G. Beasley, *The Meiji Restoration*, Stanford: U.P., 1972, p. 310.
48. Ibid, p. 344.
49. *tozama daimyō*, literally 'outer lords' in contrast to the *fudai daimyō* who were related to, or close supporters of, the Tokugawa.
50. Fox, pp.179, 423/4.
51. Satow, p. 160.
52. Fox, pp.248/9.
53. Fox, p. 487.
54. Fox, p. 493.
55. Fox, p. 494.
56. G. Daniels, 'Sir Harry Parkes and the Meiji Government, 1868–83', in *Proceedings of the Japan Society*, 115 (March 1990), p. 20. (Hereafter referred to as Daniels.)
57. Hazel Jones, *Live Machines: Hired Foreigners and Meiji Japan*, Tenterden: Paul Norbury Publications, 1980, pp.148–9. (Hereafter referred to as Jones.)
58. R.H. Brunton, *Building Japan, 1868–76* (edited by Sir Hugh Cortazzi), Folkestone: Japan Library, p. 9.
59. Fox, p. 375.
60. Fox, p. 544.
61. Jones, p. 61.
62. Daniels, p. 24.
63. Dickins, p. 319.
64. Dickins, p. 322.
65. Fox, p. 477.
66. Daniels, pp.22/3.
67. Daniels, p. 24.
68. Jones, p. 182, quotes from a letter from Okuma Shigenobu 'that it was a pity that the Japanese always tended to heap the blame upon the English and former Minister Parkes in particular. Parkes' contributions were quickly forgotten.'

69. Daniels, p. 25.
70. Fox, p. 435.
71. Dickins, p. 278.
72. Dickins, p. 279.
73. Dickins, p. 273.
74. Fox, p. 267.
75. Daniels, p. 25.
76. Dickins, p. 343.
77. Basil Hall Chamberlain, *Things Japanese*, London and Tokyo, 1890, p. 267.
78. Daniels, p. 26.

Chapter 2 JAMES HOARE *British Journalists in Meiji Japan.*

1. P. Clarke, 'The Development of the English-language Press on the China Coast, 1827–1881', M A Thesis, University of London, 1961; F.H.H. King (ed.) and P. Clarke, *A Research Guide to China-Coast Newspapers* (Cambridge, Mass: Harvard University Press, 1965).
2. J.R. Black, *Young Japan: A narrative of the settlement and the city from the signing of the treaties in 1859 to the close of the year 1879* (Yokohama: Kelly and Walsh; London: Trubner and Co., 1880–81; reprinted in the Oxford in Asia Series, Tokyo, 1968); J.E. Hoare, 'The Japanese Treaty Ports 1868–1899: A Study of the Foreign Settlements', Ph D thesis, University of London, 1971, pp.348–63; G. Raymond Nunn, compiler, *Japanese Periodicals and Newspapers in Western Languages: An International Union List* (London: Mansell Publishing, 1979).
3. G. Raper, 'The English-language press of Japan', *Sell's Directory of the World's Press* (London, 1893), pp.148–9.
4. Foreign Office Embassy and Consular Archives Japan, Miscellaneous (FO345)/27, 'The Press of Japan', by J. H. Gubbins, 4 April 1885; Nagasaki consulate records (FO796)/15, R. Foster to R.A. Mowat, 11 Jan. 1897.
5. H.E. Wildes, *Social Currents in Japan, with special reference to the Press* (Chicago, Ill: University of Chicago Press, 1927), pp.288–9; Embassy and Consular Records China, Records of the Supreme Court for China and Japan (FO656)/69, Schroeder vs. Brooke, 20 June 1884.
6. *Japan Daily Herald*, 11 June 1880; *New York Review*, n.d.; *Japan Weekly Mail*, 9 June 1883.
7. *Eastern World*, 11 Jan. 1902.
8. King and Clarke, *Research Guide*, p. 158; *Who's Who in the Far East*, 1906–7; *Eastern World*, 1 Aug. 1908.
9. G. Fox, *Britain and Japan 1858–1883* (Oxford: Oxford University Press, 1969), pp.415–17; Hoare, 'Japanese Treaty Ports', p. 349.
10. Embassy and Consular Records Japan (FO262)/627, Hugh Fraser to Lord Salisbury, 15 Sept. 1890.
11. Olavi K. Fält, *The Clash of Interests: The Transformation of Japan in 1861–1881 in the eyes of the local Anglo-Saxon press* (Rovaniemei: Northern Finland Historical Society, 1990), p. 188; Yokoyama Toshio, *Japan in the Victorian*

Mind: A Study of Stereotyped Images of a Nation, 1850–80, (Basingstoke and London: The Macmillan Press, 1987), p. 117.

12. *New York Nation*, n.d. in *Japan Weekly Mail*, 9 June 1883.

13. Fält, *Clash of Interests*, p. 17; Fox, *Britain and Japan*, p. 428.

14. *Nichi Nichi Shimbun*, n.d. in *Japan Weekly Mail*, 1 Nov. 1890; *Japan Weekly Mail*, 13 June 1891; 'Scotus' to editor, *Kobe Chronicle*, 5 March 1898.

15. *Japan Gazette*, 15 and 17 July 1879; Public Record Office, Satow Papers (PRO30/33)/11/5, Satow to F.V. Dickins, 4 Feb. 1880; *Japan Gazette*, 18 Jan. 1884; *Japan Weekly Mail*, 19 Jan. 1884.

16. 'A seeker' to editor, *Tokio Times*, 6 Sept. 1879; *Japan Weekly Mail*, 7 Nov. 1885.

17. Fält, *Clash of Interests*, pp.205, 297; W.H. T[albot], *The currency of Japan* (Yokohama, *Japan Gazette*, 1882); 'Mr Dohmen's appointment', *Japan Gazette*, 2 April 1879; 'Our contemporaries on Mr Dohmen's Appointment', *Japan Gazette*, 8 April 1879.

18. D.M. Kenrick, 'A century of Western studies of Japan: The First Hundred Years of the Asiatic Society of Japan 1872–1972', *Transactions of the Asiatic Society of Japan*, Third series vol. 14, December 1978, pp.128–9; *Who's Who in the Far East*, 1906–7; *Kobe Chronicle*, 16 July 1898; Wildes, *Social Currents*, p. 305.

19. Fält, *Clash of Interests*, pp.17–18; Fox, *Britain and Japan*, p. 424 et seq; FO656/7, US Consul Fisher to Flowers, 13 Nov. 1865 in M. Flowers to Hornby, Shanghai, 1 Dec. 1865; Parliamentary Papers House of Commons, 1867, vol. lxxiv (3758), *Correspondence respecting the revision of the Japanese Commercial Tariff*, p. 390 et seq, Parkes to Lord Clarendon, 16 July 1866.

20. S. Hirose, 'British attitudes towards the Meiji Restoration as reflected in the "Japan Times" ', *Papers of the Ann Arbor Conference on Japanese History* (Ann Arbor Mich: 1967) and W.G. Beasley, *The Meiji Restoration* (Stanford, Ca: Stanford University Press, 1972), pp.268–9.

21. 'Kicker [Rickerby] in the Triumph of the Arena', *Japan Punch*, August 1878. Rickerby is depicted as a charioteer with two horses labelled *Japan Mail* and *Japan Times*, and a mule labelled *Japan Gazette*. See also *Tokio Times*, 28 Sept. 1878; obituaries in *Hiogo News*, 13 Sept. 1879; *Japan Daily Herald*, 10 Sept. 1879.

22. Endō, M. and Shimomura, F., *Kokushi bunken kaisetsu: zoku* ['A collection of materials for national history: second series'] (Tokyo: Asakura shoten, 1965), pp.434–5; Fält, *Clash of Interests*, pp.18–19; Jonathan Spence, *The China Helpers: Western Advisers in China 1620–1960* (London, Sydney and Toronto: The Bodley Head, 1967), p. 96 et seq; PRO30/33/11/4, F.V. Dickins to Satow, 18 July 1908.

23. FO262/627, Fraser to Salisbury, 15 August 1890.

24. Rickerby vs. Howell, *Japan Weekly Mail*, 17 and 25 July 1871; 'Subventions', *Tokei Journal*, 25 July 1874; Howell vs. Anglin and Moss, *Japan Mail*, 23 Jan. 1875; W.G. Howell to the editor, *Japan Gazette*, 5 June 1881; Fox, *Britain and Japan*, pp.429–30; Endō and Shimomura, *Kokushi bunken kaisetsu*, p. 435; Hoare, 'The Japanese Treaty Ports', pp.335–6.

25. *Tokio Times*, 27 Jan. 1877; FO345/32, Russell Robertson, Yokohama, to Parkes, private, 30 Dec. 1877; *Japan Weekly Mail*, 16 Oct. 1886.
26. *Tokio Times*, 27 July 1878; PRO30/33/11/4, Dickins to Satow, 19 March 1910; Kenrick, 'A century of Western studies', p. 51.
27. H.J. Jones, *Live Machines: Hired Foreigners in Meiji Japan* (Tenterden Kent: Paul Norbury Publications, 1980), pp.75 and 179 n. 8; A. D'Anethan, *Fourteen Years of Diplomatic Life in Japan* (London: Stanley Paul and Co., 1912), p. 92; PRO30/33/11/7, Satow to F.V. Dickins, 21 Nov. 1912: 'As you know, perhaps, I did not trust him.'
28. Jones, *Live Machines*, p. 75. No source is given.
29. Brinkley in Japanese costume with bag marked 'Japan Mail, Japanese Legation, Peking' and the caption: 'Why doesn't his excellency Count "above the well" [Inouel]'s retainer imitate Herr Höllendorf [sic – von Möllendorf] and wear an appropriate costume?', *Japan Punch*, March 1885.
30. *Japan Weekly Mail*, 1 Dec. 1883; *Japan Weekly Mail*, 10 Feb. 1881; *Japan Mail*, 1 Sept. 1881; 'The latest outbreak of the "Japan Mail" – a personal statement', *Kobe Chronicle*, 31 Jan. 1899.
31. *Japan Punch*, Oct. 1882; *Eastern World*, 20 October 1906.
32. J.-P. Lehmann, *The Roots of Modern Japan* (London and Basingstoke: The Macmillan Press Ltd., 1982), p. 292.
33. *Japan Times*, 29 Oct. 1912; *The Times*, 31 October 1912.
34. King and Clarke, *Research Guide*, p. 117; FO796/10, J.J. Quin to R.A. Mowat, Shanghai, 25 May 1892. For Norman and Morphy, see papers in FO796/15; *Who's Who in the Far East*, 1906–7.
35. Wildes, *Social Currents*, pp.262–3, 269.
36. *Eastern World*, 14 May 1904; Wildes, *Social Currents*, p. 270, n.19.
37. 'The latest outbreak of the "Japan Mail" – a personal statement', *Kobe Chronicle*, 31 Jan. 1899.
38. *Who's Who in the Far East*, 1906–7; *Japan Echo*, 15 Nov. 1890.
39. FO262/626, Fraser to Salisbury, 4 Jan. 1890; *Japan Mail Summary*, 17 Feb. 1893. The Yokohama Archives of History held an exhibition about Palmer to mark the centenary of the waterworks in 1987.
40. John Clarke, 'Charles Wirgman (1835–1891)', in Hugh Cortazzi and Gordon Daniels, eds, *Britain and Japan 1859–1991: Themes and Personalities* (London and New York: Routledge, 1991), pp.54–63; *Japan Weekly Mail*, 14 Feb. 1891; Yomiuri Shimbunsha, eds, *Kanagawa no rekishi* ('History of Kanagawa') (Kanagawa: Yomiuri Shimbunsha, 1966), II, 75.
41. *Far East*, 16 May 1871.
42. Hoare, 'Japanese treaty ports', p. 305.
43. Albert A. Altman, 'Shimbunshi: The Early Meiji Adaptation of the Western-Style Newspaper', in W.G. Beasley, ed., *Modern Japan: Aspects of History, Literature and Society* (London: George Allen and Unwin, 1975), pp.52–66.
44. J.E. Hoare, 'The "Bankoku Shimbun" Affair: Foreigners, the Japanese Press and Extraterritoriality in Japan', *Modern Asian Studies*, Vol. 9, no. 3 (1975), pp.289–302.

45. Fält, *Clash of Interests*, pp.25–6; T. Nishida, *Meiji jidai no shimbun to zasshi* ['Newspapers and Magazines of the Meiji period'] (Tokyo: Shibundō, 1961), pp.5–8.

Chapter 3 HELEN BALLHATCHET *British Missionaries in Meiji Japan*

★ Most of the material on which this paper is based comes from the archives of the Church Missionary Society (CMS) and the United Society for the Propagation of the Gospel (USPG), and I am very grateful for the access which I was given. Both archives have recently been moved, to the Universities of Birmingham and Oxford (Rhodes Library) respectively, but all my references are to the former cataloguing system.

1. For a perceptive monograph of one group of High Church Anglican missionaries in Japan, see C.H. Powles, *Victorian Missionaries in Meiji Japan: The Shiba Sect: 1873–1900* (Toronto: Univ. of Toronto-York Univ. Joint Centre on Modern East Asia, 1987). For an impressively broad survey, see A.H. Ion, *The Cross and the Rising Sun: 2 The British Protestant Missionary Movement in Japan, Korea, and Taiwan, 1865–1945* (Waterloo, Ontario: Wilfrid Laurier University Press, 1993).

2. W. Awdry to Tucker, 21 July 1896, USPG LR Far East 1896 B.

3. C.F. Warren to Wright, 27 Jan. 1875, CMS C J/0 16/7; E.C. Hopper, Annual Report for 1881, Kobe, 7 Oct. 1881, USPG MR 1881.

4. H.B. Plummer to Bullock, 5 Sept. 1877, USPG D45 India and Far East B 1877.

5. C.F. Warren to Wright, 29 August 1876 CMS C J/0 16/15.

6. H. Maundrell to Fenn, 30 Dec. 1890, CMS G.1 J/1890/263.

7. Sermon on 1 Cor.9: 22, 23, preached by H. Evington at the United CMS Conference, 1898, CMS G.1 J/1898/237.

8. CMS 13th Conference of the Japan Mission, March 1892, CMS G.1 J/ 1892/129.

9. W. Awdry to Tucker, 1–30 Dec. 1896, USPG LR Far East 1896 B.

10. C.H. Basil Woodd, 'Holiday Notes', *CMS Japan Quarterly* 33, Oct. 1904, pp.2–4.

11. 'Evangelistic Methods by the Rev. W. Andrews. A Paper read at the United Conference of the CMS Japan Mission, April–May 1898', CMS G.1 J/1898/205.

12. A.M. Cox to Baring-Gould, 10 June 1905, appended to Miss A.M. Cox, 'Report of Women's Work in Nagasaki, 1904–1905', CMS G.1 J/1905/176; also, e.g. H. Price to Furness Smith, 21 Feb. 1900 CMS G.1 J/1900/133.

13. G.H. Pole to Fenn, 17 April 1882, CMS G.1 J/1882/23.

14. A.C. Shaw to Bullock, 26 March 1878, USPG LR Asia A 1878.

15. C.H. Basil Woodd, 'Holiday Notes', loc.cit.

16. E. Bickersteth, 'Memorandum on the Location of CMS Missionaries in Japan, 1887', CMS G.1 J/1887/92.

17. H. Maundrell to Wigram, 25 July 1883, CMS G.1 J/1883/138.

18. W.P. Buncombe to Fenn, 10 Feb. 1890, CMS G.1 J/1890/60.

19. P.K. Fyson to Wright, 23 April 1875, CMS C J/0 12/2.

20. P.K. Fyson to Fenn, ? 1875, CMS C J/0 12/10.
21. C.F Warren to Fenn, 4 Jan. 1879, CMS C J/0 16/40.
22. A. C. Shaw to Bullock, 22 Oct. 1873, USPG LR 1868–74; H. Maundrell to Fenn, 13 Dec. 1875, CMS C J/0 14/25.
23. C.F. Warren, 'Extracts from Journal', 1 July 1875–30 June 1876, CMS J/0 16/31.
24. J. Williams to Fenn, 'Annual Letter', 1878?, CMS C J/0 17/12.
25. 'Medical Mission – Notes by Dr Faulds', d. 21 June 1878, *Missionary Record of the United Presbyterian Church* (Nov. 1878), p. 326.
26. In Christian periodicals and in book form: *Hensenron* (On Evolution) (Kobe: Beikoku-ken denkyoshi jimukyoku, 1881).
27. He is one of only three missionaries mentioned by Kozaki Hiromichi as having influenced the thought of early Japanese Protestants in *Reminiscences of Seventy Years: The Autobiography of a Japanese Pastor*, trans. by Nariaki Kozaki (Tokyo: Kyobunkan, 1928), p. 373.
28. A.L. Sharpe, 'Foreign Service', p. 80, *South Tokyo Diocesan Magazine* 7 (Dec. 1903), pp.80–3.
29. B.M. Nottidge, 27 Nov. 1904, CMS, *Extracts from the Annual Letters of the Missionaries for the Year 1904–5*, p. 381.
30. A.M. Tapson, 'Not Enough!', *Church Missionary Gleaner* (Aug. 1905), p. 125.
31. H. Peacocke, 30 Nov. 1896, CMS, *Extracts from the Annual Letters of the Missionaries for the Year 1896–97*, p. 456.
32. V.H. Patrick, ? Jan. 1901, CMS, *Extracts from the Annual Letters of the Missionaries for the Year 1900–1901*, p. 800.
33. H.S. Jackson, 10 Dec. 1903, p. 659, CMS, *Extracts from the Annual Letters of the Missionaries for the Year 1903–1904*, pp.658–9.
34. 'Among Factory Girls. Letters from Miss H.S. Jackson, Osaka', p. 101, *Church Missionary Intelligencer* (Feb. 1904), pp.101–2.
35. 'Report. Conference 1897' (from J. Hind), CMS G.1 J/1897/127.
36. e.g., E.B. Boulton, 5 June 1905, CMS G.1 J/1905/183; Bickersteth to Tucker, 15 January 1895, USPG LR Asia II 1895; 'Hakodate Station Report, First CMS Conference Hokkaido', 5 Aug. 1895, CMS G.1 J/1895/202; 'Editorial Notes', *CMS Japan Quarterly* No. 34, Jan. 1905, p. 1.
37. P.K. Fyson to Fenn, 26 Dec. 1877, CMS C J/0 12/12.
38. V.H. Patrick to Baring-Gould, 4 June 1901, CMS G.1 J/1901/202; T. Warren to Baring-Gould, 12 May 1899, CMS G.1 J/1899/130.
39. Barclay F. Buxton, 'The Baptism of the Holy Ghost' (London: Partridge and Co., nd), pp.3, 8; B. Godfrey Buxton, *The Reward of Faith in the Life of Barclay Fowell Buxton, 1860–1946* (London: Lutterworth Press, 1949), pp.34–5.
40. 'Work Among Japanese Students. From a Private Letter from the Rev. Barclay F. Buxton' (Kyoto, 27 Feb. 1891), *Church Missionary Intelligencer* (Sept. 1891), pp.670–3.
41. Buxton, *The Reward of Faith*, pp.104, 110–11.
42. Ibid., p. 73.

43. Miyakoda Tsunetarō, *Buxton to sono deshitachi* (Buxton and his Disciples) (Tokyo: Buxton kinenseikai, 1968), pp.7, 230; Kozaki Hiromichi, *Nihon kirisutokyōshi* (A History of Christianity in Japan), first published posthumously in *Kozaki zenshū* 2 (Tokyo: Kozaki Zenshū Kankōkai, 1938), pp.122, 160.
44. e.g. E. Bickersteth to Wigram, 1 May 1891, CMS G.1 J/1891/181.
45. Sermon on 1 Cor.9: 22, 23, preached by H. Evington at the United CMS Conference, 1898, CMS G.1 J/1898/237.
46. 'A Sermon preached before the United Conference of the CMS Japan Mission, 28 April 1898, by the Right Rev. Bishop Evington D.D.', CMS G.1 J/1890/194. See also, 'Evangelistic Methods by the Right Rev. Bishop Evington D.D. A Paper read at the United Conference of the CMS Japan Mission April–May 1898', CMS G.1 J/1898/204.
47. J. Batchelor, 'Some Ainu Religious Ideas', *Church Missionary Gleaner* (Oct. 1890), p. 160.
48. See, e.g. Amy C. Bosanquet, 'Japan of Today: An Address to the Northumberland and Durham Church Missionary Union, Newcastle-upon-Tyne', 14 Dec. 1899, *Church Missionary Intelligencer* (March 1900), pp.193–9.
49. Arthur Lloyd, *Shinran and his Work: Studies in Shinshu Theology* (Tokyo: Kyobunkan, 1910), p. 8.
50. See, e.g., 'Kurotani no shōnin' (The Holy Priest of Kurotani) in *Uemura Masahisa zenshū* 7 (Tokyo: Uemura Masahisa zenshū kankōkai, 1932).
51. See Shōwa Joshi Daigaku Kindai Bungaku Kenkyūshitsu, *Kindai bungaku kenkyū sōsho* 12 (Tokyo: Shōwa Joshidai Kōyōkai, 165), pp.261–2; Powles, op.cit., p. 80.

Chapter 4 OLIVE CHECKLAND *'Working at their Profession': Japanese Engineers in Britain before 1914*

1. For further information see O. Checkland, *Britain's Encounter with Meiji Japan, 1868–1912*, (Macmillan, 1989).
2. William John McQuorn Rankine (1820–1872) had been professor at the University of Glasgow since 1855.
3. S. Fujita, *Gojūkunen mae no Kōbu Daigaku ni tsuite no Kioku* (Recollections of the Institute of Technology some fifty years ago).
4. W.J.M. Rankine, *Manual of Applied Mechanics*, (1858), pp.8–10.
5. The Imperial College of Engineering (Kobū Dai Gakkō) was also called College of Engineering, or College of Technology.
6. Henry Dyer (1848–1918), CE, BSc, MA, was an ideal practical engineer for Japanese purposes in 1873. He had the Certificate of Engineering, the degree of Bachelor of Science, and the degree of Master of Arts from the University of Glasgow. He had also served a full engineering apprenticeship at James Aitken and Co., foundrymen of Cranstonhill, Glasgow, while also attending evening classes at Anderson's College, Glasgow.
7. Fred T. Jane, *The Imperial Japanese Navy*, (London, 1904), p.284.
8. A.E. Seaton, *Transactions of the Institution of Naval Engineers*, (Jubilee Volume), 1911, p.200.
9. There is an entry for K. Kawada 'serving from 8 January to 2 March 1915'

in Apprentice Time Book of Simon Lobnitz but this is exceptional, and probably an error, Glasgow University Archives, Upper Clyde Shipyards Archive 4/7/1.

10. Vickers, the armament makers, certainly had agreements with the Japanese, see Vickers Archive, University of Cambridge Library, Vickers' film, Reel No.307.

11. A.G. Clement and R.H.S. Robertson, *Scotland's Scientific Heritage*, (Edinburgh, 1971), p.127.

12. See Henry Dyer, *Dai Nippon, the Britain of the East: A Study in National Evolution*, (London, 1905), p.2.

13. BSc degree was introduced by the University of Glasgow in 1873. Henry Dyer was the first to take this qualification. The Certificate of Engineering was the general 'degree' in engineering.

14 University of Glasgow, Class Prize Lists, 1881–2, Glasgow University Archives.

15. Further details and references can be found in O. Checkland, *Britain's Encounter with Meiji Japan, 1868–1914*, Chapter 9.

16. In March/April 1901 the candidates in Japanese were Fukuzawa Sampachi, Kajima Tatsuzō and Satō Konji.

17. University of Glasgow Court, Minutes, 7 February 1901, Glasgow University Archives.

18. H.E. Roscoe, *The life and experiences of Sir Henry Roscoe*, (London, 1906), pp.113 and 114.

19. See J. Hunter, 'British Training for Japanese Engineers: the case of Kikuchi Kyōzō (1859–1942)' in *Britain and Japan*, (ed. H. Cortazzi and G. Daniels), (1991), pp.137–46.

20. Haramiishi Motereru (1870–1934) see Obituary in *Transactions of the North East Coast Institution of Engineers and Shipbuilders*, Vol.52, 1935, pp.142–3.

21. J.H. Biles, memo on visit to Japan and China, October 1895, Glasgow University Archives, UCS 1/21/85.

22. Dr S. Yokota in correspondence with William Denny's, Dumbarton, Glasgow University Archives, UGD 3/5/0422.

23. There is some information held in the Diplomatic Archives in Tokyo, for Glasgow file see M2–1–0, 14–30.

24. The A.R. Brown Archive, which is useful but not extensive, is held in Glasgow University Archives.

25. A.R. Brown Archives, University of Glasgow.

26. K. Koizumi, 'The Emergence of Japan's First Physicists, 1868–1900', *Historical Studies in the Physical Sciences*, Vol.6, (1975), pp.3–108.

27. Kelvin papers, University Library, Cambridge, NB 168, 25 June 1904.

28. Nagaoka's original letter is in the Tanakadate Papers, National Science Museum, Tokyo, but see also K. Koizumi, 'The Emergence of Japan's First Physicists, 1869–1900', *Historical Studies in the Physical Sciences*, Vol.6, (1975), p.87.

Chapter 5 JANET HUNTER *Maejima Hisoka (1835–1919) – Founder of Japan's Postal System*

1. A full account of Maejima's career, from which most of the information in this paper is drawn, can be found in J.E. Hunter, 'A Study of the Career of Maejima Hisoka, 1835–1919', D.Phil. thesis, Oxford University, 1976. The basic sources for Maejima's life and activities are Maejima Hisoka, *Kōsōkon* (Tokyo, repr. 1955), which is Maejima's autobiography, and Maejima Hisoka, *Yūbin Sōgyō Dan* (Tokyo, 1936). More recent secondary works are Hagihara Tatsu, *Nihon Yūbin no Chichi: Maejima Hisoka* (Tokyo, 1947) and Yamaguchi Osamu, *Maejima Hisoka* (Tokyo, 1990). The only English language source to consider Maejima's role in the development of the postal service is D. Eleanor Westney, *Imitation and Innovation: The Transfer of Western Organizational Patterns to Meiji Japan* (Cambridge, MA, 1987), ch.3.

2. Maejima's birth name was Ueno Fusagorō. He changed his name three times subsequently, eventually taking the name Maejima when in 1866 he became the adopted son (*yōshi*) of Maejima Teijirō, a Shizuoka samurai and direct retainer of the Tokugawa family. For clarity the name Maejima will be used throughout this paper.

3. Shimane Kiyoshi, *Tenkō – Meiji Ishin to Bakushin* (Tokyo, 1969), p.81.

4. Maejima Hisoka, 'Genji no Yūbin Seido wa Ikaga ni Shite Umaretaru ka?' *Tsūshin Kyōkai Zasshi* 1, April, 1908, p.39.

5. For information on Tokugawa communications, see Maejima Hisoka, 'Japanese Communications in the Past' in S. Ōkuma (ed.), *Fifty Years of New Japan* (2 vols., London, 1909); Edwin L. Neville Jr., 'The Development of Transportation in Japan: a Case Study of Okayama Han, 1600–1868', Ph.D. thesis, University of Michigan, 1959; Constantine Vaporis, 'Post Station and Assisting Villages: Corvee Labour and Peasant Contention', *Monumenta Nipponica*, 41, 4, Winter, 1986.

6. For information on the development of the postal system in Britain see Christopher Browne, *Getting the Message: the Story of the British Post Office* (London, 1990); Douglas N. Muir, *Post Reform and the Penny Black: a New Appreciation* (London, 1990).

7. Quoted in Carmen Blacker, *The Japanese Enlightenment* (Cambridge, 1964), p.7.

8. The text of the submission can be found in Yūseishō, *Yūsei Hyakunen Shi* (Tokyo, 1971), p.57; Yūseishō, *Yūsei Hyakunen Shi Shiryō* (Tokyo, 1971), vol.29, p.8.

9. Except where stated, the information on the trip comes from Kaneko Ichirō, 'Maejima Hisoka no Tōkō Jijō no Kyūmei', *Kitte Kenkyū* 207–211, 1968–9.

10. Letters from Ueno to Ōkuma, October, 1870, in Imperial Palace Archive, Ōkuma Kōshaku-ke Monjo (Tei) 375–6.

11. For information on the loan problem and the building of the railway, see Nihon Kokuyū Tetsudō, *Nihon Kokuyū Tetsudō Hyakunen Shi* (10 vols., Tokyo, 1969–72) vol.1, pp.61–70; Tanaka Tokihiko, *Meiji Ishin no Seikyoku to Tetsudō Kensetsu* (Tokyo, 1963).

12. Maejima Hisoka, *Yūbin Sōgyō Dan* (repr. Tokyo, 1951), p.25.
13. *Ibid.*, pp.25–27.
14. *Ibid.*, p.29.
15. Letter from Maejima to Samejima, 24th Nov., 1871.
16. Yamamoto Yokichi, *Japanese Postage Stamps* (Tokyo, 1962), p.13.
17. Maejima Hisoka, *Yūbin Sōgyō Dan*, pp.96–7.
18. Quoted in *ibid.*, p.67.
19 Letter from Maejima to Takagi Saburō, 23rd January, 1875.
20. Morita Eiji, 'Yūbin Chokin Seido to Maejima Danshaku', *Teishin Kyōkai Zasshi* 132, June 1919, p.26.
21. For further information see Yūseishō, *Yūsei Hyakunen Shi Shiryō* vol.30.
22. I have recounted the process of these negotiations more fully in 'The Abolition of Extraterritoriality in the Japanese Post Office, 1873–1880', *Proceedings of the British Association for Japanese Studies* vol.1, pt.1, 1976.
23. Maejima Hisoka, *Yūbin Sōgyō Dan*, pp.53–4.
24. Public Record Office, F.O.46/168.
25. Public Record Office, F.O.46/269, Parkes to Derby, 14th Sept., 1876.
26. For information on the Universal Postal Union, see George A. Codding, *The Universal Postal Union: a Coordinator of the International Mails* (New York, 1964).
27. Cutting enclosed in F.O.46/269, Parkes to Salisbury, 5 Feb., 1879.
28. Memorial included in F.O.46/269, Kennedy to Salisbury, 31 Jan., 1880.
29. Maejima Hisoka, *Yūbin Sōgyō Dan*, pp.57–8.

Chapter 6 PAT BARR *Isabella Bird, 1831–1904*

1. Extracts from these first appeared in magazines and were published in book form in 1875 and 1879. The publisher was John Murray who remained Isabella's publisher and friend for the rest of her life.
2. *Unbeaten Tracks in Japan* (London: John Murray, 1880), p.15. Published in two volumes and five editions.
3. *Ibid*, p.22.
4. *Ibid*, p.44.
5. Dr John Bishop – see later.
6. *Ibid*, p.50.
7. *Ibid*, p.48.
8. *Ibid*, p.52.
9. *Ibid*, p.31.
10. *Ibid*, p.80.
11. For more explanation of Isabella's relationship with her sister, see *A Curious Life for a Lady* by Pat Barr, a biography published by Macmillan and Murray in 1970.
12. *Unbeaten Tracks*, p.120.
13. Missionaries of the Church Missionary Society.
14. Isabella is not forgotten in the north. There are two memorials to her in Yamagata Prefecture (in Kanayama-machi and Kawanishi-machi) and a permanent exhibition about her in the Hygiea Park Hotel near Nanyo-city,

also in Yamagata.
15. *Unbeaten Tracks in Japan, Vol. II*, p.169.
16. *Ibid*, p.177.
17. Well known author of *Things Japanese*.
18. *Ibid*, p.122.
19. Anna Stoddart, *The Life of Isabella Bird* (London: John Murray, 1906), p.105.
20. *Unbeaten Tracks*, p.202.
21. *Ibid*, pp.204/7.
22. For details of Isabella's stay with the Gulicks and other American missionaries, see *Six Months in the Sandwich Isles* (London: John Murray, 1974).
23. *Ibid*, p.220.
24. *Ibid*, p.221.
25. *Ibid*, p.211.
26. For more details of Isabella's wedding and her short married life see *A Curious Life for a Lady*.
27. A. Stoddart, p.304.
28. *Ibid*, pp.326/7.
29. Baroness d'Anethan was the sister of Rider Haggard and the wife of the Belgian Minister to Japan. *Fourteen Years of Diplomatic Life in Japan* (London: Stanley Paul, 1912), p.147.
30. A. Stoddart, p.331.

Chapter 7 CARMEN BLACKER *Minakata Kumagusu, 1867–1941: a Genius now Recognized*

1. Tsurumi Kazuko, *Minakata Kumagusu*, Tokyo 1978. For earlier works see also Kasai Kiyoshi's useful biography, *Minakata Kumagusu*, Tokyo, 1967, and Itagura Shōhei (ed.) *Minakata Kumagusu, Hito to Shisō*, Tokyo, 1974, and the vivid reminiscences of his daughter Minakata Fumie, *Chichi Minakata Kumagusu wo kataru*, Tokyo, 1981.

For a short study of his life and folklore writings in English, see my 'Minakata Kumagusu: a Neglected Japanese Genius'. *Folklore*, Vol, 94, ii, 1983.
2. A selection only from these later writings should include Tsurumi Kazuko, *Minakata Mandara*, Tokyo, 1992; Kōsaka Jirō, *Shibarareta Kyōjin: Minakata Kumagusu no Shōgai*, Tokyo, 1987, a biography with a good many semi-fictional conversations and scenarios; a special number of *Gendai Shisō*, Vol. 20–7 (1992), which includes valuable studies of Minakata's thought; Matsui Ryūgo, *Minakata Kumagusu Issaichi no Yume*, Tokyo, 1991, is a valuable study of Minakata's search for 'whole knowledge'.

I am very grateful to Mr Shimoguchi Hiroshi and Mr Nakase of the Tanabe Shiyakusho for allowing me to inspect Minakata's library in 1990 and 1991, and for showing me the dangerous cave where Minakata ventured to collect specimens of a rare spider.
3. The *Wakan Sansai Zue*, by Terashima Ryōan, modelled on a Ming encyclopaedia, has been reprinted (Tokyo, 1906). The *Yamato Honzō*, 1709,

describing 1,362 varieties of plant, is in *Ekken Zenshū* Vol. 6, 1911. There is an excellent Japanese reprint of the *Pen-tsao kang-mu, Kokuyaku Honzō Kōmoku,* which includes an index of the Latin binomials of all the plants listed.
4. Kasai, op.cit., pp.38–92.
5. For example, *On Palimpsest Sepulchral Brasses,* 1848.
6. All Minakata's writings in English are collected in volume 10 of *Minakata Kumagusu Zenshū (MKZ).*
7. Dr Matsui Ryūgo has made an exhaustive index of all the books in the Library from which Minakata copied passages. I am grateful to Dr Matsui for a copy of this list.
8. *MKZ,* Vol. 10, p.159, published 5 December 1908.
9. *MKZ,* Vol. 10, pp.291, 295, 299, 301.
10. *MKZ,* Vol. 10, pp.3–25.
11. An account of the rescue of Sun by Dr James Cantlie can be found in Sun Yat-sen, *Kidnapped in London,* London, 1969, and Jean Cantlie Stewart, *The Quality of Mercy: the Lives of Sir James and Lady Cantlie,* London, 1983.
12. *Rondon Nikki, Minakata Kumagusu Nikki,* Vol. 1, p.310.
13. Kasai, op.cit., pp.112–13.
14. Matsui Ryūgo, op.cit.
15. *Minakata Kumagusu Nikki,* Vol. 2, p.16.
16. Accounts of these incidents can be found in Makita Kenji, 'Minakata Kumagusu no Dai Ei Hakubutsukan-nai Ōda Jiken,' *U.P.* (Tokyo University Press), Vol. 9 (1987), no. 179. Matsui Ryūgo, 'Minakata Kumagusu no Eikoku Hakubutsukan no Tsuitō wo megutte shinshiryō: "Chinjōsho" no zenyaku oyobi kaisetsu'. *U.P.* Vol. 6, (1991), no. 224. Matsui also discusses the incidents in his *Issaichi no Yume,* pp.165–84. I am grateful to Mr Hamish Todd of the British Library, Oriental Collections, for details of the Minutes of the Standing Committee.
17. I am grateful to Dr Matsui for a copy of this original document, now known as the *chinjōsho.*
18. Arthur Diosy was an active member of the Japan Society, rising to be chairman in 1901.
19. Matsui, op.cit.
20. Kasai, op.cit., pp.151–6.
21. 'When I see the island of Kashima misty in rain, I remember Minakata Kumagusu who was born in the country of Kii.'
22. See Matsui Ryūgo's article in *Gendai Shisō,* 1992, Vol. 20–7, pp.55–66: 'Keiseiki no Minakata Kumagusu'.

Chapter 8 MARIE CONTE-HELM *Armstrong's, Vickers and Japan*

1. J. MacDonald, 'From Yeddo to London with the Japanese Ambassadors', *Cornhill,* 7 (1863), p.620.
2. For a fuller account of this episode (and north-east shipbuilding links with Japan), see M. Conte-Helm, *Japan and the North East of England: From 1862 to the Present Day* (1989), pp.8–9.
3. Sugiyama Shinya, 'Glover & Co: A British Merchant in Nagasaki, 1861–

1870', in Ian Nish (ed.), *Bakumatsu and Meiji Studies in Japan's Economic and Social History* (1982), p.7.

4. Conte-Helm, op.cit., p.15.

5. Minutes of Board Meetings, 24 April 1884 and 2 November 1884, Armstrong Papers, Tyne and Wear Archives, Blandford House, Newcastle (TWAS), 130/1264.

6. Conte-Helm, op.cit., pp.24–5.

7. David Dougan, *The Great Gun-Maker* (1970), p.128.

8. Yamanouchi Masuji, *Kaikoroku* (Memories of the Past) (1914).

9. *Newcastle Weekly Chronicle*, 28 April 1906.

10. Olive Checkland, *Britain's Encounter with Meiji Japan 1868–1912* (1989), p.155.

11. *Ibid.*, p.288 (Note 44).

12. J.D. Scott, *Vickers, A History* (1962), p.85.

13. *Ibid.*

14. Minutes of Directors' Meeting, 25 May 1911, *Armstrong Papers*, TWAS 130/1268.

15. *Armstrong Papers*, TWAS 2001/3/2.

16. Minutes of Directors' Meeting, 20 February 1913, *Armstrong Papers*, TWAS 130/1269.

17. Amie Noble, *Memoirs* (1955), unpublished.

18. *Ibid.*, as for all references to follow.

19. *Newcastle Daily Chronicle*, 20 July 1911.

20. *Ibid.*

21. *Programme of Variety Entertainment*, in Local Studies Collection, Newcastle City Libraries.

22. *The (Barrow) News*, 28 December 1901.

23. *Newcastle Weekly Chronicle*, 28 April 1906.

24. Scott, op.cit., p.146.

Chapter 9 KIYOSHI IKEDA *The Silent Admiral: Tōgō Heihachirō (1848–1934) and Britain*

1. Ogasawara Nagayo ed., *Seishō Tōgō Zenden*, Tokyo: Tosho-Kankōkai, 1987, Vol. I, p.19.

2. *Ibid.*, p.49.

3. *Ibid.*, p.73.

4. Ikeda Kiyoshi, *Nihon no Kaigun*, Tokyo: Asahi Sonorama, 1987, Vol. I, pp.190–2.

5. Ogasawara, op.cit., Vol. 1, p.138.

6. Ikeda, op.cit., pp.243–4.

7. Satō Kunio, *Tōgō Heihachirō-Gensui no Bannen*, Tokyo: Asahishinbunsha, 1990, pp.15–16; letter from Adm. J.A. Fisher to J. Leyland, 22 Sept. 1907 (cited in A.J. Marder, ed., *Fear God and Dreadnought*, London: Cape, 1956, Vol. II, 1956, p.137).

8. Ogasawara, op.cit., pp.341–76.

9. Satō, op.cit., pp.95–115; Katō Kanichi (ed.), Katō Kanji's 'Secret Diaries

on the London Naval Conference' (unpublished).
10. Ikeda, op.cit., Vol. 2, p.106.
11. Ogasawara Nagayo, *Life of Admiral Togo* (translated by Inoue Jukichi and Inoue Tozo), Tokyo: Seitō-Shorin, 1934, pp.469–70.
12. *Ibid.*, p.473.

Chapter 10 NORIO TMAKI *Japan's Adoption of the Gold Standard and the London Money Market 1881–1903: Matsukata, Nakai and Takahashi*

1. Matsukata was in Britain between 28 April and 24 May, and between 22 and 29 June 1902.
2. *The Times*, 29 April 1902.
3. *The Bankers' Magazine*, May 1902, p.748.
4. *The Times*, 25 December 1901. For Itō's visit, see I. Nish, *The Anglo-Japanese Alliance: the Diplomacy of Two Island Empires* (London, 1966), chapter 9.
5. *The Times*, 9 May 1902.
6. See Olive Checkland's chapter in this volume.
7. *Matsukata Masayoshi Kankei Bunsho* [The Archives of Matsukata Masayoshi] (Tokyo, 1979/81), Vol. 5, pp.19–35. Hara Matsukata Reischauer, *Samurai and Silk* (Cambridge (Mass), 1986), pp.133–4.
8. Former President of the Royal Economic Society. Fellow of St John's, Cambridge. Professor of Political Economy in the University of London but who always lived in Cambridge. Foxwell's brother had been a professor in the University of Tokyo in the 1890s. He was a notable collector of economics books, which became the core of the Goldsmith Library, London.
9. Fellow of St John's, Cambridge. Professor of Political Economy, Cambridge. His *Principles of Economics* (1890) was very influential and had been translated into several languages.
10. *Matsukata Masayoshi Kankei Bunsho*, Vol. 5, p.45–6. *Jōdo Shin* (or Pure Land) Sect, was, and still is, one of the most influential Buddhist groups in Japan. The Ōtani faction is one of the ten in the Sect and is also influential.
11. *Ibid.*, p.93. *The Times*, dated 19 July 1902, covers an interview of the correspondent with Matsukata.
12. I. Nish (1966), p.254.
13. I. Tokutomi, *Kōshaku Matsukata Masayoshi Den* (Biography of the Prince Masayoshi Matsukata) (Tokyo, 1935), Vol. 2, p.673.
14. For the business of the Yokohama Specie Bank, see the next section.
15. They were Sonoda Kokichi (1847–1923), president of the Specie Bank, Soyeda Juichi (1864–1929) and Sakatani Yoshio (1863–1941), both of whom were high Finance Ministry officials. Of the three, Soyeda was essential. For Soyeda, see Olive Checkland, 'Soyeda Juichi, 1864–1929, a banker for modern Japan.' (Paper to be presented at the 11th International Economic History Congress.)
16. Although Japan was officially on the silver standard, it was in fact on a bimetallic basis using gold for settlements in Western financial centres.
17. *Matsukata Masayoshi Kankei Bunsho*, Vol. 4, pp.49, 97, 111–12.

18. Yokohama Specie Bank, *Yokohama Shōkin Ginko Shi* (History of the Yokohama Specie Bank) (hereafter *YSG*) (Tokyo, 1919), pp.68–9. *The Bankers' Magazine*, December 1884, pp.1295–8.

19. *YSG*, pp.75–6. There was an important personality in the Alliance Bank (later Parr's Bank), Alexander Allan Shand, who played an essential role in the making of Japanese banking and the Anglo-Japanese banking alliance. The fact that the Specie Bank's first contact was with the Alliance Bank plausibly suggests the role of Shand. However, Shand, a close friend of Okuma Shigenobu who was once a formidable rival of Matsukata, never made a formal appearance before the Japanese as long as Matsukata was in power. For Shand, see Olive Checkland, *Britain's Encounter with Meiji Japan* (London, 1989), pp.37–8.

20. For further details, see N. Tamaki, 'The Yokohama Specie Bank', in G. Jones, ed., *Banks As Multinationals* (London, 1990), p.194.

21. The Japanese-consul turned president was Sonoda, one of the three right-hand men of Matsukata (see above note 15). There can be no doubt that the personnel changes were organized by Matsukata himself.

22. Koizumi came from Wakayama or *Kishu Han* to Keio College founded by Fukuzawa Yukichi (1835–1901) and was the first vice-president of the Specie Bank in 1880. Koizumi resigned as one of the directors at the Bank in 1883 in the aftermath of the 'Meiji 14 Political Change' which affected the Bank, which had originally been founded by Ōkuma himself, the main target of the crisis.

23. Nakai, the son of a Kishu samurai, followed his senior, Koizumi up to Tokyo to study at Keio College. In 1878 Nakai became the manager of a bank in Wakayama, but shortly he was recruited in 1880 by Koizumi to be the chief officer in the foreign exchange department at the head office of the Specie Bank. Although his banking career spread over two decades, Nakai left neither diaries nor letters. However, fortunately, two others, Minakata Kumagusu and Horie Kiichi (1876–1927), professor of economics at Keio, left diaries which detail Nakai's life in London where they were warmly welcomed by Nakai Yoshigusu and Ryu. For Minakata and for the Nippon Club, see Carmen Blacker's chapter in this volume and N. Koyama, 'Rondon no Nihonjin (the Japanese in London)', *Libellus*, December 1992.

24. Here again the shadow of Shand can be seen. '84 Bishopsgate' is only five minutes walk from Shand's Alliance Bank in Bartholomew Lane alongside the Bank of England. 'Streatham Hill' is also very close to Lower Streatham, where Shand lived. The Specie Bank office moved to 120 Bishopsgate Street later in 1900.

25. Matsukata was, as we have discussed, feted by Ōtani, who himself was among Nakai's guests at Streatham Hill.

26. Ministry of Finance, *Meiji Zaiseishi* (Financial History of Meiji) (1925/28), Vol. 2, pp.187–8.

27. *Ibid.*, pp.190–1.

28. *Ibid.*, pp.193–4, 209.

29. *The Bankers' Magazine*, 1898, p.863.

30. R.S. Sayers, *The Bank of England* (Cambridge, 1986) p.40.
31. Takahashi succeeded in August 1895 since Koizumi had died in December 1894. See below.
32. *YSG*, pp.171–6.
33. *Ibid.*, pp.171–6.
34. Ministry of Finance (1925/28), Vol. 2, pp.725–7.
35. *The Bankers's Magazine*, 1897, p.585.
36. Takahashi may have been financially competent but he was also ruthless in his actions against those he did not regard as his friends. Another example is given by Olive Checkland in her paper on Soyeda. (See above note 15.)
37. *The Bankers' Magazine*, January 1903, p.86. *Matsukata Masayoshi Kankei Bunsho*, Vol. 10, p.387. Matsukata's name was in the list of honours announced on King Edward's birthday, January 1903, but the conferment took place at Tokyo on 23 February. Later in July that year, he was awarded 'The Grand Cross of the Order of Red Eagle' by the Kaiser. (*Ibid.*, pp.457–8.)

Chapter 11 IAN NISH *Sir Claude and Lady Ethel MacDonald*

1. J.A.S. Grenville, *Lord Salisbury and Foreign Policy: The Close of the Nineteenth Century*, London, 1964, p.305.
2. T.H. Hohler, *Diplomatic Petrel*, London, 1942, p.65.
3. P.D. Coates, *The China Consuls: British Consular Officers, 1843–1943*, Hong Kong, 1988, p.166.
4. Shiba Goro, *Pekin rōjō* [Siege of Peking], Tokyo: Heibonsha for Tōyō Bunkō, 53, 1965, pp.20–2; Suyematsu Kenchō, *The Risen Sun*, London, 1905, p.45.
5. MacDonald to Salisbury, 24 Sept. 1900 in British Foreign Office Records (Public Records Office, Kew, London) FO 405/94–5. See also Coates, *China Consuls*, p.365.
6. MacDonald's semi-official letters are to be found in FO 800 (Lansdowne, Grey etc.) and among the correspondence of Sir Charles Hardinge at Cambridge University Library, Sir John Jordan and Sir Ernest Satow at the Public Records Office, Kew. Jordan who was a close friend wrote the entry on MacDonald for the *Dictionary of National Biography*.
7. I.H. Nish, *Anglo-Japanese Alliance: The Diplomacy of Two Island Empires, 1894–1907*, London, 1966, pp.144–53.
8. FO Japan 577, MacDonald to Campbell, 18 Feb. 1904. A.M. Pooley (ed.), *Secret Memoirs of Count Hayashi*, London, 1915, pp.121–4.
9. See e.g. Itō to Katsura, 6 Dec. 1901, from *Itō Hirobumi Hiroku*, no. 35 translated in Nish, op.cit., pp.385–6.
10. F.S.G. Piggott, 'Ethel, Lady MacDonald, DBE, RRC', in *Trans. Proc. Japan Society of London*, 37 (1939–41), xxii–xxiii.
11. Hugh Cortazzi (ed.), *Mitford's Japan: Memoirs and Recollections, 1866–1906*, London, 1985, pp.195–237. I.H. Nish (ed.), *British Documents on Foreign Affairs*, Part I, series E, Vol. 10, doc. 19, 'Mr Lampson's private diary of the Garter Mission to Japan, 1906', pp.61–100.
12. MacDonald to Grey, 11 May 1907, in Grey Papers, FO 800/29.

13. MacDonald to Campbell, private, 4 Nov. 1907, FO 371/272.

14. Rumbold diary, 1 Dec. 1910, quoted in M. Gilbert, *Sir Horace Rumbold: Portrait of a Diplomat, 1869–1941*, London, 1973, p.87.

15. 'The Reminiscences of Sir George Sansom', Oral History Research Office, Columbia University, New York, 1957, p.7.

16. D'Anethan to Davignon, 23 June 1910, in G.A. Lensen (ed.), *The D'Anethan Dispatches from Japan, 1894–1910*, Tokyo: Sophia, 1967, pp.254–5.

17. MacDonald to Grey, 5 April 1991, in G.P. Gooch and H.W.V. Temperley (eds), *British Documents on the Origins of War, 1898–1914*, Vol. 8, no. 417.

18. Ibid., no. 420.

19. Ibid., no. 445.

20. G. Feaver, *The Webbs in Asia: The 1911–12 Travel Diary*, London, 1992, pp.111–12.

21. MacDonald to Grey, 28 Sept. 1912, in FO 410/61[38854].

22. *Meiji Hennenshi*.

23. Gilbert, *Rumbold*, p.95.

24. C.M. MacDonald, 'The Japanese detachment during the defence of the Peking legations, June–August 1900', in *Trans. Proc. Japan Society of London*, 12 (1913–14), pp.1–20.

25. Hohler, *Diplomatic Petrel*, p.65.

26. Gilbert, *Rumbold*, p.81.

27. Piggott, 'Lady MacDonald', *Trans. Proc. JSL*, 37 (1939–41), p.xxv.

28. MacDonald to Lansdowne, 24 Oct. 1905 in Lansdowne Papers, FO 800/134.

29. Nish (ed.), *British Documents on Foreign Affairs*, Part I, series E, Vol. 9, 'Annual Reports on Japan, 1906–13'.

30. *Jiji Shimpō*, various dates, Oct.–Nov. 1912.

Chapter 12 AYAKO HOTTA-LISTER *The Japan-British Exhibition of 1910: the Japanese Organizers*

1. I.H. Nish, *Japanese Foreign Policy, 1869–1942: Kasumigaseki to Miyakezaka*, London, 1977, pp.60–1, 71.

2. Okamoto Shumpei, 'Japan's attitude towards China during Meiji Japan – the case of Komura Jutarō', in Satō Seizaburō and R. Dingman (eds), *Kindai Nihon no Taigai Taido* (Diplomatic Attitudes of Modern Japan), Tokyo, 1974.

3. Gaimushō (ed.), *Komura Gaikō-shi* (History of Komura's Foreign Policy), Vol. II, Tokyo, 1953, p.292; Gaimushō (ed.), *Nihon Gaikō Nempyō narabini Shuyō Bunsho*, Vol. I, Tokyo, 1955, pp.305–8.

4. Gaimushō (ed.), *Gaimushō no Hyaku-nen* (Hundred Years of the Foreign Ministry), Vol. I, Tokyo, 1969, p.568.

5. National Diet, *Teikoku Gikai, Shūgi-In Giji Sokki-Roku*, 23 (The 23rd Stenographic Record of the Lower House of the Diet) on 10 March 1909 for the decision and approval of the Additional Budget presented by Kurihara Ryōichi; Gaikō Shiryō Kan Shozō (Diplomatic Records Office), *Eikyō London ni okeru Nichi-Ei Hakuran-Kai kaisetsu no ikken, Dai-Ikkan* (Matters

Concerning the Opening of the Japan-British Exhibition in London, the capital of Britain, Vol. I) (hereafter cited as *Kaisetsu*), Cabinet decision of 16 Nov. 1908 for holding the exhibition.
6. *Kaisetsu*, 'Japan-British Exhibition, Its Paternity, Promotion and Prospects', by the editor of *London Shimpō* in May 1910. *Kaisetsu*, a letter from Mutsu to Komura, 28 March 1910. According to Mutsu, Katō Satori had been a Christian priest in Japan, but, after he moved to London, he had misrepresented himself as an employee of Murai Trading Co. which dealt with tobacco, and later established a newspaper company called *Nichiei Shimpō* (Anglo-Japanese Newspaper). He is believed to have been disliked by fellow Japanese residents in London because of his vulgar sarcastic views of Anglo-Japanese relations, often disregarding the Japanese authorities. Mutsu warned Komura that Katō might try to obstruct or discredit the exhibition in some way. Indeed, his articles often appeared in the press during the period of preparations and opening of the exhibition, most of them with harsh criticisms of the event or the relations between the two countries.
7. *The Japan Magazine*, April 1910, p.224.
8. Seiji Keizai Shi Gaku-Kai (Society for Political and Economic History), *Seiji Keizai Shi Gaku* (March 1982), p.22, 'About the Japan-British Exhibition of 1910 (III)', by Kawamura Kazuo, who also thinks that the exhibition was initiated by Komura for his political and diplomatic purposes.
9. *The Japan Magazine*, Feb. 1910, p.21, by Hirayama Seishin; Hirayama Seishin, *Sakumu Roku – Kaiko Gojū-nen* (Memoir of Yesterday's Dreams – the Past Fifty Years), Tokyo, 1924.
10. *Kaisetsu*, letter from Katō to Komura, 7 April 1909.
11. *Kaisetsu*, letter from Katō to Komura, 11 Nov. 1909; letter from Komura to Katō, 11 Jan. 1910. In reply to Katō's letter, Komura explained that the intention of including the Chinese exhibits had been purely for business purposes to promote the South Manchurian Railway Company by showing the scenery along the railway for prospective British travellers. He did offer, to avoid misunderstandings, to relocate these exhibits into more appropriate departments. In a letter from Mutsu to Katō and Komura, 30 April 1910, Mutsu reported on his visit to the Chinese Consul in London who had expressed his great regret that for the Chinese exhibits from Manchuria to be treated in just the same way as those from Taiwan would offend the Chinese in general and that this would affect the relationship between the two countries.
12. K. Bourne and D.C. Watt (gen. eds), *British Documents on Foreign Affairs: Reports and Papers from the Foreign Office Confidential Print*, I.H. Nish, (ed.), Part I (Series E), Asia (1860–1914) Vol. 10, Document 149, C. Greene to E. Grey, 27 June 1914, p.439.
13. Uehara Etsujirō, *Yasoji No Omoide* (Memoir of Travels). Incidentally, while he was working at the exhibition, an invitation letter addressed to him from the LSE for the post of lecturer there arrived at the Japanese embassy, but it was withheld by Count Mutsu, who regarded Uehara as so indispensable for the exhibition that, he thought, Uehara could not be released, so the invitation was withdrawn. Uehara, upon hearing this fact later, was furious

with Mutsu and left the job immediately and went back to Japan.
14. Nishimura Tokihiko (ed.), Ōbei Yūranki (Diary of Travelling Around Europe and America), 'The Japan-British Exhibition', by Nyozekan, Tokyo, 1910; Hasegawa Nyozekan (trans. John Bester), *The Japanese Character*, Tokyo, 1983, comments about Nyozekan by Kaji Ryūichi. See Hirokichi Mutsu, 'Diplomatic and Consular Service of Japan', *Trans. Proc. Japan Society of London* (1907–8).

Chapter 13 IAN NISH *'In One Day Have I Lived Many Lives': Frank Ashton-Gwatkin, Novelist and Diplomat, 1889–1976*

This essay is based on a paper published originally in Japanese in Iriye Akira and Aruga Tadashi (eds), *Senkanki no Nihon gaikō*, Tokyo: University Press, 1984, under the title 'Ashton-Gwatkin and Japan'. That essay contains a more detailed account of the period down to 1935 than is here given.
1. F. Gwatkin, 'The promise of greater things to come', in P. Norbury (ed.), *Introducing Japan*, Tenterden: Paul Norbury Publications, 1977, p.43.
2. Ibid., pp.49–50. Gwatkin was not unique in this posting. M.B.T. Paske-Smith, a consular official in Japan since 1907, was transferred to Manila (1915–21), becoming acting consul-general there in 1919.
3. The Morrison papers in the Mitchell Library, Sydney, contain many letters exchanged between Gwatkin and Morrison between 1917 and the latter's death in 1920. Morrison was an Australian like Gwatkin's wife. See Morrison to Gwatkin, 2 Feb. 1920, in Lo Hui-min, *The Correspondence of G.E. Morrison*, Vol. 2, *1912–20*, Cambridge: University Press, 1978, pp.787–8.
4. *Documents on British Foreign Policy, 1919–39*, first series, Vol. 6, no. 789. (Hereafter cited as *DBFP*.)
5. *Gaimushō no 100-nen*, Tokyo, 1969, p.772.
6. Gwatkin diary.
7. Gwatkin diary.
8. F. Gwatkin, 'Japan Revisited', in *Bulletin of the Japan Society of London*, 76 (1975), p.10. (Hereafter cited as *BJSL*.)
9. Letter to the author.
10. See *DBFP*, 1 (xiv), no. 521. In general, the Japanese wanted their home islands to be included in the Quadruple Pact, while the Americans spoke with differing voices but tended to want their exclusion, in view of the strong attitude likely to be taken by Congress over the ratification of the Pact.
11. Gwatkin, 'The meeting of John Paris and Japan', in *Tsuru*, 3/1 (1973), p.6.
12. Anonymous (F. Gwatkin), 'Japan and the War', in *Quarterly Review*, Vol. 234 (Oct. 1920), pp.395–410.
13. F. Gwatkin, 'The Life and Times of John Paris', in *BJSL* 31 (1967), pp.11–16, especially 13.
14. Ibid.
15. Hayashi Gonsuke *Waga 70-nen wo kataru* (Tokyo, 1935).
16. Minute by F. Gwatkin, 8 Aug. 1928, in British Foreign Office Records (hereafter FO) 371/13170 [F4168/7/10].

17. Gwatkin, 'John Paris', in *BJSL*, 31 (1967), p.13.

18. Nitobe Inazō, *Bushido, The Soul of Japan*, London, 1899; and Okakura Kakuzō, *The Book of Tea*, 1906, and *The Awakening of Japan*, New York, 1921.

19. Gwatkin, 'John Paris', in *BJSL*, 31 (1967), p.13.

20. Ibid., p.16.

21. Minute by Gwatkin, 2 April 1933, in FO 371/17166 [F1571/1571/23].

22. Randall of the Far East department took a similar view. Analyzing the causes of the decline in Anglo-Japanese relations in 1933, he wrote that one reason was 'the fact that an Englishman was principally associated with the League's report in which Japan felt herself to be held up to worldwide criticism and condemnation'.

23. Gwatkin, 'John Paris', in *BJSL*, 31 (1967), p.11: 'Sansom was my friend from my first day in Japan; so were Edward Crowe and Colin Davidson. I want to emphasize here and now my good fortune and my privilege in having known these marvellous men, known them as friends and colleagues, and as the guides of my first faltering footsteps in Japan.'

24. FO 371/17318; note by Sansom, 10 June 1933, in FO 371/17166 [F4628/583/23].

25. Minute by Gwatkin, 3 Aug. 1933, in FO 371/17166 [F4954/1652/237].

26. Minute by Randall, 15 Dec. 1933, in FO 371/17166 [F7764/1571/23].

27. Memorandum by Gwatkin, 5 Dec. 1933, in FO 371/17166 [F7764/1571/23].

28. Obituary in *The Times*, 31 Jan. 1976 attributed to Ashley Clarke.

29. F. Gwatkin, *The British Foreign Service*, Syracuse: University Press, 1949.

30. F. Gwatkin, 'Japan Revisited', in *BJSL*, 76 (1975), p.12.

31. Ibid., p.11.

32. Ibid., pp.8–12.

33. John Paris, *A Japanese Don Juan: Narihira at the Temple*, London: Collins, 1926. (Republished, with a Foreword by P.G. O'Neill, London, Paul Norbury Publications, 1974. Another little known poetic work by Ashton-Gwatkin is *Max: Poet of the Final Hour, being the Elegies of Maximianus the Etruscan*, translated from the Latin, with an Epilogue by Sir Robert Parr, London, Paul Norbury Publications, 1975.)

Chapter 14 CARMEN BLACKER *Yoshio Markino, 1869–1956*

1. This chapter is a revised and expanded version of my 'Yoshio Markino: a Recollection', *Proceedings of the Japan Society*, 115 (March 1990). I must reiterate my deep gratitude to Mr John Shephard, who gave me the letters sent to his sister Betty by Makino and Shigemitsu after the war, together with Betty's unpublished accounts of her friendship with Makino which she wrote shortly before her death in 1984. Also to Mrs Helena Wayne, who passed on to me all the papers collected by her late husband, Donald Burke, for his intended biography of Makino. Mr Burke tragically died while he was still at the stage of collecting material. Also to Dr John Clarke, for his scholarly cooperation, and for supplying valuable biographical material.

Yoshio Markino was the name adopted by Makino in England to prevent people calling him 'Mr Maykino'.

2. His promotion both in England and Japan is largely due to the enterprise of Mr Sammy Tsunematsu, who has republished with a biographical essay, *A Japanese Artist in London*, London: In Print 1991, and a collection of his essays, *Alone in the World*, 1993, in which Betty Shephard's memoir is printed for the first time. Mr Tsunematsu has further established a Makino Corner in his Soseki Museum of London, 80 The Chase, SW4. Also published in Japan, the charming book of pictures *Makino Yoshio Gashū*, 1922, and with Miyazawa Shinichi, *Rondon no Nihonjin Gaka Makino Yoshio*, 1990.

3. Published in 1956 under the title *Asaki Yume Mishi*.

4. Miss, later Dame, Christabel Pankhurst was imprisoned three times for her suffragist activities, but only on the first occasion, in 1905, was she put into the Third Division where prison dress was obligatory. This garb she described as '. . . of antique pattern, scrubby texture, and incredible thickness in layers and layers of pleats'. See her account of the Women's Suffrage Movement, *Unshackled*, London, 1959, p. 53. She was never, as was her sister Sylvia, subjected to the horrors of forcible feeding. See E. Sylvia Pankhurst, *The Suffragette Movement*, London, 1931, pp.443–4.

5. Betty Shephard's memoir. The exhibition at Cottars Studio Gallery, 134 Brompton Road, was arranged by Amelia Defries and featured thirty-five pictures by Makino in New York, Boston and London. It included 'First Impression of New York seen from the Boat', which made New York look like fairyland, an 'impression' which was dispelled on closer view.

6. *A Japanese Artist*, chapters 1–3. Also *When I was a Child*, 1912, for details of his years in San Francisco.

7. *Japanese Artist*, p. 14.

8. Ibid., pp.24–5.

9. Ibid., p. 36.

10. Ibid., pp.40–1.

11. Ibid., pp.111–14.

12. Ibid., pp.48–56.

13. *The Colour of London*, by W.J. Loftie, introduction by M.H. Spielmann, illustrated by Yoshio Makino; essay by the artist. London, 1907, pp.v–vi. Also *Japanese Artist*, pp.76–80.

14. Douglas Sladen, *Twenty Years of My Life*, London, 1915. Mr Sladen also wrote what he claimed to be 'the first travel book about Japanese', *The Japanese at Home*, 1892.

15. *The Colour of Paris*, by L. Descaves, London, 1908; *The Colour of Rome*, by Olave Potter, London, 1909; *Oxford from Within*, by Hugh de Selincourt, London, 1910.

16. *Japanese Artist*, pp.104–5.

17. Reprinted in *John Bullesses*, where a whole chapter, 'Suffragettes', expresses his feelings on the subject.

18. *My Recollections and Reflections*, 1913, p. xi.

19. Ibid., pp.142–3.

20. He learned enough Greek and Latin to be able to write his lesser known

book *Thinkers and Thoughts of East and West*. Here the main text discusses virtuous Chinese Sage Kings such as Yao, Shun and the Great Yu, while copious footnotes offer parallels from Greek and Latin philosophy and literature. He read not only Plato, but also Aeschylus, Xenophon, Seneca, Dio Cassius, Tacitus, Petronius and Marcus Aurelius. He was unable to find a publisher in England and sent the manuscript in 1934 to Shigemitsu, who arranged for a deluxe edition by the Sanseido Co. in 1936. It is an odd man among his books, much of it written in biblical English.

21. BS's memoir.
22. Ibid. Divina's young brother John Pini recalled in 1969 that Heiji used to come every evening into the shop, often in evening dress, and would sit at a table sketching. He mopped the floor every evening. The cab drivers thought him a 'fool' because he was always giving away cigarettes and food, and often tried to tease him. But he was too innocent to be hurt. Personal communication to Donald Burke, 20 September 1969.
23. YM to Divina, 12 February 1947.
24. This long typed letter is undated.
25. From a six-page letter, undated by probably written early in 1946.
26. YM to Divina, ibid.
27. Shigemitsu to BS, 20 April 1952.

Chapter 15 SIR HUGH CORTAZZI *The Mingei Movement and Bernard Leach*

1. Yanagi Sōetsu, *Mingei Yonjūnen*, Tokyo: Iwanami Shoten, 1984, p.159. Quoted by Elizabeth Frolet in the Catalogue to the exhibition of Mingei during the Japan Festival in the United Kingdom in 1991.
2. Published by Kodansha, Tokyo, 1972.
3. *The Unknown Craftsman*, Tokyo: Kodansha, 1972, p.104.
4. Ibid., p.131.
5. Quoted by Dr Brian D. Moeran from a piece by Yanagi Sōetsu in *Kogei* 115: 1-22, in 'Yanagi Muneyoshi and the Japanese Folk Craft movement', *Asian Folklore Studies*, Nagoya, Vol. XL–l (1981).
6. *The Unknown Craftsman*, p.197.
7. Ibid., p.135.
8. Ibid., p.200.
9. Ibid., p.105.
10. Ibid., p.200.
11. Ibid., p.141.
12. Ibid., p.109.
13. Ibid., p.148.
14. Ibid., p.120.
15. Ibid., p.114.
16. Bernard Leach, *Beyond East and West*, London: Faber and Faber, 1978, p.59.
17. *The Unknown Craftsman*, p.130.
18. Bernard Leach, *A Potter in Japan*, Faber and Faber, 1960, p.49.
19. *The Unknown Craftsman*, p.186.

20. Ibid., p.187.
21. Ibid., p.97.
22. Ibid., p.98.
23. Bernard Leach, *The Potter's Challenge*, London: Lund Humphreys, 1951, p.21.
24. *The Unknown Craftsman*, pp.133–5.
25. *Beyond East and West*, p.74.
26. The Shirakaba Society or 'White Birch School' was founded by such important literary figures as Mushanokōji Saneatsu and Shiga Naoya.
27. *The Unknown Craftsman*, p.93.
28. Ibid., p.76.
29. *Beyond East and West*, p.266.
30. *The Unknown Craftsman*, p.74.
31. *Beyond East and West*, p.84.
32. Comment made by William Blake in about 1808 in the margin of Sir Joshua Reynold's *Discourses on Painting*, as quoted in Kathleen Raine, *William Blake*, London: Thames and Hudson, 1970, p.41.
33. Kathleen Raine, *William Blake*, p.113.
34. Helen Dore, *William Morris*, London: Pyramid Books, 1990, pp.8/9.
35. Ibid., p.10.
36. *The Unknown Craftsman*, pp.205/6.
37. Dore, *William Morris*, p.25.
38. Ibid., p.33.
39. *The Unknown Craftsman*, p.88.
40. Ibid., p.141.
41. Ibid., p.110.
42. Ibid., p.149.
43. Ibid., p.131.
44. *Beyond East and West*, p.266.
45. Ibid., p.119.
46. Ibid., p.139.
47. Ibid., p.140.
48. *The Potter's Challenge*, p.19.
49. *The Unknown Craftsman*, p.9.
50. *Beyond East and West*, p.182.
51. Ibid., p.184.
52. Kawai's later pots were not in the mingei tradition. They could considered modernist and symbolic.
53. *Beyond East and West*, p.54.
54. Ibid., p.58.
55. Ibid., p.76.
56. Ibid., pp.187/8.
57. *A Potter in Japan*, p.194.
58. Ibid., p.205.
59. *Beyond East and West*, p.255.
60. *A Potter in Japan*, p.52.

61. Ibid., p.80.
62. *Beyond East and West*, p.148.
63. Ibid., p.149.
64. Ibid., p.153.
65. Ibid., pp.156/7.
66. Ibid., p.144.
67. Ibid., p.222.
68. Ibid., p.247.
69. *A Potter's Book*, Introduction, xiii–xvii.

Chapter 16 IAN NISH *Matsudaira Tsuneo, Diplomat and Courtier (1877–1949)*

1. I. Nish 'Hayashi Tadasu', in H. Cortazzi and G Daniels (eds), *Britain and Japan: Themes and Personalities, 1859–1991*, London: Routledge, 1991, pp.147–56.
2. Article by Admiral Yamanashi Katsunoshin, in *Matsudaira Tsuneo Tsuisō-roku*, published privately, 1961, pp.530–2. (Hereafter *Tsuisō-roku.*) F.S.G. Piggott, *Broken Thread*, Aldershot, 1950, pp.8, 60. Because of Shidehara's indisposition, much of the work of the Japanese delegation at Washington had to be organized by Matsudaira.
3. J.C. Grew, *Turbulent Era: A diplomatic record of forty years, 1904–45*, 2 vols, London: Hammond, 1953, Vol. I, ch. 24 passim.
4. A. Henderson to J. Tilley, 15 March 1930: '. . . hitherto Mr Wakatsuki and Mr Matsudaira have not been able to win over their naval colleagues in the delegation', in W.N. Medlicott et al., *Documents on British Foreign Policy, 1919–39*, London: HMSO, 2nd series, Vol. I, no. 156. (Series hereafter cited as *DBFP.*)
5. Kobayashi Tatsuo, 'London Naval Treaty, 1930', in J.W. Morley (ed.), *Japan Erupts: The London Naval Conference and the Manchurian Incident, 1928–32*, New York: Columbia UP, 1984, pp.90–4.
6. *DBFP*, 2 (viii), no. 749.
7. R.H. Tawney et al., *The Reorganization of Education in China*, Paris: League of Nations, Institute of Intellectual Cooperation, 1932, p.11.
8. *Nihon gaikō bunsho, Manshū jihen*, I/3, no. 557. (Hereafter *NGB-MJ.*)
9. *NGB-MJ*, I/3, no. 810.
10. I. Nish, *Japan's Struggle with Internationalism: Japan, China and the League of Nations, 1931–3*, London: 1993, pp.50–1.
11. *NGB-MJ*, I/3 no. 595.
12. Article by Sawada Setsuzō, in *Tsuisō-roku*, pp.269–70.
13. Nish, *Japan's Struggle*, pp.171–2.
14. Fukai Eigo, *Kaiko 70-nen*, Tokyo: Iwanami, 1949, pp.279, 295; Article by Shimazu, in *Tsuisō-roku*, pp.322–3.
15. D.C. Watt, *Personalities and Policies*, London: Longman, 1965, pp.83–99. The most recent study is Gill Bennett, 'British Policy in the Far East, 1933–6: Treasury and Foreign Office', in *Modern Asian Studies*, 26 (1992), pp.545–68.
16. Hosoya Chihiro, in I.H. Nish, *Anglo-Japanese Alienation, 1919–52*, Cambridge: UP, 1982, p.19.

17. *Transactions and Proceedings of the Japan Society (London)*, 32 (1934–5), xx–xxiv.

18. Matsudaira to Japan Society, 9 March 1936, in *Transactions and Proceedings of the Japan Society (London)*, 33 (1936), xxi.

19. R.L. Craigie to K. Fujii, 24 Oct. 1935, in *DBFP*, 2 (xiii), no. 538.

20. F. Leith-Ross, *Money Talks*, London: Hutchinson, 1968, p.201.

21. *Transactions and Proceedings of the Japan Society (London)*, 33 (1936), xxi.

22. *DBFP*, 2 (xx), no. 506.

23. Leith-Ross, *Money Talks*, p.221.

24. S.S. Large, *Emperor Hirohito and Showa Japan*, London: Routledge, 1990, passim. It is understood that one of Matsudaira's actions as Household Minister was to arrange the appointment of Admiral Yamanashi Katsunoshin whom he had known from the time of the Washington Conference of 1921 as president of Gakushuin in 1940.

25. Diary of Sir George Sansom, 22 Jan. 1946, in K. Sansom, *Sir George Sansom and Japan: A Memoir*, Tallahassee: Diplomatic Press, 1972, p.151. Also Piggott, *Broken Thread*, p.365. Some writers were under the impression that Matsudaira continued as Household Minister under the occupation; but this was not so.

26. *Bulletin of the Japan Society (London)*, no. 1 (1950), pp.7–8. Also to be found in *Tsuisōroku*, pp.456–7, where it is stated (speaking of him and his wife) that no foreign representatives were more popular, '. . . not only in the London society where they occupied a special place, but wherever they went'.

27. Shiotani and Mushakoji Kintomo, articles in *Tsuisōroku*, pp.298–9 and 506–7.

28. M. Gayn, *Japan Diary*, Tokyo: Tuttle, 1981, p.280.

29. J Tilley, *London to Tokyo*, London: Hutchinson, 1944, pp.180–1.

Chapter 17 JANE WILKINSON *Gordon Munro: Ventures in Japanese Archaeology and Anthropology*

1. E.S. Morse, 'The Omori Shell Mounds', in *Nature*, London, 15 April 1880.

2. N.G. Munro, *Prehistoric Japan*, Yokohama: private, 1908.

3. N.G. Munro, *Coins of Japan*, Yokohama: private, 1904; London: Kegan, Paul, 1905.

4. *Prehistoric Japan*, p. 41.

5. Kuwahara Chiyoko, *Waga Manrō-den: Aru Eijin ishi kenkyūka no shogai* [My biography of Munro: The life of an English doctor and scholar], Tokyo, 1984.

6. *Shigaku Zasshi*, Vol. 19/4 (1908).

7. *Yorodzu Chōhō*, 10 May 1908.

8. *Japan Times*, 25 Feb. 1908.

9. *Japan Daily Advertiser*, 9 May 1908.

10. *Prehistoric Japan*, p. 239.

11. C.G. Seligman (1873–1940), Professor of Ethnology, London School of Economics, visited the East in 1929–30 and later addressed the Japan Society

of London on 'The Japanese Temperament and Character' [*Proceedings of the Japan Society of London*, 28 (1931)]. He was the editor of the Cresset Historical series on China and Japan and was a friend of Sir George Sansom.

12. F. Maraini, *Gli iku-bashui degli Ainu*, Tokyo, 1942.
13. N.G. Munro (ed. Brenda Seligman), *Ainu Creed and Culture*, London: Routledge and Kegan Paul, 1962.
14. A.H.S. Landor, *Alone with the Hairy Ainu or 3800 miles on a pack saddle in Yezo and a cruise to the Kurile Islands*, London: Murray, 1893.
15. F. Maraini, 'Life of Dr Munro', in *Japan Times & Advertiser*, 24 April 1942.
16. Katherine Sansom, *Sir George Sansom and Japan: A Memoir*, Tallahassee: Diplomatic Press, 1972, p. 7.
17. Ibid.

OTHER WRITINGS

Kuwahara Chiyoko. *Waga Manro-den: Aru Eijin ishi kenkyūka no shogai*. (My Biography of Munro, The life of an English doctor and scholar), Japan, 1984.
Munro, N.G. (ed. Seligman, Brenda Z.), *Ainu Creed and Cult*, London, 1962.
Munro, N.G., ed., *Ainu Past and Present*, MS.
Munro, N.G., 'Primitive Culture in Japan', in *Transactions of the Asiatic Society of Japan*, Vol. 34 (1906).
   'Reflections on some European Palaeoliths and Japanese Survivals', in ibid., Vol. 37, 1909.
   'Some Origins and Survivals', in ibid., Vol. 39, 1911.
Munro, N.G., *The Soul in Being*, 1918.
Letters from Munro to Seligman C.G. (Held at the Royal Anthropological Institute Library, London.)

Chapter 18 ANTONY BEST *Sir Robert Craigie as Ambassador to Japan 1937–1941*

1. For recent critical judgements of Craigie, see K. Satō, 'The Historical Perspective and What is Missing', in K. Satō, *Japanese and Britain at the Crossroads, 1939–1941. A Study in the Dilemmas of Japanese Diplomacy*. (Tokyo: Senshu Univ. Press, 1986), pp.207–8, and S. Olu Agbi, 'The Pacific War Controversy in Britain: Sir Robert Craigie Versus the Foreign Office', in *Modern Asian Studies*, Vol. 17, pp.489–517.
2. For recent broadly favourable assessments of Craigie, see D.C. Watt, *How War Came: The Immediate Origins of the Second World War, 1938–1939*. (London: Heinemann, 1989), p.350; P. Calvocoressi, G. Wint and J. Pritchard, *Total War. The Causes and Courses of the Second World War. Vol. 2: The Greater East Asia and Pacific Conflict* (London: Penguin, 1989), pp.256–7; and P. Lowe, 'The Dilemmas of an Ambassador: Sir Robert Craigie and Japan', in *Proceedings of the British Association of Japanese Studies*, Vol. 1, no. 2, 1977, pp.34–56.
3. Sir R. Craigie minute 24 December 1936, on Sir R. Clive to A. Eden, 24 December 1936, in Public Record Office Kew (PRO) Foreign Office 371/20279, F7963/89/23. (Hereafter cited as FO.)

4. P. Fleming to Sir A. Clark Kerr, 12 July 1938, in Inverchapel Papers, Bodleian Library, Oxford, General Correspondence 1937–8.

5. Sir R. Craigie to Lord Halifax, 18 June 1939, in *Documents on British Foreign Policy*, Series 3, Vol. IX, no. 227. (Hereafter *DBFP*.)

6. Sir R. Craigie to Lord Halifax, 16 November 1939, in FO371/23534, F11946/6457/10.

7. Sir R. Craigie to Lord Halifax, 14 July 1940, in FO371/24925, F3465/23/23.

8. Sir R. Craigie minute 22 December 1936, on Sir R. Vansittart memorandum, 'The World Situation and British Rearmament', 16 December 1936, in FO371/19787, A9996/9996/51.

9. Behind these rumours lies the suggestion that Chamberlain and Craigie were close personal friends; the lack of any letters from Craigie to Chamberlain in the latter's papers deposited in Birmingham University Library would, however, suggest that this relationship may have been exaggerated.

10. Sir R. Craigie to Lord Halifax, 15 June 1939, in FO371/23399, F5883/1/10.

11. Sir R. Craigie memorandum, 5 October 1938, in FO262/1978, 8/234/38. I am indebted to the late Anthony Haigh for initially putting me on to the trail of this memorandum.

12. Sir R. Craigie to Lord Halifax, 30 January 1939, in FO371/23555, F2215/76/23.

13. See Sir R. Craigie to Lord Halifax, 1 January 1939, in *DBFP* 3 (VIII), no. 382.

14. On Sansom, see G. Daniels, 'Sir George Sansom', in Sir H. Cortazzi and G. Daniels (eds), *Britain and Japan 1859–1991: Themes and Personalities* (London: Routledge, 1991), pp.227–38.

15. For Hornbeck's views, see Lord Lothian to Lord Halifax, 9 December 1939, in FO371/23551, F12625/4027/61.

16. Sir R. Craigie to Lord Halifax, 1 January 1940, in FO371/24708, F297/193/61.

17. On Piggott, see C. Blacker, 'The Two Piggotts', in Cortazzi and Daniels (eds), *op.cit.*, pp.118–27.

18. Sir R. Craigie to R. Howe, 30 June 1939, in FO371/23485, F8566/372/10.

19. Sir R. Craigie to Lord Simon, 1 August 1940, in Simon Papers, Bodleian Library, Oxford, Mss Simon 86.

20. Sir R. Craigie to Lord Halifax, 11 October 1940, in FO371/24737, F5295/626/23.

21. On the issue of Canadian wheat, see Sir R. Craigie to A. Eden, 11 March 1941, in FO371/27918, F1836/122/23. On copra see Sir R. Craigie to A. Eden, 30 May 1941, in FO371/27895, F4964/18/23.

22. Sir R. Craigie to A. Eden, 3 June 1941, in FO371/27895, F4810/18/23.

23. Sir R. Craigie to A. Eden, 4 February 1943, in FO371/35957, F821/821/23.

24. For Grew's arguments at this point, see W. Heinrichs, *American Ambassador: Joseph C. Grew and the United States Diplomatic Tradition*. (New York: Oxford University Press, 1966), pp.345–50.
25. Sir R. Craigie to A. Eden, 9 September 1941, in FO371/27883, F9172/12/23.
26. For the global situation in November 1941, see W. Heinrichs, *Threshold of War: Franklin D. Roosevelt and American Entry into World War II* (New York: Oxford Univ. Press, 1988), p.213.
27. On the issue of appeasement, see R.J. Grace, 'Whitehall and the Ghost of Appeasement: November 1941', in *Diplomatic History*, Vol. 3 (1979), pp.173–91.
28. W. Churchill to A. Eden, 19 September 1943, in FO/371/35957, F2602/751/23.

Chapter 19 ADRIAN PINNINGTON *R.H. Blyth (1898–1964)*

1. *Kaisō no Blyth*, ed. Kawashima Yasuo, Tokyo, 1984.
2. *Zen in English Literature and Oriental Classics*, Tokyo, 1942, p.85.
3. *Kaisō no Blyth*, p.28. See also Frederick Franck (ed.), *Zen and Zen Classics: Selections from R.H. Blyth* (1978), Union City, 1991, p.xii.
4. *Edo Satirical Verse Anthologies*, Tokyo, 1961, Preface.
5. R.H. Blyth, 'Zen to Suzuki Daisetsu', *Suzuki Daisetsu no hito to gakumon*, Suzuki Daisetsu Zen Senshu Bekkan, Tokyo, 1992, p.37.
6. *Kaisō no Blyth*, pp.105–12.
7. See Haruko Fukuda, 'The Peaceful Overture: Admiral Yamanashi Katsunoshin (1877–1967)', in *Britain and Japan 1859–1991: Themes and Personalities*, eds Sir Hugh Cortazzi and Gordon Daniels, London, 1991, pp.198–213.
8. William P. Woodard, *The Allied Occupation of Japan 1945–1952 and Japanese Religions*, Leiden, 1972, pp.249–68, 314–21. See also the article by Otis Cary, 'Ningen Sengen o kaita otokotachi', reprinted in *Kaisō no Blyth*, pp.44–50; and the article by Haruko Fukuda cited in n.8 above. I have been unable to see Hirakawa Sukehiro, 'R.H. Blyth and Hirohito's denial of the divine character of the Tenno', British Association for Japanese Studies, *Proceedings*, 1985, pp.33–41.
9. *Kaisō no Blyth*, pp.33–9.
10. See *Kaisō no Blyth*, pp.165–6.11.
Elizabeth Gray Vining, *Windows for the Crown Prince, Akihito of Japan* (1952), Tokyo, 1989, p.28.
12. Blyth also left a number of unpublished writings at his death; see Frederick Franck (ed.), *The Buddha Eye, an Anthology of the Kyoto School*, New York, 1982, p.75.
13. See *Haiku, Volume I*, pp.126–44.
14. A famous example is Shibata Shokyoku's *Koku o Miru* (1945).
15. See Frederick Franck, *Zen and Zen Classics*, 1991, p.xiv.
16. See note 5 above.
17. See for example Luis O. Gomez, 'D.T. Suzuki's Contribution to Modern

Buddhist Scholarship', in *A Zen Life: D.T. Suzuki Remembered*, ed. Masao Abe, Tokyo, 1986, pp.90–4.

18. D.T. Suzuki, *Zen and Japanese Culture (1959)*, Princeton, New Jersey, 1970, p.228.
19. *Haiku, Volume I*, p.iii.
20. See, e.g. *Zen in English Literature*, pp.28, 32, 99, 109, 228.
21. *Haiku, Volume I*, p.vii.
22. *A History of Haiku, Volume I*, Tokyo, 1963, p.13.
23. Hiroaki Sato, *One Hundred Frogs*, New York, 1983, pp.129–31; by contrast Sato Kazuo, *Haiku kara HAIKU e*, Tokyo, 1987, p.4.
24. *A History of Haiku, Volume I*, p.110.
25. Ibid., p.v.
26. For Blyth's poems see *Kaisō no Blyth*, p.56ff.
27. H.G. Henderson, *The Bamboo Broom*, London and Kobe, 1933, p.2.
28. William J. Higginson, *The Haiku Handbook*, New York, 1985, pp.58, 63, 65.
29. See especially Sanahide Kodama, *American Poetry and Japanese Culture*, Connecticut, 1984, p.158ff.
30. J.D. Salinger, *Raise High the Roofbeam Carpenters / Seymour: an Introduction* (1963), Harmondsworth, Middlesex, p.91; cf. p.53.

Chapter 20 RONALD DORE *Frank and Otome Daniels*

1. Oba Sadao, *Senchu Rondon Nihongo-gakko*, Tokyo, Chuko-shinsho, 1988
2. 'Japanese studies in the University of London and elsewhere', *Japan Society of London Bulletin*, no. 4 (1963).
3. *Japan Society of London Bulletin*, no.75 (1975), p.20.

Chapter 21 PETER LOWE *Sir Alvary Gascoigne in Japan, 1946–1951*

1. See R.W. Buckley, *Occupation Diplomacy: Britain, The United States and Japan, 1945–1952* (Cambridge, 1982), pp.41–53. See also Buckley, 'Working with MacArthur: Sir Alvary Gascoigne, UKLIM and British Policy towards Occupied Japan, 1945–52' in Ian Nish (ed.), *Aspects of the Allied Occupation of Japan*, International Studies (STICERD, LSE), 1986/4, pp.1–14.
2. For two comprehensive and illuminating accounts of MacArthur's work in Japan, see D. Clayton James, *The Years of MacArthur*, vol. III, *Triumph and Disaster, 1945–64* (Boston, 1985) and R.D. Finn, *Winners in Peace: MacArthur, Yoshida, and Postwar Japan* (Oxford, 1992).
3. Clayton James, III, 693.
4. For a discussion of British views towards MacArthur during the Korean war, see Peter Lowe, 'An Ally and a Recalcitrant General: Great Britain, Douglas MacArthur and the Korean War, 1950–1', *English Historical Review*, vol. CV (July 1990), 624–53.
5. See Douglas MacArthur, *Reminiscences*, paperback edition, (Greenwich, Conn., 1965), p.323.
6. See H.B. Schonberger, *Aftermath of War: Americans and the Remaking of*

Japan, 1945–1952 (London, 1989), pp.134–60.

7. Gascoigne to Dening, 9 January 1948, FO 371/69885/1368, Public Record Office, Kew.
8. Minute by F.S. Tomlinson, 28 January 1948, ibid.
9. Minute by M.E. Dening, 29 January 1948, ibid.
10. See G.F. Kennan, *Memoirs, 1925–50* (London, 1968), pp.384–94.
11. Foreign Office to Tokyo, 18 March 1948, FO 371/69885/4213.
12. Gascoigne to Bevin, 30 June 1948, FO 371/69911/7609.
13. Tokyo to Foreign Office, 1 July 1948, FO 371/69911/9266.
14. Tokyo to Foreign Office, 1 September 1948, FO 371/69823/12111.
15. Ibid.
16. Ibid.
17. See Sir John Figgess, 'Japan under Occupation: A Personal Reminiscence', in *Proceedings of the Japan Society*, 121 (1993), 120.
18. Gascoigne to Bevin, 18 December 1948, FO 371/76178/7527.
19. Ibid.
20. Ibid.
21. Gascoigne to Bevin, 13 February 1948, FO 371/69819/3508.
22. Minute by Tomlinson, 17 February 1949, on dispatch from Gascoigne to Bevin, 2 February 1949, FO 371/76179/2420.
23. For a valuable assessment of Yoshido, see J.W. Dower, *Empire and Aftermath: Yoshida Shigeru and the Japanese Experience, 1878–1954* (London, 1979), pp.273–492.
24. Conversation between Gascoigne and Yoshida, 22 January 1951, FO 371/92521/4.
25. Gascoigne to Bevin, 2 February 1949, FO 371/76179/2420.
26. Gascoigne to Younger, 12 June 1950, FO 371/83831/93.
27. Gascoigne to Dening, 21 November 1949, FO 371/76214/23G.
28. Foreign Office to Washington, 8 December 1949, ibid.
29. Gascoigne to Younger, 12 June 1950, FO 371/83831/93.
30. Ibid.
31. Gascoigne to Bevin, 22 June 1950, FO 371/83831/97.
32. See Peter Lowe, 'Great Britain and the Japanese Peace Treaty, 1951', in Peter Lowe and Herman Moeshart (eds), *Western Interactions with Japan: Expansion, the Armed Forces, and Readjustment, 1859–1956* (Folkestone, 1990), pp.91–104.
33. Gascoigne to Bevin, 9 July 1950, FO 371/83832/103.
34. Gascoigne to Scott, 9 October 1950, FO 371/83834/148.
35. Gascoigne to Bevin, 18 November 1950, FO 371/83816/63/G.
36. Ibid.
37. Record of interview between Sansom and MacArthur, communicated in Gascoigne to Scott, 22 January 1951, FO 371/92521/3.
38. 'Trend of Events in Japan from July 1946 to February 1951', in Gascoigne to Bevin, 6 February 1951, FO 371/92521/5.
39. Ibid.
40. Ibid.

41. Ibid.
42. Clutton to Strang, 13 February 1951, FO 371/92657/4.
43. Clutton to Strang, 17 February 1951, FO 371/92657/2, enclosing typed extract from *Sydney Sun*, no name or date.
44. Franks to Strang, 26 February 1951, FO 371/92657/5.

Chapter 22 ROGER BUCKLEY *Split Images: Occupied Japan through the Eyes of British Journalists and Authors*

1. 'British Cultural and Propaganda Activities in Japan', 22 June 1950, FJ1021/93(FO371/83831).
2. See Buckley, *Occupation Diplomacy: the United States and Japan, 1945–1952* (Cambridge, 1982), Ch. 3 'British Diplomacy and the Allied Control of Japan, 1945'.
3. For statements on the problems involved see Michael S. Howard, *Jonathan Cape, Publisher* (London, 1971). On the domestic background see Robert Hewison *Under Siege: Literary Life in London, 1939–45* (Oxford, 1977).
4. Reproduced in *The New Yorker Book of War Pieces* (New York, 1947 and subsequently reprinted). On Hersey see his obituary in *The Times*, 26 March 1993. This states that the British edition of *Hiroshima* quickly sold a quarter of a million copies for Penguin. Its explanation for the phenomenal success of the short book is perceptive – arguing that Hersey's reporting background '. . . let the unvarnished facts speak for themselves. They did so with terrible eloquence'.
5. Christmas Humphreys *Via Tokyo* (London, 1948), p.VIII.
6. He continues: 'As at present practised they have no part in the world of the good, the beautiful and the true with which I am alone concerned, and are the cause of most of our suffering.'
7. Hawley's confidential letter to Imperial and Foreign Department, *The Times*, 27 May 1947. The accompanying distribution list names only seven staff members when circulated by Foreign Editor Deakin. I am grateful to *The Times* Archives for the opportunity to inspect their material on Hawley.
8. Ibid. See also Hawley's report on MacArthur's speech of March 1947 for an accurate account of the changes envisaged in occupation objectives from then on. *The Times*, 18 March 1947.
9. Ibid.
10. Hawley confidential letter to *The Times*, 17 September 1948. Hawley throughout his term as correspondent always address his foreign editor as 'Mr Deakin' and signed such letters 'Frank Hawley'.
11. Ibid.
12. Ibid.
13. Ibid.
14. The NPR is discussed most recently in Richard B. Finn's *Winners in Peace: MacArthur, Yoshida and Postwar Japan* (Berkeley, 1992). Yoshida apparently assumed that MacArthur's proposals were to form a new police force on the lines of 'the London Metropolitan Police'. Finn, p.263.
15. Richard Hughes *Foreign Devil*, quoted in *No. 1 Shimbun* (Tokyo, April

1993).

16. Tiltman co-authored this with Colonel P.T. Etherton. Their book went through seven impressions in its first year of publication from January 1933. It attempted to weigh Japan's national interests against the criticisms of world opinion, by noting that some form of 'adjustment' was necessary that recognized that 'the future of Manchuria will be fashioned in Tokyo'. The concluding sentence warns that: '. . . nothing short of a national defeat in war can rob Japan of' the fruits awaiting the nation which develops the riches of the Manchurian plains'.

17. Again written in collaboration with Etherton; published in London in 1933 it too quickly came out in a cheap edition.

18. Tiltman, who died in August 1976, left no personal papers. Information from Mrs Marjorie Tiltman.

19. I am grateful to M. Alfred Smoular for his recollections of Tiltman and Hawley in the post-war years.

20. Richard Mason, *The Wind Cannot Read* (London, 1947 and 1979).

21. Lord Beaverbrook's *Daily Express* led this virulent campaign throughout the 1950s.

22. See Buckley, 'The Emperor Question Again: Anglo-Japanese Relations, 1945 and 1989', *The Journal of Social Science* (ICU), March 1991.

23. Mason, *op.cit.*, p.200 (1979 edition).

24. Honor Tracy, *Kakemono* (London, 1950).

25. Tracy felt it was only through the Emperor's authority that law and order were maintained for the Americans.

26. *Op.cit.*, p.36.

27. See Finn, *op.cit.*, pp.256–7.

28. Morris added that the war had effectively silenced such voices but he still expected these leaders to reappear after defeat in order that 'reorganizing the administration' of Japan under a new government be accomplished. Success would also require the 'indispensable' and 'whole-hearted cooperation of the Emperor'.

29. *The Phoenix Cup: some notes on Japan in 1946* (London, 1947), p.ix.

30. John Morris, *Traveller From Tokyo* (London, 1943), p.150.

31. *The Phoenix Cup*, p.92. He inspected Sugamo prison and saw Kido writing his memoirs in English while in gaol.

32. Ibid., p.196.

33. Ibid., p.229.

34. *Via Tokyo*, p.vii.

35. Ibid., p.22.

36. Ibid., p.28.

37. Ibid., p.82.

38. Ibid., p.84.

39. For a cautious review of Barry Webb's *Edmund Blunden: a Biography* (London, 1990) see *The Economist*, 8 December 1990. Webb's biography necessarily drew on Sumie Okada's *Edmund Blunden and Japan* (London, 1988).

40. Sumie Okada, *Edmund Blunden and Japan*, p.171.

41. I am indebted to Professor Saito Makoto of ICU for these points. It was Professor Saito's father who had originally invited Blunden to Tokyo in 1924.

42. Edmund Blunden, *Shakespeare to Hardy* (Tokyo, 1948) and *Addresses on General Subjects* (Tokyo, 1949).

43. Edmund Blunden, *Undertones of War* (London, 1928). It has been frequently reprinted in Japan; Kenkyusha's edition had seen eight reprints by 1980.

44. G.S. Fraser, *Impressions of Japan* (Tokyo, 1952). The Foreword is by Blunden.

45. G.S. Fraser, *The Modern Writer and his World* (Tokyo, 1951). It became a popular paperback in Britain when published by Penguin. Its length and detail on the novel, drama and poetry are remarkable considering that Fraser wrote it under taxing conditions in Japan during 1950; parts were based on lectures given at Tokyo University.

46. *New Republic*, 26 August 1946.

47. *The Nation*, 2 June 1951.

48. See *The Times*, 20 June 1950.

49. *The Times*, 28 June 1950. The same backbencher noted that as a result of imprisonment by Japan during the war, Hawley had 'suffered considerably' and was now 'an embittered man', who '. . . saw at every corner and under almost every table the possibility of the old Japanese militarist element coming up again'.

50. See Buckley 'Gambling on Japan: the British Press and the San Francisco Peace Settlements, 1950–1952', *Bulletin of the Graduate School of International Relations, International University of Japan*, No. 2 (December 1984). The most adequate coverage came from *The Financial Times*.

I am grateful to Dr Keiko Sueuchi of the Social Science Research Institute of ICU for assistance in the preparation of this essay.

Index

Abo Kiyokazu, Admiral Baron, 208
Acheson, Dean, 287
Adachi Montarō, 225
Ainu, ch. 17 passim, 71
Aitken, Robert, 253, 257
Akihito, Emperor Heisei, as Crown Prince,
    257-60, 304-5
Alcock, Sir Rutherford, 1-2, 9-10
Allen, Louis, 301
d'Anethan, Baron Albert, 140
    Baroness, 76
Anglin, J.R., 23, 24
Anglo-Japanese alliance, 38, 104-5, 115-16,
    118, 123, 160-3, ch. 11 passim,
    ch. 12 passim
Anglo-Japanese postal convention (1880), 63-5
Aoki Shūzō, 112
Araki Hachirō, 245
Arisugawa, Prince, 104
Armstrong, Sir William, 93-4, 96-7
Armstrong Whitworth & Co, ch. 8 passim, 50,
    122
Arnold, Matthew, 253, 265
Asiatic Society for Japan, vii, 4, 24, 69, 70, 223
Ashida Hitoshi, 298
Atkinson, George A., 100
Aston, William G., 223, 252
Australia, 283-4, 288-9, 292
Ayrton, William, 49

Bailey, Rev. Buckworth, 30
Barnby, Lord, 212
Batchelor, Rev. John, xii, 42-3, 218-19, 229,
    232
Battle of Japan Sea (1905), 106, 117-18
Beale, J.E., 21, 26
Beasley, William G., 11
Beppu Ushitarō, 149, 153-4
Bevin, Ernest, 286-7
Bickersteth, Bishop Edward H., 75
Bigot, Georges, 29
Biles, Sir John Harvard, 51
Bird, Isabella (Mrs Bishop), viii, 2, ch. 6 passim
Bird, Henrietta, 69-70, 73-5
Bishop, Dr John, 75
Bizen incident (1868), 7
Black, John Reddie, 20-3, 28-30
Blake, William, 198, 205
Blunden, Edmund, 293, 301, 307-8

Blyth, R.H., ch. 19 passim
Boshin civil war, 108
Bowen, H.G., 128
Brandt, Max von, 6
Brinkley, Captain Francis, 26-7
British journalists in Japan, ch. 2 passim
British Museum library, ch. 7 passim
Brooke, John H., 21-2
Brown, Albert R., 52
Browne, Sir Thomas, 200
Buddhism, chs 15 & 19 passim, 305-10
Burma Road crisis (1940), 241
Bush, Lewis, 257
Buxton, Barclay, 34, 40-2
Byron, Mary, 184

Cadogan, Sir Alexander, 242-3
Canada: wheat, 247
Cantlie, Dr James, 84
Capel, Rev. A.S., 109
Cardew, Michael, 204
Cezanne, 196
Chamberlain, Basil H., 3, 7, 72, 223, 252
Chamberlain, Neville, 212, 242, 250
Chichibu, Prince, 207
China: Indemnity, 125, 127ff
Christianity, ch. 3 passim;
    'hidden Christians', 12
Church Missionary Society (CMS), 41-2
Churchill, Winston S., 238, 249
Clark, Aiko, 273-4
Claudel, Paul, 252
Clive, Sir Robert, 239
Clutton, George, 293-4
Cole, A.H., 23
Comyns-Carr, A.S., 305
Connaught Mission (1906), 118
Cox, Melville, 247
Cragside, ch. 8 passim
Craigie, Sir Robert, ch. 18 passim, 248ff
Cromer, Lord, 132-3
Crowe, Sir Edward, 159, 169
Cumming, Gordon, 72

Daniels, Frank, ch. 20 passim
Daniels, Gordon, viii, 14, 16
Daniels, Otome (Nishide), ch. 20 passim
Dawes, General Charles, 209-10
Dening, Sir Esler, 281-2, 285

345

INDEX

Shand, Alexander A., 126
Shaw, Patrick, 284
Shephard, Betty, 176, 182-6, 188
Shiba Gorō, 134-5
Shibusawa Eiichi, 54-5, 146
Shida Rinzaburō, 49
Shidehara Kijūrō, 210-11, 259
Shigemitsu Mamoru, xii, 185-8
Shinki Shonosuke, 252-3, 260, 262
Shirakaba Society, 196-7
Siebold, Philipp F. von, 8
Simon, Sir John, 209, 216, 246
Sino-Japanese war (1894-5), 110-11, 121, 125
Sladen, Douglas, 178-80
Society for Propagation of the Gospel (SPG), 43
Spielman, M.H., 179-80
Stoddart, Anna, 75, 77
Strang, Sir William, 293, 294
Suematsu Kenchō, 149
Sugimura Yokarō, 209-10, 217
Sugiura Yuzuru, 58
Sun Yat-sen, 84-5
Sutton, A.E., 46
Suzuki Daisetsu, 194, 254ff, 263, 266, 306
Sydney Sun, 293-4

Takahashi Korekiyo, 121, 129-32
Takahata Toku, 224
Takakusu Junjirō, x
Takami Jun, 188
Takarabe, Admiral Takeshi, 119-20, 207-8
Takayama Naomoto, 49
Taki Zensaburō, 7
Talbot, W.H., 23
Tanakadate Aikitsu, 52-3
Terajima Munenori, 14
Terashima Ryōan, 80
Thomson, William (Lord Kelvin), 48, 49, 53
Tientsin crisis (1939), 238-42, 245-6
Tilley, Sir John, 217
Tiltman, Hessell, 300, 308-9
Ting Ju-ch'ang, Admiral, 113-14
Togi Hōryū, 90
Tōgō Heihachirō, Admiral, ch. 9 passim, 101-3
Tokio Times, 65
Tokyo Imperial University, 45-6, 80-1
Tokyo-Yokohama railway, ix, 57
Tomimoto Kenkichi, 200-2
Tomlinson, F.S., 282
Tracy, Honor, 301-3
Truman, President Harry S., ch. 21 passim
Tsuboi Kōzō, Admiral, 111, 113
Tsuboi Shōgorō, 225
Tsuboichi Shoyo, 157

Tsurumi Kazuko, 78

Uehara Etsujirō, 156-7, 329
Uemura Masahisa, 43
Ueno Kagenori, 57-9, 110
Ugaki Kazushige, 245
Ukhtomskii, Admiral, 116
United States, 12-13, 58, 81, 126-7, ch. 21 passim

Vaughan-Smith, Alice M., 22, 23, 29
Vickers Sons & Maxim Ltd, ch. 8 passim
Vining, Elizabeth, 260

Wada Hikojirō, 149, 153-4
Wade, Sir Thomas, 16
Wakatsuki Reijirō, 207-8
Walters, Frank, 210
Washington Conference (1921-2), 105, 119, 207
Watanabe Hitoshi, 234
Watkins, A.W., 21, 28
Weale, Putnam (B. Lennox Simpson), 140
Webb, Sidney, 141
Westlake, Dr J.,112-13
Whitman, Walt, 198
Whitney, General Courtney, 303, 309
Williams, William C., 264-5
Williamson, Alexander, 47
Willis, Dr William, 2, 4-5, 6
Wirgman, Charles, 28-9
Witgeft, Admiral, 116
Woodard, William P., 258-60
World Economic Conference (1933), 170, 212-14

Yagi Shozaburō, 224
Yamagata Aritomo, General, 118
Yamamoto Gombei, 114-15, 118, 139
Yamamoto Isoroku, Admiral, 244
Yamamuro Gumpei, 41
Yamanashi Katsunoshin, Admiral, 120, 257-61
Yamanouchi Masuji, 97
Yamao Yōzō, 47, 48
Yamaza Enjirō, 152, 157
Yanagi Sōetsu, 190, ch. 15 passim
Yanagita Kunio, 83, 90
Yezo, 71
Yokohama:
    Chamber of Commerce, 24
    1923 earthquake, 222, 226-8
    General Hospital, 228
    Orchestra, 222
    Specie Bank, ch. 10 passim
    Tokyo railway, 57

349